# ELECTRONIC EMPIRES

# ELECTRONIC EMPIRES

*Global media and local resistance*

edited by

## DAYA KISHAN THUSSU
*Senior Lecturer, Communication,
Culture and Media,
Coventry University, UK*

A member of the Hodder Headline Group
LONDON · NEW YORK · SYDNEY · AUCKLAND

First published in Great Britain in 1998 by
Arnold, a member of the Hodder Headline Group,
338 Euston Road, London NW1 3BH

http://www.arnoldpublishers.com

Co-published in the United States of America by
Oxford University Press Inc.,
198 Madison Avenue, New York, NY 10016

*British Library Cataloguing in Publication Data*
A catalogue record for this book is available from the British Library

*Library of Congress Cataloging-in-Publication Data*
Electronic empires: global media and local resistance/edited by
Daya Kishan Thussu.
    p.    cm.
Includes bibliographical references and index.
ISBN 0–340–71895–1.—ISBN 0–340–71896–X (pbk.)
1. Communication, International.    I. Thussu, Daya Kishan.
P96.I5EA    1998
302.2—dc21                                      98–7877
                                                 CIP

ISBN 0 340 71895 1 (hb)
     0 340 71896 X (pb)

1  2  3  4  5  6  7  8  9  10

Production Editor: Wendy Rooke
Production Controller: Priya Gohil
Cover Design: Andy McColm

Typeset in 10/12pt Sabon by Phoenix Photosetting, Chatham, Kent
Printed and bound in Great Britain by MPG Books Ltd, Bodmin, Cornwall

What do you think about this book? Or any other Arnold title?
Please send your comments to **feedback.arnold@hodder.co.uk**

# Contents

# Notes on contributors

**Oliver Boyd-Barrett** is Professor at California State Polytechnic University, Pomona. He has authored and edited many books and articles on international communication and education, including *The International News Agencies* (1980), *Contra-Flow in Global News* (with D. K. Thussu, 1992) and *The Globalization of News* (with Terhi Rantanen, 1998). He has pioneered international distance-learning courses in mass communications at the Open University, UK, and at Leicester University, UK.

**Stuart Cunningham** is Professor and Head of the School of Media and Journalism, and Deputy Director, Australian Key Centre for Cultural and Media Policy, Queensland University of Technology, Brisbane. He is co-author with Elizabeth Jacka of *Australian Television and International Mediascapes* (1996), and co-editor, with John Sinclair and Elizabeth Jacka, of *New Patterns in Global Television – Peripheral Vision* (1996).

**Tony Dowmunt** is an independent producer with APT Film and Television. He is author of *Video with Young People* and has produced a number of programmes on the politics of television for Channel 4. He is editor of *Channels of Resistance: Global Television and Local Empowerment*, published by the British Film Institute in conjunction with the Channel 4 series.

**John Downey** is Senior Lecturer in Communication, Culture and Media at Coventry University and editor of the forthcoming publication *TechnoCities: the Culture and Political Economy of the Digital Revolution*.

**Peter Golding** is Professor of Sociology and Head of the Department of Social Sciences at Loughborough University. He is Chair of the Standing Conference on Cultural, Communication and Media Studies in Higher Education, a co-editor of the *European Journal of Communication*, and

Chair of the European Sociological Association Media Research Network. His books include *The Mass Media* (1974); *Making the News* (with Philip Elliott, 1979); *Images of Welfare* (with Sue Middleton, 1982); *Communicating Politics* (edited, with Philip Schlesinger and Graham Murdock, 1986); *Taxation and Representation* (with David Deacon, 1994); *The Political Economy of the Media* (edited, with Graham Murdock, 1997); *Beyond Cultural Imperialism* (edited, with Phil Harris, 1997); and *Cultural Studies in Question* (edited, with Marjorie Ferguson, 1997).

**Edward S. Herman** is a Professor Emeritus of Finance, Wharton School, University of Pennsylvania, and the author of a number of books, including *Corporate Control, Corporate Power* (1981); *Triumph of the Market* (1995); *Manufacturing Consent* (with Noam Chomsky, 1988); and *The Global Media* (with Robert McChesney, 1997).

**Elizabeth Jacka** is Dean of Faculty of Humanities and Social Sciences and Professor of Communication Studies, University of Technology, Sydney. She is co-author with Stuart Cunningham of *Australian Television and International Mediascapes* (1996). She is co-editor with John Sinclair and Stuart Cunningham of *New Patterns in Global Television – Peripheral Vision* (1996).

**Anandam Philip Kavoori** is Assistant Professor of Telecommunications, College of Journalism and Mass Communication, University of Georgia, Athens. His research interests include television news, reception theory, media globalisation and transnational cultural studies. He is co-editor of *The Global Dynamics of News: Studies in International News Coverage and News Agendas* (forthcoming).

**Robert W. McChesney** is Research Associate Professor in the Institute of Communications Research and the Graduate School of Library and Information Science at the University of Illinois. He has published over fifty articles and book chapters, and is the author or editor of six books, including *Media in Crisis, Democracy in Retreat: Communication Politics, History, and Scholarship in Dubious Times* (1999).

**Jim McGuigan** is Senior Lecturer in Sociology at Loughborough University. He is the author of *Cultural Populism* (1992) and *Culture and the Public Sphere* (1996), co-editor of *Studying Culture* (2nd edn 1997), and editor of *Cultural Methodologies* (1997) and a thematic issue of the *International Journal of Cultural Policy* on cultural analysis and cultural policy. His forthcoming publications include *TechnoCities: the Culture and Political Economy of the Digital Revolution* and *Modernity and Postmodern Culture*.

**Ali Mohammadi** is Reader in International Communication and Cultural Studies at Nottingham Trent University. He is editor of *International Communication and Globalisation* (1997), co-author with Annabelle Sreberny-Mohammadi of *Small Media, Big Revolution* (1994) and co-editor of *Questioning the Media* (1995).

**Herbert I. Schiller** is Professor Emeritus of Communication at the University of California at San Diego and Adjunct Professor, Department of Culture and Communication, New York University. Professor Schiller is author of over a dozen books on the structure, control and consequences thereof, of the information system in the United States. Among his books are the hugely influential *Mass Communications and American Empire* and most recently *Information Inequality* (1996).

**John Sinclair** is Professor in International Communication, Sociology and Cultural Studies in the Faculty of Arts at Victoria University of Technology, Melbourne. He has written widely on Latin American media and is co-editor with Stuart Cunningham and Elizabeth Jacka of *New Patterns in Global Television – Peripheral Vision* (1996).

**Colin Sparks** has written widely about the public sphere. He is Professor at the Centre for Communication and Information Studies, University of Westminster and is co-editor of the journal *Media, Culture & Society*.

**Annabelle Sreberny** is Professor and Director of the Centre for Mass Communication Research at the University of Leicester. Her books include *Small Media, Big Revolution: Communication, Culture and the Iranian Revolution* (1994), *Globalisation, Communication and Transnational Civil Society* (1996) and *Media in Global Context* (1997). She edited a special issue of the *Journal of International Communication* on 'International Feminism(s)' and is concerned to engender debates within International Communication.

**Daya Kishan Thussu,** editor of *Electronic Empires*, is Senior Lecturer in Communication, Culture and Media at Coventry University. A former Associate Editor of Gemini News Service, a London-based international news features agency, he is the co-author (with Oliver Boyd-Barrett) of *Contra-Flow in Global News* (1992).

**Anuradha Vittachi** is a founding Director of OneWorld Online, the world's leading Internet site on human rights and sustainable development, a multilingual, international partnership. She is also a Director of the OneWorld Broadcasting Trust, and an internationally published journalist and author. Her books include *Earth Conference One* (1988) and *Stolen Childhood: In Search of the Rights of the Child* (1989).

# Introduction

DAYA KISHAN THUSSU

The villain in the 1997 James Bond movie *Tomorrow Never Dies* is a power-hungry media mogul who believes triggering a third world war would send the stock value of his media empire soaring, so sets about manipulating the world's news through his vast chain of newspapers and satellite systems. Such dangerous powers in a popular fictionalised character – Elliot Carver – and the vision of a 'digital dictatorship' may be wildly exaggerated for melodramatic effect but fears that reality may be imitating art are already audible in some parts of the world.

It is now routine practice in the mainstream media and academic writing to use the term 'empire' in referring to the increasingly powerful transnational media corporations and their steadily growing global reach and influence. The convergence of telecommunications, computing and media industries as a result of neo-liberal policies of deregulation and privatisation, coupled with the rapid globalisation of new information and communication technologies, have enabled the building of new kinds of empires, supported by electronic delivery systems.

The virtual empires of the electronic age do not depend on territorial conquest, on gunboat diplomacy or on ideas of nationalism or racial difference. The Robert Clives and the Cecil Rhodes of the twenty-first century, such as Rupert Murdoch, Bill Gates and Ted Turner, are constructing their electronic empires by colonising the imagination of the increasingly depoliticised and atomised consumers of media products. Unlike the empires of the nineteenth century which shaped the modern world, these new empires are not ultimately based on coercion or military might. Their aim is not to subject alien populations to imperial dictates but to persuade consumers, through their global electronic networks, to use their media or buy the products advertised and to accept as inevitable the global progress of the market.

They are building on the linguistic legacy of the British empire, the grandest of the modern empires which at its height governed – directly or indirectly – over a quarter of the human race and encompassed more than a fifth of the globe. Besides transforming a small damp island off the edge of Europe into a leading industrial and military power, the British empire also gave the world a language which has evolved into a lingua franca, at least among the global political, intellectual and commercial elite. From electronic commerce to electronic publishing and electronic media, English is the language of globalisation, which the new empire-builders are using to create transnational communications networks.

In modern history, imperial power has changed hands from Spaniards and Portuguese to the Dutch; from the British and the French to the Americans – and from mercantile capital to state power and increasingly back to corporate capital. Similarly, the commodities which formed the basis of empires have changed – from spice to textiles; from precious gold and silver to oil; and to electronic media and cultural products. As Asia marks the five-hundredth anniversary of its 'discovery' by the Portuguese explorer Vasco de Gama, harbinger of colonial empires to Asia, and starting what an eminent historian has called the 'Vasco de Gama epoch of Asian History' (Panikkar, 1953), it may be possible to discern a new type of colonisation, a corporate colonialism – controlled by transnational capital rather than states – in the world's biggest continent and indeed across the globe.

Harold Innis argued that the concept of empire could be used as an 'indication of the efficiency of communication' (Innis, 1972: 9) and concluded that major empires have tended to go hand-in-hand with media monopolies. Communications networks and technologies were key to the mechanics of distributed government, trade and military campaigns. In the nineteenth century, telegraphy played a crucial role in imperialist expansion and consolidation, while, in the early part of this century, control of the airwaves was a key factor in the propagation of the idea of empire. In the years after the Second World War, with the decline of the European empires and the ascendancy of the United States, broadcasting made America a felt presence throughout the world. Radio was a powerful instrument of propaganda, used by both camps during the Cold War – from the BBC World Service, Voice of America, Radio Free Europe and Radio Liberty, to Radio Moscow's own cruder version for the battle to win hearts and minds. The availability and expansion of television made the Eastern bloc countries see for themselves how life was in the capitalist West, a contributing factor in the ending of East–West ideological confrontation.

The coming of satellites for communications and broadcasting and the development of global information (and control) systems opened up infinite scope for the delivery of electronic goods, transcending physical and political constraints. The increasing concentration of media control in large, integrated, predominantly Western-based transnational media empires, and the beaming of mainly American cultural products (or their locally made clones) to traditional societies, raises important questions about cultural autonomy. Like the empires of the past, which were, to a large extent, responsible for the destruction of the cultures, traditions, knowledges and social structures of the colonised territories, the new empires too may undermine national media systems, cultural identities and cultural sovereignty.

However, it is impossible to make sense of cultural globalisation without understanding the processes behind the internationalisation of production and labour and of financial transactions, which are being carried out by the transnational corporations (TNCs) who are the biggest beneficiaries of neo-liberalism. Between 1993 and 1995, the value of foreign assets of the top 100 TNCs (sixty-nine of which are based in the West, another eighteen in Japan) increased by 30 per cent and their foreign sales by 26 per cent (UNCTAD, 1997: 28). Media and communications corporations figure prominently in the world's top companies listed in the FT500 at the end of 1997, with Microsoft Corporation being placed at number three, Disney at number 40, Sony at 75, Time Warner at 96, Reuters at 183 and News Corporation at 408 (*Financial Times*, 1998). Electronics is the most important industry as far as the largest TNCs are concerned, accounting for some 16 per cent of all firms' foreign assets (UNCTAD, 1997: xviii).

Globalisation has moved economics beyond the authority of the state to the suprastate bodies such as the World Bank, the International Monetary Fund and the World Trade Organisation. The policies enunciated by such organisations, especially the World Bank, often in alliance with the TNCs, have eroded the economic powers of states, particularly in the southern hemisphere. As Susan George and Fabrizio Sabelli argue, the World Bank is a 'secular empire' which has 'managed to make its own view of the world appear the norm'. 'Its real success,' they write, 'has been not so much economic – however great the economic power it wields – as cultural [and] ideological . . .' (1994: 3).

Herbert Schiller's seminal *Mass Communications and American Empire*, published in 1969, examined the dimensions of US cultural and media domination. He argued then that the US informational facilities and products were deployed worldwide to support the American empire that came into existence after the Second World War. Over the last two decades that power has acquired enormous new strengths, given the corporatisation even of the institutions of the United Nations. In September 1997, Ted Turner, the founder of Cable News Network, the world's only global news channel, stunned the world by announcing that he was to donate one billion dollars to the UN – the highest on record – to fund educational projects across the world. That the UN is now following the corporate agenda was evident in February 1998 when UN Secretary General Kofi Annan hosted a meeting for the International Chamber of Commerce (Tran, 1998).

The greatest impact of the new media empires is likely to be on the 'majority world' – the former colonies of the European empires – which has become a site of a contest renewed with the end of the Cold War. The breakup of the Soviet Union and the 'triumph' of market capitalism over state socialism has considerably weakened the position of the Southern countries in the global arena. Such Southern groups as the Non-Aligned Movement are in disarray, and the governments themselves are increasingly following the economic agenda set by the TNCs in conjunction with supranational institutions like the World Bank. In addition, the countries which were recipients of economic or military aid and diplomatic support from the Eastern bloc now feel more inclined to toe the line of the remaining military and 'information' superpower – the USA.

The European Commission sees no point in 'resisting the process of globalization', calling any such attempts 'quixotic and suicidal'. A recent report from the Commission counsels: 'Countries are better advised to adapt to this inevitable process and adopt development strategies which allow them to participate in the world economy and benefit from globalization' (European Commission, 1997: 75).

Like the empires of the past, when liberals could accommodate themselves with the imperial idea, calling themselves 'liberal imperialists', today's postmodernists view globalisation as an inevitable, and even positive, development. This uncritical support for globalisation can be seen in an article by David Rothkopf entitled 'In praise of cultural imperialism?' published in the influential US journal *Foreign Policy*. According to Rothkopf, managing director of Kissinger Associates, a professor at Columbia University and a former senior official in the Clinton administration:

> The homogenizing influences of globalisation that are most often condemned by the new nationalists and by cultural romanticists are actually positive; globalisation promotes integration and the removal not only of cultural barriers but of many of the negative dimensions of culture. Globalisation is a vital step toward both a more stable world and better lives for the people in it.
>
> (Rothkopf, 1997: 39)

The enthusiasts of the new open global societies, which know no cultural barriers or physical frontiers, see media playing a key role in the globalisation of democratic ideas. The globalisation of the telecommunication industry, they argue, is facilitating the free flow of information, a prerequisite for the development of a global public sphere, where issues of international significance – democracy, human rights, gender and ethnic equality, the environment and sustainable development – could be discussed, and which promises empowerment in a pluralistic and democratic world citizenry.

Since the introduction of mechanical printing into Europe in the fifteenth century, mechanised technologies of communication have influenced the formation of pan-European ideas. The advent and expansion of electronic media – first radio and then television – had a profound impact on increasing international awareness. The globalisation of the electronic media has undoubtedly made citizens aware of the wider world. Global networking and computer-mediated communications, especially the Internet, have helped to enable individuals and groups to overcome geographical and cultural boundaries and evolve a 'global civil society'.

Strobe Talbot, a former *Time* magazine journalist and at present under-secretary of state in the Clinton administration, even went to the extent of proclaiming the 'birth of a global nation' in which 'collective action on a global scale will be easier to achieve in a world already knit together by cables and airwaves' (Talbot, 1992: 63). Such euphoric belief in the power of technology is not new. All through the history of modern media – telephone, phonograph, motion pictures, radio, television, camcorder, cable, satellite – similar sentiments were expressed. Developments in media technology were seen as contributing to the broadening of democracy and a civil society. More often than not, possible benefits of new technologies were emphasised rather than their misuse – from propaganda to 'virtual' wars.

Nevertheless, globalisation has created an unprecedented number of new media outlets, which in turn have led to job opportunities for media workers, as new programming is needed to fill in the burgeoning channels, increasingly using local programming in local languages. Global media have given the audience much greater choice in programmes than was hitherto available. This has forced governments to introduce a greater degree of plurality in news and current affairs, since they now realise they cannot maintain a monopoly over broadcasting when satellite-based networks can beam signals over vast areas regardless of borders, challenging definitions of national identity.

In addition, the new media ecology of the 1990s has opened up spaces for non-metropolitan centres of media production to international audiences, although their access may be comparatively much smaller than that of media TNCs dominated by US programming. The Central Asian republics, at last free from another type of empire, now receive Turkish television; South African programmes are available in China; Indian films are widely viewed across Asia; and the Latin American television giants Globo and Televisa export television soap operas around the world, including to Russia.

Just as the British, Dutch and French state empires, though based upon exploitation of the human and natural resources of the colonies, nevertheless brought ideas on social and political mobilisation, on democracy and political pluralism to scattered parts of imperial territories, the new private empires may also provide potential for cultural resistance. As in the past, democratic resistance is bound to keep raising its banner even if it is unable to withstand in the short run the combined efforts of imperial power and corporate colonialism.

The new media have undermined state control of the media and challenged censorship and hierarchies across the globe. There are instances where the new technology has been used to broaden the dominant media agenda or even provide an alternative agenda: Deep Dish's community TV/satellite link-up in the USA; Aboriginal TV in Australia; El Salvador's rebel radio – Radio Venceremos; al-Manar, the television station of Lebanon's Islamic resistance movement Hizbullah; Med-TV, the Kurdish satellite station – these are some of the examples of this kind of activism. Communication by satellite is playing an increasingly significant role in the development of indigenous electronic media, 'both as an aid to distribution of programming *to* indigenous stations and to the exchange of programming *among* them' (Browne, 1996: 42).

However, these few, though vitally important organisations and groups face extraordinary odds. The questions that Barnouw raised in the 1970s in the context of the growth of cable television in the USA are even more relevant today in an age of globalised communications networks.

> Who will be the gatekeeper of the evolving system? Who will man the control points? Will the multiplicity of choices provide diversity, or only seem to? Who will decide what will be stored in the electronic archives and information banks available to pushbuttons? Our history teaches us that these are crucial questions. Underlying them all is another: what role will sponsorship – and the financial control it involves – play in the system to come?
>
> (Barnouw, 1978: 178)

One of the gatekeepers of global information in the twenty-first century is likely to be Rupert Murdoch, whose News Corporation perhaps best exemplifies the concept of electronic empires. Given its global reach and unrivalled capacity to provide programming and delivery systems, Murdoch's deterritorialised media empire will define the emerging contours of a new global media, especially in digital satellite television, which is likely to dominate broadcasting in the next century.

The digital globe under construction by Murdoch will lead to empires which have no territories but span the world, with the potential of being more powerful than the territorial-based ones of the past. Already, News Corporation operates in nine different media on six continents, achieving this global dominance by focusing on entertainment – sports and movie-based programming. Murdoch controls 132 newspapers across the globe and his British-based Sky network now has affiliates in the USA, Japan, Latin America and India. This global empire has been created by linking up with local media corporations, such as US cable giant Tele-Communication Inc., Mexico's Televisa, India's Zee network and China's Phoenix. As a media commentator put it: 'Murdoch is . . . the personification of millennial global business where international frontiers do not exist, national politics are irrelevant and regulatory laws are minor hazards. The only thing that matters for him is the exploitation of markets for profit . . .' (Greenslade, 1998).

What distinguishes Murdoch, apart from his business acumen and a willingness to take risks, is an extensive knowledge of media operations, a very pragmatic political agenda and an instinctive feel for the market. In pursuing such an approach Murdoch has arguably created a new kind of global media empire based on entertainment and infotainment. Such an approach can be summarised in what might be termed the 'Murdochisation' of media – the process which involves the shift of media power from the public to privately owned, transnational, multimedia corporations controlling both delivery systems and the content of global information networks. This should not be read literally but is of the same order as 'McDonaldisation' where one famous example of a phenomenon comes to stand for a general process. 'Murdochisation' embraces all the faceless impersonal media corporations that are part of the same project.

'Murdochisation' could be characterised by a combination of the following factors: a convergence of global media technologies; a tendency towards a market-driven journalism thriving on circulation and ratings wars; transnationalisation of US-inspired media formats, products and discourse; and lastly, an emphasis on infotainment, undermining the role of the media for public information. 'Murdochisation' could be said to have contributed to the global standardisation of media products. At the same time, the project is able to adapt global products to local circumstances, incorporating/imitating imported genres, leading to hybridity.

Inevitably, as in any collection of essays, a range of viewpoints will emerge in this book. However, there are a number of themes running through it. One of its major concerns is to examine and assess who is driving media globalisation, who is benefiting from it and who is losing out. The other major theme is to weigh the question of democratisation and the public-sphere role of the media against the gradual privatisation of public communication spaces. The dynamics between the global and the regional, the global and the local are analysed. Theoretical critiques of media globalisation, from the perspectives of both political economy and cultural studies, are offered. The issue of how media messages are received by a increasingly heterogeneous audience is analysed and case studies are included to link the theoretical domain with the real world.

The book has been divided into four sections. The first section sets the scene, analysing the historical evolution of the media industries and the role of the US government in promoting its media and cultural industries. Key media empires are discussed and their impact on global territories – Eastern Europe and the developing world – is examined. The second section focuses on the concept of the public sphere and whether globalisation is helping or hindering the creation of public space for debate. It explores such questions as how global the globalisation of media is and whether a global public sphere is possible and if so, whether is it compatible with the emerging electronic empires. The third section critiques the concepts of globalisation, with contributors examining media imperialism, regional/global dynamics, reception of global media and feminist readings of media globalisation. In the final section, perspectives from activists from non-governmental organisations and media practitioners are included to broaden the range of what is a vital and challenging area of critical enquiry. The chapters in this section explore alternatives to media empires, with case studies from the Internet and youth movements; Islamic encounters with modern media are discussed and news content of a popular Indian television channel is analysed to examine how local media adapt to or resist electronic empires.

Many of the chapters that follow were first outlined at an international conference organised by the Communication, Culture and Media Subject Group of Coventry University in March 1997. I am very grateful for the valuable support of my colleagues, especially Peter Every, and postgraduate students – Roshni Luthra and Phaik Yin Tang – and to the contributors to that very stimulating and successful event. I am thankful to Roshni for research assistance on the chapter on Zee TV and to Anandam Kavoori for his insightful comments on an earlier draft of that chapter. I am indebted to Oliver Boyd-Barrett, who has been supportive throughout, for his feedback on a draft of my chapter on infotainment. I also owe sincere thanks to senior colleagues in my Subject Group for granting me study leave to work on the book. My gratitude, too, to Lesley Riddle and Elena Seymenliyska at Arnold, for their professionalism.

Most important, this volume could not have been possible without the help of my wife, Elizabeth, who despite a broken ankle, a job and looking after Shivani, 6, and Rohan, 3, was magnificent in her unstinting support.

# References

Barnouw, E. (1978) *The Sponsor: Notes on a Modern Potentate*, Oxford University Press, New York.

Browne, D. R. (1996) *Electronic Media and Indigenous Peoples*, Iowa State University Press, Ames.

European Commission (1997) *The Future of North–South Relations: Towards Sustainable Economic and Social Development*, Luxemburg.

*Financial Times* (1998) FT 500, 22 Jan., pp. 5–6.

George, S. and Sabelli, F. (1994) *Faith and Credit: The World Bank's Secular Empire*, Penguin, Harmondsworth.

Greenslade, R. (1998) Overlord of the media jungle, *Guardian*, 28 Feb., p. 3.

Innis, H. (1972) *Empires and Communications*, University of Toronto Press, Toronto, originally published by Clarendon Press, Oxford in 1960.

Panikkar, K. M. (1953) *Asia and the Western Dominance*, George Allen & Unwin, London.

Rothkopf, D. (1997) In praise of cultural imperialism? *Foreign Policy*, 107, summer, pp. 38–53.

Schiller, H. (1969) *Mass Communications and American Empire*, Augustus M. Kelley, Chicago.

Talbot, S. (1992) The birth of the global nation, *Time*, 20 July, pp. 62–3.

Tran, M. (1998) UN boosts its brand identity, *Guardian*, 23 Feb., p. 16.

UNCTAD (1997) *The World Investment Report 1997: Transnational Corporations, Market Structure and Competition Policy*, United Nations Conference on Trade and Development, Geneva.

SECTION

I

# GLOBALISATION OF ELECTRONIC EMPIRES

# Introduction to Section I

The rapid globalisation of electronic media in the 1990s has become one of the key subjects of contemporary debate. For its supporters, media globalisation opens up new vistas of democratic international communication which would end state censorship of the media and help evolve a global civil society. However, for critics, it indicates yet another form of domination – of global information and entertainment networks – by a few Western-based media empires.

The growing power of such media conglomerates, which control both delivery systems and the content of global media networks, is a central theme of this book and Section I examines the forces shaping and driving media globalisation. The contributors analyse the political and economic context of the expansion and consolidation of media empires as a result of globalisation and their strategies to open up markets in international territories, from Eastern Europe to the developing world. Among the key concerns in this section are to identify the main players in global media, to examine the reasons for their ascendancy and finally to evaluate the implications for public information of increasing privatisation of global networks.

Herbert Schiller sets the globalisation of transnational media corporations and communication industries in the historical context of US dominance and sees continuities in this process in the late twentieth century. Far from being undermined by forces of globalisation, Schiller argues that, in the case of the USA, the state is still in charge, representing the core interests of capital, especially in the expanding and critical area of the economy – the communication sector. Schiller analyses US government policy since the end of the Second World War. The American global cultural/informational domination was achieved and maintained, Schiller argues, by US government support, including state-subsidised research and development in such areas as information technology, computing, the 'special effects' industry and worldwide surveillance systems.

This global ascendance, according to Schiller, was made possible largely through the 'free flow of information' doctrine which has been used, more often than not, to undermine national sovereignty. Schiller goes on to review the role of information in the era of transnational capital; concentration of capital; and privatisation and commercialisation of communication industries under the influence of neo-liberal ideology. Criticising the current tendency to ahistoricism in the rush to embrace the new information technologies, Schiller sees an ideological agenda in the rejection of the past, and in efforts to extend US global cultural hegemony, founded on electronic mastery. A political economy of culture – of its production and its consumption – Schiller contends, remains a vital site for research into such issues.

Robert McChesney, co-author of a widely cited study of global media, also sees the rise of the global media market in the context of a more integrated global capitalist economy. Chronicling the rise of the global media system and its core attributes, he examines the convergence of media industries across traditional lines of production, with the expansion of transnational media corporations. He then analyses in detail what he calls the Holy Trinity: Time Warner, Disney and News Corporation – the world's three most important media empires. McChesney traces the interconnections between the largest media firms – which share major shareholders or have overlapping boards of directors.

What distinguishes the global media system, he argues, is transnational control not only over exported media content, but over media distribution as well. In the late 1990s, the logic of the global commercial system dictates that global concerns define the national strategies of media empires. The close relationship between the global media system and the global capitalist political economy, can be seen, first, as a direct result of the deregulatory policies that have assisted in the formation of global markets for other goods and services. Advertising, conducted disproportionately by the largest firms in the world, is the second way in which the global media system is linked to the global market economy. Finally, McChesney considers how new information technologies such as the Internet may play the role of a wild card in the global media deck, although he concedes that it has already been taken over to some extent by corporate clients.

In his contribution, John Downey examines a new form of media colonisation taking shape in the former socialist countries once under the Soviet empire but now increasingly being integrated into Western corporate capitalism. He analyses the changes in the media systems in these countries, within the framework of the debate on media and cultural imperialism.

Downey argues that these nations have become post-colonial states and a new site for media colonisers. As an example, he analyses a BBC documentary which followed the fortunes of a Kazakhstan soap opera, made with the help of a production team from a popular BBC soap under a scheme financed by Britain, part of the British government's 'humanitarian aid' to the newly independent states of the former Soviet Union. He sees this experiment in cultural cooperation as an attempt by the government to make the capitalist project acceptable to the Kazakh people, which demonstrated neatly the relationship between capital, power and narrative form.

The chapter also outlines the changes in the media systems of central and Eastern Europe in the post-Cold War era, focusing on contemporary developments in Germany, since it remains the dominant media power in the region. The majority of privatised newspapers in central and Eastern Europe, Downey notes, have been bought by German media corporations or their affiliates, effectively creating a quasi-monopoly position, with Hungary, Bulgaria and the Czech Republic being the extreme examples of Western colonisation of the press. Countries like Bulgaria and Romania, still experiencing profound difficulties associated with the transition to capitalism, have not attracted much interest from Western media investors. The West's influence in broadcasting, Downey argues, is more complex and can be detected in the supply of capital and broadcasting technology and export of Western or Westernised programming on terrestrial television.

While satellite and cable television are in private hands, terrestrial television has remained under the control of the governments, which are now using the electronic media to promote capitalist lifestyles. In this context, Downey sees the state as coloniser which is drawing on its legacy of an authoritarian approach to media policy. Downey argues that while formal democracy has been introduced to the countries in this region, many of the elements of liberal democratic culture are missing and consequently the public sphere has remained underdeveloped. The chapter argues that the development of more democratic media is dependent upon the creation of a robust civil society to counter the power of the state and the media empires.

Daya Kishan Thussu looks at the implications of the expansion of Western-owned transnational media corporations for the South, with particular reference to news media. He argues that having nearly saturated markets in the North, media empires are now exploring new ones for their products in the South, especially in Asia and Latin America. The chapter examines the strategies of media conglomerates to expand in these new territories, which emphasise entertainment-based programming at the expense of information.

The focus of the chapter is on global television news. The

increasingly market-driven television news, Thussu argues, is contributing to the trivialisation of public information and, given the Southern dependence on television news from Western media organisations, this has serious implications for the development of democracy in the countries of the South. Claims that the globalisation process will lead to the 'free flow' of ideas, products and technologies need to be looked at in the context of the increasing control of news and information channels by Western-owned media organisations. Will this 'free flow' of information promote democracy and contribute to a public sphere in the South or will it create new empires based on corporate colonialism? Viewed in a North–South context, he argues, the competition is far from fair. From print to broadcasting, from online to specialised services, the Northern media, and more specifically its Anglo-American axis, continue to dominate global information and the global news agenda.

The overriding objective of the media TNCs is to get their products to the largest number of people. The logic of global television demands the creation of global programming and global markets. At the same time, in order to operate effectively, they also need to be a vehicle for creating new consumers and markets for their advertisers. In the name of globalisation, cable and satellite can now deliver the values of a consumer society across the world. Visual images overcome limitations of language and literacy to target universal human desires and aspirations.

The chapter examines the rise of 'infotainment' and how this is affecting the production and presentation of news in the South. Increasingly, news values are driven by the procurement of dramatic television pictures rather than the nature of the issue. This is particularly relevant in societies where the majority population has moved directly from oral to visual cultures. Thussu considers the implications of the globalisation of infotainment for news agendas and news discourse and how this might be harmful to the interests of the world's poor countries and may affect the evolution of a public sphere in the South.

# |1|

# *Striving for communication dominance*

## *A half-century review*

### HERBERT I. SCHILLER

Today, the United States exercises mastery over the sphere of global communication and culture. How did it happen? What can be done to challenge it? Reviewing the last half-century of tumultuous change in the arena of communications and culture, a few sweeping generalisations seem to be warrantable.

The first is that the US (capitalist) state, contrary to many reports, is alive and, if not well, at least still in charge. This conclusion does not apply necessarily to other states in the global economy. But in the USA, very significant functions are still performed by the state. Certainly in the sphere of communication it is no paper tiger. To the contrary, representing the core interests of capital, the state has demonstrated unusual vision. It has acted frequently, with initiative and decisiveness, to assure the promotion of the ever-expanding communication sector – to what now has become a central pillar of the economy.

A second feature of this period is the effort – marked by many variants – to persuade the public that a new era has arrived, one which breaks the connection to earlier times. The argument generally dismisses many existing structural or institutional relations as obsolete, e.g. the adversary relation between labour and capital. The game, it is said, is a new one, with no roots in the past. History, by this criterion, is not only useless for understanding the present. It is totally irrelevant. This is an especially destructive ideological notion, for it undermines any understanding of the social process and how to change it.

A third conclusion, coming from five decades of witnessing continuous changes in the structure, content and dissemination of the cultural/communication industries, and their ever-expanding concentration, is the legitimacy and essentiality of political economy as a means of grasping ongoing developments. The ever-popular proposition that the cultural/

media sector can be regarded as autonomous and free-standing has been belied by the material conditions that have produced a configuration of cultural production that simply cannot be explained without recourse to political economy. I now examine these propositions in more detail.

# The state and the promotion of US communication mastery

In the late 1990s there is strong insistence, in governing and academic circles, that the market is the solution to all problems, that private enterprise is the preferred means to achieve solid economic results, and that government is, as one economic analyst recently put it, 'the enemy' (Roberts, 1997: 26). This widely held credo hardly squares with the last half-century's record of government initiative, support and promotion of information and communication policies. These have conferred advantage and global mastery on the now powerful sector engaged in cultural production, transmission and dissemination. It is important to understand that this has been deliberate policy, pursued by every administration from the Second World War up to, and including, the Clinton White House. (Current adulation of market forces cannot be attributed solely to hypocrisy. Capital, and its administrators, have consistently denied the legitimacy of government intervention on behalf of social needs, while being most solicitous for expenditures that improve the coercive and money-making sectors.)

The principle of the 'free flow of information' – vital to the worldwide export of American cultural products – has been a construction which has made a universal virtue out of the cultural industries' marketing requirements. John Foster Dulles, possibly the most aggressive secretary of state in the postwar years (though bellicosity has been a mark of most secretaries of state), regarded this 'free flow' as the single most important issue in foreign policy (Schiller, 1976).[1] Even before the end of the Second World War, the Pentagon made military aircraft available to US publishers and senior editors to circle the globe and hector leaders in eleven allied and neutral countries on the virtues of a free press – defined as a privately owned one – and the free exchange of information (*New York Times*, 29 November 1944).[2]

The government did everything in its considerable power in the early postwar years to establish the 'free-flow' doctrine as a universally accepted objective. In 1946, Assistant Secretary of State William Benton, for example, put it this way:

> The State Department plans to do everything within its power along political or diplomatic lines to help break down the artificial barriers to the expansion of private American news agencies, magazines,

motion pictures, and other media of communications throughout the world ... Freedom of the press – and freedom of exchange of information generally – is an integral part of our foreign policy.
(Department of State Bulletin, 1946)

In Congress, in international fora such as the UN and UNESCO and at international conferences, US representatives pressed relentlessly for the free flow. To be sure, there was another benefit from this advocacy. Besides the material advantages it offered to US companies, it facilitated an ongoing propaganda windfall at the expense of the non-market sector of the world (USSR et al.) which was organised on a completely different basis. Free flow, as articulated by US officials, invariably emphasised the unacceptability of the doctrine to state-managed societies and easily made it appear that virtue was being rejected for evil.

State support for the cultural industries, however, was not limited to ideological initiatives. A wide-ranging programme of US material assistance to many countries came into operation after the war. The Marshall Plan, 1948–51, for example, was a model for all the foreign 'aid' programmes that succeeded it. Among the many features of the plan was one tying dollar grants to a recipient's acquiescence to opening its market to US cultural exports, film in particular (Guback, 1969). Fifty years later, Harvard University professor Jeffrey D. Sachs, free-market missionary to several former socialist countries, offered a similar view of the Marshall Plan that has generally been obscured. He noted: 'The Marshall Plan had two key features: it was conditional on policy changes in the countries that received assistance, and it was temporary' (Sachs, 1997). Seemingly unaware that this has been, and remains, US policy in all its overseas dealings, Sachs was recommending this as a new idea.

Stipulations of this nature have remained a feature of US foreign aid in its many forms. They have become the basis of US world trade policy as well, and have been incorporated in the recently concluded World Trade Organisation agreements. In the economic débâcle in East and Southeast Asia in the fall/winter of 1997–8, US economic pressure, which was once relatively concealed, has become overt. Gloatingly, the *New York Times* headlined the weakened condition of the region: 'Asia's surrender: reeling from blows to their economies, countries agree to financial concessions' (Sanger, 1997).

In another sphere, more indirect but of enormous significance, are the huge subsidies for state-funded research and development. Astronomical sums have been allocated by the Pentagon, from the public's tax money, to underwrite technological developments. The fruits of these outlays – estimated at over one trillion dollars since 1945 – among many others, have included the rapid development of computers and the fields of computer science and artificial intelligence. These industries and fields of study have contributed incalculably to US ascendancy in information technology, computer networks, database creation, the special effects industry and worldwide surveillance systems – the underlying infrastructure of what is now benignly termed 'the information age'. Without huge amounts of government money this could not have happened.

Still another planned and direct state action to further US communication primacy in the postwar years was the communication satellite undertaking. In this instance, the objective of this costly enterprise was explicit. It aimed to wrest global information control from America's 'special partner', Great Britain, which at that time exercised worldwide domination of undersea cable. Testifying before Congress in 1966, McGeorge Bundy, former chief aide to President Kennedy, and later the president of the Ford Foundation, recollected:

> I was, myself, a part of the executive branch during the period which led up to the establishment of Comsat [Communication Satellite Corporation] . . . I do clearly remember what the record fully confirms – that Comsat was established for the purpose of taking and holding a position of leadership for the United States in the field of international global commercial satellite services.
>
> (Progress Report on Space Communications, 1966)

The State Department's legal adviser at the time, A. Chayes, was even more explicit. He noted that it was the rapid growth of US satellite technology in the 1950s that undercut Britain's chance to extend control of cable communications for another several decades (Satellite Communications, 1964: 360 and 364).

In sum, the US state has played a pivotal role in achieving and maintaining American global cultural/informational domination over the last 50 years, a domination enduring to this day. This has been a fully conscious and deliberate effort, carried out by each administration, from Truman's to Clinton's.

# The discontinuity fable and the survival of history

In *Theories of the Information Society*, Frank Webster makes a crucial distinction, in the study of contemporary communication theory, between those writers who see today's world as a rupture with the past and those who find 'historical antecedents and *continuities*' (Webster, 1995: 217, emphasis in original). Webster comes down firmly on the side of historical continuity. Yet his is by no means a majority view in recent times.

In the postwar decades, at least three variants of the rupture of history theory have had a powerful influence in fortifying the ideology of capitalism. One of the early expressions of this thinking came from Daniel Bell and those who took up his lead. Bell set the stage for what was to follow with his study of what he called post-industrial society (Bell, 1973). The appearance of a huge white-collar workforce, to which Bell gave prominent recognition, was taken to mean, by many interpreters, that the old industrial system, along with all its defining characteristics and institutions, was dead. The far-reaching restructuring of labour and industry could easily be pushed further (and it was) to conclude that a new age had emerged – one in which old forms and relations disappeared.

Interest in discovering how this new social order differed from, but still related to the industrial system, was not a priority concern of the proponents of post-industrial society. Difference, yes! Connectedness, no! Writing about this disinclination, Dan Schiller noted: 'Post-industrial theory utilised its exceptionalist premise [the uniqueness of "information" and its production] to invoke a comprehensive but undemonstrable historical rupture, and therefore to draw back decisively from the predominating social relations of production and into schematic and false models of social development. "Information" itself was given an aura of objectivity' (Schiller, 1996: 167 and 169).

The collapse of the Soviet Union and the global 'triumph' of United States capitalism that the collapse signified, prompted a second version of a new age to be articulated. This was the thrust of Francis Fukuyama's book on the 'end of history' (Fukuyama, 1992). In this work, Fukuyama, to the delight of those tired of confrontation and polarities, also heralded a new era. It is one, according to the author, in which serious social conflict is absent, and a steady incrementalism toward social improvement can be expected. Fukuyama considered this a boring but inevitable process.

In the post-industrial age, labour is seen as essentially uninvolved in the social process because there is no need for assertive labour. Its needs will be satisfied by the ongoing process of social betterment, driven by well-disposed pluralistic forces. Inconveniently for this theory, the 'benign' social forces foreseen by Fukuyama are rapidly reversing the century-long push towards greater social welfare. Triumphant capitalism has unleashed a powerful drive towards inequality in the social sphere.

Today, therefore, the latest theory of historical rupture is represented by the claims of the electronic crowd – who now comprise a strident chorus. In this group may be included the communication hardware and software people who speak mostly with market expectations in mind. But there is also the academic contingent, centred in the high-tech universities, and, most consequentially, political figures in the highest reaches of the government. One of the earliest proponents of the theory of a new electronic age, and its alleged break with the past, is Alvin Toffler. In a series of books, beginning in 1970 – which received mass circulation and wide, national attention – Toffler breathlessly described the computer-using society as the Third Wave (Toffler, 1980), displacing the preceding industrial one, which, in turn, came after the agricultural era.

More recently, feverishly enthusiastic accounts of the networked age have been served up by *WIRED* magazine, a monthly with a sizeable readership.

*WIRED*'s editorial posture is to present itself and the material it publishes as bold, fresh, innovative and indispensable for clues about what is happening in a culture undergoing digitisation. According to *WIRED*'s contributors and editors, we are on the threshold of, if not already in, a new and wonderful world. The magazine's outlook was thus described by an outsider: 'Computers lead to a kind of Utopia; a better future through symbiosis between man and machine . . . a religion that sees cyberspace as a transcendental medium which will usher in a Golden Age, an age where being digital frees the mind, allowing us to transcend the body and ascend to a higher plane of consciousness' (Bennahum, 1996).

When such a transcendental fantasy is accepted, on-the-ground problems that have endured since the beginning of industrialisation – insecurity, poverty, unemployment, exploitation – fade from sight and consideration. The class struggle, for example, is transformed into an opposition between those who support, and those who are unreceptive to the Internet (Barlow, 1996).

Yet *WIRED*, and the many other equally fervent media and academic voices claiming transformative power for electronic networks are, at most, only a cheering section for processes underway that are energised by powerful political and economic forces. Far more influential in affecting actual developments in the restructuring of the economy, is government – much maligned, incidentally, by *WIRED* and other, now numerous, laissez-faire advocates in the country.

The Federal initiatives and massive financial support for new communication technologies over the last half-century have already been noted. This lavish underwriting of research and development for informational projects has scarcely diminished in the present digital period. To the contrary, communication has been elevated to a top government priority since the beginning of the Clinton administration in 1993. The President, and Vice-President Al Gore, no less than *WIRED* magazine, rhapsodise over the capability of the new information technologies to transform everyday life and to overcome the pervasive economic and social disabilities that scar modern existence.[3]

Yet Washington's view, no less exuberant than those of other electronic believers, out of necessity retains an acknowledgement of history. This is so because the exercise of power, in any period, cannot overlook past experience. In the current American situation, a glance backward to 1941 is in order, because that was the year in which Henry Luce proclaimed the advent of the American Century. In the late 1990s, a reconstituted American Century is contemplated, one founded on electronic mastery.

This is the core of the argument offered by two formerly highly placed officials in the first Clinton administration, Joseph S. Nye, Jr. and Admiral William A. Owens, respectively former assistant secretary of defense for international affairs, now dean of the Kennedy School at Harvard, and former vice chairman of the Joint Chiefs of Staff. According to Nye and

Owens, 'the twenty-first century, not the twentieth, will turn out to be the period of America's greatest preeminence. Information is the new coin of the international realm, and the United States is better positioned than any other country to multiply the potency of its hard and soft power resources through information.' Further, 'The one country that can best lead the information revolution will be more powerful than any other. For the foreseeable future, that country is the United States ... its ... subtle comparative advantage is its ability to collect, process, act upon, and disseminate information, an edge that will almost certainly grow over the next decade' (Nye and Owens, 1996: 20).

Another voice, one from the computer software industry, is no less enthusiastic about prospects for American information global primacy in the time ahead. Daniel F. Burton, Jr., vice-president of government relations at Novell and the former president of the private-sector Council on Competitiveness, has this to say:

> As the pioneer of the [networked] economy, the United States will play a defining role in how it develops. No other country combines the diverse set of assets necessary to drive its evolution – a towering software presence, a world-class hardware business, a dynamic content industry, a telecommunications sector that is rapidly being deregulated, a strong venture capitalist base, flexible labour markets, and an unparalleled university system.
>
> (Burton, 1997: 23)

From this, Burton concludes: 'It will be a networked world comprised of electronic communities of commerce and culture – a world that ironically will strengthen the position of the United States as a nation among nations, even as it disrupts the system of nation-states' (ibid.: 37).

This thinking comes close to being a blueprint of current United States strategic communication policy. President Clinton put it this way: 'To keep the United States on the cutting edge, my job is to adjust America so we can win in the twenty-first century' (Markoff, 1993). Charlene Barshevsky, the US trade representative, after the recently concluded World Trade Organisation negotiations on worldwide telecommunications, struck an almost identical note. The government, no less than industry and happy networked academics, confer on the new electronics a revolutionary role. Industry and university voices are more inclined to claim that the technology is producing a totally new world. The state and its administrators, more aware of power relations, nationally and globally, announce their intention to incorporate the new technologies into historically familiar structures of control and domination.

However strongly, therefore, the electronic faithful insist on the totality of difference the new instrumentation provides, the state authority, matter-of-factly, reveals the historical continuities in its quest for systemic power and control. The goal of electronic mastery fits smoothly into recognisable patterns of earlier imperial structures of privilege and exploitation. This hardly escapes the attention of those most vulnerable to this power. The Canadian deputy prime minister, for example, openly challenged what she termed 'American cultural imperialism' and stated that 'If the Americans insist in pursuing their domination of the world culture community by using all the instruments at their disposal, they will expect the same in return' (Turner, 1997). Easier said than done!

## Emergence of the transnational symbolic factory: the consequent necessity for a political economy of culture

Finally, what has been the culmination, to date, of the US state's interventionist role in communications developments, and the denial of history in the ideological sphere? Can anyone still doubt the centrality of the communication (production) sector in the United States economy? In 1996, for example, two giant firms, one in software and the other in hardware, Microsoft and Intel, reported net profits that totalled $11 billion. This colossal return catapulted Intel into second place in the national corporate profitability scale, behind GE (General Electric) and ahead of Exxon. 'In a sense,' the report stated, 'the duopoly is already the world's most successful commercial enterprise' (Takahashi, 1997).

Yet this is no aberrant example. The 1990s have seen an incredible system-wide concentration of capital, the communication/media sector in particular being in the forefront. In 1996, for example, 'the volume of [all] mergers and acquisitions done worldwide . . . added up to $1 trillion, . . . and more than $650 billion in the US' (Lipin, 1997).

Growth through merger, consolidation and capital expansion in the symbol-producing industries has been especially active. Time Warner and Disney-ABC Capital Cities, two $20 billion-plus communication/cultural conglomerates, among other symbolic production, manufacture films, TV programmes, books and magazines, and recordings. At the same time, their holdings extend to the circuits that disseminate these products, e.g. cable systems, TV networks, theme parks, etc. To understand the stakes involved, the returns to the 'Star Wars Trilogy' offer some perspective. Beyond its $1.3 billion in movie tickets sold, there was $500 million in video sales, $300 million in CD-ROM and video games, $1.2 billion in toys and playing cards, $300 million in clothes and accessories and $300 million in books and comics (Sterngold, 1997). Four billion dollars is hardly small change!

Accordingly, a few dozen mega hardware and software corporations increasingly fill US and global space with their manufactured symbolic products. How is this rationalised, if it is, by the cultural oligarchs? If the chief executive officer of Time Warner, for example, were asked, 'Don't you think there is a potential danger in having such an aggregation of cultural power, of so much media power, in the hands of one company?' he might reply: 'Our subsidiary companies make their own decisions', implying that there is no such thing as centralised control.[4]

But this fails to take into account a fundamental law at work in a market system. Seemingly autonomous decision-makers still have to bring in a profit. In ways that are not necessarily crudely interventionist or manipulative, they will fashion their media product to guarantee that profit. You don't need a cultural police in a market system. The market system is the 'KGB' and it works very effectively.

The effect on the viewer, reader or listener of the consumption of conglomeratised corporate cultural outputs cannot be explored here. Yet one conclusion seems indisputable. Just as cultural production, in its basic forms and relations, becomes increasingly indistinguishable from production in general, a political economy of culture – its production and its consumption – becomes an obligatory and vital site for research and analysis. To ignore or minimise the value of this field of inquiry is to relinquish understanding of, and therefore the capability for resistance to, the latest crucially important terrain of capitalism. The political economy of cultural production and consumption is the core element in a twenty-first-century political economy of capitalism. This is especially so in this age of 'triumphant capitalism'. How else to begin to challenge its material and symbolic authority?

# Notes

1 The first critique of the 'free flow' doctrine was written by this author and published in *Le Monde Diplomatique* in the early 1970s.

2 Also published in *Editor and Publisher*, 21 April 1945.

3 *The National Information Infrastructure: The Administration's Agenda for Action*, Washington, DC, 15 September 1993. For a critique of this agenda, Herbert I. Schiller, *Information Inequality*, Routledge, New York (1996).

4 Frank Rich reports in his *New York Times* column, 6 March 1997, page A-19, that 'the powers that be at NBC and ABC, both said that their corporate bosses, Jack Welch and Michael Eisner respectively, stay out of programming'.

# References

Barlow, J. P. (1996) The powers that were, *WIRED*, Sept., pp. 197–9.

Bell, D. (1973) *The Coming of Post-Industrial Society*, Basic, New York.

Bennahum, D. S. (1996) The myth of digital nirvana, *Educom Review*, Sept./Oct., 31.5, pp. 24–5.

Burton, D. F., Jr. (1997) The brave new wired world, *Foreign Policy*, 106, Spring, pp. 23–37.

Department of State Bulletin (1946), 14 (344), p. 160.

Fukuyama, F. (1992) *The End of History and the Last Man*, Free Press, New York.

Guback, T. (1969) *The International Film Industry*, Indiana University Press, Bloomington.

Lipin, S. (1997) Corporations' dreams converge in one idea: it's time to do a deal, *The Wall Street Journal*, 26 Feb., p. 1.

Markoff, J. (1993) Clinton proposes changes in policy to aid technology, *New York Times*, 23 Feb., p. 1.

Nye, J. S., Jr. and Owens, W. A. (1996) America's information edge, *Foreign Affairs*, Mar./Apr., pp. 20–36.

Progress Report on Space Communications (1966) Hearings before the Senate Subcommittee on Communications, 89th Congress, 2nd Session, August 10, 17, 18 and 23rd, 1966. Serial 89-78, Washington, p. 81.

Roberts, P. C. (1997) Newt should keep his eye on the enemy: big government, *Business Week*, 13 Jan., p. 26.

Sachs, J. (1997) When foreign aid makes a difference, *New York Times*, 3 Feb., p. A-19.

Sanger, D. E. (1997) Asia's surrender, *New York Times*, 14 Dec., p. 1.

Satellite Communications (1964) (Part 1), Hearings, Committee on Government Operations, 88th Congress, 2nd Session, Washington, pp. 360 and 364.

Schiller, D. (1996) *Theorizing Communication: A History*, Oxford University Press, New York.

Schiller, H. I. (1976) *Communication and Cultural Domination*, International Arts and Sciences Press, White Plains, NY.

Sterngold, J. (1997) The return of the merchandiser, *New York Times*, 30 Jan, p. C-1.

Takahashi, D. (1997) Intel's net doubles on overseas demand, *Wall Street Journal*, 15 Jan., p. 3.

Toffler, A. (1980) *The Third Wave*, William Morrow, New York.

Turner, C. (1997) Canadian official hints at trade war on Hollywood, *Los Angeles Times*, 11 Feb., p. 1.

Webster, F. (1995) *Theories of the Information Society*, Routledge, London.

# 2

# *Media convergence and globalisation*

ROBERT W. McCHESNEY

By the end of the 1990s a major turning-point was reached in the realm of media. Whereas media systems had been primarily national before the 1990s, a global commercial media market was emerging in full force by the dawn of the twenty-first century. In the past, to understand any nation's media situation, one had to first understand the local and national media and then determine where the global market – which largely meant imports and exports of films, TV shows, books and music – fits in. Today one must first grasp the nature and logic of the global commercial system and then determine how local and national media deviate from the overall system.

The rise of a global commercial media system is closely linked to the rise of a significantly more integrated 'neo-liberal' global capitalist economic system. To some extent the rise of a global media market is encouraged by new digital and satellite technologies that make global markets not only cost effective but also lucrative. It is also encouraged by the institutions of global capitalism – the World Trade Organisation (WTO), the World Bank, the International Monetary Fund (IMF) – as well as those governments, such as that of the United States, that advance the interests of transnational corporations (TNCs). Moreover, media and communication more broadly have become a much more significant sector for business activity during the past generation (Mandel, 1997).

The rise to dominance of the global commercial media system is more than an economic matter; it also has clear implications for media content, politics and culture. In this chapter I briefly chronicle the rise of the global media system and its core attributes. It is a system that, in the end, is dominated by less then ten global TNCs with another three or four dozen firms filling out regional and niche markets. I examine the activities and holdings of the three most important global media firms – Time Warner, Disney and News Corporation – in detail. In my view the general trajectory of the global commercial media system is quite negative if one wishes to preserve and promote those institutions and values that are conducive to meaningful self-government. I conclude by assessing where the Internet fits into the emerging global media system. Some argue that the Internet will 'set us free', and undermine corporate domination of not only communication but the overall political economy. I think that notion is flawed but, as I discuss, there are other signs that the system is meeting resistance.

# The rise of the global media system

The global markets for film production, TV-show production, book publishing and recorded music have been oligopolistic markets for much of their existence. Although there are important domestic industries in many of these industries, the global export market is the province of a handful of mostly US-owned or US-based firms. These not only remain important markets, but they all are tending to grow faster than the global economy.

The motion-picture and TV-show production industries are absolutely booming at the global level (Peers, 1997a). The major film studios and US TV-show production companies (usually the same firms) now generate between 50 and 60 per cent of their revenues outside of the USA (Goldblatt, 1997). A key factor that makes these global oligopolies nearly impenetrable to newcomers is their extensive distribution systems (Rawsthorn, 1997b). Although the Dutch-owned Polygram is attempting to establish a global distribution system for its films, for most other independents the smart move is to link to one of the existing giants (Dawtrey, 1997b; Rawsthorn, 1997a). The global film industry is the province of seven firms, all of which are part of larger media conglomerates. Likewise, the global music industry is dominated by five firms, all but one (EMI) that are part of larger media TNCs (Sandler, 1997).

What distinguishes the emerging global media system is not transnational control over exported media content, however, as much as increasing TNC control over media distribution as well as content. Prior to the 1980s and 1990s, national media systems were typified by nationally owned radio and television systems, as well as domestic newspaper industries. Newspaper publishing remains a largely national phenomenon, but the face of television has changed almost beyond recognition.

The rise of cable and satellite technology has opened up national markets to scores of new channels. The primary providers of these channels are the media TNCs that dominate cable television channel ownership in the USA, and have aggressively established numerous global editions of their channels to accommodate the new market (see, for example, Williams, 1997). Neo-liberal 'free-market' policies have opened up ownership of stations as well as cable and satellite systems to private and transnational interests. As the *Wall Street Journal* notes, 'the cable colonialists continue to press on in Europe, Asia and Latin America, betting on long-term profit' (Frank and Rose, 1997: A1). Likewise, the largest media TNCs are invariably among the main players in efforts to establish digital satellite TV systems to serve regional and national markets (DeGeorge and Malkin, 1997; McElvogue, 1997a). Television is rapidly coming to play the same sort of dominant role in Europe, Asia and worldwide that it has played in the USA for two or three generations. After reviewing the most recent research, one observer noted in early 1998: 'Europe hasn't caught up to American TV consumption levels, but Europeans are spending more time than ever watching television' (Hils, 1998: 41).

The close connection of the rise of the global media system to the global capitalist political economy becomes especially clear in two ways. First, as suggested above, the global media system is the direct result of the sort of 'neo-liberal' deregulatory policies that have assisted in the formation of global markets for other goods and services. At the global level, for example, the WTO ruled in 1997 that Canada could not prohibit Time Warner's *Sports Illustrated* from distributing a Canadian edition of the magazine (Urquhart and Bahree, 1997). Although there is considerable pressure for open media markets, this is a sensitive area and there are strong traditions of protection for domestic media and cultural industries. Nevertheless the trajectory is clearly in the direction of opening markets to TNC penetration. There are often strong commercial media lobbies within nations that see as much to gain by opening up their orders as they do by maintaining any form of protectionism.

The European Union (EU) and European Commission (EC) provide an excellent case study in the evolution of media policymaking to a largely market *über alles* position. Historically, European nations have enjoyed prominent and well-financed national public broadcasters as well as a variety of other mechanisms to protect and promote domestic cultural production. The EU and EC are hardly commissioned to advance the interests of US-based media TNCs, but they are devoted to establishing strong European firms and a regional open commercial market. By this logic, the traditional notion of public-service media, meaning nonprofit media with public subsidy, is something of a square peg. The EC sees its mission as encouraging more competitive media markets, rather than promoting public-service media (Tucker, 1997c; Tucker, 1997d; Buckley and Gapper, 1997).

Nevertheless, there was considerable concern that US-based media firms would quickly overwhelm Europe unless regulations to protect European content were enacted. The EU nearly passed a law in 1997 requiring that 50 per cent of TV content be European-made, but after a 'ferocious lobbying' campaign by European media interests dependent upon US fare, the wording was watered down to be meaningless (Tucker, 1997a; Tucker, 1997b). The EU system has been more effective in spreading commercial values; on two occasions in 1997 the European Court of Justice ruled that member states could not prohibit cable TV channels that featured advertising to children, even though this violated national statutes

(*Financial Times*, 1997a; *Financial Times*, 1997b). An indication of the shifting terrain of European policymaking came in June 1997 when the European summit found it necessary to include a protocol to the EU treaty formally acknowledging that public-service broadcasters had a right to exist (Leclercq, 1997).

Advertising is the second way that the global media system is linked to the global market economy. Advertising is conducted disproportionately by the largest firms in the world, and it is a major weapon in the struggle to establish new markets. For major firms like Procter & Gamble and Nike, global advertising is arguably the most important aspect of their campaigns to maintain strong growth rates (Tomkins, 1997). In conjunction with the 'globalisation' of the economy, advertising has grown globally at a rate greater than GDP growth in the 1990s (Cardona, 1997). The most rapid growth has been in Europe, Latin America and especially East Asia, although the economic collapse of the late 1990s has doused what had been characterised as 'torrid ad growth' (Wentz and Herskovitz, 1997; Wentz, 1998). Advertising in China has been growing at annual rates of 40–50 per cent in the 1990s, and the singularly important sector of TV advertising is expected to continue to grow at least at that rate, with the advent of sophisticated audience research that now delivers vital demographic data to advertisers, especially TNC advertisers (Stein and Daswani, 1997). It is this TNC advertising that has fuelled the rise of commercial television across the world, accounting, for example, for over one-half of the advertising on the ABN-CNBC Asia network, which is co-owned by Dow Jones and General Electric (Lucas, 1997).

The advertising agency business itself has consolidated dramatically on a global basis in the 1990s, such that the three largest firms – WPP Group, Omnicom Group and Interpublic Group – have a combined income 15 per cent greater than that of the ad organisations ranked 4 through 10, and the size of ad organisations falls precipitously after one gets past the first dozen or so (*Advertising Age*, 1997). The fifteenth largest advertising organisation in the world does barely 10 per cent of the business of the WPP Group. The consolidation is encouraged by globalisation, as the largest advertisers increasingly prefer to work with a single agency worldwide. When Citibank consolidated its global advertising into one agency in 1997, an observer noted that 'they want to have one brand with one voice – that's their mantra' (Cardona and Arndorfer, 1997). Global consolidation is also encouraged because the larger an ad agency, the more leverage it can have getting favourable terms for its clients with global commercial media (Smith, 1997). Put together, all of this suggests ever more consolidation in the years to come, and the largest advertising organisations are scurrying about purchasing almost all of the remaining viable independent agencies around the world (Elliott, 1997; Fannin, 1997b). And this, in turn, suggests increased advertising influence over media operations.

But the most important corporate concentration concerns the media industry itself, and here concentration and conglomeration are the order of the day. In short order the global media market has come to be dominated by nine or ten TNCs, which rank among the largest firms in the world: Time Warner, Disney, Bertelsmann, Viacom, Tele-Communications Inc. (TCI), News Corporation, Sony, Seagram (owner of Universal Studios), General Electric (owner of NBC) and the Dutch Philips (owner of Polygram). The largest media firm in the world, Time Warner, is some fifty times larger in terms of annual sales than the world's fiftieth largest media firm.

These firms all have global distribution networks and have major interests in more than one – usually several – media sectors. The global media market is rounded out by a second tier of some three or four dozen firms that are national or regional powerhouses, or which have strong holds over niche markets, like business or trade publishing. About one-half of these second-tier firms come from North America and most of the rest come from Western Europe and Japan. In combination, these fifty or sixty firms control most of the media – book publishing, magazine publishing, music recording, TV-show production, TV station and cable channel ownership, cable/satellite TV system ownership, film production, motion picture theatre ownership, newspaper publishing – in the world (Herman and McChesney, 1997).

There are tremendous economic advantages to size and prudent conglomeration in the global media market, so firms are aggressively expanding through mergers and acquisitions, or putting themselves in the position to be purchased at a premium by another giant. Small firms operating in one market simply cannot compete, unless they are formally linked to a giant. Sony, for one example, has hired the investment banking Blackstone Group to help it identify media takeover candidates (Shapiro, 1997).

To compete in the global market, a firm needs the scale that comes with being a major player in Europe and, especially, the USA. 'We want to be a world-class media company', the CEO of the UK's Pearson TV stated, 'and to do that, we know we've got to get bigger in America' (Littleton and Peers, 1997). Firms like the music powerhouse EMI are invariably on the market; they are worth considerably more merged with one of the other five global music giants that are all part of huge media conglomerates, or with another media TNC that wants a stake in the music market (Rawsthorn, 1997c).

But corporate growth, oligopolistic markets and conglomeration barely reveal the extent to which the global media system is extraordinarily noncompetitive in the economic sense of the term. On the one hand, many of the largest media firms share major shareholders, own pieces of each other, or have interlocking boards of directors. When *Variety* compiled its list of the fifty largest media firms for 1997, it observed that 'merger mania' and cross-ownership had 'resulted in a complex web of interrelationships' that will 'make you dizzy' (Peers, 1997b). On the other hand, the market strongly encourages firms to establish equity joint ventures where the media giants each own a part of an enterprise. This way firms reduce competition and risk, and increase the chance of profitability. In the burgeoning realm of satellite television, for example, even the potentially most lucrative markets like Japan, Germany and the USA have seen joint ventures and mergers reduce the number of viable entrants to two or one. In Germany, former arch-enemies Kirch and Bertelsmann buried the hatchet in 1997 to co-own Premiere (Hils, 1997). In Japan, News Corporation's joint venture Japan Sky Broadcasting (JSkyB) has already merged with one of its two potential competitors (Nakamoto, 1997b). The CEO of Fuji Television, Japan's biggest media company and a partner in JSkyB, states that 'eventually there will only be one satellite broadcaster' (McElvogue, 1997b: 53).

Satellite broadcasting is a very small example of the joint-venture phenomenon. The ten largest media TNCs have joint ventures on average with six of the other nine media giants. Often, the media TNCs enjoy multiple joint ventures with each other. News Corporation has joint ventures with each of the other nine media giants. News Corporation heir Lachlan Murdoch expressed the rational view when explaining why News Corporation is working more closely with Kerry Packer's Publishing and Broadcasting Ltd., the company that with News Corp. effectively controls much of Australian media. It is better, Murdoch the younger contends, if they are not 'aggressively attacking each other all the time' (Groves, 1997c).

The global media market is one where the dominant firms compete aggressively in some concentrated oligopolistic markets, are key suppliers to each other in other markets, and are partners in yet other markets. As the headline in one trade publication put it, this is a market where the reigning spirit is to 'Make profits, not war' (Hall and McConville, 1997: 3). In short, the global media market looks much more like a cartel than it does a competitive marketplace.

# The Holy Trinity of the global media system

The nature of the global media system seems less abstract when one examines the recent growth, activities and strategies of its three most important TNCs: Time Warner, Disney and News Corporation. Time Warner and Disney are the two largest media firms in the world, with 1998 sales in the area of $23–26 billion. News Corporation is in contention with Viacom for the status as fourth largest global media firm, with sales slightly more than one-half those of Time Warner and Disney, but under its CEO Rupert Murdoch it has led the way in media globalisation. These are global empires constructed largely in the 1990s, and they are a long way from completion.

Time Warner is the outgrowth of the 1989 merger of Time and Warner Communications and the 1996 acquisition of Turner Broadcasting. It will do around $26 billion in business in 1998, and its sales are expected to continue to grow at double-digit rates for the foreseeable future. With 200 subsidiaries worldwide, Time Warner has seen its non-US income increase from around 15 per cent in the early 1990s to 35 per cent in 1997. Early in the twenty-first century, Time Warner expects to earn a majority of its revenues outside of the USA. That is where the most dramatic growth can be found. What is also striking about Time Warner is how it is a dominant global player in virtually every single important media sector except newspaper publishing and radio broadcasting. Time Warner's challenge is to develop its synergies; to mesh its extremely lucrative parts to increase the size of the profit whole (*Economist*, 1997a). But it has an unparalleled combination of content production and distribution systems to work with.

Here are some of Time Warner's holdings:

- majority interest in the US WB television network
- largest cable broadcasting system operator in USA, controlling 22 of 100 largest markets
- controlling interest in cable TV channels CNN, Headline News, CNNfn, CNN International, TNT, TBS, Turner Classic Movies, CNNSI, The Cartoon Network, Court TV, HBO, HBO International, Cinemax
- partial interest in cable TV channel Comedy Central
- minority stake in US satellite TV service PrimeStar
- Warner Brothers film studios, one of the half-dozen studios that dominated the global market
- Warner Brothers TV production studios, one of largest TV-show production companies in the world
- New Line film studios
- the largest US magazine publishing group, including *Time*, *People*, *Sports Illustrated* and *Fortune*
- Warner Music Group, one of the six firms that dominate the global recorded music industry
- second largest book publisher in the world, with 42 per cent of sales outside the USA
- 150 Warner Bros. retail stores
- Six Flags theme-park chain
- the Atlanta Hawks and Atlanta Braves US professional sports teams
- Hanna-Barbera animation studios
- 10 per cent stake in France's Canalsatellite, a digital TV service
- one of largest movie-theatre-owning companies in the world, with over 1000 screens, all outside the USA
- 23 per cent stake in Atari
- 14 per cent stake in Hasbro
- minority stakes in the following non-US broadcasting joint ventures: Germany's N-TV, New Zealand's Sky Network Television, European music channel VIVA, and Asian music channel Classic V.

Even this list fails to do justice to Time Warner's global reach. CNN International is the dominant global TV news channel, broadcasting in several languages to some 200 nations (Anderson, 1997). HBO is a global powerhouse as well, having expanded successfully into Western Europe, Latin America, Eastern Europe and all across Asia. As one observer notes, HBO's International division 'gobbles up new countries' (Klapwald, 1997; see also Groves, 1997a; Nadler, 1997; Meils, 1997; Dutz, 1998). The Warner Bros. film studios has established relations with Australian, German, French and Spanish companies to co-produce films, often not in English (Dawtrey, 1997a; Weiner, 1997; Karon, 1997). Even the US-based magazine division is going global, with non-US editions of its publications and planned acquisitions of European magazines (Fannin, 1997a; Brown, 1997).

But what really distinguishes Time Warner and what gives it such leverage in the global market are two related things. First, in addition to arguably 'producing' more media content than any other firm, Time Warner also has the world's largest library of music, films, TV shows and cartoons to exploit. This makes Time Warner a firm that is extremely attractive to national media firms for joint ventures or simply major contracts, as it has with Canal Plus, the satellite television power in France, Spain and Italy (Vulser, 1997; Jack, 1997; Hopewell, 1998; Hopewell and Guider, 1997). Second, Time Warner arguably has more recognisable media 'brand names' than any firm in the world. Branding is considered the most crucial determinant of market success, and the one factor that can assure success in the digital world, with its myriad of choices, albeit controlled by a small number of owners. Branding also lends itself to extensive licensing and merchandising of products related to media characters, channels and programming. Time Warner considers its 'Looney Tunes' cartoons alone a $4 billion worldwide brand, and Batman a $1 billion worldwide brand. With 150 Warner Bros. retail stores and scores of licensing agreements, merchandising has become a multi-billion-dollar segment of Time Warner's annual income, and it is among the fastest-growing branches of its global operations.

But nobody understands branding and merchandising better than Disney, which runs neck-and-neck with Time Warner for the honour of being the world's largest media firm. With some 590 Disney retail stores worldwide as well as merchandising and licensing deals with numerous manufacturers and retailers, Disney is evolving into what one industry observer characterises as 'the ultimate global consumer goods company' (Mermigas, 1997). Disney has moved aggressively into China, with seven stores in Hong Kong and plans to open several more on the mainland in 1998 and 1999 (Groves, 1997e). Disney has carefully intertwined its media brands with its retail activities, and has done so on a global basis. It has major Disney theme parks in Japan and France as well as the USA, a Disney passenger cruise-ship line, and is launching DisneyQuest, a chain of 'location-based entertainment' stores – i.e. high-tech video arcades – based around Disney brands (Voland, 1997). Disney has even launched a planned community near its Disney World resort in Orlando, Florida, replete with Disney-run schools and social services. Disney is also the master of synergies, the process of taking a media brand and exploiting it for all the profit possible. Its animated films routinely generate vastly more income and profit from merchandising and other sources than they do from box-office receipts. In 1998 Disney will also launch an *ESPN Sports Weekly* magazine (to compete with Time Warner's *Sports Illustrated*) and a chain of ESPN Grill restaurants to capitalise upon the ESPN trade name.

Here are some of Disney's holdings:

- the US ABC television and radio networks
- ten US TV stations and twenty-one radio stations
- US and global cable TV channels – Disney Channel, ESPN, ESPN2, ESPNews, ESPN International, and major stakes in Lifetime, A&E and History Channels
- a stake in Americast, an interactive TV joint venture with several US telephone companies
- major film studios, Miramax and Walt Disney Pictures
- TV production and distribution through Buena Vista
- magazine publishing through its Fairchild and Chilton subsidiaries
- music recording, including the Hollywood, Mammoth and Walt Disney labels
- world's largest theme parks and resorts, including Disneyland, Disney World and a stake in Euro Disney
- Disney cruise line
- DisneyQuest, chain of high-tech arcade game stores
- controlling interest in Anaheim Mighty Ducks and Anaheim Angels US professional sports teams
- 590 Disney stores worldwide
- 50 per cent stake in Super RTL, a joint venture with Bertelsmann
- 20–33 per cent stakes in the following commercial media companies: Eurosport TV network, the Spanish Tesauro SA, the German terrestrial channel RTL2, the German cable TV channel TM3, Scandinavian Broadcasting Systems SA, and Brazilian TVA, a pay-TV company.

Disney, like Time Warner, has globalised its production and has signed production and distribution deals with firms in France, Japan and Latin America, to mention but a few (Nakamoto, 1997a; Orwall, 1997b; Paxman, 1997). Disney's Miramax is launching a European film studio to be based in Britain (Parkes, 1997). And Disney is making a full-scale assault on the global television market, operating on many fronts. It is the largest shareholder in Scandinavian Broadcasting Systems (SBS), the company which owns and operates major commercial terrestrial TV channels in Norway, Sweden, Denmark, Finland, Belgium and the Netherlands. The

SBS goal is to corner 25–40 per cent of the TV advertising revenue in each of those markets, and it has already been successful in that regard in Norway and Belgium (Westcott, 1997; Edmunds, 1997). Disney also has distributed its Disney TV Channel in numerous nations around the world, customising it to local cultures and languages. Most important, Disney's ESPN International has become the world leader in televised sport, broadcast in 21 languages to over 165 countries.

Sport is arguably the single most lucrative content area for the global media industry, a point understood best of all by Rupert Murdoch, CEO of News Corporation. Sport was crucial in making his British Sky Broadcasting (BSkyB) the most successful satellite TV service in the world and in making the US Fox TV network a full-fledged competitor to ABC, NBC and CBS. Murdoch, more than any other figure, has been the visionary of a global corporate media empire. Using as a base his newspaper empires, first in his native Australia where he controls 70 per cent of the daily circulation, and later in Britain where he is the largest newspaper publisher, Murdoch has expanded into film, publishing and especially television on a global basis (*Economist*, 1997b). He has established a major film studio in Australia to serve the global market (Groves, 1997b; Groves, 1997d). Murdoch remains the most aggressive media mogul, and he has turned to joint ventures to expand his empire without using much of his own capital. 'We don't see ourselves as a large corporation', Murdoch informed a closed meeting of investors in 1997. 'We see ourselves as tiny compared to the worldwide opportunities for media.' Murdoch has devoted inordinate attention to developing media properties in Asia and Latin America, even though News Corporation will receive the majority of its income from the USA for at least another decade. 'He views these investments in multiyear terms,' a securities analyst states, 'even multigenerational' (Lippmann, 1997).

Here are some of News Corp.'s holdings:

- the US Fox television network
- twenty-two US television stations, covering 40 per cent of the US population
- Fox News Channel, US and international TV network
- 50 per cent stake in fx, fxM, Fox Sports Net, Fox Kids Worldwide, Family Channel TV channels
- film studio Twentieth Century Fox
- Twentieth Television, US and international TV production and distribution group
- over 130 daily newspapers, including *The Times* (of London) and the *New York Post*
- twenty-five magazines, including *TV Guide*
- book publishing, including HarperCollins
- Los Angeles Dodgers professional baseball team

- controlling interest in British Sky Broadcasting (BSkyB) satellite TV service
- numerous Sky TV channels distributed across Britain and parts of Europe, including Sky News
- Latin American TV channels El Canal Fox and Fox Sport Noticias
- partial stake in Latin Sky Broadcasting satellite TV service to Latin America, joint venture with Televisa and Globo
- 80 per cent stake in New Zealand's Natural History Unit, world leading producer of nature and wildlife documentaries
- Heritage Media, leading US direct marketing company, with 1996 revenues over $500 million
- 30 per cent stake (nonvoting) in Primestar, US satellite TV joint venture with major cable companies
- Asian Star TV satellite TV service
- pan-Asian TV channels: ESPN and Star Sports (four Asian channels), Channel V music channel (with four Asian channels) joint venture with major record companies, Star World, Star Plus, Star Movies (nine Asian channels)
- 50 per cent stake in Indian TV channels Zee TV, El TV and Zee Cinema
- partial stake in Indian cable TV company Siti Cable
- partial stake in Indonesian pay TV venture Indovision and Film Indonesia pay-TV channel
- partial stake, with Sony, Fuji TV and Softbank, in Japan Sky Broadcasting satellite TV system
- Star Chinese Channel, broadcast across Taiwan
- 45 per cent interest in Phoenix Chinese Channel, satellite TV service for mainland China
- partial interest in Golden Mainland Productions, TV joint venture with Taiwan Sports Development
- Australian TV channels FoxTel
- partial interest in ChinaByte, website joint venture with China's *People's Daily*
- India Sky Broadcasting, satellite TV service.

The defining feature of Murdoch's global push is the establishment of satellite television systems, along with the channels and programming to be displayed on them. By 1998 Murdoch claimed to have TV networks and systems that reached more than 75 per cent of the world's population, with his launch of satellite systems in Latin America, Japan and India to complement his other activities. 'The borderless world opened up to us by the digital information age will afford huge challenges and limitless opportunities', Murdoch contends (Gapper, 1997a). The archetype will be BSkyB, which not only dominated British pay television, but also has launched film and programme production facilities and has channels to be broadcast not only in Britain but also on European TV systems and eventually across the world (Clover, 1997; Boehm, 1997). His two other main TV 'brands' are the Fox channels, connected to his US TV network, cable channels and major film and TV production studios, and his Star Television service, which News Corp. purchased in 1993, for all of Asia.

The list above barely gives a sense of how quickly News Corporation has made Asian television its own fiefdom. In India, for example, it has equity stakes of either 50 or 100 per cent in eight different networks. In combination these channels constitute 45 per cent of the total viewership in cable and satellite homes in India. News Corp. has six networks in China, and its Phoenix joint venture has already been cleared in 36.2 million Chinese cable TV households. In Taiwan, News Corp. has seven channels and dominates the market (Davey, 1997). When Prince Al-Waleed invested $400 million to purchase a 5 per cent stake in News Corp. in 1997, he commented that 'News Corp. is the only real global media company that covers the world' (Frank, 1997). Whether News Corp. ever fulfils its ambitions remains to be seen, and it faces numerous obstacles along the way. In India, for example, the government in 1997 cracked down on foreign ownership of media after Murdoch hired scores of former government employees to be his top local executives (Karp, 1997; Wanravi, 1997).

But News Corp. has enjoyed tremendous successes and its persistence has paid off just about everywhere, including China, where Murdoch had got into hot water in 1994 by stating that new communication technologies 'were a threat to totalitarian regimes everywhere' (Walker and Snoddy, 1997). And as firms like News Corp. expand through mergers and acquisitions, they run the risk of taking on large levels of debt that leave them exposed, especially if there is a business recession. Nevertheless, all of the media giants are emulating News Corp.'s strategy of getting bigger and going global with a vengeance. If they wish to maintain or expand their profitability – and avoid getting swallowed up by a competitor – they have no choice. And in the current political environment, the global media giants are in position to make dramatic strides in short order. The world is being remade before our eyes.

## Conclusion: the two wild cards in the global media deck

The discussion to this point has emphasised the strength and power, the almost 'irreversibility' of the emerging global commercial media system. If one is concerned with the promotion and expansion of participatory democracy, or some sort of civic life and values aside from those of the market, this is a fairly depressing scenario. But in tumultuous times like these, no one can speak with certainty with regard to the future. In mainstream debate, in fact, the tumult is largely associated with the dramatic technological revolution in computing and communication, most significantly represented by the rise of the Internet in the middle and late 1990s.

With the Internet 'wild card', the traditional concentrated control over communication on technological grounds effectively ends. Accordingly, the Chinese government has gone to considerable lengths to limit the ability of Chinese to get online and to prevent the dissemination of politically dissident websites (Eckholm, 1997). But the Internet does not merely threaten governments; it also holds the potential to undermine corporate control of media. If anyone can produce a website at minimal cost and it can be distributed worldwide via the World Wide Web, it will be only a matter of time (expansion of bandwidth, improvement of software) until the media giants find themselves swamped by countless high-quality competitors. As one *New York Times* correspondent put it: 'To hear Andy Grove [CEO of Intel] and Reed Hundt [former chair of the US Federal Communications Commission] talk, the media industry is about where the horse-and-buggy business was when Henry Ford first cranked up the assembly line' (Landler, 1998: 9).

This is nonsense. Although the rise of the Internet and digital communication introduces instability to the media industry, in the current neo-liberal political environment, the Internet is being developed on nearly purely commercial grounds, meaning whoever can make the most money wins. The real action with the Internet at present comes less on the media side than on the telecommunication and computing side, and with the corporate economic order in general. The easiest and most lucrative manner for the Internet (and digital communication networks) to be exploited is to serve the wealthiest corporate clients who have the most to gain by rapid, global communication (Schiller, forthcoming). 'It may seem as if the two year old Internet industry is mounting a takeover of corporate America', the *Financial Times* noted in 1998. 'The reality is more like a merger' (Denton, 1998). Indeed, the Internet and digital communication network are in some ways the defining features of the emerging global economic order. Already, electronic commerce and marketing are booming, with strong projections of continued rapid growth (Wheelwright, 1998). And this is how the Internet is being exploited as it rapidly evolves from being primarily a US medium to being a global medium. As *Business Week* notes, 'it's a nifty way to expand a company's markets without spending a bundle on foreign subsidiaries' (Browne and Green, 1997).

It remains to be seen exactly where the Internet and/or any other digital communication network will fit into the global media landscape 10 or 20 years down the road. If it remains, as Time Warner CEO Gerald Levin puts it, 'not clear where you make money on it' (in Landler, 1998: 9), the web might become primarily a means of selling digital media products directly to the consumer. To the extent that it is aggressively developed as a commercial medium by cable, satellite and terrestrial television companies, all signs point to its becoming increasingly like the existing commercial broadcasting system. Something along these lines tends to be the prevailing wisdom among the media giants. 'I believe the electronic revolution is simply one new form of communications that will find its place in the food chain of communications and will not displace or replace anything that already exists,' the president of Time, Inc. stated, 'just as television did not replace radio, just as cable did not replace network television, just as the VCR did not replace the movie theatres' (Snoddy, 1997). At any rate, in this type of scenario, the existing media giants should have little problem using their current market position to incorporate the Internet into their existing empires. There may be some reshuffling of the deck between them, but little likelihood of the industry being overturned.

Ironically, the most striking feature of digital communication may well be not that it opened up competition in communication markets, but that it has made it vastly easier, more attractive and 'necessary' for firms to consolidate and strike alliances across the media, telecommunication and computer software sectors. In the 1990s almost all the media giants have entered into joint ventures or strategic alliances with the largest telecom and software firms. Time Warner is connected to several of the US regional Bells telephone giants, as well as AT&T and Oracle. It has a major joint venture with US West. Disney, likewise, is connected to several major US telecommunication companies as well as to America Online. News Corp. is partially owned by WorldCom (MCI) and has a joint venture with British Telecom (Herman and McChesney, 1997; Flaherty, 1997). The global media cartel may become something of a global communication cartel.

At any rate, the global corporate media giants are leaving nothing to chance with the Internet. Bertelsmann and Sony, the third and sixth largest global media firms respectively, have made development of the Internet a main strategic focus (Studemann, 1997). Consider the activities of Time Warner and Disney, for example. Time Warner produces nearly 200 websites, which it aggressively promotes to its audiences through its existing media (Landler, 1998). Its CNN website is now available in Swedish, with other languages to follow (Jakobsen, 1997; Galetto, 1997). Time Warner uses its websites to go after the youth market, to attract sports fans, and to provide entertainment content similar to that of its 'old' media (Griffith, 1998; Shaw, 1997). Time Warner is bringing advertisers aboard with long-term contracts, and giving them equity interest in some projects (Sharkey, 1997). Its most developed relationship with advertisers is the ParentTime website joint venture it has with Procter & Gamble (Riedman, 1997).

Disney's vision of the digital future also sees a major role for advertising. 'With a click of a remote-control button', ABC president Preston Padden enthused in 1997, 'customers will be able to tell us if they want a free sample of a new headache remedy or wish to test-drive a new car' (Pope, 1997). Disney has been as aggressive in cyberspace as Time Warner and the other media giants; in 1997, as part of a 'blitz by Disney to establish Internet beachheads for many of its products', it launched a subscription website for its 'Daily Blast' children's website, exclusively available on the Microsoft Network (Orwall, 1997c).

By the end of the 1990s, while it remains unclear where the Internet will fit into or how it might alter the global media system, this much can be concluded. Despite the much ballyhooed 'openness' of the Internet, to the extent it becomes a viable mass medium, it will likely be dominated by the usual corporate suspects. The media giants have enormous advantages over any other Internet 'content providers'. These include their abilities: to use their existing programming; to promote their websites on their traditional media; and to draw in major advertisers. Moreover, as the possessors of the hottest 'brands', the media firms have the leverage to get premier location from browser software makers and Internet service providers (Orwall, 1997a).

The ultimate aim of the corporate media giants, as the president of Starwave, the website producer linked to Disney, stated, is 'to create the destination which contains everything someone could want . . . It's the brand power that we have' (Sacharow, 1997). To the extent that the Internet develops as a commercial medium worldwide, these patterns would hold true as well. Indeed, aimed at the affluent consumers that would attract web advertising, the Internet might even increase information and communication inequality in the developing world, if not everywhere (Browne and Green, 1997). The dissident and noncommercial voices will remain and have the potential of being extraordinarily important. But they will hardly challenge the hegemony of the corporate communication giants, as they will exist largely on the margins with what at this point in time is an indeterminable amount of influence in the big scheme of things.

But it does not have to be this way. The second wild card in the global media deck is the world's people, constituted as organised citizens rather than as consumers and couch potatoes. It can be difficult, especially from the vantage-point of the USA or the wealthy nations, to see much hope for public opposition to the global corporate media system. As one Swedish journalist noted in 1997, 'unfortunately, the trends are very clear, moving in the wrong direction on virtually every score, and there is a desperate lack of public discussion of the long-term implications of current developments for democracy and accountability' (Wennerberg, 1997). Yet, there are indications that progressive political forces in nations around the world are increasingly making media issues part of their political platforms. As the global media system is increasingly intertwined with global capitalism, their fates go hand in hand. And despite much blathering about the 'end of history' and the triumph of the market in the commercial media and among Western intellectuals, the actual track record is quite dubious. Asia, the long-celebrated tiger of twenty-first century capitalism, is now mired in a deep economic depression. Latin America, the other vaunted champion of market reforms since the 1980s, has also seen what a World Bank official terms a 'big increase in inequality' (Colitt, 1997). The ecologies of both regions are little short of disastrous. If, and perhaps only if, the reigning spirit of profits *über alles* ever comes under political challenge, it seems likely that the corporate media system will be subject to a well-deserved public examination as well.

# References

*Advertising Age* (1997) Top 10 ad organizations, 21 April, p. s2.

Anderson, K. (1997) CNNI's money makers, *Cable & Satellite Express*, 8 May, p. 6.

Boehm, E. (1997) BSkyB eyes move into UK film market, *Variety*, 21–7 April, p. 8.

Brown, M. (1997) A whiff of the exotic, *Financial Times*, 8 Sept., p. 11.

Browne, L. and Green, H. (1997) Welcoming Spanish speakers to the web, *Business Week*, 29 Dec., p. 50E8.

Buckley, N. and Gapper, J. (1997) Publishing merger plan probed by Brussels, *Financial Times*, 12 Dec., p. 15.

Cardona, M. M. (1997) Coen: Ad spending in '98 will outpace overall economy, *Advertising Age*, 15 Dec., p. 6.

Cardona, M. M. and Arndorfer, J. M. (1997) Citibank's global plum lands at Y&R, *Advertising Age*, 11 Aug., p. 4.

Clover, J. (1997) Sky launches Nordic package, *European Television Analyst*, 12 March, p. 5.

Colitt, R. (1997) Latin America reforms 'fail to cut income disparities', *Financial Times*, 13 Nov., p. 7.

Davey, G. (1997) Star TV, *Asia Research* (a Goldman Sachs publication), 24 Oct., pp. 5–14.

Dawtrey, A. (1997a) Warners Intl. favors local flavor, *Variety*, 26 May–1 June, p. 19.

Dawtrey, A. (1997b) Polygram sets sail for American market, *Variety*, 15–21 Dec., pp. 11, 40.

DeGeorge, G. and Malkin, E. (1997) Satellite TV: still a fuzzy picture, *Business Week*, 29 Dec., p. 50E4.

Denton, N. (1998) Mainstream.com, *Financial Times*, 3–4 Jan., p. 6.

Dutz, V. (1998) HBO takes first steps with Romanian service, *TV East Europe*, Jan., p. 1.

Eckholm, E. (1997) China cracks down on dissent in cyberspace, *New York Times*, 31 Dec., p. A-3.

*Economist* (1997a) Ted Turner's management consultant, 22 March, p. 86.

*Economist* (1997b) Let battle commence, 26 April, pp. 60, 63.

Edmunds, M. (1997) Buying sizzles for Scandi TV, *Variety*, 7–13 April, p. M14.

Elliott, S. (1997) In a further push into Latin America, DDB Needham is buying a stake in a Brazilian agency, *New York Times*, 16 June, p. C-12.

Fannin, R. (1997a) Every title a pearl, *Advertising Age International*, May, p. i16.

Fannin, R. (1997b) DDB Needham takes majority interest in Brazil hot shop DM9, *Advertising Age*, 16 June, p. 12.

*Financial Times* (1997a) TV restrictions unlawful, 3 June, p. 25.

*Financial Times* (1997b) Broadcasting across borders, 15 July, p. 11.

Flaherty, N. (1997) Diving in at the deep end, *Cable and Satellite Europe*, March, pp. 61, 63.

Frank, R. (1997) Prince Waleed invests $850 million in News Corp., Netscape, Motorola, *Wall Street Journal*, 25 Nov., p. B4.

Frank, R. and Rose, M. (1997) A massive investment in British cable TV sours for US firms, *Wall Street Journal*, 17 Dec., pp. A1, A10.

Galetto, M. (1997) CNN spots online gold and starts speaking Swedish, *Electronic Media*, 17 March, p. 28.

Gapper, J. (1997a) News Corporation raises coverage, *Financial Times*, 15 Sept., p. 23.

Goldblatt, H. (1997) The universal appeal of schlock, *Fortune*, 12 May, p. 32.

Griffith, V. (1998) Get them while they're young, *Financial Times*, 5 Jan., p. 19.

Groves, D. (1997a) Hooks and 'faith' helped delivery, *Variety*, 9–15 June, p. 63.

Groves, D. (1997b) Fix Oz studios eye int'l biz, *Variety*, 25–31 Aug., p. 18.

Groves, D. (1997c) Heir power, *Variety*, 8–14 Sept., p. 8.

Groves, D. (1997d) Bowing complex courts new synergies, *Variety*, 15–21 Sept., pp. 21, 27.

Groves, D. (1997e) Tough going: sino the times, *Variety*, 1–7 Dec., pp. 1, 86.

Hall, L. and McConville, J. (1997) Time Warner, News Corp.: make profits, not war, *Electronic Media*, 28 July, pp. 3, 38.

Herman, E. and McChesney, R. (1997) *The Global Media: The New Missionaries of Corporate Capitalism*, Cassell, London.

Hils, M. (1997) DF1 in Premiere fold, *Variety*, 1–7 Sept., p. 29.

Hils, M. (1998) Tube time on the rise in Europe, *Variety*, 5–11 Jan., pp. 41, 48.

Hopewell, J. (1998) WB creates Spanish axis, *Variety*, 5–11 Jan., p. 28.

Hopewell, J. and Guider, E. (1997) Sogecable, WB in pact, *Variety*, 14–20 July, p. 33.

Jack, A. (1997) Warner to purchase 10% of Canal Satellite, *Financial Times*, 18 Nov., p. 20.

Jakobsen, L. (1997) CNN interactive in Swedish, *Cable & Satellite Express*, 20 March, p. 8.

Karon, P. (1997) WB, Village ink prod'n pact, *Variety*, 15–21 Dec., p. 20.

Karp, J. (1997) India may pull plug on News Corp.'s TV, *Wall Street Journal*, 2 Sept., p. A15.

Klapwald, T. (1997) Int'l division gobbles up new countries, *Variety*, 3–9 Nov., p. 56.

Landler, M. (1998) From gurus to sitting ducks, *New York Times*, 11 Jan., Section 3, pp. 1, 9.

Leclercq, T. (1997) Europeans give blessing to public service, *Television Business International*, July/Aug., p. 13.

Lippmann, J. (1997) News Corp.'s Murdoch is shopping to expand empire, *Wall Street Journal*, 16 April, p. B10.

Littleton, C. and Peers, M. (1997) All American raises Brit flag, *Variety*, 6–12 Oct., p. 36.

Lucas, L. (1997) Business television in Asia receiving mixed signals, *Financial Times*, 11 Dec., p. 14.

Mandel, M. J. (1997) The new business cycle, *Business Week*, 31 March, pp. 58–68.

McElvogue, L. (1997a) Digging for gold in Latin America, *Television Business International*, Sept., p. 92.

McElvogue, L. (1997b) Developing Fuji, *Television Business International*, Dec., pp. 52–3.

Meils, C. (1997) HBO goes sat for Slovak launch, *Variety*, 17–23 March, p. 35.

Mermigas, D. (1997) Strong profit picture for animation, *Electronic Media*, 22–9 Dec., p. 14.

Nadler, J. (1997) HBO gets sat hookup, *Variety*, 7–13 April, p. 66.

Nakamoto, M. (1997a) Walt Disney presents: A Japanese story, *Financial Times*, 17 July, p. 5.

Nakamoto, M. (1997b) JSkyB confirms talks on PerfecTV merger, *Financial Times*, 23 Dec., p. 17.

Orwall, B. (1997a) On-line service by Disney's ABC unit will be promoted by AOL, Netscape, *Wall Street Journal*, 4 April, p. A5.

Orwall, B. (1997b) Disney's Miramax signs pay-TV pact with Canal Plus, *Wall Street Journal*, 16 May, p. B6.

Orwall, B. (1997c) Disney blitzes cyberspace with 'Daily Blast' service, *Wall Street Journal*, 28 July, p. B4.

Parkes, C. (1997) Disney hires once more, to keep the Brits a'coming, *Financial Times*, 4 Nov., p. 5.

Paxman, A. (1997) It's a smaller world already for Disney in Mexico, *Variety*, 17–23 March, p. 32.

Peers, M. (1997a) Movie biz enjoys global warming, *Variety*, 7–13 April, pp. 1, 32.

Peers, M. (1997b) The global 50, *Variety*, 25–31 Aug., p. 31.

Pope, K. (1997) High-definition TV is dealt a setback, *Wall Street Journal*, 13 Aug., p. B5.

Rawsthorn, A. (1997a) Put to the screen test, *Financial Times*, 30–1 Aug., p. 7.

Rawsthorn, A. (1997b) Film industry focuses on distribution scene, *Financial Times*, 4–5 Oct., p. 5.

Rawsthorn, A. (1997c) Playing in a minor key, *Financial Times*, 22–3 Nov., p. 22.

Riedman, P. (1997) ParentTime 1st family channel for PointCast, *Advertising Age*, 18 Aug., p. 19.

Sacharow, A. (1997) Star power, *Adweek*, 5 May, p. 48.

Sandler, A. (1997) BMG's potent portfolio boosts market share, *Variety*, 15–21 Dec., pp. 38, 78.

Schiller, D. (forthcoming) *The Enchanted Network: How Digital Capitalism is Remaking the World*.

Shapiro, E. (1997) Sony says it's weighing digital moves and hires Blackstone Group to assist, *Wall Street Journal*, 21 Nov., p. B6.

Sharkey, B. (1997) Warner's web, *IQ*, 18 Aug., pp. 10–14.

Shaw, R. (1997) CNN/SI challenges ESPN site, *Electronic Media*, 21 July, p. 20.

Smith, A. (1997) Strength through unity, *Financial Times*, 10 Nov., p. 15.

Snoddy, R. (1997) Programmer turned publisher, *Financial Times*, 9 June, p. 7.

Stein, J. and Daswani, M. (1997) Counting China, *Television Business International*, Dec., pp. 30–1.

Studemann, F. (1997) Online and on top, *Financial Times*, 18 Nov., Germany section, p. 9.

Tomkins, R. (1997) P&G to get ahead by marketing, *Financial Times*, 5 June, p. 21.

Tucker, E. (1997a) EU media initiative bogged down, *Financial Times*, 13 March, p. 3.

Tucker, E. (1997b) TV law finds the off-switch, *Financial Times*, 17 April, p. 3.

Tucker, E. (1997c) German groups to halt digital TV promotion, *Financial Times*, 16 Dec., p. 3.

Tucker, E. (1997d) EU tells telecoms groups to isolate cable TV, *Financial Times*, 17 Dec., p. 3.

Urquhart, J. and Bahree, B. (1997) WTO body orders Canada to change magazine rule, *Wall Street Journal*, 1 July, p. B8.

Voland, J. (1997) Disney sets sights on new games, *Variety*, 11–17 Aug., pp. 7–8.

Vulser, N. (1997) Time Warner to put 10% stake in Canal satellite, *Cable & Satellite Express*, 20 Nov., pp. 1–2.

Walker, T. and Snoddy, R. (1997) Murdoch woos China on satellite TV, *Financial Times*, 16 May, p. 1.

Wanravi, A. (1997) Star in a storm, *Television Business International*, Oct., pp. 82–3.

Weiner, R. (1997) 'H'wood's euro fever, *Variety*, 19–25 May, pp. 1, 70.

Wennerberg, T. (1997) Letter to Edward S. Herman, 18 Aug., p. 3.

Wentz, L. (1998) Happy new year? Asia drops long shadow over forecast, *Ad Age International*, Jan, pp. 3, 6.

Wentz, L. and Herskovitz, J. (1997) Asian economic turmoil douses torrid ad growth, *Advertising Age*, 8 Dec., p. 18.

Westcott, T. (1997) SBS moves in from the margin, *Television Business International*, Oct., pp. 77–80.

Wheelwright, G. (1998) Money-makers on the Internet, *Financial Times*, 7 Jan., IT section, p. 15.

Williams, M. (1997) NBC Europe enters Spain, eyes France, *Variety*, 8–14 Sept., p. 33.

# 3

# *Full of Eastern promise?*

## *Central and Eastern European media after 1989*

JOHN DOWNEY

The media in the former state socialist regimes of Central and Eastern Europe were largely bypassed in the media- and cultural-imperialism debate generated by media scholars in the 1970s (Schiller, 1976; Boyd-Barrett, 1977; Tunstall, 1977). Mattelart and Dorfman's classic cultural-imperialism text (1975), for example, set about deconstructing the transmission of the ideology of the US military–industrial complex via Disney cartoons in South America. The imperialists were the huge US media conglomerates, ably assisted by the US state, and were perceived to be undertaking a deeply ideological as well as, of course, financial project (Golding and Harris, eds, 1997). The victims of this export trade were numerous – the 'third world' as well as states in Western Europe. Of course, the USA tried very obviously to use media to intervene on an ideological level in Central and Eastern Europe, but this received much less attention. Perhaps this was because the attempts were so obvious that scholars did not feel the need to enlighten; perhaps it was because of the difficulties of carrying out such research (however, audience research was never a strong point of the media-imperialist theorists); perhaps it was because of an unwillingness to side with the Soviet Union and its satellite states.

The theoretical support for the proponents of the media-imperialist thesis is Marxism and a variety of neo-Marxisms. Fundamental to this discourse is an analysis of the forces and relations of production (indeed Mattelart and Dorfman were unusual in that they indulged in textual critique). This was very much an ethical and political project; engaged intellectuals labouring on behalf of the oppressed. With respect to Central and Eastern European states, the media imperialists inherited the thorny problem of Western Marxism. After the Hungarian uprising in 1956 and the Stalin revelations, Western Marxism set out to steer a course between the two evil empires – a course that concentrated largely on a critique of contemporary capitalism but without siding with the Soviet Union. The relationship between US media and the states in Central and Eastern Europe was too much of an ambivalent subject for scholars of media imperialism.

The fall of the state socialist regimes in Central and Eastern Europe in 1989, however, reduces this ambivalence while also making critical empirical research a possibility. In terms of media studies, 1989 meant the opening up of new possibilities for the media-imperialism thesis. Critical studies of the impact of US and Western European media on the changes occurring in Central and Eastern Europe could unambiguously side with democracy. That said, there has not been an avalanche of monographs and journal articles investigating this issue. Partly this is due to the waning of the popularity of the media-imperialist thesis and the brand of Marxism on which it depends and the fact that post-colonial theorists have not found the events in the newly post-colonial Central and Eastern European states to be an engaging subject.

The work that has been published has largely been conducted by Central and Eastern European media scholars, many of whom are closely connected with media developments in their respective states and some of whom were intimately involved in the media systems of the state socialist societies. Some of this work has been translated into or, indeed, was originally written in English (a phenomenon worthy of investigation in itself). Most has not been. Publishers of media studies books and journals have not seen a demand for such work. In addition, there is a modest German secondary literature. This is partly down to the comparative strength of mass communications approaches in Germany relative to cultural-studies-type work and partly down to the fact that for obvious geographical and historical reasons German media scholars are often more interested in the media events of Central and Eastern Europe than their counterparts in the rest of Western Europe and the United States.

This chapter is essentially a review of the English and German secondary literature on the media changes in Central and Eastern Europe since 1989, focusing on the issue of media imperialism (although this is not a term to be found widely in the literature). It cannot pretend to be either exhaustive or conclusive. There are many differences as well as similarities in the conditions of the media in Central and Eastern Europe. It is perhaps inevitable that an overview will pay more attention to the similarities while empirical monograph research will redress this balance. However, as well as reviewing the extant secondary literature, it will seek to establish a framework which may prove helpful both to students aiming to come to grips with the inordinate complexities of Central and Eastern Europe and to researchers considering undertaking empirical research in this still largely unexplored field.

# Framing the issue

The majority of Central and Eastern European states have become post-colonial states since 1989. The control of the Soviet Union over these societies first diminished and then collapsed. Soviet troops were withdrawn and the states embraced the Sinatra doctrine of 'doing it their way'. Only the majority may be called post-colonial, as some, for example the former Yugoslavia, had more or less successfully resisted Soviet domination. These post-colonial states, however, it is claimed, have potentially become sites for a new imperialism. If colonialism may be characterised as a direct physical presence of a colonising power coming in from the outside, imperialism may be seen as all the other forms of intervention but stopping short of direct political domination. Imperialism is both the ancestor of and successor to colonialism. Imperialism has a myriad of forms and guises, one of those being media imperialism.

Imperialism and colonialism are often associated with the behaviour of the great powers and thought about in terms of nations and states. In this chapter, however, I would like to suggest an alternative. The subject of this chapter is the occupation of spaces, the spaces of the media in Central and Eastern Europe. It is also about how these occupations have attempted to create new media spaces different from the spaces that existed during state socialism. However, the imperialists and colonisers are not just transnational media conglomerates, but also the 'native' economic and political actors in Central and Eastern Europe.

Using this framework, both the newly created state and political machineries and citizens' groups may be seen as potential imperialists and colonisers. What I am seeking to describe is a complicated war of position conducted in media spaces between various groups of would-be imperialists and colonisers. It is complicated because in Central and Eastern Europe there are similarities and differences; there is a patchwork of rivalries and alliances between the potential conquistadors. There are situations in which states see themselves as bitter rivals to transnational media conglomerates that are perceived to be a threat to national culture and sovereignty. There are other situations in which states see themselves as allies of transnational media in the attempt to establish capitalism. In both types of situation, however, it would seem that those groups seeking to develop democratic media spaces have been squeezed out.

Another difference from the conventional media-imperialism approach is that the almost conspiracy-theory-like argument that TNCs are working in tandem with their 'host' states as part of a seamless military–industrial complex is put to one side. That is to argue not that the involvement in Central and Eastern Europe of TNCs is never motivated by more than the prospect of financial gain (although it would appear that this is a prerequisite for such involvement) but that the link between TNCs and states is more complex than the one often implied in the media-imperialist thesis. TNCs are of course keen on creating an ideology of consumerism similar to that in Western Europe and the USA in order to provide a fertile ground for their products, but it is hard to see this as a grand ideological project rather than piecemeal measures to strengthen markets. It is largely the governments and states of Central and Eastern Europe who are seeking to use the media for grander and more abstract ideological purposes, that is, establishing their own legitimacy and the legitimacy of capitalism.

## From Stepney with love

A rich example to consider from the perspective of the cultural-imperialism thesis is presented by the 1997 BBC documentary, *East of Eastenders*, which followed the genesis of a Kazakhstan soap opera, *Crossroads*, the first of its kind in Kazakhstan, made with the help of the production team from one of the most popular British soaps, *Eastenders*. This case demonstrates clearly the complexities of cultural imperialism and the importance of understanding the relations between capital, power and narrative form.

The project was financed by the British government's Know-How Fund to the tune of $2.25 million. This was seen as 'humanitarian' development aid with the aim of winning the hearts and minds of the Kazakh people for the economic reforms begun after the collapse of the Soviet Union in 1991, that is, the transition to capitalism. This in itself reflects a transition in the status of soap operas. Originally seen as trivial, as a way of selling soap to 'housewives', the genre is now widely perceived in the UK as popular moral education, as a way of discussing societal issues by means of popular narrative.

The cultural-imperialism thesis is often couched in terms of a military vocabulary. Western culture is perceived as an invasion. This may serve to over-simplify matters (Tomlinson, 1991). For example, in this case, the humanitarian aid was welcomed by the government of Kazakhstan, which was eager to encourage the acceptance of capitalism amongst the people. This shows us that the cultural-imperialism thesis must examine the economic and political context, and particularly the balance of forces at play, in states that are supposedly victims of cultural imperialism. One may read, for example, the popularity of Western forms as symptomatic of cultural conflict within the states concerned. This is often neglected in the debates concerning cultural imperialism.

The *Eastenders* production team, although there ostensibly to help their Kazakh peers, effectively made all the decisions concerning the production. Although *Eastenders* has been acknowledged as a social democratic text in many ways critical of the popular ideology of Thatcherism into which the programme was born in the UK, this did not translate into a questioning of the values of capitalism or the values of British broadcasting when the production team were confronted by cultural difference. For example, a popular soap narrative device is the personalisation of history, of showing historical trends through the lives of particular characters. This is a distant descendant of nineteenth-century bourgeois realist novels. It is ironic that an aesthetic movement that struggled precisely against this form of representation marked the early history of the Soviet Union. Rather than seeking to make history somehow individual, Eisenstein, for instance, strived to make his characters representatives of historical forces through typology, using cultural symbols to stand for classes and emphasising class not individual characteristics.

When contemplating how to represent Kazakhstan's historical predicament it was no great surprise to discover that the *Eastenders* writers decided to use a new-born baby. (It is interesting to contemplate how ideologically inappropriate it would have been to start with a death, which is how Eastenders began in the UK.) This is not just about using personal narratives to represent history. It is about how the specificity of these narratives is not recognised by the writers, who see their way of doing things as the 'right' way. This is reminiscent of Edward Said's point that it is the confident realism of 'the West' which is so indicative of cultural imperialism. It is precisely here, where no ambiguity or ambivalence is apparently to be found, that one may examine cultural imperialism in its purest form. This was compounded in the *Eastenders* case by the fact that it is against Kazakh custom for babies to be displayed publicly for forty days. Rather than respect Kazakh culture, however, the immediate solution to this problem was to find a heavily pregnant woman and pay her enough money to entice her to break with the culture. This shows the intrinsic relation between money, power and narrative. An analysis of cultural imperialism which concentrates entirely on economics and politics risks again overly simplifying matters.

There were a number of conflicts between the *Eastenders* writers and the team of Kazakh writers. While the *Eastenders* team saw a quick turnover of characters and plots as essential, Kazakh writers suggested characters who would take themselves off to the hills for weeks at a time and then return. Bakhtin's concept of 'chronotope' is useful here: what was essentially at issue was time itself and its meaning. Western soap-opera time is accelerated time; time has been annihilated by form. The Kazakh writers who could not adapt to this version of time were dismissed.

This conflict was indicative of an ideological conflict between the two groups of writers. The Kazakh writers wanted to show intellectual characters who would speak of the spiritual situation of Kazakhstan. They wanted to use the programme to express their analysis of the politics of Kazakhstan without making concessions to the popular. This in itself is symptomatic of the absence of 'popular culture'. On the one hand, there is the high aesthetic culture of the writers and, on the other, the folk traditions of 'the people'. This experiment in cultural co-operation was in reality more of an attempt to transplant popular culture.

At the party to celebrate the screening of the first episode of *Crossroads* much vodka was consumed (Smirnoff was one of the sponsors of the programme), and a Beatles song was sung as a reminder of the power of popular culture to create a bond between West and East. However, the Kazakh writer whose name appeared in the credits was distraught because the story was so banal and had been completely changed from her original intentions by the production values of the *Eastenders* team. She asked whether she could take her name off the programme, commenting that she 'wasn't prepared for the rules of the game'. Eighteen months later *Crossroads* was the sixth most popular programme in Kazakhstan, with an audience share of 26 per cent, representing the triumph of the popular, of Western narrative form, and of a popular accommodation with capitalism.

# 1989 and all that

Journalist and historian Timothy Garton Ash has coined the term 'refolution' to describe the events of 1989 in Central and Eastern Europe, arguing that the events may be characterised as partly reform from above and partly revolution from below. Most state socialist regimes saw the need for reform, given the precarious nature of their command economies and the almost total absence of legitimacy of the states in the eyes of the people, especially when the traditional barrier to such reforms, the Soviet Union, had essentially paved the way through the policies associated with glasnost and perestroika. The reforms, however, did not have the desired effect of securing the support of the people but rather served to open up cracks which could be exploited by opponents.

While the opposition movements in 1989 appeared to be gloriously and spontaneously united, overwhelming the regimes through a show of popular morality and utter contempt for the culture of pretence of state socialism, in hindsight one can see that these movements were only united in their opposition to state socialism. Once these regimes were out of the way, consensus disappeared very quickly. This was nowhere more apparent than in East Germany, where oppositionists made for really quite strange bedfellows. On the one hand, there were radical dissident intellectuals who sought a third way for a new East Germany between the capitalist social market of West Germany and the command economy of the authoritarian East. On the other, there were protesters, much more numerous though individually less prominent, who believed that West Germany, all things considered, was about as good as it could get. While the exodus of East Germans to the West (ostensibly on holiday in Czechoslovakia and Hungary) was taking place, the people took to the streets of Leipzig and other cities in the East in ever greater numbers chanting 'Wir bleiben da' (We're staying here), signifying both their opposition to the state socialist regime and to the exiles. The fall of the Berlin Wall, the collapse of the regime, and the overwhelming and somewhat surprising election victory of the conservative parties in the March 1990 elections leading to reunification in October 1990 are well known. The reunification and the subsequent capital transfers from West to East does, however, make East Germany a special case, very different from the situation in say Poland, Hungary and the Czech Republic.

From the establishment of state socialist regimes in the late 1940s to 1989, the media in Central and Eastern Europe was organised along strictly Leninist lines. Liberal notions of journalism see the media as watchdogs, educating the people to be distrustful of the overbearing state. The independence or freedom of the press is seen as paramount, although paradoxically, of course, the media in liberal capitalist democracies are largely subordinate both to capital and to the state. The Leninist model sees the media, however, as really an arm of the state; it is the sector of the state that aims to secure legitimacy by enlightening the people as to what their true needs really are. Control of the media by the state in Central and Eastern Europe was very pronounced. Some indication of this is given by comments that Manfred Pohl, editor of the leading East German daily evening TV news programme, *Aktuelle Kamera*, made at a conference he attended in London in 1990: 'Every afternoon there was a meeting between the news editors of the newspapers and of Aktuelle Kamera and the Agitation department of the Central committee where the next day's headlines were decided' (Nowell-Smith and Wollen, eds, 1991: 33).

A culture of pretence was prevalent in Central and Eastern Europe. The state socialist regimes pretended that they were loved by the people. The media were the conduits of this pretence and, therefore, did not enjoy the respect of the people. Media coverage did change in 1989, particularly in the last weeks of the state socialist regimes, but this should be seen as more of a media reflection of changes in society rather than as events in themselves which helped to precipitate opposition. The opposition that arose invented itself with the help of other media – word-of-mouth; samizdats and flyers; and media broadcasts from the West (roughly 90 per cent of East Germans watched West German TV). While there were calls, and there still are, for a democratisation of the media in Central and Eastern Europe, undoubtedly, in general terms, the lack of a history of independence, or even an ideology of independence, has meant that in the aftermath of 1989 the media is often still perceived to be an instrument of political control. The master may have changed but the function, for the most part, has not.

## The state of media spaces

One of the central themes of the cultural-imperialism debate at the moment is the impact of information and communication technologies. These new media are conceived as new avenues of imperialism, enabling the metropolitan areas to secure their ideological control of 'the rest'. While it is undoubtedly important for critical scholars to examine the implications of these new media, this discussion of new information and communication technologies is not, however, of central importance for understanding what is happening in Central and Eastern Europe. Slavko Splichal comments that 'whereas information and communication technologies mark revolutionary changes in West Europe, North America, Japan, and some newly industrialised countries – the "four tigers" in Asia, for example – East-Central Europe largely remains a typical peripheral zone in terms of technology' (1994: xi).

Because much of Central and Eastern Europe remains peripheral to these debates (although the situation has changed somewhat since 1994), this chapter will concentrate largely on print and terrestrial radio and television broadcast. However, it is worth noting that satellite technology is becoming more important in those states in Central and Eastern Europe which are experiencing significant growth (Hungary and the Czech Republic in particular), although still the media landscape is dominated by 'old' media technologies. The debates about new media technologies still appear very distant from the perspective of Central and Eastern Europe. In the aftermath of 1989, for example, a combination of economic collapse and the sudden increase in the costs of newsprint and newspapers meant that overall circulation plummeted in many states. Many new publications that began life so optimistically went quickly to the wall, as did many established newspapers. Many functions which are taken for granted in Western Europe, such as distribution, are still major headaches for media publishers in East and Central Europe.

At this stage, it is necessary to point to vastly differing circumstances in Central and Eastern Europe. One difference is due to the modern history of the region. The reunification of Germany marks off former East Germany clearly from the rest of Central and Eastern Europe (for example, eastern Germany now has one of the most advanced telecommunications infrastructures in Europe as a result of massive investment after 1990). Hungary, Poland and the Czech Republic may be grouped together, as their economic performance and situation is perceived by foreign media investors to be encouraging in the longer term. The third category of states, such as Bulgaria and Romania, are still experiencing some of the profound difficulties associated with the transition to capitalism and have not attracted much interest from Western media investors.

One may characterise these differences in terms of distance from the 'centre': former East Germany is closest to the centre (although undoubtedly experiencing protracted economic and social problems); Hungary, Poland, and the Czech Republic are attempting to move closer to the centre (for example, through membership of the European Union); 'the rest' remain on the periphery (although there has been some movement). This chapter is concerned primarily with the first two categories, although I will bring in occasional examples drawn from the third category. This is because the first two categories are more pertinent to the subject of this chapter – cultural imperialism. It does not represent a privileging *per se* of the more central over the peripheral.

The changes that have occurred in the media since 1989, however, are not just dependent upon geographical location and historical specificity. Many of the changes have been influenced by perceived differences between the power of media to influence opinion. While newspapers have often been privatised and left to the mercy of the free market, terrestrial television has generally been closely controlled by the fledgling states (the situation of satellite and cable is different). This has been so for essentially good old Leninist reasons: television is a powerful weapon in the propaganda war. This in itself should indicate to us that in the midst of revolutionary economic and social upheaval the function of television has not significantly changed.

## Transnational corporations as colonisers

In contrast to television, the press in former East Germany was abandoned to market forces (Hagen, 1997). While West German newspapers and magazines have not proved to be popular in the East, only three of the seven major newspapers in the East before 1989 have survived. West German publishers have not been influential because their titles have been popular in the East but because they have simply bought up Eastern newspapers and installed West Germans in managerial and editorial positions. The four largest West German publishers (Axel Springer, Gruner and Jahr, Heinrich Bauer, and Burda) were allowed to buy only one newspaper each, but in total 85 per cent of the Eastern German press is owned by West Germans. The press structure that has evolved guarantees a limited pluralism. Although rarely in decision-making positions do the newspapers employ journalists who were working before 1989 and those subsequently educated in the East (particularly at the renowned institute at Leipzig University). Consequently, the revival in fortunes of the PDS (the successor party to the SED) is mirrored in terms of favourable coverage in eastern German newspapers (Hagen, 1997) and offers a significant contrast to the coverage of the party on television news.

The privatisation of the press in eastern Germany was a far more structured and considered ideological process than in Hungary. In 1990 the Socialist Workers' party sought to solve its financial problems by selling, or even giving away, its newspapers to Western publishers. Axel Springer took over seven provincial newspapers and 90 per cent of profits without paying a penny (Splichal, 1994: 37). It is important at this point to correct the impression of an apparent contradiction between the different attitudes of the states to television, on the one hand, and the press, on the other. The states were, by and large, prepared to privatise the press because they could almost guarantee that the ideology of the newspapers would be favourable to their policies of transition to free-market capitalism. In Hungary the government intervened in discussions to ensure that a paper was sold not to a (politically) liberal Swedish publisher but to the right-wing Hersant group in France (ibid.: 38–9). Rather than establish democracy, the overriding objective was to create capitalism and integrate Hungary into a world market. Colin Sparks sums this up more than adequately: 'I prefer to call it an unfinished attempt to make the shift from autarchic nomenklatura state capitalism to nomenklatura private capitalism' (in ibid.: 23).

In Bulgaria, WAZ (Westdeutsche Allgemeine Zeitung) followed the same business model that it has employed so successfully in Germany. Its strategy has been to buy newspapers competing for the same market segment (usually defined geographically) and then amalgamate the titles, thus creating a quasi-monopoly position in that market sector. In 1996–7 WAZ bought a controlling interest in the second largest Bulgarian publishing house to add to its 70 per cent ownership of the country's biggest publisher. In such circumstances, it is not unreasonable to speak of an effective press monopoly (Roper, 1997). In the Czech Republic 75 per cent of dailies and periodicals are foreign-owned. Only three dailies of more than 100,000 circulation are still in Czech hands (Muller, 1995).

Hungary, Bulgaria and the Czech Republic are the most extreme examples of Western colonisation of the press. Not only did Western capitalists see the economic situation in Hungary as more appealing, but also the Hungarian government had fewer qualms about losing Hungarian cultural sovereignty. In Poland the press is largely owned by two political parties and there are statutory limits concerning the amount of foreign ownership (Goban-Klas, 1994).

While the Western colonisation of the press in some countries can be understood in straightforward terms of ownership and control, Western influence in broadcasting is more complex. Splichal (1994) identifies three categories of involvement, to which I would add a fourth (and amend the third to include the influence of television form):

- direct broadcasting by satellite
- supply of capital and broadcasting technology
- Western programming on national terrestrial television (and influence of form, for example, introduction of soap operas)
- ownership of terrestrial stations.

The first category of influence has been limited because of the relatively low number of people able to receive Western satellite channels in Central and Eastern Europe. This is compounded by the fact that Western satellite broadcasters for the most part do not see central and Eastern Europe as a significant market as yet and so do not tailor their broadcasts accordingly.

In addition, the language barrier is often a factor (with some exceptions – many Albanians understand Italian and Italian broadcasts are very popular in Albania). However, the elites of these countries, the emerging capitalist class, not only have access to the technology but also possess the language skills (English and particularly German are the business languages) to decipher the broadcasts.

This is, of course, different in eastern Germany, where German-owned or part-owned satellite broadcasters (RTL, SAT 1, etc.) have made considerable inroads (as in western Germany) (Pfetsch, 1996). In recent years there has been increasing interest from Western media companies in the possibility of broadcasting satellite channels in the national languages of Central and Eastern European states. In 1993, Polonia 1, which was previously a network of local media companies in Poland, was taken over by Marciano Volani and the channel is now transmitted from Italy but in Polish (there are about 2.5 million cable subscribers in Poland). In Hungary, Time Warner and United Communication International own a pay-TV cable channel, Kabelkom.

The second factor, supply of capital and broadcasting technology, has been prevalent in markets where the future is decidedly uncertain thereby making substantial investment unwise. Rather than going to the huge expense of starting up their own channels (logistically as well as culturally also very difficult), Western broadcasting companies have supplied equipment to East and Central European broadcasters.

The third category of involvement is much more difficult to quantify and it is very difficult to obtain credible empirical evidence. Anecdotal evidence suggests that the amount of Western programming and Western-style programming is substantial. Some countries have imposed quotas on foreign programming. In the Ukraine, 50 per cent of broadcasts must be domestically produced; in Poland, 60 per cent on public TV and 35 per cent on private TV must be of Polish origin. Two points can be made here: quotas are only infrequently obeyed and the quotas themselves indicate a very large volume of Western programming. In some countries there are no limits. This is the case in Latvia, Romania, Slovakia and the Czech Republic.

The influence of Western TV forms is obvious and media landscapes in both Western and Eastern Europe are awash with low-budget game and chat shows. Czech media researcher Vaclav Markoul detects a turn away from intellectually demanding programming to mass entertainment. From a Western perspective such a conclusion is hardly surprising given the experience of the last 40 years or so. For Eastern commentators, however, having grown up in authoritarian states that heavily subsidised high culture, this trend is rather shocking. The depoliticisation of life (and media) which Habermas (1995) notes is a phenomenon shared by both Western and Eastern Europe.

The fourth category of involvement, ownership of terrestrial stations, is growing. Obviously a substantial investment is required to start up terrestrial television broadcasting. Given that the objective of private broadcasting is to make a profit, it is only a viable option in countries whose economies are potentially strong enough to support a vibrant advertising market. Only three countries in Central and Eastern Europe are attractive to potential investors: Poland, Hungary and the Czech Republic. In Poland, Berlusconi and Bertelsmann have a stake in the third, commercial terrestrial TV channel. In the Czech Republic, TV Nova, owned by Central European Development Corporation (US-owned), has a 60 per cent market share (Muller, 1995). At the beginning of 1997, the Hungarian government invited bids for two private TV channels (26 per cent to remain in state hands). While there is no limit or quota on ownership in the Czech Republic the limit for foreign ownership in Poland is 33 per cent.

# The state as coloniser

After 1989 states were far more cautious about relinquishing control of broadcasting than was the case for print media. However, rather than attempt to establish quasi-independent public-service television along the lines of the BBC and ARD, states were eager to use the power of broadcasting for their own ends (East Germany is once more a special case). This may be seen as essentially a continuation of an authoritarian approach to media policy rather than an introduction of a liberal model. The behaviour of governing parties post-1989 has been similar in intent, though not in extent, to that of pre-1989 regimes.

Most commentators put this down to the absence of a democratic political culture (Splichal, 1994: 101). Because of the historical trajectory of capitalism in Western Europe, particularly the role played by the bourgeoisie in building a public sphere (Habermas, 1989), many commentators assumed that the transition to capitalism would be accompanied by a transition to democracy. While formal democracy has been introduced many of the elements of liberal democratic culture are missing. The difficult transition to capitalism has meant that there is no substantial middle class and, therefore, the public sphere remains undeveloped. Although the economic and political circumstances of many Central and Eastern European states remain turbulent (especially given the revival of fortunes of reformed communist parties), it appears that competing political actors are in agreement about the function that broadcasting ought to play. Political competition is not restricted to elections but extends to a battle for control of the media. The continued state control of broadcasting is antithetical to the intentions of many of the revolutionaries in 1989.

In July 1990 in East Germany a new media law paved the way for the abolition of the 'public-service' broadcasting institution, the DFF. Its TV channels were taken over by the two West German public-service channels,

ARD and ZDF. After a brief flowering of critical programming following *die Wende*, the takeover by the West stifled optimism. Richard Kilborn concludes: 'if the immediate post-*Wende* period had been characterised by a spirit of optimism and enthusiasm, the general mood among broadcasters in the East after unification was one of resignation and even despair' (1993: 464). Many jobs were lost in the reorganisation; many of the influential posts were taken over by West Germans. In addition to the national stations, provincial broadcasters (MDR and ORB) were established by means of co-operation between the eastern German states (Länder). The most important is MDR, which has a potential audience of 10 million. Again the media colonisation of the East by the West is apparent. Kilborn notes that 'the vast majority of the top positions in the MDR were occupied by those who had gained their broadcasting spurs in the West' (ibid.: 465). The adoption of West German media law and organisational structures does mean, however, that public-service television is obliged, at least in theory, to cater for the needs of all citizens and reflect the plurality of interests in German society. In addition, all significant groups in civil society are represented on the controlling boards of provincial television (political parties, trade unions, religious organisations, etc). However, the danger of this proportional representative system (whereby political parties are represented according to their numbers in regional parliaments) is that television may be used to serve ruling political interests (Kepplinger and Hartmann, 1989).

The battle for the media has been particularly fierce in Hungary. At the beginning of 1993 the chief executives of both television and radio resigned in protest at the increasing control the government was seeking to exert over editorial matters. Towards the end of 1993 and shortly before national elections, leading right-wing TV and radio journalists attempted to seize control of broadcasting in order to support extreme nationalist and fascist political parties. This is indicative of a general problem in Central and Eastern Europe, one view of which is that political parties seek to control broadcasting directly and journalists have 'not yet learnt' to exercise critical distance from parties with whose platforms they sympathise. This is a rather patronising and deeply flawed attitude. It takes as its model the supposed objectivity and neutrality central to the ideology of journalism in Western Europe and North America. It is based on discredited positivistic and empiricist epistemologies and the claim that knowledge may be value-free. Neutrality in the BBC public-service tradition, for example, appears to mean that journalists do not explicitly side with the views of competing political parties, but in fact the journalism produced is implicitly value-laden. Advocacy journalism is unavoidable and desirable. The problem in Central and Eastern Europe is really one of pluralism and separation of powers. The concentration of media power in either private or state hands has restricted the development of a democratic culture.

Censorship is also widely practised in many Central and Eastern European states, again reminiscent of the behaviour of the state socialist regimes before 1989. In 1995, for example, the Romanian Broadcasting Council forbade the transmission of BBC news, contravening the Romanian constitution. In 1993, the long-awaited Polish broadcasting law contained the condition that both private and public broadcasters should respect Christian values, indicating the immense influence of the deeply conservative Catholic Church in Polish politics.

# Conclusion

Privatisation of the press and continued state control over the majority of broadcasting, together with the difficult economic conditions experienced during the transition to capitalism, have meant that a liberal democratic public sphere is yet to emerge in Central and Eastern Europe. The development of more democratic media is dependent upon the creation of a robust civil society to counter the power of the state and media moguls. This is, in turn, dependent upon the success of economic reform. This incremental development of liberal democratic culture and politics is probably the 'best-case' scenario and is still a far cry from what many leaders of the 'refolutions' in 1989 were demanding. Indeed, many of these people after 1989 have been marginalised and denied access to the media: 'the access of oppositional parties and autonomous groups from civil society to national broadcast media and mainstream print media is being limited' (Splichal, 1994: 30). The 'refolutions' in 1989 were not just about living standards, they were not just about wanting to mimic the 'consumer heaven' of the West, they were also about winning democratic freedoms. Some, indeed, have been won but, very importantly, a democratic culture has not been created. Many of the leaders of the various citizens' initiatives in East Germany wanted to create a people's democracy qualitatively different from both liberal capitalism and state socialism, and part and parcel of this was the demand for a democratic media ensuring independence from the state and plurality of representation. The heady optimism of 1989 has turned into despair.

The interest of the Western media in Central and Eastern Europe is likewise dependent upon the success of economic reform. Their interest is primarily economic rather than ideological. Immediately post-1989 there was great interest in the potential of the new eastern markets, but this waned considerably as the economies of the East collapsed. Private media requires quite a mature capitalism, one that can generate advertising revenues. The revival of certain Central and Eastern European economies, notably the Czech Republic and Hungary in recent years, has spawned renewed interest. Future media colonisation, counter-intuitively, is dependent upon economic growth. As this is also a precondition for the development of a liberal public sphere, we are likely to witness a sharpening of this conflict in years to come.

# References

Becker, J. (1996) Between censorship and commercialisation: structural changes in the public sphere in Eastern Europe, *Balkan Media*, 1–2.

Boyd-Barrett, O. (1977) Media imperialism: towards an international framework for the analysis of media systems, in Curran, J. and Gurevitch, M. (eds) *Mass Communication and Society*, Edward Arnold, London, pp. 116–35.

Dries, J. (1995) Nach Mauerfall auch Sprachbarrieren weiter abbauen, *Das Bulletin Europaisches Institut für Medien*, 1.

Goban-Klas, T. (1994) *The Orchestration of the Media: The Politics of Mass Communication in Communist Poland and the Aftermath*, Westview, Boulder, Colo.

Golding, P. and Harris, P. (eds) (1997) *Beyond Cultural Imperialism: Globalisation, Communication, and the New International Order*, Sage, London.

Habermas, J. (1989) *The Structutural Transformation of the Public Sphere: An Inquiry into a Category of Bourgeois Society*, Polity, Cambridge.

Habermas, J. (1995) *Facticität und Geltung*, Suhrkamp, Frankfurt am Main.

Hagen, L. (1997) The transformation of the media system of the former German Democratic Republic after the reunification and its effects on the political content of newspapers, *European Journal of Communication*, 12.1, pp. 5–26.

Hallenberger, G. and Krzeminski, M. (eds) (1994) *Osteuropa: Medienlandschaft im Umbruch*, ISTAS, Berlin.

Kepplinger, H. and Hartmann, T. (1989) *Stachel oder Feigenblatt? Rundfunk- und Fernsehrate in der Bundesrepublik Deutschland: Eine Empirische Untersuchung*, IMK, Frankfurt am Main.

Kilborn, R. (1993) Towards utopia – or another Anschluss? East Germany's transition to a new media system, *European Journal of Communication*, 8, pp. 451–70.

Mattelart, A. and Dorfman, A. (1975) *How to Read Donald Duck: Imperialist Ideology in the Disney Comic*, International General, New York.

Muller, J. (1995) untitled, *Das Bulletin Europaisches Institut für Medien*, 4.

Nowell-Smith, G. and Wollen, T. (eds) (1991) *After the Wall*, BFI, London.

Pfetsch, B. (1996) Convergence through privatisation? Changing media environments and televised politics in Germany, *European Journal of Communication*, 11.4, pp. 427–51.

Roper, H. (1997) Formationen deutscher Medienmultis, *Media Perspektiven*, 5/97.

Schiller, H. (1976) *Communications and Cultural Domination*, M. E. Sharpe, New York.

Skwierawski, F. (1993) Satellitenfernsehen in Polen, *Rundfunk und Fernsehen*, 2.

Splichal, S. (1994) *Media Beyond Socialism: Theory and Practice in East-Central Europe*, Westview, Boulder, Colo.

Tomlinson, J. (1991) *Cultural Imperialism: A Critical Introduction*, Pinter, London.

Tunstall, J. (1977) *The Media are American*, Constable, London.

# |4|

# Infotainment international

## A view from the South

### DAYA KISHAN THUSSU

This chapter examines the implications of the expansion of mainly Western-based electronic empires in the South as a result of media globalisation. It analyses this within the framework of the economic liberalisation policies prescribed by Western governments and Western-dominated multilateral organisations and discusses the strategies of the key media players to penetrate the emerging markets of the developing world. Focusing on television news, the chapter investigates whether market-driven 'infotainment' channels are undermining the public-service role of the media in the South. In addition, it argues that by projecting news as entertainment the media empires are acting as ideological messengers for transnational corporations (TNCs).

Nearly two decades of neo-liberal policies of deregulation and privatisation, aggressively promoted by the World Bank and the International Monetary Fund (George and Sabelli, 1994), coupled with developments in communications technologies, especially satellites, have enabled the globalisation of media markets and given free rein to mainly Western-based media conglomerates to become truly global in their operations. With the imposition of Structural Adjustment Programmes, Southern countries have been obliged to open up their media and communications industries to media conglomerates. Having almost saturated their markets in the North, these are increasingly looking towards the 'emerging markets' of the South, especially Asia and Latin America, to exploit the latent demand for their products.

Television is seen as the 'cornerstone of the media empires under construction' (Maidment, 1995). The possibilities for growth are enormous given that in much of the South broadcasting was traditionally state-owned and controlled and resources limited, constraining the availability of indigenously conceived and locally relevant television programming.

While acknowledging the diversity of the media in the South – from the thriving commercial enterprises of India's film industry and Latin America's television giants, to information-starved Malawi – there are still fundamental factors which they have in common, most notably their continuing dependence on Western, or more accurately, Anglo-American media empires, both for content and delivery systems. Post-Cold War media globalisation has ensured that US-made or -inspired news and entertainment programmes have come to dominate the mediascape of much of the South. Moreover, global television has a much wider reach – visuals transcend barriers of language – than the elite Western news agencies, newspapers and magazines which have traditionally dominated media-imperialism debates (Boyd-Barrett, 1977; Tunstall, 1977).

The gradual privatisation of television news, which has 'moved from being mostly a publicly owned service to being mostly a privately owned service' (Paterson, 1997: 153), makes this expansion vulnerable to charges that, to maximise profits, television companies may turn news into infotainment. Will global television news – increasingly driven by entertaining visuals and profit motives, as we note below – be used to promote a corporate agenda? Is there a future for the electronic media as a source of public information and empowerment? What about the original educational role of television in the South – a much neglected, though vital, area?

Such questions have revived debates about information imbalances and inequalities, issues which exposed bitter divisions between the information-rich North and the information-poor South during the 1970s New World Information and Communication Order (NWICO) discussions (Masmoudi, 1979; McBride, 1980; Roach, 1997). While NWICO has been consigned to history, the 'free flow of information' insisted on by the West, led by the United States, during often acrimonious debates within UNESCO, has increased tremendously with the rapid convergence between telecommunications, media and computing industries, and the expansion of Western satellite and cable television to the South.

The media empires, the channels for this information flow, are aiming to consolidate their reach in the South, exploiting the commodification of global information and communication, which is likely to accelerate as agreements to liberalise trade in information technology, telecommunications and financial services (signed in December 1996, February and December 1997 respectively, under the auspices of the World Trade Organisation) come into effect.

As the leading manufacturer and distributor of the global entertainment and information products, the USA is set to benefit most from the 'free trade' in cultural commodities. Enthused by US domination of the 'global traffic in information and ideas', David Rothkopf, managing director of Kissinger Associates and a former senior official in the Clinton administration, writes: 'American music, American movies, American television, and American software are so dominant, so sought after, and so visible that they are now available literally everywhere on the Earth. They influence the tastes, lives, and aspirations of virtually every nation' (Rothkopf, 1997: 43).

As Edward Herman and Robert McChesney point out, the global media market is dominated by about ten mainly US-based and vertically integrated media conglomerates (Herman and McChesney, 1997: 104). Such domination of all spheres of global communication and the resultant information imbalance is seen by critics to be detrimental to the interests of Southern countries (Schiller, 1996; Hamelink, 1997). Not only do these conglomerates have the power, reach and influence to set and then build a global news agenda that reflects Western geo-strategic and economic interests, they could also become the vehicles for promoting infotainment to a global audience. This may contribute to the eclipsing of public-service news media in the South, where state monopolies on broadcasting have been challenged by transnational media players, such as Hong Kong-based STAR (Satellite Television Asian Region, part of Rupert Murdoch's News Corporation), BBC World (the commercial television channel of the British Broadcasting Corporation) and the Atlanta-based Cable News Network (CNN: since 1996, part of Time Warner, the world's biggest media corporation).

# Why the South is important to electronic empires

With the near saturation of markets in North America and comparatively tougher regulatory structures of the European Union, media empires have turned their attention to the South, where an estimated 2.5 billion people have regular access to a television, constituting the majority of the global viewing public. With its huge numbers of potential consumers, Asia provides the media empires with unrivalled opportunities – it is the fastest-growing and potentially biggest media market in the world for both hardware and software. Satellites can provide cheaper and quicker nationwide coverage of broadcasting in continental-size countries like India and China or scattered island states like Indonesia and the Philippines. In addition, the diversity of cultures in Asia means that demand for a wide array of satellite channels, catering to different languages and tastes, is even stronger than in Europe or the USA. In Asia, the number of homes reached by cable or satellite TV will grow from 44 million in 1994 to 206 million by 2004, according to industry estimates (Levinson, 1995).

Television advertising revenues are forecast to nearly triple from $7.6 billion in 1995 to $20 billion in 2003 (Lucas, 1995). As one commentator put it: 'The scope for expanding television advertising on the back of Asia's new middle class consumers is vast. Corporate ad dollars should easily support the many new cable and satellite channels being put up around the region' (Maidment, 1995). J. Walter Thompson, one of the biggest advertising companies in Asia, is now focusing its operations on huge population markets like China, Indonesia and India. According to JWT's Asia-Pacific president, Alan Fairnington, the company's China operation is growing by 60 per cent annually, while in Indonesia the growth is by 40 per cent and in India by 30 per cent (Fannin, 1997).[1] In Latin America the industry is forecast to reach $32 billion in 1999, up from about $17 billion in 1995. As *Advertising Age International* commented in a special report on the region, 'the growing band of panregional media is offering marketers new ways of reaching similar and increasingly affluent audiences across Latin America, whether that target audience is business executives, children or avid buyers of hi-tech gadgets' (1997).

The main beneficiaries of this expansion have undoubtedly been the TNCs, as prime media advertisers. In 1996, the largest 100 TNCs (87 of which were based in the USA, European Union and Japan) ranked on the basis of size of foreign assets, owned $1.7 trillion assets in their foreign affiliates, controlling an estimated one fifth of global foreign assets; and their foreign sales amounted to $2 trillion (UNCTAD, 1997a: xvii).

The TNCs' already considerable power will increase tremendously if the Multilateral Agreement on Investment (MAI), currently being negotiated within the Organisation for Economic Cooperation and Development (OECD), comes into force. The MAI, which will include cultural clauses, intends to outlaw restrictions and controls that governments might wish to impose on TNCs, and will be entitled to sue governments at an international court if they object to a regulation, while governments will have no reciprocal rights (Rowan, 1998).[2]

It is an indication of the importance that the TNCs give to the new markets of the South that foreign direct investment (FDI) has been increasing to Asia and Latin America at a record level. In 1996, according to the *World Investment Report 1997*, FDI flow to Asia rose by 25 per cent to $81 billion, about 60 per cent of all developing-country inflow. The increase to Latin America and the Caribbean was by 52 per cent to nearly $39 billion, accounting for 30 per cent of all FDI inflow received by the South. In contrast, Africa barely received $5 billion (UNCTAD, 1997a: 78, 71 and 56).[3]

Such free movement of capital could not have been possible without support from the TNCs' host governments, keen on extending their spheres of influence to parts of the world where it has hitherto been limited, such as China. In the so-called information age, the information-driven industries can play a crucial role in enabling the expansion of Western influence by 'soft power'. Joseph S. Nye, Jr., a former chairman of the National Intelligence Council, assistant secretary of defense for international affairs in the Clinton administration and the president's ideologue on Asia, defined 'soft power' as the 'ability to achieve desired outcomes in international affairs through attraction rather than coercion. It works by convincing others to follow, or getting them to agree to, norms and institutions that produce the desired behaviour. Soft power can rest on the appeal of one's ideas or the ability to set the agenda in ways that shape the preferences of others' (quoted in Nye and Owens, 1996: 21). A recent report from the European Commission also takes up this theme:

> The complexity of the distribution of power and the role of public opinion make it increasingly difficult for governments to impose unilaterally policies on their own people and on other countries. Therefore, multipolarity will be less hegemonic and less hierarchical, and leadership will increasingly be based on the exercise of soft power, by stimulating and convincing other actors to go in a certain direction.
> (European Commission, 1997: 20)

Given that the media conglomerates, carriers of 'soft power', are not only dependent on TNCs as advertisers, but that several key players – Time Warner, Disney/ABC, Microsoft/NBC, Sony and News Corporation – are themselves TNCs, the question arises of the potential of these media as conduits for corporate propaganda in the South.[4]

# Key global media players and their strategies in the South

Globalisation has ensured that the already considerable domination in the South of the US–UK media axis – in print, broadcast and online media – has increased substantially, with US-based media TNCs getting the biggest share of the global entertainment and media market. Specifically, the Anglo-American domination of global television news – both trade in raw footage and completed news and current affairs programming – remains overwhelming (see Table 4.1). Although some Southern media organisations, notably Mexico's Televisa and Brazil's Globo, are emerging as powerful presences in the global media export market, they tend to play a subservient role to the truly global actors such as News Corporation. The media TNCs have used an array of strategies to access the existing markets and create new ones in the South, where it is easier for vertically integrated media conglomerates to exploit the synergies between their different sectoral interests, as the regulations on cross-media ownership, where they exist, are not strict and are not rigorously enforced. For example, CNN can use its news channels to promote its Cartoon Network or Warner Brothers movies while STAR can draw popular Hollywood films from its Twentieth Century Fox library, part of News Corporation.

The most profitable areas of television content are films, sports and children's programmes, which transcend barriers of culture and language, unlike news and current affairs which demand advanced language skills and knowledge of or interest in political and international affairs. One field of

Table 4.1   Key players in global television news

| TV news channels | Bureaux | Correspondents | Ownership | Viewership |
|---|---|---|---|---|
| BBC World | 42 | 250 | BBC | 54m homes/187 countries and territories |
| CNN International | 32 | 150 | Time Warner | 120m homes/ 220 countries and territories |
| Sky News* | 6 | 90 | News Corporation | 70m viewers/ 40 countries |

| TV news services | Subscribers | Countries | Ownership |
|---|---|---|---|
| Reuters Television | 290 | 91 | Reuters Holdings |
| Worldwide Television News | 1000 | 110 | ABC (Disney) |
| Associated Press Television | 170 | 55 | Associated Press |

*Sky, STAR and Fox are planning to merge their news operations into a single news network
Sources: company annual reports, websites, trade press

assured success in the South is the children's television market, which in much of the developing world has been hugely neglected, with a paucity of indigenous programming and poor production values in what is broadcast. Walt Disney Corporation, which dominates the market, is cashing in on this demand – in 1994, just under a quarter of Disney's $10.1 billion in revenue came from outside the USA, but by 2006, it is aiming to generate half of its revenue from abroad (Higgins and Walker, 1996). Disney is also the 'worldwide leader' in sports coverage: its Entertainment and Sports Network (ESPN) remains 'the world's most profitable network' (Gunther, 1998). With its rivals CNN-SI (Sports Illustrated) and News Corporation, it has realised that exclusive broadcasting of live sports events is something only television can deliver, providing a constant source of revenue from fans, generally young men with money, subscribing to a sports channel.

News and current affairs, on the other hand, are usually not profitable (profitable news organisations such as Reuters earn most of their revenues by selling financial information to clients globally) and have to be cross-subsidised from entertainment programming. As Table 4.1 shows, the major news operations are owned by entertainment empires – News Corporation/Sky News, Disney/WTN, Time Warner/CNN – leaving open the question of how committed they are to news as public information. News is usually included as part of a broader package, dominated by entertainment, to gain a semblance of respectability and attract a more upmarket audience interested in international or regional issues – the first syndicated pan-Asian cable and satellite TV survey found that CNN

International was the most watched programme among high-income Asians (Wentz, 1997).

However, although they do not earn much revenue for the conglomerates, news channels are important vehicles for political influence, as they can reach the decision-makers in a society, especially the small, though highly influential, English-speaking metropolitan elite. In the words of Bob Ross, president of Turner International: 'With CNN International we have an English product that is distributed globally and we go after the three per cent or five per cent or 10 or 12 per cent or whatever it is in each country, which is, first, English fluent, and second of all, has an interest in receiving global news, international news, produced by an American network' (Channel 4 Television, 1995).

However, other media TNCs are aiming to increase their audience base beyond the elite by making programmes in languages accessible to the average television viewer in the South. STAR TV has taken the lead in this regard, as Rupert Murdoch himself admitted: 'Everywhere I go it is local programming which is proving to be most popular. The majority of our staff everywhere are local. Local producers and editors provide the concepts and ensure the cultural priorities' (ibid.). In line with this strategy, STAR has developed Phoenix, a Mandarin-language service for China, and STAR Plus, the mainly Hindi-language-based channel for India – both drawing on indigenously made programmes. In 1998, it was claiming to distribute programming in eight languages, targeted to 260 million viewers, across Asia. Using STAR network in Asia, BBC World, keen to capitalise on its reputation in news and current affairs, started focusing on country-specific programming. In January 1997, it launched a Hindi TV News, broadcast on Home TV, a private channel.[5]

In March 1997, CNN also adopted a regionalisation strategy, launching a twenty-four-hour Spanish service, broadcast from its Atlanta headquarters. CNN en Espanol, CNN's first non-English language news channel, is distributed by cable operators and as a Direct to Home (DTH) service by Galaxy Latin America (also known as DirecTV) in the region. Carlos Diaz, president of Turner International Latin America says: 'We have the global news gathering infrastructure to lower operational costs below the level of our competitors' (quoted in Kepp, 1997). CNN can potentially overshadow its rival in the continent's main twenty-four-hour, pan-regional Spanish-language pay-TV news programmes, CBS Telenoticias, a Westinghouse/CBS owned channel, which is delivered to 10 million households in eighteen countries (ibid.).

Another plank in the media TNCs' expansion strategy is to control the delivery systems, as important as providing content to the burgeoning television channels in the South, and News Corporation so far has a competitive advantage in this. In Asia, News Corporation, which already dominates the satellite television market with STAR reaching 61 million affluent homes, is in 1998 to launch DTH digital services. News

Corporation entered an agreement in 1995 with Brazil's Globo and Mexico's Televisa and US cable giant Tele-Communications Inc. (TCI) to provide an array of direct satellite channels to Latin America. The resultant Sky Entertainment Services ('the only satellite television system with infinite possibilities', as its publicity material proclaims) gives the corporation an important breakthrough in direct satellite transmission to the region. Given the continent's rugged terrain, satellite is expected to emerge as the dominant delivery system. By joining the two biggest producers of television programming in the region Murdoch hopes potentially to have a market of 400 million people to make his empire truly global.[6]

## 'Infotainment': news as entertainment

In order to make news and current affairs more profitable and to reduce their dependence on entertainment-based channels, there is an increasing tendency to dilute the news content and make it more like entertainment, accessible to a heterogeneous global audience; in other words, globalised infotainment.

One of the world's most recognised journalists, Larry King, host of 'Larry King Live', CNN's highest-rated show, defines himself as an 'infotainer'. CNN, like other media TNCs in their quest for new audiences in the South, is under pressure to be 'entertaining' even with news, current affairs and documentaries. The overriding concern is to keep up the ratings and advertising revenue by giving the audience easily accessible, dramatic and visually arresting news material (McManus, 1994). The key characteristics of television news – its immediacy, superficiality and intimate nature, and the passivity of its audience (Winch, 1997: 36–7) – make even the best of television newscasts rather limited. Highly 'imagistic in nature' (Kellner, 1990: 112), it invariably depends on visuals to tell a story, putting pressure on news reporters and their editors to come up with eye-catching reports, often personalised and sensationalised for maximum global impact. In this era of what the late British media commentator Malcolm Muggeridge called 'newszak', news is converted into entertainment (Franklin, 1997: 5).

Apparently it works. During the fifteen-month trial of US sportsman and actor O. J. Simpson, in 1995, three cable networks, CNN, Court TV and the E! (Entertainment) Channel gave 'wall-to-wall coverage, with CNN reporting a five-fold jump in ratings' (Cornwell, 1995). During this period Simpson accounted for more minutes of coverage on ABC, CBS and NBC prime-time news than Bosnia. Robert Macneil, former co-anchor of the Macneil/Lehrer NewsHour, argues that the lack of interest in Bosnia was an indictment of the US media: 'If you are covering O. J. Simpson so much, clearly you're not covering other things. You've decided, "we will give less time to Bosnia because surveys show the American public does not give a damn about Bosnia"' (quoted in Moran, 1995).

Covering celebrities, scandals and personalising 'human interest' stories helps international networks to sell their reports across the globe. According to company estimates, CNN would generate about $540 million in advertising and subscription revenue in 1997 – an increase of 78 per cent since 1990 when ratings began to run up to historic heights due to its high profile in covering the Gulf war (Farhi, 1997).[7] The worldwide media audience which watched the funeral of Diana, Princess of Wales, in September 1997, was estimated to be 2.5 billion. BBC World provided coverage of the funeral for 187 countries while ITN supplied another 45. CNN made the pictures available to 210 countries (McCann, 1997). Similarly, Sky News, which cleared its schedules to broadcast the trial of British nanny Louise Woodward, indicted for murder in the USA in 1997, reported that more than 6 million people watched it, 'with its ratings increasing by up to 1,000 per cent at key moments' (Midgley, 1997).

Such stories increasingly dominate television news schedules, where news agendas are constantly narrowing. In the USA, where news has increasingly to compete with entertainment programming (Hallin, 1996), television news has been further localised, with the South experiencing even less exposure – 'time and money dictates we must bypass some stories', is how Roger Ailes, chairman and chief executive of Murdoch's Fox News Network, explains this phenomenon (Wittstock, 1998). Garrick Utley, a former chief foreign correspondent for ABC News and NBC News, points out that the US networks have, over the past decade, more than halved their foreign coverage. ABC, which is supposed to have best overseas reporting, has reduced its coverage from 1410 minutes in 1988 to 918 minutes in 1996 (Utley, 1997: 5). 'Foreign news is expendable,' Utley reports, 'unless it is of compelling interest to a mass audience. The new litmus test at network news programmes is whether viewers (in the producer's opinion) will instinctively "relate" to the story' (ibid.).

In Britain, *5 News,* the half-hour news bulletin of the country's newest terrestrial channel, Channel 5, which goes under the name of 'modern mainstream', is read by a woman newscaster precariously perched on the edge of a table. With its fast-paced, glitzy and glamorous presentation, and an agenda of connecting with the audience by focusing on consumer issues, *5 News* has forced other British channels to repackage their news programmes. Tim Gardam, the channel's head of news and current affairs, argues that it has become 'a sort of "Public Interest Broadcasting"', where one identified the point of intersection between public affairs and the things that mattered in the viewer's private life' (Gardam, 1997: 17).

The BBC, the guardian of public-service broadcasting and a model for many in the South, has not been unaffected by a market-driven news agenda. Its *News 24*, a round-the-clock news service ('The Now O'Clock News', after its main evening news *Nine O'Clock News*, giving, in its own words, 'The whole picture, the whole time'), thrives on short and snappy news items, devoid of analysis. Its presenter, having shed his jacket for a trendy shirt, told the viewers in a promotional video released during its launch in November 1997 that this new news channel was 'not going to be stuffy . . . it might even be fun.' This emphasis on making news 'fun' to watch has been necessitated, in part, by audience attitudes towards the news. According to an internal BBC programme review document, leaked to the press, most of its audiences are not interested in international affairs. 'World economics, wars and famines make little impact unless there is some frothy presentation', the report, *Reflecting the World*, says. 'The groups at the bottom are looking for entertainment, not information. Any educational message to this group cannot be explicit' (Culf, 1997). Consequently, there is pressure, in the words of one disgruntled producer, to 'dumb down' even BBC's flagship news programme *Newsnight* (Harris, 1998).

## Implications of infotainment in the South

The process that started in the metropolitan centres is now acquiring global dimensions. With the expansion of media empires, the US model of commercial television has been globalised and with it the emphasis on entertainment-led news. This has serious implications, since news is of fundamental importance, a form of 'public knowledge' (Schudson, 1995), an essential source of information to enable citizens to function effectively. TV news is particularly influential because of its widespread reach and its credibility: viewers tend to trust it; it gives them a feeling that they are witnessing the events as they unfold. In addition, in the Southern context, where a large section of the population is still illiterate, visuals can be a very powerful form of persuasion.

Advances in media technology, especially satellites and the development of communications systems worldwide, have ensured that the international broadcasters can deliver more news and information to more channels and to greater numbers of people than ever before. However, given the commercial pressures among competitive media, the emphasis is increasingly on entertainment at the expense of public information. As one broadcaster concedes: 'It's saleable, it's like cornflakes, it's like washing powder, you've got to find a new improved formula . . . It's the new improved news' (quoted in MacGregor, 1997: 201).

The emphasis on personality, the unusual and the grotesque, rather than on any attempt to explain or analyse a particular event, situation or issue, has further marginalised public information. Channel surfing, which is becoming the norm among audiences, militates against news consumers concentrating on a given subject and can lead to a cursory examination of the news. In the age of what Walter Cronkite, the CBS evening news anchor, calls 'soundbite journalism', viewers may stay tuned to just get the headlines – CNN already offers a syndicated news programme called *Headline News*.

Given that news has to be made meaningful to a wide variety of audiences internationally, with varied socio-political situations and educational standards, the tendency among transnational news organisations is to aim for easily digestible 'sightbites' and an undemanding narrative – a simple, 'good vs. bad' tale and almost a professional requirement for a sensationalist and eye-catching headline, therefore contributing to the trivialisation of serious public concerns. More ominously, it can also make the public easier to manipulate for governments and corporations.

Television journalists filing stories from the South work under tremendous pressure to meet the increasingly shorter and more frequent deadlines (every hour, with the growth of 'rolling newsday' and 'continuous news on demand' channels). This can jeopardise the contextual and linguistic, if not factual accuracy of often complex events and make journalists vulnerable to manipulation by vested interests. Unsurprisingly, they tend to follow the news agendas often set by providers of pictures – it could be a staged event such as a Western aid agency flying in a television news crew to show their humanitarian work in an emergency situation in Africa, or the Pentagon displaying its 'smart weapons' against the 'rogue states' of the South, or lobbyists and media managers putting their case for 'corporate efficiency'. The emphasis on speed and immediacy, coupled with the cost of news gathering and distribution, ensures that only media TNCs can provide instant coverage of world events, making Southern countries buy 'white' news about their own affairs or those of their neighbours (Fiske, 1987: 289). Given the overwhelming dependence of Southern media on Anglo-American news sources, such pictures and the news agendas they help build become global news agendas. The broadcasters in Asia use the same footage as their counterparts in Latin America and Africa – supplied by Western television news agencies.

For the often unrepresentative governments in the South, infotainment is good news, as long as it is non-controversial and they get their share of the revenue from the taxes that the media TNCs have to pay them to operate in their territories. In addition, as Gitlin (1979) has suggested, entertainment encourages political passivity and even depoliticisation. For their part, the media conglomerates tread the line carefully. When Disney, traditionally dominant in entertainment, entered the global television news arena by taking over ABC in 1995, its chief executive officer, Michael Eisner, commented: 'There are many places in the world, like China, India, and other places, that do not want to accept programming that has any political content. But they have no problem with sports, and they have no problem with Disney kind of programming' (quoted in Utley, 1997: 8).

However, despite its dilution by entertainment, news still remains an intensely political entity and has occasionally created problems for media TNCs in the South, notably in countries with undemocratic media systems. For example, in late 1994, just 3 years after its launch, STAR TV summarily removed the BBC from its northern beam that reached China, after the Chinese authorities complained of the BBC's coverage of the country. News Corporation used its synergies to placate the Chinese authorities, including setting up, in 1995, an information technology joint venture with the Communist Party mouthpiece, the *People's Daily*, publishing (under the HarperCollins imprint) the English translation of a biography of the Chinese leader Deng Xiaoping, written by his daughter Deng Rong, and showing on Phoenix Channel, in 1997, a series of twelve one-hour episodes on the life of Deng, made by China Central Television (Poole and Vines, 1997).[8] Similarly, in 1995, BBC Arabic Television was discontinued after the BBC broadcast a critical programme about human rights in Saudi Arabia of which the Saudi government disapproved. However, the Saudis still broadcast BBC comedies, wildlife programmes and game- and chat-shows.

Despite such attempts at censorship, global satellite/cable television channels can override the capacity of nation states to determine national or public interest judgements in broadcasting news, creating unease among the Southern elite. The Kuala Lumpur-based Asian Broadcasting Union has formulated a series of voluntary guidelines for transnational broadcasters (Goonasekera, 1997: 29). Southern governments are aware of the power of media TNCs to challenge the docility of domestic media, not uncommon in the South, where traditionally the media, especially the airwaves, were seen, at least by the ruling elites, as instruments for development and an agent in 'modernisation' – a 'bridge to a wider world' (Schramm, 1964: 41–2).

With some exceptions, Southern media generally lack international credibility, since in much of the South, the media were wholly or partly controlled by the state or the ruling parties, broadcasting news mainly about state visits and the inauguration of 'developmental' projects, so-called protocol news. In addition, state control, through draconian censorship laws, or at the very least interference, severely restricted journalists' freedom to critically examine government policies. The explosion of private, commercial television has given Southern journalists a new space to engage in critical reporting. At the same time it has made the state broadcasters' role of education and public information more difficult, since they now have to provide popular entertainment to remain competitive. In Asia, STAR TV's entertainment-oriented programming has necessitated a rethinking of public-service broadcasting and, in some nations, led to charges of 'cultural invasion' (Chan, 1994: 128). In Latin America, the region's two main players – Brazil's Globo and Mexico's Televisa – are thriving on a diet of commercial programming (Sinclair, 1996: 33). In Africa, the state-run media, once used for both formal education and general information on health and agriculture, is now eclipsed under mostly Western programming, threatening the continent's nascent media industries (Okigbo, 1995: 377).

# Infotainment as corporate propaganda?

As news presentation and content are increasingly driven by advertisers' demand for consumers, and given that television can be a powerful instrument for propagating dominant ideology (White, 1992; Glasgow Media Group, 1995), the question arises of how far the media are being used as a vehicle for promoting the free-market capitalism that enables their corporate clients to operate. Behind the mask of viewing pleasure, are the electronic empires pursuing their own agenda – to promote corporate colonialism?

As well as advertising the products of TNCs and helping to create demand among the burgeoning middle classes in the South who have aspirations to a 'Western' lifestyle, at a state level they present the process of privatisation and deregulation with almost missionary zeal, using favourable and value-laden terms – such as 'reform', 'freedom' and 'modern' – which have become staple items in the daily media vocabulary, while ignoring issues of vital concern to the South. Despite routine and robust support among media TNCs for economic liberalisation of the South, there is ample evidence to demonstrate that the much-vaunted 'reforms' are not working (Chossudovsky, 1997). As the 1997 *Human Development Report*, published by the United Nations Development Programme, points out, 'new global pressures are creating or threatening further increase in poverty' (UNDP, 1997: 3).[9]

Global television news has followed the mantra of free trade which says that everyone ultimately benefits from globalisation. It tends to give disproportionate attention to the views of political and economic elite proponents of a certain political disposition, rarely challenging the free-market dogma. Global television news rarely contests assumptions of the inevitability of globalisation, or raises questions about whether eliminating national constraints on investors and producers (but not on workers) is favourable to the majority of the population in the South. The dearth of such coverage reflects the success of the purposeful insulation of international trade negotiations and agreements, and multilateral economic bodies such as the IMF, World Bank and WTO, from public comprehension. Chakravarthy Raghavan, chief editor of the Geneva-based *South-North Development Monitor*, says that in his 18 years' experience of following the GATT, he had never previously found as much secrecy as today. 'The lack of transparency and democracy in decision-making', comments the veteran observer of international trade negotiations, 'had made the WTO and its agreements illegitimate' (quoted in Khor, 1997: 77).

It is unrealistic to expect commercial television news networks to be interested in a thorough survey of the South. Yet the way the South is covered – with more programmes about Africa's wildlife on the world's television networks than about its people – raises fundamental questions about Western news agendas and news values and their implications for the

South. Issues of major concern to the developing countries, such as the GATT negotiations (Raghavan, 1990) and the subsequent actions of the WTO in relation to trade in agricultural and industrial commodities and textiles (Raghavan, 1996), in biodiversity (Shiva, ed., 1991) and intellectual property rights (Bettig, 1996), are almost totally absent from global television news. Instead, journalists tend to legitimise the economic agenda of the West. A notable example of this was the first Ministerial Conference of the WTO in Singapore in December 1996, where the Information Technology Agreement (which was, in fact, already decided at the EU/US summit in 1995) and was not even on the agenda of the meeting, became its 'centre-piece'. As the Third World Network, a Malaysia-based international group, remarked, the conference was hijacked by the West to 'put liberalisation of their information technology products on a super-fast track' (Third World Network, 1997). A year later, when the WTO, under pressure from the USA and Western Europe, forced the Southern countries to open up the financial-services market under a major new agreement on financial liberalisation, television news generally ignored the story, as it continues to do the MAI negotiations.[10]

Southern efforts to establish parallel sources of news and an alternative global news agenda have met with little success, to wit the news exchange mechanisms (NEMs) set up with support from UNESCO as a result of the NWICO debates. The NEMs – both international, such as the Non-aligned News Agencies Pool, and regional, like the Pan African News Agency and the Organisation of Asian News Agencies – failed to make any significant impact on global or even regional newsflow, primarily because they consisted of little more than exchange of official information among member countries (Boyd-Barrett and Thussu, 1992: 140–1).

However, an agenda free from government and corporate pressures is crucial for the growth of news media in the South and the evolution of a public sphere. Yet the growing commercialisation of national media in the South, it can be argued, is undermining their public-service ethos. The increasing emphasis on entertainment in news programmes contributes to the trivialisation of vital public concerns and undermines the concept of a public sphere in which the media helps to create a forum for public discourse and the articulation of public opinion (Habermas, 1989).

In a Southern context it is questionable whether there has ever existed a public sphere (the non-Western world scarcely informs any discussion of Habermas's concept of the public sphere). In countries where it might exist, the idea of a public sphere is still in its infancy, given the historical legacy of authoritarian colonial governments and the post-independence experiences of one-party states – whether of right or left disposition – evident in much of the South during the Cold War. While the multi-party system, in operation in most Southern countries in the late 1990s, and consequently the growth of pluralistic media, offers possibilities of a public space for political debate, the gradual privatisation and take-over by mainly Western-based media empires of Southern media threatens to undermine any nascent public sphere in the South.

An alternative to the rapid globalisation of infotainment is more significant today than were the newsflow debates of the heady days of NWICO, given the encroachment on media cultures by the electronic empires. It is imperative for the Southern media to make use of the limited openings that liberalisation has provided it with to investigate and analyse the impact of market 'reforms' on the people of the South and the workings of such institutions as the World Bank, the IMF and the WTO, whose prescriptions often dictate government policy in many developing countries. The need to evolve such an alternative is vital to broaden the debate about the impact of neoliberalism on the South, and, more importantly, for the development of the 'majority world' and the empowerment of its peoples.

# Notes

1 Among the world's top ten advertisers in 1996, four were based in the USA, four in Europe and two in Japan, with the US-based Procter & Gamble being the highest spender on international advertising – $5.1 billion. The company's advertising spending in China showed an extraordinary increase – 278 per cent, from $4.5 million in 1995 to $17.2 million in 1996. In Taiwan the yearly increase was nearly 24 per cent, while in India it was 15 per cent (*Advertising Age International*, November 1997, pp. 9–10).

2 It is remarkable how little attention was given to this, one of the most significant multilateral agreements, by the global media, especially television. The MAI was supposed to be discussed by the WTO but the US government felt that WTO was 'too unwieldy' and decided to negotiate it within the OECD. If the agreement is ratified, it will further erode the already fragile sovereignty of Southern governments, and yet it has hardly been mentioned in the Southern media. For a discussion of MAI see Daly, 1997.

3 The currency crisis in East and Southeast Asia in late 1997 may reduce this flow temporarily (although it was the Western bankers who benefited most from the turmoil while the IMF forced the Asian nations to further tighten their belts), but it is likely that Western investments will increase, especially if the MAI comes into effect.

4 According to the *Fortune Global 500*, of the world's 500 largest corporations in terms of revenues in 1996, only twenty-eight were from the South, of which South Korea had thirteen, Brazil five, China three, Hong Kong two, and Taiwan, Malaysia, Mexico, Venezuela and India one each. The largest number, 162, were from the USA, followed by Japan which had 126. The media corporations among the top 500 included Sony (ranked 33), Walt Disney (ranked 192), Viacom (ranked

365), Time Warner (ranked 457) and News Corporation (ranked 462) (*Fortune*, 4 August 1997). However, *FT 500*, the world's top 500 corporations ranked by market capitalisation, showed on 31 December 1997 that 222 were from the USA, seventy-one from Japan and fifty-one from the UK. Only thirty-nine belonged to the South (*Financial Times*, supplement, 22 January 1998, p. 3).

5 However, the agreement came to an end in November 1997 as, in the words of Shobhana Bhartia, chairperson of Home TV, 'we now want to focus on home-grown Hindi entertainment programming' (*Asian Age*, 1 December 1997). BBC World takes a robustly commercial approach to global broadcasting, reflected in its signing deals with private companies for delivery of its programming or for joint productions. Most important of these was the October 1996 agreement with the US documentary network, Discovery channel (which serves 111 million subscribers in 145 countries), a subsidiary of TCI, to co-produce programmes and share cable and satellite channels round the world. In 1996–7, BBC World's sales were at £354 million, 4 per cent higher than in 1995–6, and the net profit was £73.5 million (*BBC Annual Report and Accounts, 1996-97*, BBC, London, 1997, pp. 50–1).

6 In its success in the South, News Corporation benefited from its experience in Britain, where it made subscription television a reality. Using BSkyB, Britain's multi-channel TV company and Europe's most profitable broadcaster, Murdoch is developing, designing and marketing the set-top boxes required to decode digital signals into high-quality pictures on TV screens. This will make him the gatekeeper controlling the digital TV market, which is likely to dominate broadcasting in the twenty-first century, prompting the *Guardian* to call him the 'digital dictator' in an editorial on 29 October 1996. Murdoch made it to the top 25 with a net worth of $3.9 billion according to the *Forbes* magazine (*Forbes*, 'The Top 25', 13 October 1997).

7 According to *Business Week* (17 November 1997, p. 91) Time Warner showed a 49 per cent increase in sales from 1996, at $9.4 billion at the third quarter of 1997.

8 Only a year later, Rupert Murdoch backed out of a contract to publish the memoirs of Chris Patten, the controversial last governor of Hong Kong, presumably for fear of prejudicing his attempts to penetrate China's potentially enormous cable television market (Ahmed, 1998: 2).

9 The UNDP says that more than ninety developing countries are likely to have a per capita income below what it was a decade ago. The United Nations' *The Least Developed Countries 1997 Report* shows that some of the poorest countries on earth, mainly in sub-Saharan Africa, have experienced 'regress' – their economies have declined (between 1980 and 1994, the world's twenty-two poorest countries have suffered a fall in per capita GDP of more than 10 per cent), social conditions (food availability, access to education, health status) have worsened markedly,

and they have become increasingly marginalised from the mainstream of the world economy (UNCTAD, 1997b, pp. vi–vii). For how the IMF/World Bank policies have increased poverty see Chossudovsky, 1997.

10 Such omissions by television news can also be detected in the coverage of stories which impinge on Western geo-political interests. For example, during the 1991 Gulf conflict, Western television played a key part in the propaganda war (Mowlana et al., eds, 1992). Since then, television coverage of Iraq has broadly followed the agenda set by the Pentagon, with scarcely any reports about the devastating impact of UN sanctions on the Iraqis. This selective approach to news was evident in November 1997, when while international headlines were dominated by alleged Iraqi misdemeanour towards UN weapons inspectors, an important defence agreement between the USA and Kazakhstan – billed to become the world's fourth largest oil producer – went largely unreported, as did the first ever military exercises by NATO's rapid reaction force in Central Asia – an area outside the remit of NATO (Meek and Whitehouse, 1997: 16–17).

# References

*Advertising Age International* (1997) Special Report: Latin America Media, Jan., p. 123.

Ahmed, K. (1998) Caught up in Rupert Murdoch's Chinese puzzle, *Guardian*, 28 Feb., pp. 2–3.

Bettig, R. V. (1996) *Copyrighting Culture: The Political Economy of Intellectual Property*, Westview Press, Boulder, Colo.

Boyd-Barrett, O. (1977) Media imperialism: towards an international framework for the analysis of media systems, in Curran, J. and Gurevitch, M. (eds) *Mass Communication and Society*, Edward Arnold, London.

Boyd-Barrett, O. and Thussu, D. K. (1992) *Contra-Flow in Global News*, John Libbey, London.

Chan, J. M. (1994) National responses and accessibility to STAR TV in Asia, *Journal of Communication*, 44.3, pp. 112–31.

Channel 4 Television (1995) *Bazaar Television*, part 2 of *Satellite Wars* series, broadcast on 2 April, Channel 4, UK.

Chossudovsky, M. (1997) *The Globalisation of Poverty: Impacts of IMF and World Bank Reforms*, Zed Press, London.

Cornwell, R. (1995) The tendency to moralise, the appetite for trash, *Independent*, 4 Oct., p. 3.

Culf, A. (1997) Here is the news – read by Vic Reeves, *Guardian*, 22 July, p. 1.

Daly, M. (1997) Some taxing questions for the Multilateral Agreement on Investment (MAI), *The World Economy*, 20.6 (Sept.), pp. 787–808.

European Commission (1997) *The Future of North–South Relations: Towards Sustainable Economic and Social Development*, Luxemburg.

Fannin, R. (1997) Flat market, falling yen hit Japanese agencies hard, *Advertising Age International*, June, p. i18.

Farhi, P. (1997) CNN confronts a news crisis – itself, *International Herald Tribune*, 3 Sept.

Fiske, J. (1987) *Television Culture*, Routledge, London.

Franklin, B. (1997) *Newszak and News Media*, Arnold, London.

Gardam, T. (1997) Television news you can use, *New Statesman*, 14 Nov., p. 17.

George, S. and Sabelli, F. (1994) *Faith and Credit: The World Bank's Secular Empire*, Penguin, London.

Gitlin, T. (1979) Prime time ideology: the hegemonic process in television entertainment, *Social Problems*, 26.3, pp. 251–66.

Glasgow Media Group (1995) *Glasgow Media Group Reader, Volume 2: Industry, Economy, War and Politics*, Routledge, London.

Goonasekera, A. (1997) Asia and the information revolution – an introductory perspective, *Asian Journal of Communication*, 7.2, pp. 12–33.

Gunther, M. (1998) What's wrong with this picture? *Fortune*, 12 Jan., p. 60.

Habermas, J. (1989) *The Structural Transformation of the Public Sphere*, Polity, Cambridge.

Hallin, D. (1996) Commercialism and professionalism in the American news media, in Curran, J. and Gurevitch, M. (eds) *Mass Communication and Society*, 2nd edn, Arnold, London.

Hamelink, C. (1997) International communication: global market and morality, in Mohammadi, A. (ed.) *International Communication and Globalization*, Sage, London.

Harris, S. (1998) News nightmare, *Guardian* (Media), 16 Feb., p. 2.

Herman, E. and McChesney, R. (1997) *The Global Media*, Cassell, London.

Higgins, A. and Walker, M. (1996) Here comes Mickey Mao, *Guardian* (The Week), 30 Nov., p. 2.

Kellner, D. (1990) *Television and the Crisis of Democracy*, Westview, Boulder, Colo.

Kepp, M. (1997) News addicts, *Cable and Satellite Europe*, Aug., p. 41.

Khor, M. (1997) The World Trade Organisation and the South: fighting against the tide, *Development*, 40.4, pp. 73–7.

Levinson, M. (1995) It's an MTV world, *Newsweek*, 24 April, p. 46.

Lucas, L. (1995) Asia TV race is a marathon, not a sprint, *Financial Times*, 27 July, p. 25.

MacGregor, B. (1997) *Live, Direct And Biased? Making Television News in the Satellite Age*, Arnold, London.

Maidment, P. (1995) Pax Mickeyana?, *Newsweek*, 14 Aug., p. 30.

Masmoudi, M. (1979) The new international information order, *Journal of Communication*, 29.2, pp. 172–85.

McBride, S. (1980) *Many Voices, One World: International Commission for the Study of Communications Problems*, UNESCO, Paris.

McCann, P. (1997) Worldwide coverage for the greatest media star of all, *Independent on Sunday*, 7 Sept.

McManus, J. (1994) *Market Driven Journalism*, Sage, New York.

Meek, J. and Whitehouse, T. (1997) Where madness seeps out of the earth, *Observer*, 23 Dec., pp. 23–4.

Midgley, C. (1997) The courtroom and the camera, *The Times*, 7 Nov., p. 39.

Moran, M. (1995) The Balkans? US news media has not educated the public, *International Herald Tribune*, 22 Nov., p. 8.

Mowlana, H., Gerbner, G. and Schiller, H. (eds) (1992) *Triumph of the Image*, Westview, Boulder, Colo.

Nye, J. S., Jr. and Owens, W. A. (1996) America's information edge, *Foreign Affairs*, March/April, 75.2, pp. 20–36.

Okigbo, C. (1995) Africa, in Smith, A. (ed.) *Television: An International History*, Oxford University Press, Oxford.

Paterson, C. (1997) Global television news services, in Sreberny-Mohammadi, A., Winseck, D., McKenna, J. and Boyd-Barrett, O. (eds) *Media in Global Context*, Arnold, London.

Poole, T. and Vines, S. (1997) Murdoch dreams of a Chinese empire, *Independent*, 10 Jan.

Raghavan, C. (1990) *Recolonization: GATT, the Uruguay Round and the Third World*, Zed Books, London.

Raghavan, C. (1996) *The Role of Multilateral Organisations in the Globalisation Process*, Third World Network, Penang.

Roach, C. (1997) The Western world and the NWICO: united they stand?, in Golding, P. and Harris, P. (eds) *Beyond Cultural Imperialism: Globalisation, Communication and the New International Order*, Sage, London.

Rothkopf, D. (1997) In praise of cultural imperialism? *Foreign Policy*, 107 (summer), pp. 38–53.

Rowan, D. (1998) Meet the new world government, *Guardian*, 13 Feb., p. 15.

Schiller, H. (1996) *Information Inequality*, Routledge, New York.

Schramm, W. (1964) *Mass Media and National Development*, Stanford University Press, Stanford, Calif.

Schudson, M. (1995) *The Power of News*, Harvard University Press, Cambridge, Mass.

Shiva, V. (ed.) (1991) *Biodiversity: Social and Ecological Perspectives*, Zed Books, London.

Sinclair, J. (1996) Mexico, Brazil, and the Latin World, in Sinclair, J., Jacka, E. and Cunningham, S. (eds) *New Patterns in Global Television: Peripheral Vision*, Oxford University Press, Oxford.

Third World Network (1997) WTO conference a big let-down, *Third World Resurgence*, 77/78, Jan.–Feb., p. 28.

Tunstall, J. (1977) *The Media are American*, Constable, London.
UNCTAD (1997a) *The World Investment Report 1997: Transnational Corporations, Market Structure and Competition Policy*, United Nations Conference on Trade and Development, Geneva.
UNCTAD (1997b) *The Least Developed Countries 1997 Report*, United Nations Conference on Trade and Development, Geneva.
UNDP (1997) *Human Development Report*, United Nations Development Programme, Oxford University Press, Oxford and New York.
Utley, G. (1997) The shrinking of foreign news: from broadcast to narrowcast, *Foreign Affairs*, 76.2 (March/April), pp. 2–10.
Wentz, L. (1997) Pan-Asian TV survey represents baby step for regional research, *Advertising Age International*, Oct., p. 3.
White, M. (1992) Ideological analysis and television, in Allen, R. C. (ed.) *Channels of Discourse, Reassembled*, Routledge, New York.
Winch, S. (1997) *Mapping the Cultural Space of Journalism: How Journalism Distinguishes News from Entertainment*, Praeger, Westport, Conn.
Wittstock, M. (1998) Hi there! And here's tonight's non-news, *Guardian* (Media), 19 Jan., p. 7.

# Discussion questions

1 In what ways do electronic empires resemble or differ from empires in the past?

2 What role has the United States government played in the expansion of American media and communications industries outside the USA?

3 Summarise the key points in Chapter 1. Do you agree with Herbert Schiller's view of the USA as a hegemonic power?

4 How do transnational media corporations use synergies to cross-promote their products? Think of some examples from your country.

5 How have developments in communications and information technologies enabled the expansion of electronic empires into global markets?

6 Does it matter who owns the media? Analyse the coverage of a newspaper: how far does its ownership influence and shape its agenda?

7 In what ways can the concept of cultural imperialism be applied to the post-1989 media in Eastern Europe?

8 Critically examine the claim that television news is increasingly driven by infotainment. Monitor a news programme to see how the stories are being covered.

9 What strategies have the transnational media corporations adopted to enter the media markets in the South? Why is the South important for them?

10 What options are open to the media in developing countries to counter media empires?

# SECTION II

# GLOBAL MEDIA: A GLOBAL PUBLIC SPHERE?

# Introduction to Section II

The second section of the book evaluates the usefulness and validity of the concept of a global public sphere in relation to the impact of globalisation of the media. The concept of a public sphere is best known in its formulation by the German critical theorist Jurgen Habermas in the early 1960s, signifying both an historical phenomenon – the bourgeois nation's forum of debate during the emergence of Western capitalism – and a generally applicable measure of democratic communications.

There has been renewed and growing interest in the concept in the post-Cold War era, with the 1989 English translation of Habermas's 1962 book *The Structural Transformation of the Public Sphere* coinciding with the collapse of state socialism in Eastern Europe and the rapid globalisation of the media and cultural industries. It has been argued by some critical scholars that the concept of the 'public sphere' has replaced 'hegemony' as a key focus of attention in international communication. The contributions in this section raise the question of whether the expansion of the free flow of information in the post-communist world is helping to create a global public sphere in the Habermasian sense.

Examining the concept of the public sphere as a critical tool of cultural analysis, Jim McGuigan analyses the usefulness of the concept at a time when, with the increased globalisation of communication and media industries, it has been extended to the ideal of the global community. He makes a distinction between universalistic and particularistic usages of the concept, arguing that in its cognitive universalistic usage it is concerned typically with the national and international circulation of information in relation to political decision-making. Particularistic usages of the concept, on the other hand, such as a feminist public sphere, tend to a greater concreteness and 'sense of affectivity' than does universalistic usage.

McGuigan points out that while the public sphere may appear to be something of intellectual interest to the political class, it is of debatable relevance from a popular point of view. Although there are signs of the actualisation of public spheres, such as campaigns by new social movements and the deluge of information on issues of humanitarian concern delivered routinely by global media, these often seem remote from people's daily lives, generating a response of apparent indifference to media representations of atrocities and suffering in the world. What is needed, McGuigan argues, is a 'softer' conception of the public sphere and one that takes account of 'affective' as well as effective communication, entailing a reconsideration of the role of entertainment.

McGuigan goes on to examine one of the comparatively rare instances of public care-at-a-distance, the phenomenon of Comic Relief, the annual television event in Britain to raise funds for 'third world' and UK aid projects. McGuigan suggests that it illustrates something of the 'effectivity of affective communication' which would be essential to popular engagement in any kind of public sphere. However, he also raises the question of whether these brief occasions of international feeling and mutuality, where 'silent majorities' speak, indicate that the public sphere so constructed is merely a phantom.

In examining whether or not there are indications of the emergence of a global public sphere, Colin Sparks critiques the very concept of public sphere, pointing out its limitations, particularly with regard to its historical validity and its far from universal scope. He questions whether it is fair to extend the concept globally when its status is contested even within modern European societies, where it is rooted.

Sparks then examines the issue of how global are the global media. He addresses some of the concrete evidence of the actual extent of a globalising tendency in the international media, reviewing the 'traditional' media of the public sphere – broadcasting and the press. Then moving on to satellite television, the key medium contributing to globalisation, Sparks argues that, if we wish to make out a case for a new global form of television, we would need to point to a service that was specifically supranational in form and content. He discusses CNN as an example and argues that its audience size remains much smaller than the national television channels in most countries where it is available. Similarly, international newspapers have a limited circulation in comparison to local newspapers, though the audience for these global media are disproportionately amongst the elite.

Sparks sees the structure of the global media as closely following the patterns of established economic and political power. The USA dominates the world trade in information goods, Sparks contends, in the same way that it dominates that in commercial aircraft, and for very similar reasons. As the existence of a tiny, rich, English-speaking class of people with access to global media and interest in global issues cannot be used as proof of a new public sphere, Sparks concludes that there is no evidence for the emergence of a global public sphere. The only way we might retain the global part of the term, he argues, is by foregrounding it as the continuation of structures of international inequality.

The growth of private media power and its increasing globalisation is at the heart of the chapter by Edward Herman, who examines the privatisation of public space in the United States and globally. Analysing the underlying political and economic dynamics behind media empires, he considers the effects of market ideology on the future of public space. Herman's basic theme is that the media conglomerates are dominated by economic forces, which tend to occupy media space and capture audiences to serve the 'best economic use'. He argues that the overwhelmingly dominant funding source for use of media space is advertising, underlying the trend towards displacement of public by commercial broadcasting and forced or self-commercialisation of public broadcasting.

Employing the economic theory of externalities, Herman examines the evolution of the commercialisation of broadcasting in the USA, analysing the transfer of public-service responsibilities to the Public Broadcasting System and its subsequent erosion. According to Herman, the US experience sheds light on privatisation of airwaves, where advertiser preferences have defined broadcasting. The chapter asks how far the US model can be extrapolated beyond its borders, given its influence, by looking at examples from Canada and Brazil. The key factors driving privatisation, Herman argues, include: enhanced domestic political power of corporate systems and corporate media; role of international financial institutions and financial stringency and pressure on public services; and downgrading of the public-service role and public goods.

Herman goes on to assess how far the 'active audience' and other forces of resistance might counteract the privatisation of the public sphere at a time when they are being fragmented by the tendency towards niche-filling while the main drift of media is towards entertainment.

The issue of democracy and the empowerment of the audience is raised in Chapter 8, in Peter Golding's investigation of the potential of the new communication and information technologies, in the form of the Internet, to contribute to the creation of a global space for democratic communication and a progressive evolution of the public sphere.

The chapter assesses the contention that technological developments like the Internet are creating a new cyberdemocracy and discusses the contradictory trends in current developments. The background to this debate is the pattern of inegalitarian access evident in existing technologies. Golding reviews the extent of such inequities, both within and between nations, against the backdrop of a diminishing public sphere for communications, and the growing consolidation of new technologies into a commercialised environment in which they are unevenly available. He then reviews the evolution of the Internet, stressing its transformation from initially a military and technological innovation, to one developed largely in the education sector. The corporate take-over and commercialisation of the Internet, Golding argues, can lead easily to a weary fatalism, accepting that another potentially liberating technology has been engulfed by the still rampant forces of the 'free market'. Golding examines four key areas to illustrate the present state of uncertainty and opportunity. First, he compares the use made of the Internet for community and progressive purposes on the one hand and for entertainment and commercial exploitation on the other. He then reviews the empirical evidence on Net use and access and compares the reality with the dream of early Net champions who saw it as a horizontal communications structure. Third, he examines the corporate reality of development of the Internet, which ends another dream of the pioneers who saw it as the playground of the inventor-entrepreneur, a place where a thousand overnight millionaires might bloom. Finally, Golding looks at claims that the new technology will bring in a new golden age of 'teledemocracy', arguing that this vision is a fundamental misunderstanding of democracy and is also at odds with the reality of Internet development.

# |5|

# *What price the public sphere?*

JIM McGUIGAN

Much of the criticism of media power, from academic and activist perspectives, depends upon commitment to a potentially realisable ideal, in effect evincing a utopian realism concerning how we might imagine and perhaps bring about a more democratic means of mass communication than the systems and practices that currently prevail. Whether stated explicitly or not, the ideal of a democratic system of mass communication can be called 'the public sphere', either in the sense in which it was theorised by Jurgen Habermas ([1962] 1989) at the beginning of the 1960s and since developed by him or in one of the various senses of the concept that have been associated with its great revival over recent years.

According to Nicholas Garnham (1995), the public sphere has replaced hegemony as the concept which defines the core problematic of media and cultural studies. This is a debatable proposition since, for one thing, a great deal of media and cultural studies is now detached from social and political criticism, and both are concepts of social and political criticism. For another thing, it would be mistaken to regard hegemony as no longer relevant to the critical analysis of media power, especially when the operations of 'global media' and local forms of subordination, resistance and negotiation are under consideration.

Although hegemony is a more complex idea than ideological domination, it nonetheless carries connotations of domination, the power of the strong over the weak, even though the winning of consent rather than crude manipulation is at stake. In comparison, the public sphere is a positive idea, a good thing, and, by definition, referencing a condition within which the power of the strong may be checked by that of the weak through access to communicational resources and participation in political debate and decision-making. For this reason, it is a less immediately plausible concept, from a realistic point of view, than hegemony.

While it is essential to have an idea of a better condition in order to criticise an actual condition, it is necessary to adduce some evidence of actualisation, if only anticipatory, either in the past or in the present. What I shall do, then, is outline the idealisation of the public sphere as a critical measure of the extent of democracy in mass communications and consider arguments concerning its existence or non-existence. I also want to call into question an excessively cognitive conception of the public sphere which characterises most usage, typified by the exclusive stress upon 'information' in much economically, socially and politically critical media analysis. I do this because I believe the aspirations linked to the public sphere must include genuinely popular involvement and, therefore, encompass emotion as well as cognition.

## A necessary concept

Habermas's ([1962] 1989) tragic narrative of the rise and fall of the bourgeois public sphere between the eighteenth and twentieth centuries in major European states, most notably Britain and France, is so well known that it hardly requires detailed recapitulation. The standard criticisms (Thompson, 1993) are also very well known. To be brief, then, crucial to the bourgeois public sphere was the articulation of principles of rational-critical debate conducted through face-to-face discussion and print media, journalism in particular but also literature more generally (see Eagleton, 1984). Quite apart from the subsequent history of decline, involving the growth and commercialisation of communications media and the increasingly sophisticated management of public opinion, the public sphere was founded in a fundamental contradiction: its universalistic claims were undermined by its particularistic functioning as a gentleman's club. Nevertheless, it has been on grounds of universal democracy and egalitarianism that popular emancipation has been sought and to an extent (however limited) achieved ever since in liberal-democratic polities.

Rather than raking over the history yet again, it is more useful to consider how Habermas has reworked his concept of the public sphere up to the present. In the 1970s Habermas (1979) formulated a general theory of communication according to what he considered to be the normal operations of ordinary language use. When we speak to one another we seek mutual understanding. We routinely make validity claims about the way things are, what should be done, and so forth, that are, in principle, open to critical questioning. We may or may not reach agreement but if we did not try to understand one another and aim to reach agreement, especially when we have something practical to do, it is difficult to imagine quite how sociality would go on at all. None of this is to deny that mutual misunderstanding is common for all sorts of reasons, including ideological, linguistic and psychological reasons. The important point is, however, that the orientation towards mutual understanding is a constitutive feature of everyday life and it is ethical to keep it going.

In developing his general theory, Habermas (1984 and 1987) makes two major distinctions: between communicative and instrumental modes of rationality; and between lifeworld and system. Participants in communicatively rational discourse construct their own purposes, whereas most participants in instrumentally rational discourse have the goals of action constructed for them. In fact, in this latter case it may appear as though nobody is actually responsible for determining the goals and purposes of action. They seem to be just there, dictated by impersonal economic and bureaucratic forces over which ordinary people have no control. These forces are systemic, bound up with complex processes of social reproduction and steered by the media of money and power. By contrast, in the everyday lifeworld we may find spaces of communicative freedom that are not dictated by impersonal and systemic forces.

The distinction between lifeworld and system can be seen and perhaps dismissed as merely another variant on the old binary opposition of community and society, with its romantic and nostalgic connotations, although I believe it does provide considerable insight into the contemporary operations of power. For Habermas, modernity is characterised by the uncoupling of lifeworld and system. The system is animated by instrumental and strategic rationality which is over and above the comprehension of most people yet with which they have to comply in order, for instance, to earn a living. In comparison, lifeworld spaces are more open to creativity and self-fulfilment. This may illuminate, for example, why so many people today find greater opportunities for self-realisation in leisure than in work. However, though they operate according to different principles, it would be mistaken to treat lifeworld and system as radically separated spaces. In this case, leisure is not free of systemic determination. It is constructive, then, to explore the interactions between lifeworld and system, such as how in, say, workplaces communicative rationality may resist, modify and humanise instrumental rationality.

With regard to his later conceptualisation of the public sphere, Habermas has proposed two successive theses on the relationship between lifeworld and system: the colonisation thesis (1987) and the sluicegate model (1996). The colonisation thesis suggests that instrumental rationality is invading the lifeworld, displacing communicative forms of sense-making with the senselessness of instrumentalism. At one time, it might have been presumed that the overthrow of systemic power would thus be the aim of radical politics. Events, however, have proved this to be less than likely in the immediate future and, in any case, system collapse does not necessarily lead to progressive outcomes. For a German like Habermas, the experience of the Weimar Republic and 'the rectifying revolution' in East Germany are deeply wrought into this anxiety about the consequences of systemic transformation. He focuses, then, on the way in which lifeworld resources are gathered together and brought to bear on systemic processes – hence the importance of the 'new social movements' as advocates of progressive policy and pressure on formally democratic governmental systems. Feminist, ecological and other movements are therefore viewed as the necessary antidote to the encroachments of the system on the lifeworld.

Perhaps becoming more conservative in his old age, Habermas now places much less emphasis on the colonisation of the lifeworld by system imperatives and resistance to it than on the communicative exchange between system and lifeworld. His mature reflections on the problem combine both a notion of multiple public spheres with reformist politics in relation to an official and unitary public sphere. This is the 'sluicegate' model whereby social movements put issues on the political agenda that would not themselves be engendered by the system and the official public sphere.

> The great issues of the last decades give evidence for this. Consider, for example, the spiralling nuclear-arms race; consider the risks involved in the peaceful use of atomic energy or in other large-scale technological projects and scientific experimentation, such as genetic engineering; consider the ecological threats involved in an overstrained natural environment (acid rain, water pollution, species extinction, etc.); consider the dramatically progressing impoverishment of the third world and the problems of world economic order; or consider such issues as feminism, increasing migration and the associated problems of multiculturalism. Hardly any of these topics were *initially* brought up by exponents of the state apparatus, large organisations or functional systems. Instead, they were broached by intellectuals, concerned citizens, radical professionals, self-proclaimed 'advocates' and the like.
>
> Moving in from the outermost periphery, such issues force their way into newspapers and interested associations, clubs, professional organisations, academies and universities. They find forums, citizen initiatives and other platforms before they catalyse the growth of social movements and new subcultures. The latter in turn can dramatise contributions, presenting them so effectively that the mass media take up the matter. Only through their presentation in the media do such topics reach the larger public and subsequently gain a place on the 'public agenda'. Sometimes the support of sensational actions, mass protests and incessant campaigning is required before an issue can make its way via the surprising election of marginal candidates or radical parties, expanded platforms of 'established' parties, important court decisions, and so on, into the core of the political system and there receive formal consideration.
>
> (Habermas, 1996: 381)

# Universalism and particularism

Beyond what Habermas himself has to say, while keeping in mind what he says, one of the main tensions in conceptualising the public sphere for current use is between universalism and particularism. In considering this tension I want to examine two contrasting arguments: Nicholas Garnham on the side of universalism and Nancy Fraser on the side of particularism.

Garnham has written two papers, both of which are entitled 'The media and the public sphere', the first originally published in 1986 (and reprinted in Garnham, 1990), the second delivered at the conference that was held in North Carolina in 1989 (reprinted in Calhoun, ed., 1992) on the occasion of the publication in English of *The Structural Transformation of the Public Sphere*, 27 years after it was originally published in German. The first version of 'The media and the public sphere' is marked by a critical response to what Garnham calls 'a reinforcement of the market and the progressive destruction of public service as the preferred mode for the allocation of cultural resources' (1990: 104). He goes on to say, 'It is very much in the interests of the controllers of multinational capital to keep nation-states and their citizens in a state of disunity and dysfunctional ignorance unified only by market structures' (ibid.: 113). Garnham is speaking out of a British experience, where there has been a very strong tradition of public-service broadcasting as an alternative to the market and as a means of regulating commercial television and radio. Although he does not exactly equate the public sphere with the institutions of public-service communication, Garnham certainly sees such arrangements as providing a necessary institutional framework for a national public sphere to flourish in a highly mediated society. He stresses the universalism of the public sphere and argues that it should be coterminous with the political sphere in the sense of the nation-state. To assume in this way that the nation-state is the relevant context of communicative and democratic universalism, an assumption held by Garnham only a decade ago, seems strangely old-fashioned now, when 'globalisation' is such a buzzword. However, Garnham concludes his first version of 'The media and the public sphere' with the following observation: 'Not only do we face the challenge of sustaining and developing the public sphere at a national level. Such a development will simply be bypassed if we do not at the same time and perhaps with greater urgency begin to develop a public sphere where at present one hardly exists at the international level' (ibid.: 114).

This is the starting point for Garnham's second disquisition on 'The media and the public sphere' where he says, 'the development of an increasingly global market and centres of private economic power are steadily undermining the nation-state, and it is within the nation-state that the question of citizenship and of the relationship between communication and politics has been traditionally posed' (1992: 361–2). It is significant that when Garnham talks of globalisation with regard to media power he stresses the economic determinations rather than the cultural aspects of 'time–space compression' (Harvey, 1989) or 'time–space distanciation' (Giddens, 1990).

For this reason, his argument is vulnerable to the kind of critique launched by Paul Hirst and Graham Thompson (1996) of the exaggerated claims that are made about *economic* globalisation and how these claims furnish a convenient alibi for the abrogation of responsibility for economic and indeed media policy by national governments. That, however, is somewhat incidental to an explication of Garnham's wish to globalise the public sphere. If economics and communications media are now 'global', then the public sphere must be coterminously 'global' as well. When confronted with the problem of cultural difference that this necessarily raises, Garnham asserts the universal validity of the public sphere and, moreover, the very principles of the European Enlightenment out of which it emerged. It is worth quoting him at some length on this point:

> To claim the Enlightenment project, out of misplaced ethnocentric guilts, as exclusively (and detrimentally) Western, for instance, or to claim rationality as exclusively (and detrimentally) male seems to me to condescend to those other cultures or subordinated social groups who are fighting our common struggle to understand and control the world in pursuit of human liberty. In Britain it has been interesting how shallow the political and intellectual positions based on cultural relativism have looked in the light of the Salman Rushdie affair. But I would go further. If we accept that the economic system is indeed global in scope and at the same time crucially determining over large areas of social action, the Enlightenment project of democracy requires us to make a Pascalian bet on universal rationality. For without it the project is unrealisable, and we will remain in large part enslaved to a system outside our control.
>
> (Garnham, 1992: 369–70)

Although I am quite sympathetic to Garnham on this point, however, I do think we have to entertain the possibility that the global public sphere is a Western fantasy and perhaps a last gasp of its otherwise shaky bid for or to sustain global hegemony. Garnham, it must be said, holds to his position consistently and honourably. He not only universalises the public sphere but insists upon its singularity. There must be one public sphere, in his view, commensurate with a unified global political economy. To be fair, I think Garnham argues this abstract, totalising and unconvincing case because of a conviction that if, say, News Corp. operates on a global scale so must the counter-forces of democratic control and accountability. National governments cannot check Murdoch so 'the world' has to do it instead.

Actually, I personally believe that national governments could have checked Murdoch a good deal more than they have ever tried to do. This kind of consideration is vital because we cannot possibly mean that a global public sphere is simply the product of the global circulation of media messages, the fact that we could all watch video games on television during the Gulf War or see *Evita* at our local cinemas. That would be a mistakenly mediacentric view of the public sphere and one which misses its idealistic function as the forum of a democratic culture.

The trouble with the concept of a global public sphere is that it lacks concreteness and compares unfavourably, therefore, with particularistic notions of the public sphere that can point with greater credibility to its actualisation. Moreover, in her feminist critique of the Habermasian position and her own reworking of the public sphere concept, Nancy Fraser has challenged the gender blindness and hence masculine bias of the whole universalising idea as it has been used theoretically and in so far as it has been actualised at all in the past. She asks, 'Should we conclude that the very concept of the public sphere is a piece of bourgeois, masculinist ideology so thoroughly compromised that it can shed no genuinely critical light on the limits of actually existing democracy?' (Fraser, 1992: 117). By the point at which she asked this question, Fraser had already answered it in saying, 'something like Habermas's idea of the public sphere is indispensable to critical social theory and democratic political practice' (ibid.: 111). Her frame of reference is not global but societal. Fraser argues that in a stratified and multicultural society a unitary public sphere can only suppress difference with its fake universalism and spurious egalitarianism. It involves 'filtering diverse rhetorical and stylistic norms through a single, overarching lens' (ibid.: 126).

It is preferable and more realistic, therefore, to think in terms of competing public spheres. Echoing Oskar Negt's and Alexander Kluge's ([1972] 1993) original critique of Habermas for exclusively attending to 'the bourgeois public sphere' and neglecting 'the plebeian public sphere', Fraser proposes a notion of 'subaltern counter-publics' and illustrates her case with reference to the actual achievements of feminism in the United States, which has its own networks and institutions, 'spaces of withdrawal and regroupment' and 'bases and training grounds for agitational activities directed towards wider publics' (ibid.: 124).

Fraser really does identify something actual, the enormous impact, though by no means total success, that feminism has had upon the national culture of the USA. However, there are a couple of critical observations that I want to make regarding lacunae in Fraser's position and a further observation on her distinction between 'weak' and 'strong' publics. While, first, she is right to point to the concrete existence of a feminist public sphere in the USA, Fraser seems strangely unreflexive about how her own claims concerning its success are substantiated by reference to the broader impact of feminism on the system as a whole and, in effect, upon a 'single, overarching' national public sphere. Second, she takes American society unproblematically as her frame of reference, which is odd when you consider that feminism is not just confined to the USA. It might be possible, for instance, to speak of an international feminist public sphere that has a certain universalism about it. Not even socialist-feminists, then, are entirely innocent of the casual and quite typical error made by Americans of confusing the USA with the world. Also, the distinction drawn by Fraser between the 'weak' publics of liberal politics, which are opinion-forming but not decision-making, and 'strong' publics, like organised feminism, which make decisions, is perhaps too rigid a distinction. Her conception of the public sphere is a very demanding one from the point of view of ordinary citizenship, requiring a civic vigilance that may be unrealistic for most people.

# Affective communication

The ideal subject of an ideal public sphere, in almost any version, seems to be that of a vigilant citizen who must be properly informed about what is going on and be extremely active politically. While I would neither want to deny the necessarily cognitive aspects of public discourse and the rigours of rational-critical debate nor defend widespread political apathy, I do believe we need a rather softer conception of the public sphere than we find in the work of Habermas, Garnham and Fraser, one that takes due account of *a*ffective and not only *e*ffective communications.

This observation must be qualified, however, with regard to Garnham since he did remark in passing and with tantalising brevity, in the second version of 'The media and the public sphere', upon what he says is 'a crucial and neglected area of media and cultural studies research', namely, 'the entertainment content of the media [which] is clearly the primary tool we use to handle the relationship between the systems world and the lifeworld' (1992: 374). Garnham is not strictly accurate here since much of the research in media and cultural studies is actually about 'the entertainment content of the media'. Yet, it is true to say that this kind of research usually operates in a very different space from research that is grounded in a problematic of the public sphere.

As Peter Dahlgren (1995) has observed in his study, *Television and the Public Sphere*, media research tends to be divided between a focus upon news and current affairs from the point of view of the public sphere, on the one hand, and popular culture from the point of view of enjoyment, on the other hand. He shuffles around the usual terminology of 'public knowledge' and 'popular culture' by talking about 'popular knowledge' and 'public culture' in order to indicate how the distinction between information and entertainment is routinely transgressed. This is not just a matter of the blurring of genre boundaries in television, which may be celebrated as 'postmodern' or denounced as 'infotainment', but may be seen to manifest a rather more fundamental interaction between cognition and emotion. Dahlgren says that, from the point of view of the public sphere, 'rational communication is necessary, but if our horizons do not penetrate beyond the conceptual framework of communicative rationality and the ideal speech situation, we will be operating with a crippled critical theory' (ibid.: 109). Moreover, he remarks, 'there is no road to representational information (or critique, for that matter) which does not, at least in part, pass through the terrain of the affective and arational' (ibid.: 150).

The affective and arational are clearly relevant to assessing how television represents suffering and how audiences respond to representations of suffering, as Kevin Robins (1993 and 1994) has argued cogently. Recently, in this connection, Keith Tester (1997) has examined the issue of televisual witnessing of genocide. Today, when it comes to genocide, as in the case of Rwanda, nobody can say they did not know because it is there for our routine consumption mundanely on the box. This may invoke vague feelings of guilt, calls that 'something must be done', declarations of innocence, and so forth, yet, according to Tester, 'the most overwhelmingly obvious reaction and response in the West to the news of genocide' is 'utter indifference' (Tester, 1997: 14). Whether this is true or not, and it is debatable, Tester clearly has a point. The televisual consumption of war, genocide and famine has become somewhat banal and may indeed invoke a blasé response. In what sense then, if any, asks Tester, are audiences who respond in this way to be found guilty? He comes to the conclusion that they are not guilty in a conventionally criminal or moral sense. Although there may be a certain amount of political guilt involved, say in the case of the Gulf War, the most important grounds for a guilty verdict are metaphysical. To quote Tester, 'If metaphysical guilt is taken to consist in doing nothing even though we are aware of the perpetration of horror and violence, if metaphysical guilt is the lack of absolute solidarity with the human being, then perhaps we can be found guilty as charged' (ibid.: 148). Television is the principal medium of such guilt, in Tester's view, since it gives us information but not knowledge.

I can think of an example, however, where metaphysical guilt of this kind is to some extent mitigated, paradoxically, through the mediation of entertainment. Before making this argument, though, it is necessary to digress for a moment on matters of ethics and morality. To return to Habermas, his discourse ethics relate to the procedures of a properly rational public sphere, in effect, an ideal public sphere. This entails a formulation of what it is to be a mature moral subject, someone with a sense of justice which transcends personal interests and contingent circumstances, that is someone who reaches the sixth and highest stage of moral development, commitment to just procedure, according to Lawrence Kohlberg's Piagetian model (see Habermas, 1990).

Kohlberg's former student, Carol Gilligan ([1982] 1993a), has famously contested this model in the name of an 'ethic of care'. In her empirical research, Gilligan finds that women do not typically reach Kohlberg's pinnacle of post-conventional morality. They fall short, usually at around the fourth stage of conventional morality. Are we to conclude from this, then, that women are morally inferior to men? The reason why women, according to Gilligan, fall short of the most elevated moral rectitude in Kohlberg's and Habermas's scheme of things, is that they pay much more attention to the feelings and experiences of others than do men. To quote Gilligan:

> Women's construction of the moral problem as a problem of care and responsibility in relationships rather than rights and rules ties the development of their moral thinking to changes in their understanding of responsibility and relationships, just as the conception of morality as justice ties the development to the logic of equality and reciprocity. Thus the logic underlying an ethic of care is a psychological logic of relationships, which contrasts with the formal logic of fairness that informs the justice approach.
>
> (1993a: 73)

As Seyla Benhabib (1995) has argued, there is no necessary incompatibility between a moral sense of universal justice and an ethic of care in particular situations, though I am also inclined to agree with Gilligan (1993b) that, experientially, it is the latter which has most force in practice and, perhaps, not only for women (see Stevenson, 1997, for a further discussion). Gilligan does not view an ethic of care as *essentially* feminine, yet it does seem to have something to do with remarkably resilient differences in the psychic formation and socialisation of girls and boys (Chodorow, 1978).

The gender issue is one thing; the issue of the public sphere and popular culture is another. However, I would not be the first to suggest that there is a certain gendering of the 'serious' and the 'popular', what is said to be of public importance and what is said to be trivial and of merely private interest in the domestic sense. The general and counter-argument being proposed here, influenced by Gilligan's ethic of care, is borne out, I believe, by Sonia Livingstone's (1994) audience research that reveals differences between male and female viewers' responses to audience-participation talk shows, which is similarly informed by Gilligan's insights concerning a 'different voice'. The issue, then, arises of how care-at-a-distance operates through the 'mediated quasi-interaction' (Thompson, 1995) of television. Does it always degenerate, ultimately, into blasé indifference? To begin to explore this question, I want to briefly consider the phenomenon of Comic Relief.

## 'Small Change, Big Difference'[1]

In 1986, the year of Cliff Richards's and the Young Ones' comic rendition of *Livin' Doll* and the first Comic Relief Show at the Shaftesbury Theatre in London, which followed the launch of the organisation the previous Christmas, Stuart Hall and Martin Jacques wrote approvingly of what they called 'People Aid' (Hall and Jacques, 1986, reprinted in Hall, 1988). They were referring specifically to Band Aid, Live Aid and Sport Aid, a wave of charitable events in Britain and elsewhere mediated by popular culture, musical performance, particularly open-air concerts, and sporting activities, most notably marathon-running, that were sparked off by famine in Ethiopia; the milieu out of which Comic Relief sprang. Hall and Jacques read 'People Aid' as signifying a 'sea change' in politics, as representing the obverse of 1980s selfishness. They were clearly mistaken in attributing such historical significance to this popular movement. It was equally well seen as yet another aspect of the revival of 'Victorian values', promoted by Margaret Thatcher, charity towards the poor, providing a salve to the guilty collective conscience in comparatively rich countries like Britain.

I was reminded of my own ambivalence towards 'People Aid' in general and Comic Relief in particular, on the morning of the latest 'Red Nose Day' (14 March 1997), by Mark Steel writing against it in the *Guardian*. He began: 'Tonight is the worst night of the year for the poor: Comic Relief. How can anyone see someone like Phil Collins saying: "Just £2,000 is all we need to feed this village" without thinking, "Well bloody well give it to them then. You have that down the back of your settee".' Steel continued in the same vein, scoring a number of telling points, such as, 'tonight managing directors will come on and buy themselves the cheapest possible advert by saying: "Um, well Anthea, it, er, gives me very great pleasure, to, er, present this 50-foot wide cheque for £2,000 on behalf of Lloyds-TSB plc with highly competitive loan rates and currently offering a fixed-interest option for first-time buyers to, er, the Comic Relief fund"' (Steel, 1997). Steel's disdainful view is valid: he highlights the various contradictions involved in Comic Relief, most importantly its substitution for official politics, in effect letting the British government's measly aid programme off the hook. And yet his satire is too cold. One wonders whether or not Steel had been invited to join in. As Mikhail Bakhtin once said: 'The satirist whose laughter is negative places himself above the object of his mockery, he is opposed to it. The wholeness of the world's comic aspect becomes a private reaction. The people's ambivalent laughter, on the other hand, expresses the point of view of the whole world; he who is laughing also belongs to it' (1968: 12). It is difficult to resist seeing Comic Relief in some sort of relation to Bakhtin's theory of carnival, worked out in his classic study of François Rabelais's *Histories of Gargantua and Pantagruel*. Bakhtin notes that the second book in the cycle, though the first written, 'was conceived during the misfortunes suffered by France in 1532' (ibid.: 339). This was a period of war and severe drought. Bakhtin observes, 'these misfortunes were not catastrophic, but they were serious enough to affect the people's consciousness and to awaken their cosmic terror and eschatological expectations. Rabelais's book was a merry answer to these fears and pious moods' (ibid.).[2]

Comic Relief, an aid organisation operating in both Africa and Britain, funding projects to alleviate distress (irrigation schemes and half-way houses for the young homeless, for instance), reaches the British public and obtains money largely, of course, through television, including the biennial Red Nose Day extravaganza on BBC1 through which credit-card giving is sought, fronted by the tireless Lenny Henry, linked also to fund-raising activities in some schools and workplaces and the sale of such items as videos and books, like *Pick of the Nose* and *Balls to Africa* in 1997. The general aim is to create a carnival atmosphere in a good cause. It carries with it the typical features of carnival identified by Bakhtin (1968: 5): 'ritual spectacle', 'comic verbal composition' and 'various genres of billingsgate'. It is utopian, jolly and caring, involving what Bakhtin calls 'a characteristic logic, the peculiar logic of the "inside out" (*a l'envers*), of the "turnabout", of a continual shifting from top to bottom, from front to rear, of humorous parodies and travesties, humiliations, profanations, comic crownings and uncrownings' (ibid.: p. 11). So, children may go to school dressed as clowns and serious television presenters play the fool.

A key concept of Bakhtin's is *tacktichnost*, usually translated as 'speech tact' and referring to the 'ensemble of codes governing discursive interaction' (quoted by Stam, 1988). Tact is of critical importance for the showbiz stars who contribute their time and energies to Comic Relief and Red Nose Day in order, somehow, to combine comedy and compassion in the discursive duality of entertainment and information. The television extravaganza is made up of studio acts, mostly comedic, mini-sitcoms, interspersed with documentary footage of visits by the likes of Billy Connolly, Lenny Henry and Victoria Wood to distressed places in Africa and Britain, reporting on how the money is eventually spent properly and on the living conditions of the very poor, so unbelievably straitened by the standards of the presumed television-viewer. We are continually reminded that the object of the exercise is serious, albeit mediated through mechanisms of popular pleasure.

A good illustration of the problem of tact is the 1997 three-part programme *Balls to Africa* shown on consecutive evenings during the week leading up to Red Nose Day. I, at first, I have to admit, was shocked by the title of this programme, the phrase, one suspects, frequently uttered around the pubs of Britain on and about Red Nose Day. This was literally, however, about taking balls to Africa. A football team of ageing comics, singers, actors, including the former *EastEnders'* star Susan Tully, and 'personalities' such as the telly chef Ainsley Harriott, some with a sporting pedigree like the rugby player Victor Ubogu, went to play football with local teams in Burkina Faso (on the edge of the Sahara Desert, the fifth poorest country in the world) and Ghana (where amongst the teams they played was an all-woman team of much greater talent than the Sporting Noses). Their first game was at Loanga in Burkina Faso where Lenny Henry had, 8 years before, reported on a 'magic stones' project designed to prevent the little rainwater that falls there from flowing away. Ironically, the game was delayed due to an unexpected and very rare downpour. The Sporting Noses' victory of 2-1 against Loanga Village was a matter of agonising by Frank Skinner over whether or not they should instead have drawn the match deliberately. The majority opinion of the team, however, was that there was no charity when it came to football, although they did give balls and kit to the village team. Wherever the Sporting Noses went they generally had a good laugh with the locals. As Nick Hancock commented:

> If I'm honest, the idea of a Comic Relief football tour to Africa originally struck me as a rather naff one – in the first place it seemed to be another unneeded passenger on an unwanted football bandwagon and in the second place I don't really relish the idea of visiting communities in desperate plight, listening to their heart-wrenching tales of woe, and then having to say 'well, sorry about the food situation and the war; things must be terrible – do you fancy a kickabout?' The truth is, to give credit to Kevin Cahill [of Comic Relief] and his team, the idea was inspired – it meant that we could visit communities on equal terms. We weren't voyeurs grandly discussing their problems and making little films they'd never see – we were the guests for a football match where we could meet as equals, not givers and receivers. The moment a football appeared we were surrounded by kids and adults alike, keen to show off their skills. I believe I was even heard to utter that naffest of all football clichés 'the international language of football'.
>
> (Deayton et al., 1997: 88)

It would be foolish to make any great claims for Comic Relief itself. However, I do wish to suggest that it does illustrate something of the effectivity of *a*ffective communication across otherwise closed borders of life experience. It also exemplifies a comparatively popular form of cultural politics, though intermittent, fragile and quite marginal politically, in what Geoff Mulgan (1994) has called 'an antipolitical age'. Unlike official politics and the discursive power of mealy-mouthed politicians and bureaucrats, such cultural politics is much less a turn-off for many people, as 'People Aid' in various manifestations has demonstrated. Finally, the fact that this kind of mediation is facilitated by what is still, in spite of its limitations, a public-service broadcasting organisation, the BBC, is not insignificant.

# Conclusion

Lest one becomes too carried away by fleeting moments of the meeting of mirth and compassion, it is necessary to consider, in conclusion, to what extent any sign of popular engagement in any kind of public sphere is merely phantasmagoric. It was Walter Lippmann who originally suggested 'the public' is a 'phantom', a democratic myth, a legitimating myth for the political system in the West (Robbins, ed., 1993). A democracy is supposed to be communicative; and, if it is not, it must be made to look so. As another comedian, Jean Baudrillard, has observed, 'the masses scandalously resist . . . [the] imperative of rational communication' (1983: 10).

The opinions of social majorities, according to this view, are fictions that are constructed in order to give the impression that politics is mediated in a meaningfully popular way. Publics are, in truth, 'silent majorities' in Baudrillard's ironic scheme of things. This is not a pathetic condition, however: it is 'the evil genius of the masses' (Baudrillard, 1988: 213) to refuse participation in the official system of meanings. Although stated in very different terms, Baudrillard's chilling insights may be said to illuminate the gulf between the lifeworld and the systems world. In a universe of 'phantom publics' and 'silent majorities', then, what is the public role of affective communication?

Stjepan Mestrovic (1996 and 1997) has offered the concept of postemotionalism as an alternative to Baudrillard's pitiless postmodernism, enunciated infamously with regard to the Gulf War (Baudrillard, 1995; Norris, 1992), in discussing the outbreak of genocidal war in the post-communist Balkans. For Mestrovic, '[p]ostemotionalism . . . refers to the manipulation of *emotionally* charged collective representations of "reality" on the part of the culture industry' (Mestrovic, ed., 1996: 11). What typically happens, according to Mestrovic, is that public emotions are displaced and misplaced by the news media's coverage of war and suffering. For example, the Gulf War became a means for Americans to get over the national trauma of the Vietnam War. And, in other cases, such as genocide in the Balkans, a 'postemotional rhetoric of concern and sympathy' is manipulated through the frameworks of Western media and politics which may have little to do with what is actually going on on the ground.

Mestrovic's argument is a complex one and it is unnecessary to explicate it further for my purpose here. Suffice it to say that I agree with Mestrovic that controversial issues of public communication, where matters of life and death are at stake, are bound up not only with rational deliberation but with deep emotion. As I have argued, an exclusively cognitive conception of the public sphere, whether singular or plural, is unsatisfactory: we have to take account of affective communication in a popular context. The example of Comic Relief, open no doubt to differences of interpretation, is meant to illustrate how the channelling of emotions through the mediation of mass communication in an international public sphere is not always and necessarily misplaced.

# Notes

1 'Small Change (in your pocket can make a), Big Difference (in people's lives!)' was the slogan of the 1997 Red Nose Day. It clearly indicates the charity frame through which Comic Relief operates, addressing the comparatively well-off in a way that suggests a tiny sacrifice will produce a much greater effect on the lives of the globally poor. This is a highly problematical frame, albeit in a marginal yet discernible way effective. In

discussing Comic Relief, I have deliberately sought to suspend this problem in order to open up issues concerning popular engagement with the suffering of others. Personally, I believe this is the difficult thing to do. I am well aware that others may doubt my judgement.

2 Habermas has himself recently commented upon Bakhtin's work on Rabelais and, indeed, its relevance to feminism: 'I must confess . . . that only after reading Mikhail Bakhtin's great book *Rabelais and His World* have my eyes become really opened to the *inner* dynamics of a plebeian culture. This culture of the common people apparently was by no means only a backdrop, that is a passive echo of the dominant culture; it was also the periodically recurring violent revolt of a counterproject to the hierarchical world of domination, with its official celebrations and everyday disciplines. Only a stereoscopic view of this sort reveals how a mechanism of exclusion that locks out and represses at the same time calls forth countereffects that cannot be neutralised. If we apply the same perspective to the bourgeois public sphere, the exclusion of women from this world dominated by men now looks different than it appeared to me at the time' (Habermas, 1992: 427).

# References

Bakhtin, M. (1968) *Rabelais and His World*, Massachusetts Institute of Technology, Cambridge, Mass.

Baudrillard, J. (1983) *In the Shadow of Silent Majorities, or, the End of the Social*, Semiotext(e), New York.

Baudrillard, J. (1988) The masses – the implosion of the social in the media, in Poster, M. (ed.) *Jean Baudrillard: Selected Writings*, Polity, Cambridge.

Baudrillard, J. (1995) *The Gulf War Did Not Take Place*, Power Publications, Sydney.

Benhabib, S. (1995) The debate over women and moral theory revisited, in Meehan, J. (ed.) *Feminists Read Habermas*, Routledge, New York and London.

Calhoun, C. (ed.) (1992) *Habermas and the Public Sphere*, Massachusetts Institute of Technology, Cambridge, Mass.

Chodorow, N. (1978) *The Reproduction of Mothering: Psychoanalysis and the Sociology of Gender*, California University Press, Berkeley and Los Angeles.

Dahlgren, P. (1995) *Television and the Public Sphere*, Sage, London.

Deayton, A., Hancock, N. and Fielding, H. (1997) *Balls to Africa: Sporting Noses on Tour*, Comic Relief, Solihull/Dillons, London.

Eagleton, T. (1984) *The Function of Criticism: From the Spectator to Post-Structuralism*, Verso, London.

Fraser, N. (1992) Rethinking the public sphere – a contribution to the critique of actually existing democracy, in Calhoun, C. (ed.) *Habermas and the Public Sphere*, Massachusetts Institute of Technology, Cambridge, Mass.

Garnham, N. (1990) The media and the public sphere, in his *Capitalism and Communication: Global Culture and the Economics of Information*, Sage, London.

Garnham, N. (1992) The media and the public sphere, in Calhoun, C. (ed.) *Habermas and the Public Sphere*, Massachusetts Institute of Technology, Cambridge, Mass.

Garnham, N. (1995) The media and narratives of the intellectual, *Media, Culture & Society*, 17, pp. 359–84.

Giddens, A. (1990) *The Consequences of Modernity*, Polity, Cambridge.

Gilligan, C. ([1982] 1993a) *In a Different Voice: Psychological Theory and Women's Development*, Harvard University Press, Cambridge, Mass.

Gilligan, C. (1993b) Reply to Critics, in Larrabee, M. J. (ed.) *An Ethic of Care: Feminist and Interdisciplinary Perspectives*, Routledge, New York.

Habermas, J. (1979) *Communication and the Evolution of Society*, Heinemann, London.

Habermas, J. (1984) *The Theory of Communicative Action, Vol. 1: Reason and the Rationalization of Society*, Beacon Press, New York.

Habermas, J. (1987) *The Theory of Communicative Action, Vol. 2: The Critique of Functionalist Reason*, Polity, Cambridge.

Habermas, J. ([1962] 1989) *The Structural Transformation of the Public Sphere: An Inquiry into a Category of Bourgeois Society*, Polity, Cambridge.

Habermas, J. (1990) *Moral Consciousness and Communicative Action*, Polity, Cambridge.

Habermas, J. (1992) Further reflections on the public sphere, in Calhoun, C. (ed.) *Habermas and the Public Sphere*, Massachusetts Institute of Technology, Cambridge, Mass.

Habermas, J. (1996) *Between Facts and Norms: Contributions to a Discourse Theory of Law and Democracy*, Polity, Cambridge.

Hall, S. and Jacques, M. (1986) People Aid – a new politics sweeps the land, in Hall, S. (1988) *The Hard Road to Renewal: Thatcherism and the Crisis of the Left*, Verso, London.

Harvey, D. (1989) *The Condition of Postmodernity*, Basil Blackwell, Oxford.

Hirst, P. and Thompson, G. (1996) *Globalization in Question: The International Economy and the Possibilities of Governance*, Polity, Cambridge.

Livingstone, S. (1994) Watching talk – gender and engagement in the viewing of audience discussion programmes, *Media, Culture & Society*, 16, pp. 429–47.

Mestrovic, S. (ed.) (1996) *Genocide After Emotion: The Postemotional Balkan War*, Routledge, London and New York.

Mestrovic, S. (1997) *Postemotional Society*, Sage, London.

Mulgan, G. (1994) *Politics in an Antipolitical Age*, Polity, Cambridge.

Negt, O. and Kluge, A. ([1972] 1993) *Public Sphere and Experience: Towards an Analysis of the Bourgeois and Proletarian Public Sphere*, University of Minnesota Press, Minneapolis.

Norris, C. (1992) *Uncritical Theory: Postmodernism, Intellectuals and the Gulf War*, Lawrence & Wishart, London.

Robbins, B. (ed.) (1993) *The Phantom Public Sphere*, University of Minnesota Press, Minneapolis.

Robbins, K. (1993) The war, the screen, the crazy dog and poor mankind, *Media, Culture & Society*, 15, pp. 321–27.

Robbins, K. (1994) Forces of consumption – from the symbolic to the psychotic, *Media, Culture & Society*, 16, pp. 449–68.

Stam, R. (1988) Mikhail Bakhtin and left cultural critique, in Kaplan, E. A. (ed.) *Postmodernism and its Discontents: Theories, Practices*, Verso, London.

Steel, M. (1997) Have You Heard the One about Comic Relief?, *Guardian*, 14 March, p. 17.

Stevenson, N. (1997) Media, ethics and morality, in McGuigan, J. (ed.) *Cultural Methodologies*, Sage, London.

Tester, K. (1997) *Moral Culture*, Sage, London.

Thompson, J. B. (1993) The theory of the public sphere, *Theory, Culture & Society*, 10.3, pp. 173–89.

Thompson, J. B. (1995) *The Media and Modernity: A Social Theory of the Media*, Polity, Cambridge.

# |6|

# *Is there a global public sphere?*

COLIN SPARKS

The major forces that shape our lives operate on a broader scale than the existing states. The flows of trade, telecommunications and people around the world across state boundaries are well documented. States, however, are the main sites of political power. Some have a democratic polity. The tendency of human affairs to cross state boundaries thus implies problems for the state system, and even more for democracy. There are no international bodies that have the powers and constitutions of states. In none of the existing bodies is the principle of the popular mandate recognised. We do not elect the secretary generals of the United Nations Organisations, UNESCO, the International Telecommunications Union or the World Trade Organisation: they are appointed by the governments of states. None of these bodies have the power directly to enforce their will: they are dependent upon the governments of states. The growth of supranational activities thus inevitably implies a diminution even of those limited forms of democratic control of our common affairs that have been established in some of the more fortunate states. The development of a global society means a crisis for the public sphere (Garnham, 1992: 361–2). This chapter investigates whether there is an emergent 'global public sphere'.

Accordingly, I begin with a brief theoretical discussion of the concepts of globalisation and the public sphere. If there is a global public sphere, it is reasonable to expect to find some evidence of it, and in order to determine what might count as evidence we need to translate the general claims of social theory into propositions about the nature of the world. Secondly, the chapter addresses some of the evidence as to the actual extent of a globalising tendency in the media. The 'traditional' media of the public sphere, broadcasting and the press, are briefly reviewed. Finally, I consider whether the evidence is adequate to support the notion that a global public sphere exists.

# Globalisation

It is one thing to point to the existence of an ever-increasing interlocking of the world and quite another to claim that this process is best theorised as 'globalisation'. The proposition that we live in an interlocking world has been a commonplace since at least the Communist Manifesto (Marx and Engels, 1976 [1848]: 488). This fact has, however, been theorised in a large number of competing ways, amongst them: the world market (as in Marx and Engels); imperialism (as in numerous later Marxist accounts, and almost as many different, non-Marxist accounts); world-systems theory; modernity and postmodernity (again in many different accounts); even the critique of socialism in one country. Globalisation, again in many varieties, is only another contender in the struggle to explain all this.

There is no one set of ideas that we can point to as constituting theories of globalisation. We can distinguish two broad groups. In one camp are those who see globalisation as an extension of a previously existing capitalist system. For them, globalisation describes 'a world patently characterised by unprecedented extremes of material experience and opportunity' (Golding and Harris, 1997: 8). The logic of the present period is that the commercial media system of the developed capitalist world, and in particular that of the United States, is increasingly the dominant international model, destroying or subverting all alternative systems (Herman and McChesney, 1997).

This is not the main current of thinking. For most writers, globalisation is a new way of analysing the world, different to that offered by concepts like capitalism and imperialism (Tomlinson, 1997). Globalisation is identified by three points:

1 That, while the processes which have been leading up to the current situation are of long standing, we are now living in a qualitatively new epoch in which a concept of 'globalisation proper' is central to an understanding of social life (Robertson, 1992: 8).
2 Theories of globalisation seek to stress their distance from determinist, and particularly Marxist, accounts of social life. The 'condition of globality' is too complex to be grasped by any theory that seeks to explain social development in terms of a single master opposition like that between labour and capital (Appadurai, 1990: 296).
3 Following directly from this, theorists of globalisation tend to stress the autonomous power of the cultural and symbolic in the explanation of social reality. In particular, they argue that the achievement of globalisation is partially the consequence of the triumph of the symbolic over the material (Waters, 1995: 9–10).

It is possible to derive four hypotheses from the above general principles:

G1 Because we are living in a globalised world, we expect to find global media. These are media that are quite distinct from those that were appropriate to the earlier age of the state system. They will not be bounded by the shape of the state system of the past, but will be responsive to suprastate needs and values.

G2   Because globalisation is a recent phenomenon, these global media are of relatively recent origin. They employ a technology, and bear a content, that is quite different from the state-bounded media of the preceding epoch. The technology is one that exceeds the limitations of state boundaries, and the content is such as to be distinct from the parochial concerns of the older media.

G3   Because the symbolic is the prime site of globalisation, we expect to find that these media are relatively well-developed compared particularly to economic exchanges. If it is true that the media are that area of social life most influenced by globalising tendencies, then their operations will be less confined by state boundaries than, say, the car industry.

G4   Because globalisation is characterised by a high level of cultural autonomy, we expect to find these media displaying a different structure to that prevailing in the economic order. Their location, their content, their relationships will be recognisably distinct from world trading relations or world political structures.

# The public sphere

The second category that we need to clarify, the public sphere, is another site of contention. Fortunately, we can be more definite about the central issues than with globalisation. The clearest definition is the one Habermas gave in 1964:

> By 'the public sphere' we mean first of all a realm of our social life in which something approaching public opinion can be formed. Access is guaranteed to all citizens. A portion of the public sphere comes into being in every conversation in which private individuals assemble to form a public body. They then behave neither like business or professional people transacting private affairs, nor like members of a constitutional order subject to the legal constraints of a state bureaucracy. Citizens behave as a public body when they confer in an unrestricted fashion – that is, with the guarantee of freedom of assembly and association and the freedom to express and publish their opinions – about matters of general interest. In a large public body, this kind of communication requires specific means for transmitting information and influencing those who receive it. Today [1964] newspapers and magazines, radio and television are the media of the public sphere. We speak of the political public sphere in contrast, for instance, to the literary one, when public discussion deals with objects connected to the activity of the state.
>
> (Habermas, 1974: 49)

In his developed account, Habermas dealt not only with this normative concept, but also with what he claimed were its historical manifestations. He identified in eighteenth-century London and Paris a number of fleeting social forms – newspapers, salons, coffee houses – that constituted the physical site of the bourgeois public sphere. As modern capitalism developed, this public sphere was destroyed. On the one hand, the transformation of the printed press into a large-scale commercial undertaking meant that it was profit, rather than public enlightenment, that dominated the thinking of media producers. On the other hand, the growth of large-scale firms and parties meant that debate was no longer concerned with the rational discussion of issues of public concern, but with wrangling over the interests of different powerful political actors. This decline Habermas called 're-feudalisation', since it represented a retreat to an earlier form of public life in which its only function was to act as an arena for the display of power.

This formulation has been subject to penetrating criticism, particularly with regard to its historical validity, and to the degree of congruence between this historical reality and the claims of the normative concept. We can identify three of these criticisms as being the most important:

1 Historians have demonstrated that the evidence does not support the existence of any such bourgeois public sphere. James Curran has shown how Habermas was misinformed about press history in Britain. As he put it: 'the newspapers celebrated by Habermas were engines of propaganda for the bourgeoisie rather than the embodiment of disinterested rationality' (Curran, 1991: 40). Of the US case, Michael Schudson writes that: 'The idea that a public sphere of rational-critical discourse flourished in the eighteenth or early nineteenth century, at least in the American instance, is an inadequate, if not incoherent, notion' (Schudson, 1992: 146).

2 It has been shown that the bourgeois public sphere was very far from universal in scope. On the contrary, it was based on systematic exclusions, in particular the exclusion of women (Fraser, 1992). The right to speak in public, and the right to be heard, were very closely restricted by the multiple inequalities of social power that characterised the birth of bourgeois society. The public sphere of eighteenth-century England and France was one that it was impossible, or very difficult, to enter unless one was a bourgeois male. This argument can be extended to embrace the claim that the rationality that is at the centre of the claims made for the public sphere was itself the product of fundamentally gender-specific construction of the social order that validated as masculine preserves public life and reason while denigrating the feminised sphere of emotion and intimate life.

3 It has been argued that the modern mass media, in extending the audience for political debate, changing the registers of political rhetoric,

and widening the scope of the nature of the political, actually constituted a massive extension of the public sphere, rather than marking 're-feudalisation'.

Contrary to Habermas's claims that the development of the welfare state and the entry of powerful commercial interests into the public sphere marked its transformation into a private, rather than a public, forum, it is argued that it is only in such conditions that the media became sufficiently inclusive as to overcome their historical limitations and permit the entry of the whole population into public life. The commercialisation of the press forced it to open its pages to new and more representative material (Le Mahieu, 1988). For its part, the nature of broadcasting meant that it was obliged to find ways of addressing issues of social life in a vocabulary and with a mode of presentation that was sufficiently demotic as to render it palatable to the mass audience (Scannell, 1989).

These criticisms mean that it is very difficult to continue with the classical model. We must recognise that Habermas's account of the historical dynamic of the bourgeois public sphere is wrong, and that the record is one of the patchy and contradictory realisation of a concept whose full potential is very much greater. When analysing any historical phenomenon in this light, we need to foreground two aspects of the original formulation. The first of these is universality: 'Access is guaranteed to all citizens.' Everybody has a right to participate. Any analysis of concrete media structures needs constantly to ask of whether they are in reality open to everyone as a matter of right. We cannot use the term 'public sphere' in anywhere near its full sense to describe a situation in which there are systematic exclusions, upon whatever grounds, of whole classes of citizens. Indeed, one might plausibly argue that, the fewer and more sporadic the exclusions from the media are, the closer a situation approximates to a public sphere.

The second issue is equality: citizens 'confer in an unrestricted fashion'. To confer is to participate in a discussion, to have the rights both of auditor and of speaker. Again, any analysis needs constantly to return to the question of whether all people in fact have an equal right to participate in both capacities. We cannot use the term 'public sphere' in anywhere near its full sense to describe a situation in which a tiny minority have the right to speak in public and the vast majority are at best consigned to the role of audience, still less when they are, for whatever reason, unable even to follow a debate conducted by others. Once again, to the extent that the right to public speech is in practice shared equally among all citizens we may say that a situation approximates to a public sphere.

We may therefore formulate two more hypotheses about the global public sphere:

P1  We would expect to find that the media that constitute the global public sphere display at least as much universality in terms of availability and access as do the existing media of state-limited public spheres. That is to say, while it would be unreasonable to expect that the very fact of globalisation has abolished all of the limits and restrictions that have accrued during the centuries of state-bounded public discourse, it would not be unreasonable to expect the new global public sphere not to be based on worse terms.

P2 We would expect to find clear evidence that built into the media of the global public sphere are mechanisms which tend to lead it beyond any current limitations it may display.

## Television and the global public sphere

The six hypotheses outlined above provide a means whereby we can test whether a global public sphere is coming into being. Before we can do that, however, we must define what parts of the media might properly be considered as having a global dimension. We need to make a distinction between the operation of media companies on a global scale and global media. Media companies that operate in more than one country, or more than one continent, are not necessarily global operations. The media empire built by Roy Thomson began in the 1930s in Canada, purchased its first US newspaper (the *Independent* of St. Petersburg, Florida) in 1952 and its first UK newspaper (the *Scotsman* of Edinburgh) in 1953. Its founder moved to Britain, and was later ennobled as Lord Thomson of Fleet. Under the directorship of his son, Kenneth, it made a major return to the US market. By the early 1980s, it had media interests in North America, Europe, Africa and Australia, and was one of the world's largest publishing companies (Goldenberg, 1985).

A recent authoritative study, however, did not include it in the 'first tier' of global media firms. This was despite the fact that its 1985 turnover was larger than some of the companies placed in that league. Instead, it was assigned to the second tier as one of the firms 'that fill regional or niche markets' (Herman and McChesney, 1997: 95). One might reformulate the distinction by arguing that, although Thomson has operations of global scope, these are not aspects of a single operation that is global in scale. Globalisation implies that there are distinctive aspects of media operations that take place across a range of countries, with the same or similar content being used in each case, thus realising economies of scale to a greater extent even than is characteristic of all media.

A similar qualification needs to be entered with regard to the technical means of delivery. Not all new techniques of media delivery constitute symptoms of globalisation. The most publicised of forms, satellite television, is in the vast majority of cases bounded by states in terms of its regulation and programming, if not in terms of its footprint. While these constitute important developments in broadcasting, that have had a major impact on existing institutions, there is little evidence that they represent a substantial shift towards a new, global, media.

There are four reasons for believing this. The first is that, despite their novel means of delivery, most of these services are simply additions to the available national broadcast television offering. As services move from the relatively primitive free-to-air model, financed through the sale of advertising or, occasionally, by public subsidy, towards a more sophisticated, and much more profitable, subscription-based revenue model, so the fit between political geography and reception-area becomes much closer. What comes to be essential in determining the boundaries of the potential audience are not the technical means of delivery but the parameters of the subscriber-management system.

The second reason is that what is true for the delivery system is also true for the content. Rights owners do not, at least if they are able to avoid it, dispose of their property in one single global deal. Rather, they will seek to subdivide the rights in as great detail as the market will bear. They will sell terrestrial rights and satellite rights, analogue rights and digital rights, and so on. They make more money that way. One of the most important ways in which content rights are divided is by the 'national' markets staked out by the boundaries of different states. Just because Channel 4 in Britain has the rights to Series A or the Tour de France for UK terrestrial television, it does not mean that it is the sole broadcasting organisation in any country with any rights on these events. So far, at least, there is little evidence that rights are being sold on a global basis.

The third reason is that the majority of satellite broadcasting, and certainly that which has been most successful in terms of audience-size, has had a distinctly national content. BSkyB is a case in point. This organisation is global in the sense that a major owner, Rupert Murdoch, operates around the world in many markets, and it is transmitted over a satellite that is registered in Luxemburg and owned by large corporations from a variety of countries. Its footprint falls over a greater area than just the UK, but there is no doubt that this is the home market. It is difficult to see how Sky News constitutes a global media form. Its language, concerns, news values and presentational style all fit the category of British national television news, albeit with a strongly marked commercial flavour. It should also be noted that it is not a particularly successful competitor for the attention of the British audience. Sky News accounted for around 0.3 per cent share of the total UK audience for television in the year ending 31 December 1996. Even in those households with satellite and cable, it only accounted for 1.1 per cent of the total share (Phillips, 1997: 30).

The fourth reason is that satellite systems are not independent of all national constraints. They are regulated by national governments. BSkyB is classified as a domestic satellite under UK law, and thus (inadequately) regulated by the ITC. Even these limited regulations, however, have real teeth. The attempts by other operators to use the potential of satellite television to get around the UK legal system, all by pornographic channels based in countries with looser restrictions on what may be broadcast, have each been defeated by the British government. In doing so, it has used national regulation, the 1990 Broadcasting Act, which gives it the power to declare particular channels 'proscribed satellite services' and put penalties on suppliers, advertisers, equipment merchants and so on, sufficient to drive the offenders out of business. What we have here is a clear example of the use of state-based regulation to prevent the erosion of taste boundaries, established precisely by the existing state system, in the face of some potential challenge located outside its boundaries. This example runs counter to the claims made for an irresistible tide of supranational globalisation.

Once we recognise that the mere existence of satellite broadcasting is not in itself evidence of globalisation, there is little in the implementation of satellite technology that points beyond the state system towards a new global public sphere. If we wish to make out a case for a new global form of television, we would need to point to a service that was specifically international in orientation and programming. The fully and properly global channel would be one that broadcast material that was specifically supranational in form and content. It would not be simply an international transmitter of material generated from within one state, or even several states. However popular such material may be internationally, it remains programming produced with a specific national audience in mind and only secondarily related to the concerns of other groups.

The major candidate for this role is CNN, although it has some other, less successful, competitors like BBC World. To be very precise, one could say that CNN is a primarily US service with a limited international content. It is not clear how much of the twenty-four-hour programme is actually international, but CNNI Europe originates four and a half hours, or less than 20 per cent of the total. We may reasonably assume that the service as transmitted in Europe does not contain more than the same proportion generated in the other major regions outside of America, so even this service appears to be somewhat less than properly global, since probably not less than 60 per cent originates in the USA (CNN, 1997a: 5).

Let us ignore this reservation and accept CNN as a global form of broadcasting for the sake of argument. If we do this, the striking fact about CNN is the very small size of its audience. According to their own figures, CNN International is available in 113 million television households worldwide, 73 million of which are in Europe, 4 million in the Middle East, and 4 million in Africa. The actual reach in terms of audience is very much smaller than the total number of households that theoretically are able to receive it. Again according to their own figures, CNN Europe reaches 1.5 million European main-income earners per day, and has a monthly reach of 11.3 million, which is around 25 per cent of European 'upscale adults' (CNN, 1997b).

Compared with the daily audiences for purely state-based broadcasters, this is very small indeed: the BBC1 News and Weather, transmitted only in the UK at 18.20 on Sunday 29 June, for example, obtained 10.31 million viewers, and this is not exceptionally large (Phillips, 1997: 29). The total combined daily audience for the main prime-time news broadcasts of the two dominant British terrestrial broadcasters alone is greater than the total monthly pan-European reach of CNN. Where CNN scores is that its audience is disproportionately upmarket.

A similar picture of the sheer marginality of globalised television can be derived from looking at examples where there is direct competition between 'global' and 'national' programming. As Table 6.1 shows, the share of all satellite channels in the total UK television audience is relatively small. In total, all non-terrestrial television accounts for around 10 per cent of audience share. Compared even with the minority terrestrial channels, BBC2 (11.5 per cent) and Channel 4 (10.2 per cent), the total BSkyB share is small. The channels that could most obviously be thought of as 'global', like Disney and MTV, have tiny audiences. Since access to these channels is relatively limited, it could be argued that a better test would be to compare the audience shares only in those households that have access to the new media.

From this perspective, and bearing in mind that the data is not strictly comparable, non-terrestrial broadcasters appear much more successful, with a total share jumping to first place at 36.7 per cent. The audience for either of the same two properly global channels cited above, however, still fails to exceed 1 per cent of the total. There is no doubt that the minority section of the UK television audience that has chosen to purchase non-terrestrial television is watching mostly global, indeed US-made, television

**Table 6.1** Estimated audience share for national and global television channels in the UK

| Channel | Percentage in all households[1] | Percentage in satellite and cable homes[2] |
|---|---|---|
| Total BBC | 44 | 31.1 |
| Total terrestrial commercial | 45.5 | 32.1 |
| Total non-terrestrial | 10.5 | 36.7 |
| Total BSkyB | 4.9 | 16.8 |
| MTV | 0.2 | 0.8 |
| Nickelodeon | 0.5 | 1.8 |
| Country Music Television | 0.1 | 0.1 |
| Discovery Channel (Europe) | 0.2 | 1.2 |
| The Disney Channel | 0.3 | 0.8 |
| The Paramount Channel | 0.1 | 0.3 |
| Fox Kids | — | 0.3 |

[1] For year ending 31 December 1996 (ITC, 1997)
[2] For week ending 29 June 1997 (Phillips, 1997: 30)

programmes, but it is not at all clear that these constitute 'global' programmes. Even MTV, once taken as the key exemplar of globalisation, has modified its programming to give it a national inflection. It therefore seems reasonable to conclude that, to the extent that satellite services are evidence of the evolution of global media, it is difficult to claim that we are discussing anything more than a marginal phenomenon.

A stronger case, in terms of sheer audience numbers, could be made out for the very old-tech BBC World Service radio, which currently has an audience of around 143 million outside of the UK. We would make two points about this, however. First, no one could possibly imagine that this is an example of a distinctive process of globalisation: the World Service is a specialised arm of a state broadcaster financed almost entirely by a grant from the British Foreign Office. Its origins, aims and contemporary practices are those of propaganda, although admittedly very subtle propaganda, on behalf of the British state. Second, according to its own audience research, the prospects of the service gaining an audience in a particular country are most closely related to the number of local stations available. If there are few local stations, the BBC gets a large audience, despite the difficulties of short-wave reception. When the number of stations increases, the BBC audience starts to drop (Mytton, 1993: 258). In media-rich markets, most obviously the USA, the audience for the BBC World Service is so tiny as to be very difficult to measure. Where it is larger, the audience has fewer alternatives. What this suggests is that the growth of viable state-based broadcasting industries undermines this very questionable representative of globalisation.

It might be objected that what we have here is an example of the importance of a concept that is invariably paired with the global: the local. What the evidence from the BBC World Service seems to suggest, though, is something rather stronger than simply that the tendency towards globalisation can only exist in and through a world in which states are by far the most powerful definers of cultural policy. The fact is that the growth of local (i.e. state-based) broadcasting systems is not achieved by mediating the existing global product, but rather by driving out that product. The stronger and more successful a local broadcaster is, the less demand there is for a global product. The clearest example of this is the USA, which is notoriously impervious to programme imports other than in niche markets, but we can find many other examples that suggest the same conclusion. If we take the case of the UK, the top forty programmes in terms of audience size in a sample week (ending 29 July) were all home-produced. The first import was the Australian soap opera *Neighbours*, at number 41. Of the top seventy programmes, only eight were from abroad, all from Australia (Phillips, 1997: 30).

There is one piece of evidence that we can adduce from a discussion of the BBC World Service that would point towards a genuine case of the interpenetration of the global and the local. There are a number of instances where the World Service sells its newscasts to local stations, who then retransmit them. These are global products (BBC World Service news broadcasts) that have been localised, first by the fact that they are produced by the BBC in 'local' languages, and second in that they are rebroadcast by genuinely local agents.

There are three points to be made about this; however, none of which give much comfort to theories of globalisation. In the first place, these examples are relatively marginal to the main business of international broadcasting. Second, the local stations enter into such deals because they lack the resources to produce an equivalent product profitably themselves. Crude and compelling economic reasons, not the autonomy of symbolic exchange, explain why even this limited amount of localisation takes place. Third, this wholesaling of news programmes represents a development of a practice that has been around as long as the modern mass media. The major news agencies are not, on any account, distinctive recent innovations. They have, since their inception, operated on as close to a global basis as was technically feasible. The major difference with this more recent development is that the news agencies began by wholesaling news items, rather than news programmes. Their original geographic scope was very heavily influenced by the imperial politics of the nineteenth century, and their major historian wrote 20 years ago of their continuing structural debt to those arrangements (Boyd-Barrett, 1980: 152–7). The global wholesaling of news is not a product of a recent period with its own distinctive dynamic, different from the past. It therefore does not provide any support for a theory of globalisation.

# The newspaper press

If we look at the newspaper press, the picture is even less promising. There are indeed two papers that aim to circulate globally: the *Financial Times* and the *Wall Street Journal*. Again, it could be claimed that these papers are basically national products that have a supplementary international dimension, like the *International Herald Tribune*, but let us once again concede the point that they are global media for the sake of argument. Here, too, the most striking features of the evidence are the small size of the operation and the affluent nature of its audience. The *Financial Times* claims a circulation of 130,000 outside of the UK, and the readers have an average gross personal income of $120,000. This is tiny, and very rich. The *Wall Street Journal Europe* has a total European circulation of 64,000, and this is even more upmarket, with an personal income of $196,000 and an average of $1,618,000 investments (*Wall Street Journal Europe*, 1997a). The market in which it competes directly against a 'national' product of a directly comparable kind is the UK. There, the *Financial Times* has a circulation of around 170,000. The *Wall Street Journal* has 13,050 (*Wall*

*Street Journal Europe*, 1997b). When faced with a choice of a more localised or a more globalised version of the public sphere, those British newspaper readers that seek this kind of material choose the less globalised by a ratio of around 13:1. The very small proportion of the population that is exercising even this choice must be stressed. The circulation of the 'global' *Financial Times* is only about 7 per cent of the circulation of the other British four quality national daily titles. It is very much smaller than that of the popular press, and constitutes around 1 per cent of the total daily national circulation.

It is further worth noting that, unlike broadcasting, where the practice of producing programmes other than in the dominant language of the broadcasting state is a characteristic feature both of properly globalised forms like CNN and international broadcasters like the BBC World Service, this is not common in the printed press. The language of the main contenders for a global presence in the newspaper press, and still more in the field of news magazines, is firmly and definitely English.

# Conclusions

On a generous interpretation, therefore, we may say that the evidence of globalisation in the mass media is weak. Some media have made some steps in that direction, but their total audiences are very small and are completely dwarfed by the scale of the audiences for purely state-based media. The most developed forms of global news production and dissemination are not of recent origin, and their distinctive features are best explained in terms other than globalisation.

What is more, the audience for these new 'global' media are disproportionately amongst the elite, and need to understand a world language (notably English or Spanish), either as native speakers or as an additional tongue, in order to benefit from this material. If there is an emerging 'CNN-watching, *Time*-reading international professional class', it is very small in numbers, very rich compared to the majority even of the population of the advanced countries, and is sufficiently well-educated as to be so entirely at home with English that it is capable of reading material that even the majority of native speakers find too difficult for easy consumption. Neither is there strong evidence that these emerging global media are seriously eroding the national media. The audiences for the state-based press and broadcasting alter without any apparent relationship to the development or otherwise of whatever global media happen to be available. The catastrophic decline of the circulation of the press in Russia, for example (down 77.19 per cent between 1992 and 1993), cannot be ascribed to globalisation. On the other hand, despite the penetration of 'global' satellite television, the nationally based press in India rose 45.59 per cent between 1990 and 1994 (FIEJ, 1995: xi).

One contrary example that might be cited is the new BBC, which, under government pressure, has certainly set itself the target of globalising its output. I have argued elsewhere why this is an illusory strategy, but even if we accepted that it had a rational basis and was likely to succeed, this would not be direct evidence of globalisation (Sparks, 1995). Rather, it would confirm that people in government and broadcasting believed that globalisation was taking place. What people, even very powerful people, believe to be the case is not firm and incontrovertible evidence that something is the case.

If we ask what the evidence suggests with regard to the hypotheses we advanced above, we are forced to draw a rather mixed conclusion. We certainly find that globalised media exist (G1).They are not self-evidently of very recent origin, nor are they clearly distinguished from the media of the state system by their technical characteristics and it is at least arguable that in their form and content they are very close to originals that were developed within particular states (G2). Whatever definition of global media we take, however, they are clearly very marginal indeed compared with the audiences for the older media bounded by the state system. It is difficult to find any precise measure that would allow us to compare the degree of globalisation of the media with any other industry, but in so far as we can tell from rough comparisons, it would be reasonable to conclude that globalisation has progressed much less in the media than in major 'material' industries like car production (G3). The structure of the global media follows very closely the patterns of economic and political power long established in other aspects of human activity. There is no evidence whatsoever that there is a different logic operating with regard to the circulation of symbolic artefacts. The USA dominates the world trade in information goods every bit as much as it does in commercial aircraft, and for very similar reasons (G4).

Those global media that do exist are even more restricted in terms of access and participation than are the dominant state-limited media. Their audiences, partly by design, are smaller, richer, better educated, and probably more male, than are the audiences for the older mass media. They speak a small number of global languages, most notably English. These media are elite, rather than mass, media. They fall very much further short of the ideals of universality and equality than do the state-bounded media (P1). The evidence as to whether there is any self-correcting mechanism built into the global media that will enable them to overcome the existing limits of access and participation is as yet inconclusive (P2). When we consider the disparities of wealth and power that mark experiences of the population of the globe, however, it is certainly the case that if any such mechanism were to emerge it would require a very long historical period for it to work through to achieve even the same degree of openness as marks the existing systems.

Overall, it seems more than merely reasonable to conclude that there is no evidence for the emergence of a global public sphere. The fact that there is a tiny, rich, educated, English-speaking class of people that do indeed have access to information and debate about the global polity is not at all evidence of a new public sphere. This group is even more sharply differentiated from the mass of the population than were the bourgeois participants in the eighteenth-century coffee houses that formed the original inspiration for this concept. By that very token, the contemporary situation is open to the same, conclusively damming, criticisms as have been levelled against the historical use of the term. We might wish to think that this class is very important, and that the kinds of discussion it engages in, the channels through which these debates take place, and the impact that they have on the world are very important indeed for discussing contemporary reality, but we certainly cannot use the concept of the 'public sphere' to aid our analysis.

It remains to consider what might best explain the phenomena that we have been examining. After all, although we have concluded that what we have observed does not correspond to the criteria necessary to constitute a global public sphere, we have certainly observed something going on. And even if the emerging media display none of the characteristics that we would expect to find in even a putative public sphere, there nevertheless are media that provide news and informed discussion about the global order. The only way we might retain the 'global' part of the term in this rethinking would be in the sense that it is used by those writers who foreground the continuation of structures of inequality and oppression. But if we accept this, are there not strong grounds for preferring the term 'imperialism'? To take a simple and obvious example: why else is English the dominant international language if not because both of the largest and most aggressive imperial powers of the last two centuries had it as their native tongue? The picture of the global media that actually do exist fits perfectly into exactly the same framework.

The use of the term 'public sphere', however, will have to be abandoned in this context, as even an approximation to reality. In its contemporary usage, the public sphere concerns debates about the nature, legitimacy, scope and direction of public power. It assumes, not the democratic right to control power, but the existence of that power as a public matter. That is the fundamental distinction between the feudal epoch, in which the state was the property of the monarch, and the bourgeois epoch when it is the property of the people. There is certainly, in the existing global media, discussion about the nature, legitimacy, scope and direction of power, but it is private, not public, power, that is the most debated site. It is the future of markets, of property, both material and intellectual, of resources, of currencies, in short of things that (rich) people own as their private possessions, that is the prime subject of the global media. They can, of course, be nothing else so long as there is no global public power. To the extent that they do discuss public issues, it is predominantly through the lens of the most powerful of states, and debates typically focus on the need to preserve Western access to oil and other raw materials in order to ensure the continuation of profitable capitalist production rather than on possible mechanisms for social change and human betterment.

It is to the concerns of those that have a direct interest in the doings of private power that the global media are primarily addressed. They are less concerned with issues of public concern than the state-based media. They are more exclusive than the state-based media. They help to constitute an elite that has definite patterns of inclusion and exclusion which we identified above. We can even go further, and propose the laws of this sphere:

1  There are three possible relations between the individual and this sphere: full participation; partial participation; effective exclusion.
2  Access to any form of participation is restricted. Full participants are selected by class, geography and language-skills. They are predominantly the ruling classes of different countries, although some other groups, like certain kinds of academics, mostly working in developed countries, also meet the entry conditions.
3  The class of partial participants is much broader. In one way or another it probably includes everyone who interacts with the mass media. This participation, however, is almost entirely restricted to consumption, and it is overwhelmingly dominated by the literary forms of the sphere. The group effectively excluded are predominantly those who are too poor to be able to have access at all regularly to the mass media. They are, of course, to be found disproportionately in the developing world.
4  Even full participation implies only limited active participation in the formation of global public opinion. The main fora, the newspapers and television programmes in which this process takes place, are highly capitalised and their columns and discussions are dominated by the views of the political and economic elite, either directly or as retailed through professional mediators.
5  These fora are distributed geographically along lines that follow the existing distributions of wealth and power. Their content reflects priorities established by that distribution. They are not the site of rational reflection upon the aims of public policy. To the extent that they are guided by reason, it is of the instrumental, rather than the critical, variety: questioning of fundamentals of the system is effectively excluded. The main subject of their reports, analysis, and opinions is private power, as embodied in the ownership of capital. The public powers of different states are considered only in so far as they impact upon the chances of good business.

If we need to abandon the term 'global public sphere' as manifestly inadequate to designate what we have been analysing, then a better one is needed. The one that fits the evidence best is 'imperialist, private sphere'. If this is unfashionable, so be it. At least it is accurate.

# References

Appadurai, A. (1990) Disjuncture and difference in the global cultural economy, *Theory, Culture & Society*, 7, pp. 295–310.

Boyd-Barrett, O. (1980) *The International News Agencies*, Constable, London.

CNN (1997a) CNN International: The CNN News Group, Jan. 1997, CNN, London.

CNN (1997b) EMS confirms CNN International as leader of the newspack: over 11 million high income viewers tune in every month, CNN, London.

Curran, J. (1991) Rethinking the media as a public sphere, pp. 38–42 in Dahlgren, P. and Sparks, C. (eds) *Communication and Citizenship*, Routledge, London.

FIEJ (1995) World Press Trends, FIEJ, Paris.

Fraser, N. (1992) Rethinking the public sphere, pp. 113–18 in Calhoun, C. (ed.) *Habermas and the Public Sphere*, The MIT Press, Cambridge, Mass.

Garnham, N. (1992) The media and the public sphere, pp. 361–2 in Calhoun, C. (ed.) *Habermas and the Public Sphere*, The MIT Press, Cambridge, Mass.

Goldenberg, S. (1985) *The Thomson Empire*, Sidgwick & Jackson, London.

Golding, P. and Harris, P. (1997) Introduction, pp. 1–9 in Golding, P. and Harris, P. (eds) *Beyond Cultural Imperialism: Globalisation, Communication and the New International Order*, Sage, London.

Habermas, J. (1974) The public sphere, *New German Critique*, 1.3, pp. 49–55.

Harman, C. (1996) Globalisation: a critique of a new orthodoxy, *International Socialism*, 73 (Winter), pp. 3–33.

Herman, E. and McChesney, R. (1997) *The Global Media: The New Missionaries of Corporate Capitalism*, Cassell, London.

ITC (1997) Estimated audience share figures for selected television channels received in the British islands in the 12 months ended 31 December 1996. Press Release, Feb. 1997.

Le Mahieu, D. (1988) *A Culture for Democracy*, Clarendon Press, Oxford.

Marx, K. and Engels, F. ([1848] 1976) The Communist Manifesto, in their *Collected Works*, Vol. 6, Lawrence & Wishart, London.

Mytton, G. (1993) How political and social circumstances determine listening to foreign radio stations, pp. 257–9 in Demers, F., Aster, H. and Olechowska, E. (eds) *La Radiodiffusion Internationale Face Ses Défis/Challenges for International Broadcasting*, Les Presses Inter-Universitaire, Quebec.

Phillips, W. (1997) Broadcast/Barb Top 70: week ending 29 June 1997, *Broadcast*, 18 July, pp. 29–30.

Robertson, R. (1992) *Globalisation: Social Theory and Global Culture*, Sage, London.

Scannell, P. (1989) Public service broadcasting and modern public life, *Media, Culture & Society*, 11.2, pp. 135–66.

Schudson, M. (1992) Was there ever a public sphere? in Calhoun, C. (ed.) *Habermas and the Public Sphere*, The MIT Press, Cambridge, Mass.

Sparks, C. (1995) The future of public service broadcasting in Britain, *Critical Studies in Mass Communication*, 12.3, pp. 325–41.

Sreberny-Mohammadi, A. (1991) The global and the local in international communications, pp. 118–38 in Curran, J. and Gurevitch, M. (eds) *Mass Media and Society*, Edward Arnold, London.

Tomlinson, J. (1997) Cultural globalisation and cultural imperialism, pp. 170–90 in Mohammadi, A. (ed.) *International Communication and Globalisation*, Sage, London.

*Wall Street Journal Europe* (1997a) The *Journal Europe* reaches an affluent and influential readership, Brussels.

*Wall Street Journal Europe* (1997b) Average daily circulation for the six months January–June 1997, Brussels.

Waters, M. (1995) *Globalisation*, Routledge, London.

# |7|

# *Privatising public space*

EDWARD S. HERMAN

Public space in the media, and in communications more broadly, is undergoing steady privatisation on a global scale, with a concurrent shrinkage in noncommercial operations and the provision of messages and programming serving the 'public sphere'. This results from the fact that the powerful economic forces, which are in virtually uncontested command of economic and political life under the New World Order, are systematically replacing nonmarket institutions and values with profit-seeking businesses and market values. In this regime of a triumphant capitalism, more intense competition and a dominant neo-liberal ideology, noncommercial media space is being taken over by those who will put it to the 'best economic use'.

## Advertiser hegemony versus the public sphere

In a market order, the potential income stream from the use of a resource tends to determine its market value, and, under competitive conditions, its price will be bid up to that value. The overwhelmingly dominant economic use of media space in capitalist economies is to advertise goods for sale, and advertising has grown rapidly and extended globally in recent decades. Global advertising increased ten-fold between 1973 and 1995 (from $33 to $335 billion), growing rapidly in the United States, but even more so elsewhere – recently, at its fastest pace in Asia, Latin America and Eastern Europe (Herman and McChesney, 1997: 58–65). In a narrow market sense, then, the 'best economic use' of noncommercial media space would be to transfer it into the commercial sector. The use of media space not funded by advertisers must depend on money provided by subscribers/listeners, donors or the government. In a world of government budget deficits, and financial pressures on ordinary citizens, noncommercial media and communications are under chronic financial stress and tend to be noncompetitive with sources able to tap the immense resources of business advertisers. And governments, under budgetary pressure and increasingly receptive to neo-liberal arguments, are more and more inclined to allow public media to be transformed into market-funded entities.

The major problem with this privatisation of public space is that advertiser and commercial media 'best use' implies an erosion of the 'public sphere', which we may define as the places and forums in which issues important to citizenship in a democratic community are discussed and debated. Advertisers, and hence commercial media managers, tend to avoid the public sphere because audiences there are smaller than for entertainment programmes and the subject matter is too serious and controversial for compatability with sales messages.

This point was stressed half a century ago by the US Federal Communications Commission (FCC) in its report on 'The Public Service Responsibilities of Broadcast Licensees', where the commission acknowledged that advertising and public-service programming are incompatible. It contended, however, that these 'irreplaceable' public-service programmes, and overall programme balance, would be maintained by broadcasters' 'sustaining programmes', funded by the broadcasters themselves. The FCC suggested that the maintenance of such balance would be assured by the commission's licensing policies, which would give substantial weight to this consideration (Federal Communications Commission, 1946: 12).

The FCC's claim that advertising-based programming and public service are incompatible is a serious one, implying that the market 'fails' in serving the 'public sphere', requiring the FCC to correct this failure by moral suasion and regulation. The economic theory of externalities throws light on this market failure, and on the implied threat of commercialisation to the public sphere. An externality is a benefit or cost of a market process that does not accrue to the source but affects others, as in the case of water pollution that kills downstream fish and makes the water unusable for swimming. Arguably, public-sphere programming represents a case where positive externalities are produced, which contribute to the public's understanding and ability to participate in a democratic order. But that benefit accrues to society at large and cannot be captured by a commercial TV station or network, which therefore does not take this social gain into account in its programming strategies. On the other hand, programmes that feature sex and violence draw and travel well, but arguably involve negative externalities, making people more fearful, insecure and violence-prone (Farhi, 1995; Gerbner, 1995). Again, the negative externality damages others, not the programme source. Noncommercial media are less eager for the large audiences that sex and violence bring, and are often brought into existence and designed to programme for public service. But in a mature market system their funding base tends to shrink and they are marginalised.

# The US experience

This process is well illustrated in the 70-year experience of broadcasting in the United States (Herman and McChesney, 1997: ch. 5). When broadcasting began in the United States in the 1920s, its proponents placed almost exclusive stress on its public-service potential – as an educational tool and means of political, religious and cultural enlightenment. Advertising was seen as a threat, or at best a necessary evil, to be kept under rigorous control. Secretary of Commerce (later President) Herbert Hoover stated in 1922 that 'It is inconceivable that we should allow so great a possibility for service to be drowned in advertising chatter' (quoted in FCC, 1946: 41). As late as 1929, the president of NBC was claiming that his was a public-service corporation that would only sell advertising to the extent needed to fund the best noncommercial programming! (See McChesney, 1993: 16.) But by a quiet coup, carried out between 1927 and 1933, the commercial stations and networks, with the help of the regulatory authorities, displaced the many early educational and religious stations and took control of broadcasting. (For a detailed account of this coup, see McChesney, 1993.) This control, and the full-blown commercial regime that ensued, was ratified in the Communications Act of 1934. In 1934 the broadcasters did pledge to provide ample public-service programming, and as noted the FCC in 1946 promised that broadcasters would meet public-service responsibilities through 'sustaining programmes', as a condition of license renewal.

But as advertising flooded in to the commercial stations and networks, sustaining programmes became more expensive, as they entailed not just production expenses but foregone advertising income. And as the FCC had suggested in 1946, advertisers preferred light entertainment to public-service programmes, which shrank steadily in importance even as broadcaster profits soared. By 1970, public-affairs programming had fallen to 2 per cent of programming time, and the entire spectrum of public-service offerings was far below that provided by public broadcasting systems in Canada, Great Britain and elsewhere in the West (Blumler et al., 1986). Profits of station owners, however, were in the range of 30 to 50 per cent of revenues, and much higher on invested capital (Bunce, 1976: 27–31, 97). However, these staggering profits did not reduce pressure for still higher profits, as the workings of the market cause profits to be capitalised into higher stock values, which become the basis for calculating rates of return for both old and new owners.

Indices of programme diversity also fell fairly steadily as the commercial broadcasting system matured and stations and networks emulated one another in their quest for formulas that would produce large audiences and high ratings (Dominick and Pearce, 1976). Under advertiser pressure, and the force of competition, not only did entertainment displace public-sphere programmes, even entertainment programmes tended to lighten up, avoiding undue seriousness, depth of thought and backgrounds devoid of lavish and upscale decor. The shrinking numbers of documentaries tended to deal with non-political and non-controversial matters like dogs, restaurants, travel, personalities and the lives of the rich. Politics was marginalised and trivialised, with news itself transformed into a form of entertainment ('infotainment') (Barnouw, 1978: parts 1–2; Andersen, 1995: chs 1–3). The hegemony of advertising and entertainment values was captured, at the time of Disney's 1996 acquisition of the giant network and media conglomerate ABC-TV, in Disney CEO Michael Eisner's description of Disney as a 'family entertainment communication company' in the business of providing 'non-political entertainment and sports' (Herman, 1996).

One of the most notable trends in US commercial broadcasting has been the long attrition and corruption of children's programming. As profits soared in the 1960s, children's programmes were removed from weekday slots and shifted to weekend mornings, and were confined increasingly to cartoons funded by advertisers of snacks and toys. Between 1955 and 1970, weekday programming for children on network affiliated stations in New York City fell from thirty-three to five hours. The situation was so bad that an organisation, Action for Children's Television (ACT), was established in 1968, and sought remedies from stations, the FCC and politicians for many years. Despite these efforts the situation reached a new low in the 1980s with the Reagan administration's further deregulation of TV, which sanctioned 'programme-length commercials' by toy manufacturers, who virtually took over children's programming (Palmer, 1988; Kline, 1993). The service to children improved somewhat with the rise of cable and the 1993 change in political administration, but not a great deal, and the downward trend of quality and central role of advertising in shaping children's programmes remains clear.

Public broadcasting was introduced with public funding in 1967, in large measure because the commercial broadcasters wanted to slough off any public-service responsibilities and were pleased to allow its shift to stations and networks paid for by the taxpayer. An interesting feature of public broadcasting has been its greater degree of political independence and courage in allowing dissent, despite its heavy reliance on government support. During the Vietnam War, for example, 'Though a groundswell of opposition to the war was building at home and throughout much of the world [1965–67], network television seemed at pains to insulate viewers from its impact … Much sponsored entertainment was jingoistic' (Barnouw, 1978: 62–3). The US networks not only made none of the seriously critical documentaries on the war, during the early war years they barred access to outside documentaries. As Barnouw points out, 'This policy constituted de facto national censorship, though privately operated' (ibid.: 138). But while the mass protest against the Vietnam War rarely found outlets on commercial TV, it did find occasional expression in public broadcasting (ibid.: 63–4). Apparently, the constraints built into the commercial operations by ownership and advertiser interest make them less bold and more subservient to establishment political desires than an institution literally on the government payroll but granted some degree of autonomy. Because of this independence, conservatives dislike public broadcasting (along with community broadcasting) and regularly urge that it be defunded and pushed into the commercial nexus. This relative autonomy also helps explain why presidents Johnson and Nixon fought to rein in public broadcasting, with Nixon quite openly seeking to force it to de-emphasise public affairs. And as the power of market interests grows, it is by no means impossible that conservatives and politicians who feel threatened by a genuine public sphere will eventually succeed in getting public stations and networks privatised and thus put to their 'best economic use'.

An important feature of the history of US broadcasting has been its increasing insulation from reform, paralleling the growth and centralization of broadcaster power. As it matured and the 'irreplaceable' public-service programmes disappeared, the FCC did nothing about it, and politicians remained silent as well – the commercial media were able to prevent the erosion of the public sphere from becoming a public issue, and politicians were too dependent on and fearful of the broadcasters to challenge them.

As another illustration of the power of the broadcasting industry to fend off virtually any threat, in the liberal environment of 1963 the FCC tried to impose a formal restraint on advertising, but only to the extent of designating as the regulatory standard the limits suggested by the broadcasters' own trade association. This enraged the industry, which immediately went to work on Congress, and the FCC quickly backed down (Krasnow et al., 1982: 194–6). Even the erosion and degradation of children's programming, paralleling record-breaking broadcaster profits, and large numbers of aroused citizens, caused no media response sufficient to make this a political issue.

The consolidations and increased media concentration of the past decade also received extremely benign (and biased) coverage as the gatekeepers protected themselves with great efficiency. The Telecommunications Act of 1996, whose primary beneficiaries are communications conglomerates like the *New York Times*, which owns five TV and two radio stations as well as newspapers, was found by the *Times* to have 'one clear winner – the consumer'! The Tyndall Report, which tracks the programming of nightly network newscasts, found that 'neither the passage nor the signing of the most sweeping telecommunications legislation in 60 years made the top ten stories in their respective weeks' (Naureckas, 1996: 17).

# Globalisation of the US model

The US model is being extended globally, partly because of US power, leadership, and plan, but more basically because it represents the advanced, if not full, product of the extension of market principles and processes to the media and communication (Herman and McChesney, 1997: ch. 6). The plan element encompasses the attempt by the US government, and sometimes its allies, to encourage private enterprise, open economies and market-based media systems throughout the world, to pry open markets and to destabilise and overthrow non-market-friendly governments. US goals and strategies were implemented by means of US economic and military aid, military and police training programmes, along with economic and political pressure, support given to indigenous forces serving US aims, and sometimes more direct interventions, as in Guatemala in 1954, Nicaragua in the 1980s and Cuba still in process today. There is a clear official record of intentionality in the pursuit of these goals (Leffler, 1984; Chomsky, 1992), which cannot be dismissed as a product of 'conspiracy theory'.

With the long dominant position of the United States in the motion picture business, and its great competitive strength in all segments of the communications industries, US politicians have been pushing for the opening up and privatization of the communications sector for decades. The great weight of the United States in the International Monetary Fund (IMF) and World Bank has been reflected in those institutions' policies serving the same ends. But the dynamics of the market has its own internal momentum, operative within the United States itself (and still working there today) and extending globally at an accelerating pace by the force of cross-border media investment and competition. Within each country the corporate system and corporate media, underwritten by advertisers, have gathered strength, with enhanced ideological and political power. Aided by the increasing force of capital's greater mobility and global financial integration, they have successfully downgraded the idea of public goods and a public-service responsibility of government, and with the help of financial pressure on governments have constrained the growth of (or shrunk) public-service and welfare budgets. Part of the new 'economic realism' has been privatisation, which raises money and placates powerful economic interests. And with the commercial media eager to capture public space and put it to better economic use, public broadcasting has been in retreat globally.

While important elsewhere in the world, the US model has had an especially profound influence on media systems in other countries of the Americas. In Canada, for example, the public-service Canadian Broadcasting Corporation (CBC) has been increasingly vulnerable to the changing economic and broadcasting environment and neo-liberal priorities. In almost an exact parallel to the United States, the Canadian right wing and neo-liberals, opposed to CBC and its cultivation of a public sphere and some modest dissent and debate on community issues, have ensured that CBC has been under attack and suffered a budget crunch for many years, with cuts aggregating 23 per cent in real terms between 1983 and 1994. The position of the CBC has also been profoundly affected by the growth of commercial television and the great proliferation of channels. Cable now reaches over 70 per cent of Canadian households, and direct satellite reception is also growing rapidly. The new flood of channels produced 'an avalanche of American programming ... now so great that Canadian children spend more time watching American television than they will spend in a Canadian school' (Taras, 1991: 192). As in the USA, the growth of the commercial broadcasting media has tended to marginalise the public sphere and erode the quality of children's programming. In-depth treatments of public issues are sparse, and the news has been affected as well. These changes have forced CBC to resort to advertising, compromising its mission and programming.

In Latin America, the US 'backyard', US influence over media evolution has been profound. The two largest media conglomerates of the region – Brazil's Globo and Mexico's Televisa – evolved from heavy dependence on US capital and programming supply to a fair degree of independence. Their own home-produced materials now occupy a large fraction of programming space, and their own telenova productions are major exports. But their formats are derivative, and foreign – mainly US – supply is still far from negligible in programming, equipment and source of advertisements. US equipment manufacturers (radio, TV and telecommunications), advertising agencies, press agencies, magazine publishers, and radio and TV broadcasters have pushed relentlessly for a commercial media in Latin America. In the continent's largest and most powerful nation, Brazil, weak and financially strapped governments did not resist the emergence of the commercial model of broadcasting in the 1920s and thereafter. As Elizabeth Fox has noted, 'The government-subsidized educational, cultural and, at times, elitist radios were unable to compete with the unregulated expansion of commercial broadcasting and were soon driven out of business or sold to the private sector' (Fox, 1988: 13). The arrival of television in the 1950s allowed the privately owned, commercially operated broadcasting 'to reach mass markets to advertise their products' (ibid.: 15).

The US government was involved in major covert subsidisation of organisations designed to produce and disseminate right-wing propaganda, contributing to the 1964 military coup, which assured a consolidation of the commercial system and an integration of the Brazilian media into the global media order. The huge inequalities built into the Brazilian economic order would be well protected by the rapidly concentrating and commercialised media, with Globo as its focal point. It would feature entertainment, in service to advertisers, and its politics would be mainly depoliticisingly blank, but under pressure would be suitably biased (Lima, 1988). A high official of Globo called it 'without any question, the best-finished product, the biggest success of the dictatorship. Globo made concrete an abstraction: Order and Progress' (quoted in Lima, 1988). Supported by the generals, the Globo system was permitted to expand both horizontally and vertically, the television system itself constituting what Roberto Amaral and Cesar Guimaraes describe as 'a private quasimonopoly of sound, image, and textual media' (Amaral and Guimaraes, 1994: 26).

Today the Globo network flourishes, absorbs some 80 per cent of TV advertising revenue and 60 per cent of all Brazilian advertising, and also controls vast other media sectors (including *O Globo*, the largest newspaper in Brazil, news and advertising agencies, record, printing and publishing companies, and all kinds of radio stations). At the heart of the formats and programming adapted from an earlier dependency regime is the 'dominance of entertainment over educational and cultural programming' (Straubhaar, 1996: 225).

# The main drift versus niche filling, and audience activism

The increasing hegemony of the market and its gradual displacement of the public sphere occurs at varying speeds and is never complete. As noted, even in the United States, public broadcasting was introduced in 1967 with commercial broadcasters' blessing, to provide cultural and educational fare of lesser market value at public expense. Furthermore, the commercial media themselves offer occasional moments of public-service broadcasting, and the proliferation of commercial cable channels and networks has made some cultural programming available to paying customers, although very little political material of value has been provided as cable strives for large audiences and advertiser favour, following in the footsteps of the larger commercial broadcasters.

Nonprofit print media and community broadcasters (mainly radio) continue to exist and do supply a public-sphere alternative and some hope for the future, but they service small audiences and do not have the resources to reach large numbers and compete with the advertising-funded media. They fill niches – as the shrinking public broadcasters and, episodically, cable broadcasters and the Internet, do as well – but at this point in history none of these is able to influence the main drift, which is being shaped by the dominant, large commercial media.

It is argued by some media analysts that audiences are 'active' and 'co-produce' materials along with programme owners and sources, so that the possibility of brainwashing and the engineering of apathy and/or consent is overrated (Fiske, 1987: 317). Audiences allegedly interpret messages from their own perspectives and producers must offer them programmes and information serving audience frames in order to attract audiences. This Pollyanna-ish view overlooks the importance of consumer sovereignty – the right to choose what is shown in the first place – as opposed to the freedom of consumers to choose among options offered them by concentrated sellers catering first to business advertisers. It also ignores the importance of the ability of the media sovereigns to study audiences, rework and repeat messages, and incorporate ideology into those messages at many levels –

ads, entertainment and news (Barnouw, 1978; Schiller, 1989: ch. 7; Seaman, 1992).

# Concluding note

The public sphere is shrinking globally under the impact of a triumphant market system, which is putting more and more public space to profitable use, as defined by the advertising community. That community wants, first and foremost, a congenial selling environment, and nothing that would, in the words of Procter & Gamble's advertising rules, 'further the concept of business as cold, ruthless, and lacking all sentiment or spiritual motivation'. This underlies the long trend towards entertainment and gradual marginalisation of the public sphere. But democracy depends on an informed public, and thus a vibrant public sphere, to function properly. The main drift of the global market system and media therefore poses the serious threat that we are allowing democracy to be subverted and, in Neil Postman's words, 'entertaining ourselves to death'.

# References

Amaral, R. and Guimaraes, C. (1994) Media monopoly in Brazil, *Journal of Communication*, 44.4, pp. 26–38.

Andersen, R. (1995) *Consumer Culture and TV Programming*, Westview Press, Boulder, Colo.

Barnouw, E. (1978) *The Sponsor*, Oxford University Press, New York.

Blumler, J., Bynin, M. and Nossiter, T. (1986) Broadcasting finance and programming quality: an international review, *European Journal of Communication*, 1, pp. 348–50.

Bunce, R. (1976) *Television in the Corporate Interest*, Praeger, New York.

Chomsky, N. (1992) *Deterring Democracy*, Hill & Wang, New York.

Dominick, J. and Pearce, M. (1976) Trends in network prime-time programming, 1953–74, *Journal of Communication*, 26, pp. 70–80.

Farhi, P. (1995) TV violence adds punch to the overseas market, *Washington Post National Weekly Edition*, Feb. 13–19, p. 21.

Federal Communications Commission (FCC) (1946) *The Public Service Responsibilities of Broadcast Licensees*, FCC, Washington, DC.

Fiske, J. (1987) *Television Culture*, Methuen, London.

Fox, E. (1988) *Media and Politics in Latin America*, Sage, Beverly Hills.

Gerbner, G. (1995) Marketing global mayhem, *the public* 2.2, p. 6.

Herman, E. (1996) The media mega-mergers, *Dollars & Sense*, 205, May–June, pp. 8–13.

Herman, E. and McChesney, R. (1997) *The Global Media: The New Missionaries of Corporate Capitalism*, Cassell, London.

Kline, S. (1993) *Out of the Garden: Toys, TV, and Children's Culture in the Age of Marketing*, Verso, London.

Krasnow, E., Longley, E. and Terry, H. (1982) *The Politics of Broadcast Regulation*, St. Martin's Press, New York.

Leffler, M. (1984) The American conception of national security and the beginning of the Cold War, 1945–48, *American Historical Review*, April.

Lima, V. A. D. (1988) The state, television, and political power in Brazil, *Critical Studies in Mass Communication*, 5, pp. 108–28.

McChesney, R. (1993) *Telecommunications, Mass Media, and Democracy*, Oxford University Press, New York.

Naureckas, J. (1996) Info-bandits, *In These Times*, 4 March, pp. 14–17.

Palmer, E. (1988) *Television and America's Children: A Crisis of Neglect*, Oxford University Press, New York.

Schiller, H. (1989) *Culture Inc.: The Corporate Takeover of Public Expression*, Oxford University Press, New York.

Seaman, W. (1992) Active audience theory: pointless populism, *Media, Culture & Society*, 14, pp. 301–11.

Straubhaar, J. D. (1996) The electronic media in Brazil, in Cole, R. R. (ed.) *Communication in Latin America*, Scholarly Resources Inc., Wilmington, Del.

Taras, D. (1991) The new undefended border: American television, Canadian audiences and the Canadian broadcasting system, in Kroes, R. (ed.) *Within the US Orbit: Small National Cultures Vis-a-Vis the United States*, VU University Press, Amsterdam.

# |8|

# *Worldwide wedge*

## *Division and contradiction in the global information infrastructure*

PETER GOLDING

Start today to realise the future – the Internet is here and is happening now, capitalise on the future today
> (advertisement in UK financial press, March 1996)

The Internet suffers from the problems often found in resources that are in common ownership: potential misuse, security problems and a lack of structure.
> (International Telecommunication Union press release,
> October 1995)

The days when the Net seemed to exist outside the laws of capitalism are just about over.
> (*HotWired* magazine, 12 March 1996)

Progressive social critics are pessimists by nature; time and again they have watched the promise of shared abundance dissipated by corporate greed and political failure. But hope survives, nourished by a mix of naivety, determination and honest endeavour as in Gramsci's succinct quip, 'pessimism of the intellect, optimism of the will'. Nothing feeds that eternal hope of progress more than technical change. The emergence in recent decades of communications forces of previously unimagined speed and flexibility has been the recurrent basis for visionary rewriting of future history.

In recent years, guerrilla television, community video, cable – the television of abundance – and citizens' band radios have all offered transient promise of providing electronic sustenance and substance for dissent and diversity. Yet each has disappeared as a serious tool of social change. The

This chapter is a revised version of an article which appeared in *The Monthly Review*, 48.3, July–Aug. 1996, pp. 70–85, by permission of *The Monthly Review*.

incorporation of technical novelty into the apparatus of oppression and inequality should come as no surprise for historians familiar with the story of the printing press, the newspaper or broadcasting. Yet as capitalism clearly arrives at something of a transitional boundary in the late twentieth century, the sense that the formidable and unprecedented potency of the new computer-based technologies may mean something quite different has once again rekindled the embers of radical optimism.

The latest repository for such optimism has been the Internet, the exponentially growing network of computer networks which has evolved its own culture, endless media hype, a growing literature and even an embryonic genre of film and novelisation. At last dreams of electronically delivered Jeffersonian ideals seem within our grasp, as politicians like Tony Blair in the UK and Al Gore in the USA scramble to become the visionaries of digital politics. No one will miss out on this transformation. We have no less than Newt Gingrich's assurance that 'this new era will see a revolution in goods and services that will empower and enhance most people' (Gingrich, 1995: 55). Note the 'most', however; even visionaries hedge their bets. It is enough to make one drool since, as Gingrich goes on, 'the United States can profit enormously by being the leader in the development of the new goods, services, systems and standards associated with a technological revolution of this scale' (ibid., 57–8).

In this chapter I want to assess more broadly the implications of the growth of the Internet, and set this assessment alongside some observations about global communications inequality more generally.

# Nerds and Net profits

There is an appealing romance about the history of the Internet, and indeed of the computer industry more generally, which would mould it into a microcosm of the American dream. Energetic and inventive young men, in backyards and garden sheds, are the driving force which kick-starts the industry taking America into the information age. With just a pocketful of risk-venture dollars, and nothing but dreams, a few borrowed gizmos and their technological wizardry, these techno-entrepreneurs are the new Carnegies, Hearsts, Edisons, DuPonts and Rockefellers of the digital age. In ecstatic endorsement of this vision, the *Economist* saw the growth of the Net as 'not a fluke or fad, but the consequence of unleashing the power of individual creativity. If it were an economy it would be the triumph of the free market over central planning. In music, jazz over Bach. Democracy over dictatorship' (1995: 4).

Like most mythologies this dramatisation has its kernel of truth. The frontier ideals of early development have bequeathed a slightly whiskery hippie taint to much Internet culture, as the networks bristle with West Coast new age rhetoric, technoshamanism and role-playing fantasy worlds.

It is a delusion. The suits were there at the beginning, and it is no surprise that devotees like Rheingold (1994) sound a wistfully fearful note. As he argues, more in hope than expectation, 'it is still possible for people round the world to make sure this new sphere of vital human discourse remains open to the citizens of the planet before the political and economic big boys seize it, censor it, meter it, and sell it back to us'.

The roots of the Internet lay elsewhere than in the nerds' backyards, however. It started life in the Pentagon's Advanced Research Projects Agency. Needing a way of linking military computer researchers led to a technique whereby data could be split up and transmitted in packets. This gave both security (parts of a message cannot be 'eavesdropped') and safety (even a nuclear attack can only hit one part of a network, so that others remain intact and take over). These early experiments in the mid-1960s paralleled work at the National Physical Laboratory in the UK. ARPANET grew from four nodes in 1969 to roughly 100 by 1975 when it was turned over to the Defense Communications Agency. In the 1980s academic networks developed under the auspices of the National Science Foundation (CSNET) and the resulting NSFNET subsequently replaced ARPANET in 1990. The privatisation of the regional NSF networks marked the emergence of a commercial basis for the interconnected networks now in place, and has been the basis for all subsequent expansion.

As the Internet grows almost exponentially, a fully commercial set of backbone systems has been constructed in place of the one developed by the government. Internet service providers have become large public companies or have merged. In 1995 all remaining curbs on commercial use disappeared. Eric Schmidt, chief technology officer for Sun Microsystems put it simply: 'customer service is the "killer application of the Internet"'. For Russ Jones, Digital's Internet programme manager, the Internet 'is a richer environment for exploring commercial capabilities'. Or to quote the *Economist*, 'The Internet had grown up' (1995: 9).

Internet size, whatever that might mean, roughly doubles every year. Put the hyperbole and the arithmetic together and everyone on the planet will be connected by the year 2003. The World Wide Web was developed at the European Centre for Particle Research in 1989, but only took off in 1993 when software developed at the University of Illinois and subsequently elsewhere created 'browsers' and graphical interfaces made the search for and interrogation of 'pages' on the WWW possible. With this arrival of multimedia possibilities for the Internet, commercial developers of such browsers, such as Netscape, became rich overnight. By 1995 there were over 30,000 websites in the Internet, and the number has doubled roughly every two or three months. The most significant change in the character of the WWW has been the irresistible rise of commercial sites.

One estimate, prepared at MIT, shows the proportion of websites devoted to commercial use to have risen from 4.6 per cent of the total in 1993 to 50 per cent by early 1996. Tracking the nature of Internet use generally can be done by watching the 'domains' into which usage fits. By 1994 'com' had replaced 'edu' as the most common domain name, as companies discovered the Web was more than a nerd's hangout. A January 1996 survey by Network Wizards shows 9.4 million host computers connected to the Internet, of which 'com' was easily the single largest domain, larger than academic (edu) and government (gov) sources combined.

# The 'big boys' join in

Two features of major corporations in the telecommunications and information sectors stand out in the late 1990s. One is the rash of mergers and incorporation that has taken place. The other is the diversification of activity. Both are designed to place the mega-corporations in pole position as the Internet's commercialisation becomes serious. According to a 1995 survey by Broadview Associates, merger and acquisition transactions in the IT industry jumped 57 per cent in 1995, with a transaction value of $134 million. IT companies sought energetically to achieve the critical mass necessary for competition in the international market, and especially sought the synergy which association with the newly deregulated telecommunications companies would allow. A presence on the WWW became more than a yuppie fashion accessory, more a business opportunity and requirement.

In Europe the activity has been mainly in telecommunications, in the USA in the audio-visual sector, and in Japan in electronics. Germany is Europe's largest telecoms market, and has seen mergers with US companies (Thyssen-BellSouth) and with British (Viag Interkom-BT, Veba-Cable and Wireless). In audio-visual sectors recent alliances include the association of France's UGC and Twentieth Century Fox, and a production accord between France Television and Time Warner. The wider trend of mega-mergers in the audio-visual sectors has included the takeover by Canadian wine and drinks giant Seagram of MCA, which controls Universal Studios; Time Warner's buy-out of Turner Broadcasting; Disney's purchase of Capital Cities (including the ABC network), and the takeover by Westinghouse of the CBS network.

The growth of vertical integration strategies which this trend represents places the audio-visual sector in a key position as distribution becomes the next priority for Internet commercialisation. This is well represented by the 1994 purchase by media giant Viacom, which controls the MTV channels, of the Paramount movie studios. Time Warner, the largest purely media corporation on the planet, includes in its activities *Time* magazine, Warner Music and Warner Bros. studios, the Home Box Office TV channel, and major holdings in cable systems and channels, as well as the mammoth operation in book-selling operated by Time Life Books.

In many ways this vertical integration may be more significant than the much-touted convergence of the telecommunications, computing and broadcasting industries. The latter is a purely technological take on what must be seen as a primarily fiscal and economic strategy. Inevitably some other familiar names come into view. Rupert Murdoch's News Corporation made its entry onto this stage with the establishment of a joint venture with long-distance operator MCI in information services, including MCI's FYI Online and e-mail services, and NewsCorp's Delphi Internet and online games service Kesmai, while Microsoft appeared with the Microsoft Network and tentative entries into the audio-visual sector through a stake in DreamWorks, an alliance with NBC network, and licensing of interactive video games. Somehow the dream of Jeffersonian democracy through optic fibres had been transposed into the slightly increased chance of saving a twenty-minute round trip to the video rental store. It is difficult to square the reality with Murdoch's promise that 'this venture will bridge different communities of interest, create opportunities to build and grow relationships and enrich the daily experience of individuals from all walks of life' (Press release, 20 February 1996, www.internetmci.com/ven).

Essentially, corporations could use the Net to market three commodities: their own goods, access to the network, and advertising. Marketing of goods on the Internet has hardly begun, stunted by the persistent difficulties surrounding security of payment. Advertising faces the problem of audience audit, to which a great deal of attention is being given. How many times has your site been accessed, or 'hit'? Despite that uncertainty, charges are beginning to stabilise. Popular sites on the Web, like *Playboy*'s, have been charging up to $100,000 for placing a postage-stamp-sized link on their pages. In the UK the Electronic Telegraph charges £25,000 for seven weeks' display on their screen of a button link. But then, by November 1995 *Playboy* could claim over 3 million 'hits' per day. Jonathan Nelson, CEO of US website specialists Organic Online, suggests 'We look at Web sites as eyeball aggregators, trying to bring people in and give them an experience. The aim is to bring in the right people in a very detailed demographic niche' (quoted in Waldman, 1996).

For the entertainment corporations the pitch is more direct. CNN Online selects stories targeted at younger upmarket males. Such services offer the possibility of seducing their clientele onto premium services beyond the main free services, in a parallel to the tariff structures of cable television. Columbia TriStar launched a website in 1995 and uses it to build viewer loyalty with such gimmicks as a poll to ask viewers whether the lead in a sitcom should become pregnant, and puzzles to back up game shows.

# Digital dilemmas: contradiction and conflict for the Internet

The corporate takeover and commercialisation of the Internet can lead easily to a weary fatalism, accepting that another potentially liberating technology has been engulfed by the still rampant forces of the 'free market'. But at this stage in its development the Net represents very starkly just those choices and contradictions which are at the heart of any political moment. Four key areas illustrate the present state of uncertainty and opportunity.

## Community use or market mechanism?

The inherent twin properties of use value and exchange value are deeply embedded in the evolution of a communication system such as the Internet. Even the most casual and serendipitous of surfers will not travel far around the Web without coming across examples of the seriously progressive potential of its social evolution. In London in 1990 McDonalds served libel writs on five activists who published a pamphlet providing less than flattering details of the food giant's employment practices and its questionable farming and food-production methods. The trial assumed Dickensian proportions, and two of the defendants, an unemployed single father and an ex-gardener turned barmaid, proved indefatigable self-taught lawyers in a seemingly endless and frustrating saga for the corporation, whose $26 billion turnover and $10,000-a-day legal team were unable to crack the pair in what became Britain's longest-ever civil trial. Not the least of the support structures for the defendants was the development of a website which made sure that the millions of words detailing McDonald's alleged failings brought out in the trial, and every critical article or cartoon which have appeared in the meantime, had the widest possible electronic circulation. When Greenpeace found themselves in dispute with Shell over the disposal of redundant North Sea oil rigs, environmental activists used the Web to drum up support. Other examples are legion.

Evidence from surveys suggests that demand for information on the Web is high, and indeed exceeds the demand for entertainment. A Harris poll in 1994 found 63 per cent of consumers wanted health or government information and other public-service material. Almost three-quarters wanted customised news, but only 40 per cent wanted movies on demand, and even fewer wanted interactive shopping. Why then is corporate strategy the opposite? Quite simply because, as Howard Besser notes, 'the industry believes that in the long run this other set of services will prove more lucrative' (Besser, 1995: 64).

What will make the Net grow, supply or demand? Consultants for the European Commission, Ovum, estimate that by 2005 the percentage of revenues from networked multimedia services in north-west Europe will derive 42 per cent from entertainment and pornography, and only 11 per cent from information services (Graham et al., 1996: 6). When Viacom bought Paramount many questioned why, at $10 billion, they should pay seventeen times the cash value of the company. But Paramount's TV and movie stock provide an invaluable resource for exploitation by seeking additional distribution channels, new user fees and extended audiences for advertising. Microsoft's alliance with NBC to create twenty-four-hour TV and Internet news is paralleled by a flocking of broadcasters to the Web. By March 1996 about 300,000 home pages on the Web had 'television' as one of their key words.

## Integration or exclusion?

Early Net dreamers saw a wired universe, in which virtual communities would offer mutual support and conviviality in a global digital commune. The Net would be a horizontal communications structure, quite unlike the hierarchical vertical structures of old. In the high profile debates about censorship and pornography on the Web there has been understandable focus on the exclusion of women from this latest 'toy for the boys'. Appalling examples of cross-national prostitution via the Web, and the arrival of such unlovely and unlikely online hucksters as 'Pimps-R-Us', have given sound bases to critiques that women are excluded from the Net by the sexist nature of chat lines and the intrinsic patriarchality of its growth. But possibly more fundamental has been the emergence of division and exclusion by price.

Inevitably the consolidation of a market structure is replicating patterns of exclusion and differentiation apparent in earlier technologies. To access the Net requires a reasonably state-of-the art computer, a phone line and a modem. In the UK many poor families do not even have telephone access. The start-up hardware would cost more than they are ever likely to afford. Online costs include the monthly payment to a company like Compuserve, currently about $27, not a princely sum, but roughly a quarter of the social security allowance for a teenage child. The growing power of the service providers was massively magnified in 1997 with the surprise marriage between Compuserve and the giant America Online, giving the new conglomerate some 11 million subscribers overall.

Recent surveys show that home-computer ownership is reaching a ceiling, with growth in 1995 virtually nil in the USA. The majority of sales are to existing owners upgrading rather than diffusion into new groups, thus exacerbating the gaps which already exist. The evidence confirms this trend. Director of the MIT Media Lab and digital visionary Nicholas Negroponte sees it this way: 'Some people worry about the social divide between the information-rich and the information-poor, the haves and the have-nots, the First and Third Worlds. But the real cultural divide is going to be generational' (Negroponte, 1996: 6). But he is wrong. A survey by Durlacher shows that the 25–34-year-old middle-class male is the biggest user group of the Internet. But an NOP survey in 1995 in the UK also shows that one-third of users are 35–54 and a third are female. The biggest differentiator is by income; roughly a third earned over £25,000 per annum.

*Financial Times* readers were the most represented on the Web. A large-scale survey by Nielsen in the USA and Canada found that WWW users have high incomes (25 per cent over $80,000), half are in professional and managerial groups and two-thirds have college degrees.

While there have been doubts cast on the accuracy of some of these surveys the picture of market differentiation by price is clear and growing. One acute analysis comes from the journal of the Association of Chief Police Officers in the UK, which has drawn its own conclusions. In an article in May 1996 it fears the arrival of an electronic underclass, 'alienated, denied access to the new society because of a lack of education and wealth'.

The emergence of new communications goods has coincided with an ever-widening profile of income inequality. In the UK changes in the labour market, Thatcherite tax and welfare policies, and industrial reconstruction and decay have produced a regime of inequalities unparalleled in a century. Between 1979 and 1993 the poorest tenth of the UK population saw their real income fall by 18 per cent, while the top tenth received an increase of a startling 61 per cent. The share of national income going to these two groups is also diverging, producing unprecedented levels of income inequality. Pay inequality is larger than at any time since records began a century ago (the worst-paid tenth received 69 per cent of average wages in 1979, 63 per cent of average in 1993; the figures for the best-paid tenth were 146 per cent rising to 159 per cent). Wealth remains equally starkly differentiated: the top 1 per cent own 18 per cent of marketable wealth, the top 10 per cent own 49 per cent. In the USA the wealthiest 1 per cent owns 40 per cent of the nation's wealth, while the top 20 per cent own four-fifths of the total.

This is not the arithmetic of community communications. The global village has become the digital bazaar. As communications are driven into the marketplace the widening inequalities of economic fortune are translated into cultural and political disadvantage. As even columnist David Kline observed in that courier of technohype, *Hotwired* magazine, 'The future may become a wonderland of opportunity only for the minority among us who are affluent, mobile, and highly educated. And it may at the same time, become a digital dark age for the majority of citizens – the poor, the non-college educated, and the so-called unnecessary' (Kline, 1995).

## Diversity or conglomeration?

Yet another dream for pioneers was the Net as the playground of the inventor-entrepreneur, a place where a thousand overnight millionaires could bloom, and everyone would be producer and consumer alike. After all, the Web was invented by a software engineer stuck away at a physics lab in Switzerland. The software which gave it its biggest boost emerged from a group of students at Illinois University, and Marc Andreesen, developer of

Netscape, the most popular browser for the WWW, became an instant multi-millionaire in his early twenties.

Not only that but the entry of the corporate giants has been far from smooth. By February 1996 NewsCorp and MCI's Online Ventures was laying off staff and saying goodbye to its chief executive. AT&T is another giant that has lost a succession of senior executives in a halting and uneven entry into the new marketplace. Apple's eWorld and Murdoch's Delphi are also distinguished in this company of stumbling Goliaths. But the point is that the giant corporations can afford to make mistakes. Watching for shooting stars on the periphery of the business they can shift risk capital into them at their point of proven take-off, allowing the start-up and R & D costs to be absorbed by the small players. The so-called boutique character of the new market, stressing subcontracting and flexible small businesses, may challenge the corporate dinosaurs, but the bulk of the new markets is still ending up in their hands.

## Electronic democracy or cyber-individualism?

Not long ago the arrival of cable TV and the imminent coming of computer networking evoked frissons of expectation about a new golden age of 'teledemocracy'. Voters would have direct access to their political masters, the electronic referendum would provide a recurrent mechanism of accountability and democratic politics, and political information for citizenship would be boundless and instantly accessible. The digital Athenian democracy this conjured up also, among sceptical observers, prompted the reminder that in Athens neither women nor slaves got much of a political look-in.

So too with the new cyberdemocracy. As Clifford Stoll in his splendidly sceptical diatribe *Silicon Snake Oil* points out, until the golden age arrives 'only the technoliterati will be enfranchised with network access' (Stoll, 1995: 32). The limited, and it would appear, stubbornly abating online community, will have privileged access to the political universe unavailable to the techno-poor. Not only that but the character of the politics envisaged in these scenarios changes the nature of democracy in its essence. As Stoll points out, 'This electronic town hall removes valid reasons for representative government. What's the purpose of a representative when each of us can vote immediately on every issue?' (ibid.: 33). There is here the potential for a fundamental individualisation of politics. In cyberdemocracy the role of representative and intermediary organisations – trade unions, community groups, political parties, pressure groups – is atrophied. As a result, as Dutch analysts van de Donk and Tops suggest, 'representative organisations may disappear . . . A direct plebiscitarian democracy becomes feasible when the *demos* . . . can come together "virtually" ' (van de Donk and Tops, 1995: 16).

But the presupposition of universal access, itself illusory, is also based on a fiction about the nature of interactivity. Home shopping on the Web has not taken off because people want to touch, see and interact with what they are buying and those from whom they purchase it. But that will change as systems become more elaborate and secure. Interactivity on the Web, far from a mechanism for democratic debate and influence, will descend, as Besser sardonically notes, to 'responding to multiple-choice questions and entering credit card numbers on a key pad' (Besser, 1995: 63). Thus individualisation, unequal access and disenfranchisement may be the outcome of Net politics, as much as an electronic Agora.

## Not so worldwide after all

The emerging electronic inequalities generated by the World Wide Web and its commercial incorporation reflect the underlying political economy of all previous communications technologies. This creates a double differentiation, both at national and at international level. As we have seen, access to an abundant resource is only of value to commercial exploitation if that access can be curtailed by the price mechanism. In other words artificial scarcity has to be introduced and barriers erected to market entry for both consumers and producers.

This scenario becomes writ large on the global scale. The 1980s were indeed the 'lost decade' for much of the poorer two-thirds of the world. At the start of the decade, roughly 60 per cent of the world's population lived in countries whose per capita income was less than 10 per cent of the world average. As the nineties arrived some were emerging from the morass of destitution. But this was a small minority, mainly in the east Asian bloc of 'newly industrialising countries'. While aid was hastily diverted to the struggling economies of Eastern Europe (prompted by commercial opportunism and American alarm at the political instability generated by collapsing economies and a power vacuum), the poorer countries, of Asia and Africa especially, listened to uncomfortable advice about 'structural adjustment' while watching over soaring debt and falling primary commodity prices. The combination of growing Northern protectionism, declining aid, higher real interest rates and growing debt has further consolidated the endemic crisis of third world economies. By the year 2000, as the rest of us gaze in wonder at millennium celebrations and ponder the luxuries of the digital future, about a billion people will be living in absolute poverty. Some 70 per cent of world income is produced and consumed by 15 per cent of the world's population.

The implications of these trends for communications have been central to global politics in the last three decades. The emergence of the Non-Aligned Movement to provide a political accompaniment to pressure for a New International Economic Order led inexorably to the cardinal involvement of

UNESCO as a forum for what became the insistent demand for a New International Information and Communication Order, culminating in the establishment of the MacBride Commission and, later, the International Programme for the Development of Communications.

It is not surprising, in this context, that the terrain occupied by communications goods and facilities is a hilly one, marked by soaring peaks of advantage and dismal valleys of privation. For example, book production continues to be dominated by Europe and the USA. The dominance of the English-language multinational publishers, especially in educational publishing, continues to sustain what has been the longest established feature of the international media. Over half the world's newspaper production remains in the industrialised West. Conversely, Africa has just 1 per cent of the world's newspaper circulation, the same proportion as a decade ago.

The growth of broadcasting as the dominant medium in most regions has been swift and dramatic. Europe and North America own two-thirds of the total of the world's TV and radio sets, though they account for just 14.9 per cent (Europe) and 5.2 per cent (North America) of the world's population. Notable for its very limited incursion into this picture is Africa, with 12.1 per cent of the world's population, but whose share of world radio and television sets is just 3.7 per cent and 1.3 per cent respectively.

The extent to which the 'lost decade' has seen the gap between rich and poor opening wider is starkly illustrated. There are over eight times as many book titles produced per capita in developed countries compared to the developing countries. The gap in newspapers per capita is of a similar ratio. The developed world has nearly six times as many radios per capita as the developing world, and nearly nine times as many television sets. The picture these figures superficially represent does not, of course, illustrate the disappointments of the 1980s. If we look at Africa again, with just 37 televisions per 1000 inhabitants in 1990 and just 172 radios, we realise how far behind some regions have been left. These figures were 17 and 104 in 1980. Yet in North America the equivalent figures for 1990 were 2017 (radio) and 798 (television), reflecting an increase in the decade greater than the African total.

In telecommunications generally the gap is enormous. Despite the pressures for deregulation imposed by the IMF, African countries lag further and further behind. Basic telephony is still an essential. In South Africa there are 60 telephones for every 100 white inhabitants, but just one per 100 blacks (the figure is only 1.6 per 100 people for the whole continent). The post-Apartheid government has resisted privatisation until this is corrected. In 1994 Europe and North America accounted for 69 per cent of global telecommunications revenues, Africa for just 1 per cent (and for just 2 per cent of international telephone traffic). South African Deputy President Thabo Mbeki put the issue in severe relief at the G7 information summit in 1995 when he simply noted that 'half of humanity has never made a telephone call. The reality is that there are more telephone lines in Manhattan, New York, than in Sub-Saharan Africa.'

The huge opportunities afforded by developments in this field, both for personal communication and liberation from constraints of time and place, and for the acceleration and facilitation of commerce, are distributed with massive inequities. Telecommunications trade grew from less than $50 billion in 1990 to $96 billion in 1995. The telecommunications services market has grown from just under $400 billion to over $600 billion in the same period. In terms of market capitalisation, the telecommunications industry ranks third in the world behind health care and banking, and it is growing at twice the rate of the global economy (ITU, 1997a).

The routing of telecommunications is a simple reflection of the global capital structure. Four of the five top international telecommunication routes have the USA as one partner, and the USA is partner to 51 per cent of international telephone traffic in the top fifty routes (calculated from ITU, 1997b). Japan and the USA dominate world telecommunication equipment exports, accounting for 48 per cent of the value of exports by the top ten nations (ITU, 1997a). Even within the developing world the overwhelming volume of traffic is among and between the major trading elites, with the top twenty-five routes including those between Hong Kong, China, Singapore and Malaysia. No African country features in the top international routes among developing nations until we get down to number 15 (Namibia and South Africa). Yet, paradoxically, the biggest users of international telephony are a small number of affluent Sub-Saharan subscribers, living in a continent where there is not even one line per hundred people. More obviously, however, '24 OECD countries, while containing only 15 per cent of the world's population, account for 71 per cent of all telephone lines' (Winseck, 1997: 234). While half the world's population have never made a phone call, a fraction are on line and in touch to great effect and benefit.

The Internet repeats this picture only too clearly. By 1994 not a single less developed country had a computer network directly connected to the Internet. Packet-switched data networks existed in only five LDCs. The Internet Society estimate that in 1994 there were 0.002 Internet users per 1000 inhabitants in India, compared to 48.9 in Sweden. Most African nations still have no Internet access, yet the possible uses for such networks, for example in electronic health and education services, are enormous. Africa One, the fibre-optic undersea cable which will create a communications ring around the continent, will not be complete before 1999 at the earliest, and it remains to be seen if it is better news for AT&T Submarine Systems, the company who developed Africa One, than it is for the potential users. No African country was involved in the development stages of the $2.6 billion project. We have heard about the 'magic multiplier' potential of communication technologies before. After all, whatever happened to the 'transistor revolution'?

# On contradiction and optimism

The jury is still out on what these innovations may mean. Just as the impact of the 'transistor revolution' in the 1960s was far from as predicted, so too for more recent gadgetry. The cassette recorder facilitated cheap and easy production, duplication and dissemination of local music and styles in many regions, yet also became the dominant form for global distribution of the ever more ubiquitous transnational music industry. Video recording gave new political energy and resource to the Kayapo and other indigenous peoples in the Amazon basin, yet also secured the full integration of the television and film industries in the further domestication of Western leisure patterns. The Internet is being heralded by aficionados as the means for horizontal communication and global networking which will revolutionise relationships both local and global, yet its commercialisation in the mid-1990s looks all too familiar to observers of past technological promise.

The contradiction inherent in these hopes and doubts is built in to international policymaking. The tension between the potential for wider access to information and the desire to own and control it is not new. At the ITU conference in 1994 US Vice-President Al Gore argued for development of the new global information infrastructure on the basis of five principles: private investment, competition, flexible regulation, non-discriminatory access and universal service. It takes no great insight to spot the incompatibility among those principles.

The same contradictions appear in the European Community, whose Ministerial Conference on the Information Society in February 1995 set out the G7 countries' visions of this future. Again we see a shopping list of principles to realise these aims including ensuring universal access; equality of opportunity; diversity of content and worldwide co-operation with special attention to the needs of less developed countries. Yet at the same time the principles included promoting dynamic competition; encouraging private investment, and an adaptable and open-access regulatory framework. Square pegs do not go into round holes, even when made from fibre optics. The essentially contradictory components of these aspirations will be the battle ground on which future policy in this area will be fought.

While the mega-corporations continue their stumbling but inexorable commodification of the Internet and allied technologies, there will be a clash of ideals. The American Libraries Association can suggest that the 'National Information Infrastructure has almost limitless potential for social empowerment, democratic diversification, and creative education' (Kranich, 1994: 2) but realistically, they also recognise that it 'will be owned, controlled and dominated by unregulated media giants that are driven by profits, not the hope for cultural understanding, greater democracy, the decrease of poverty, or educational enhancement' (ibid.: 6). Their answer is to call for a Corporation for Public Networking.

What we are witnessing is the 'mediatisation' of the new technologies, as they follow past scenarios of commercialisation, differentiated access, exclusion of the poor, privatisation, deregulation and globalisation. None of this is inevitable. We find ourselves staring at the arrival of a tool which could nourish and enhance the public sphere, or equally, which could provide another vehicle for the incorporation of progressive politics and ideals into the grubby maw of market rapacity. The call to battle may arrive along unfamiliar channels, but its tenets and tones will be all too familiar.

# References

Besser, H. (1995) From Internet to information superhighway, in Brook, J. and Boal, I. (eds) *Resisting the Virtual Life: The Culture and Politics of Information*, City Lights, San Francisco.

*Economist* (1995) The Internet, Survey, 1 July, pp. 1–20.

Gingrich, N. (1995) *To Renew America*, HarperCollins, New York.

Graham, C. et al (1996) *The Consumer in the Information Society: A Discussion Paper for Identifying Priority Issues*, Ovum Ltd., London.

ITU (1997a) *World Telecommunication Development Report*, International Telecommunication Union, Zurich.

ITU (1997b) ITU/TeleGeography direction of traffic database. (Available online at http://www.itu.int/ti/industryoverview/top50int.html.)

Kline, D. (1995) To have and to have not, *Hotwired*, 18 Dec., p. 5. (Available online at http://www.hotwired.com/market/95/51/index1a.html.)

Kranich, N. (1994) Internet access and democracy: ensuring public access on the information highway, *Open* magazine pamphlet series, No. 31, Westfield, NJ.

Negroponte, N. (1996) *Being Digital*, Coronet Books, London.

Rheingold, H. (1994) *The Virtual Community: Finding Competition in a Computerised World*, Secker & Warburg, London.

Stoll, C. (1995) *Silicon Snake Oil: Second Thoughts on the Information Highway*, Macmillan, London.

van de Donk, W. B. H. J and Tops, P. W. (1995) Orwell or Athens? Informatization and the future of democracy, in their *Orwell in Athens: A Perspective on Informatization and Democracy*, IOS Press, Amsterdam.

Waldman, S. (1996) Adland's new toy, *Guardian*, 18 March, p. 16.

Winseck, D. (1997) Contradictions in the democratisation of international communication, *Media, Culture & Society*, 19.2, pp. 219–46.

# Discussion questions

1 Using an example selected from recent news coverage, analyse the media's role in creating popular awareness about international humanitarian issues.

2 Design a questionnaire to elicit opinion about perceptions of Africa among consumers of Western-dominated global media. What kind of coverage might Africa receive if Africans were reporting from and about their own countries?

3 Is the concept of the public sphere still relevant, given the fragmented and hybrid nature of modern society?

4 Is it possible to talk of a public sphere? What evidence is there to argue that global media are helping create a global public sphere?

5 Examine the power of advertising in modern media systems. Choose a set of advertisements on television for a discussion in a group. In what ways might advertising influence programming decisions?

6 Why do you think US television products have been so successful outside the USA? Make a list of programmes available on television in your country and comment on the proportion of US and nationally produced programmes.

7 To what extent is Brazil an independent actor in the global television market?

8 Do you think a global cybercitizenship is possible with new information and communication technologies? If so what might be its uses?

9 What factors have contributed to the 'privatisation of public space'? What implications might this have for global democracy?

10 Discuss the limitations, in terms of access within and between nations, and the potential of the Internet as a new medium of empowerment.

# SECTION III

# DEBATING MEDIA GLOBALISATION

# Introduction to Section III

This section widens the theoretical debate to critique the concept of 'globalisation' in relation to the media, challenging the view of globalisation as an undifferentiated and unidirectional process, and arguing that it needs to take account of a complex set of interactions between and within regions, nations, cultures and genders.

The section begins with a robust defence of the relevance of the concept of media imperialism originally conceived in the late 1970s by Oliver Boyd-Barrett, who proposes a reformulation of the concept in the context of the complexity of the international and national media situations in the late 1990s. He argues that there are elements from the original conceptualisation that are a useful antidote to some of the 'fuzziness' that surrounds the debate on globalisation.

Challenging previous models of international communication as a process of linear intellectual development, moving from propaganda, through to modernisation and free flow, to dependency and cultural or media imperialism and globalisation, Boyd-Barrett believes that the appearance of linearity is deeply suspect. Far from being defunct, the concept of media imperialism has never seriously been tested and still has a great deal to offer as an analytical tool to critique what Boyd-Barrett calls the 'colonisation of communications space'. In addition, by incorporating some of the key concerns of globalisation theory, including hybridity and the weakening of nation-states, he argues, the concept can easily be modified for application to the present.

Boyd-Barrett believes that the concept of 'imperialism', while weighted with a great deal of ideological baggage, helps us to have regard for inequalities and to detect instances of colonisation, whether this is expressed territorially or in terms of the proportion of the world's available media resource. The chapter examines the evidence of unequal international media activity which couples strong media exporters to (unreciprocated) heavy media importers, concluding that 'in an age of democracy we have media tyranny'. Boyd-Barrett argues that, given the rapid and far-reaching changes in global media, the concept of media imperialism needs to be broadened beyond questions of simple reciprocity of cultural trade flows and to focus more on the range and diversity within given domestic markets. It also needs to take account of audiences, in particular by recognising audience preferences. In addition, Boyd-Barrett argues that a reformulated media imperialism thesis needs to encompass neo-colonialisms of inter-ethnic, inter-cultural, inter-gender, inter-generational and inter-class relations.

A contrasting position is taken in the second chapter in this section, in which Stuart Cunningham, Elizabeth Jacka and John Sinclair caution against the view of the globalisation process as an outward flow of cultural products from the dominant 'West' at the centre to the peripheral 'third world'. Instead they see the world as divided into a number of regions, each of which have their own internal dynamics as well as their global ties. Although primarily based on geographical realities, these regions are also defined by common cultural, linguistic and historical connections which transcend national boundaries. The growth of satellite television, they argue, abolishes distance and allows for the first time the linking of remote territories into new viewing communities. Such a dynamic, regionalist view of the world, the authors argue, helps us to analyse in a more nuanced way the complex and multidirectional flows of television across the globe.

Criticising the cultural-imperialism thesis – on both empirical and conceptual grounds – they argue that, in Latin America, for example, US imports have to a significant extent been replaced by local products and this pattern is replicated in Asia and in the Middle East. Each 'geolinguistic region', as they call it, is itself dominated by one or two centres of audio-visual production – Mexico and Brazil in Latin America, Hong Kong for the Chinese-speaking populations of Asia, Egypt for the Arab world and India for South Asia. The Western optic through which the cultural-imperialism thesis was developed, the authors argue, ignored these non-Western systems of regional exchange. The chapter also discusses Australia as an 'in-between' television producer: a country which shares some characteristics with US television trade (the English language and high levels of com-mercialisation), while also sharing characteristics of other peripheral nations, such as being a substantial importer of film and television. They argue that the Australian case illustrates the point that the flow of peripheral production is not so much displacing US production as finding its own intermediate level. The way is then open to inquire into what impact this might have upon the cultural identification of television audiences on a global scale.

The theme of the audience is picked up in Chapter 11 by Anandam Kavoori, who examines the reception of television news in focus groups of audiences in five different countries. Kavoori argues that while the institutional and programming aspects of media globalisation have been examined from a variety of theoretical perspectives, issues of media effect and use have been largely underexplored. Focusing on television news, his chapter presents empirical data from a media-reception project, using focus groups in the USA, UK, Israel, Germany and France to investigate both issues of the commonalties of media reception across cultures and those of local mediation. Groups in each of these countries were shown three international news stories that had been broadcast on their respective national channels, and asked to retell the story in their own terms. The findings across these countries, Kavoori reports, showed overwhelmingly a discourse of criticism of the news broadcasts rather than of the text of the news itself. In the case of Israel, discussion of the news texts, he notes, was constantly referenced back to core cultural concerns of nationhood and cultural identity. The chief finding from the analysis of the data across the Western countries was the significant similarity of the critical or 'reflexive' treatment of the news stories. Audiences across these countries showed similar trends of media referencing.

In addition, Kavoori examines the issue of whether Western-dominated global news media create a hegemonic presence in the South, suggesting that media audiences persist in traditional reading practices followed by a preference for derivative but local media products. He reports a pilot study based on in-depth interviews with consumers of global television news channels in India and concludes that despite the availability of global television, Indian newspapers and magazines remain overwhelmingly the choice for news consumption. Among television news channels too, programmes produced by Indian companies that mimic the editing and reporting styles of global news channels are preferred, indicating that, given the choice between programming developed by global media and those by local private media, audiences usually choose the latter.

The theme of complexity of global interactions is further developed by Annabelle Sreberny, who argues for a gendered perspective on the globalisation of the media, countering the perception of women as passive recipients of media messages and discussing strategies for 'globalisation from below'. Sreberny argues that gender also needs to be included in any rethinking of the overly totalising older models of international communication.

The example of the decentralised, network-based nature of the women's movement offers an alternative path for the development of a global civil society, by harnessing the potential of new communications technologies such as fax and the Internet. She proposes that the women's movement suggests a model of global activism that allows for what she calls 'a solidarity in difference', whereby broad support for general issues can be mobilised alongside specific struggles with particular or differently prioritised sets of concerns within each national and cultural context.

As a case study, Sreberny examines the Global Faxnet, a network of networks which was used by women activists to communicate globally during the 1996 UN Women's Conference in Beijing. The Global Faxnet and WomeNet – run by women for women – indicates the speed at which women are moving along the 'information superhighway'. The global interactivity of women, she argues, continues to provide support to local and national groups struggling to achieve specific goals within nation-states but also enables action on issues at an international level – the recognition of women's rights as fundamental human rights and the development of international instruments and actions to protect such rights.

# 9

# Media imperialism reformulated

OLIVER BOYD-BARRETT

During the 1990s there has been growing consensus in the literature (e.g. Tomlinson, 1991; Sreberny-Mohammadi, 1996) that previous models of international communication may be abandoned in a process of linear intellectual development that has moved through theories of international communication as propaganda, through to modernization and free flow, to dependency and cultural or media imperialism, supplanted in turn by theories of the 'autonomous reader' and culminating in discourses of globalization that play upon an infinite variety of combinations of 'global' and 'local'.

I want to argue that the narrative of linearity is suspect and that the concept of 'globalization' is a flawed conceptual tool which presumes to tell us that 'agency' no longer matters; intellectual development in the field of international communication appears not to proceed on the basis of exhaustive testing but lurches from one theory, preoccupation, dimension to another with inadequate attention to accumulative construction.

In particular I am interested in the concept of 'media imperialism'. Far from this being a now dead concept, I want to argue that (i) it has never seriously been tested; (ii) it still has much to offer as an analytical tool, and (iii) by incorporating some of the key concerns of 'globalization' theory, including hybridity and the weakening of nation-states, the concept can easily be modified for application to the present time. Even if we accept that the significance of (geographical) territory as a domain for communications control is declining, this would be a poor reason for relaxing the critique of what I call the 'colonization of communications space'.

## Two models of media imperialism

The concept of media imperialism was developed within a broader analysis of cultural imperialism and dependency. Much of the basic analysis is heavily indebted to the works of Marx, Lenin and Rosa Luxemburg (see Boyd-Barrett, 1977a). Marxist analysis of imperialism was revisited by scholars in the 1960s and 1970s wanting to investigate the continuing dependence of post-colonial states on previous imperial powers within a context of post-Second World War US dominance. Political independence had to be judged within a context of continuing economic and cultural dependence (e.g. through education, ideas, media, language), not simply on specific ex-imperial powers, but on a capitalist world order which was dominated by the prevailing US industrial–military–political coalition (Baran and Sweezy, 1970). The strength of the capitalist world order has since been consolidated by the defeat of the Soviet Union and communist bloc. The USA is still the dominant economic and political power in the 1990s, but its share of global economic activity has nonetheless been in decline. Despite set-backs to the so-called 'tiger economies' of Southeast Asia in 1997–8, this part of the world, including Japan, India and China, is expected to continue its contribution to a major redistribution of economic power in the early part of the third millennium (although we should pause to note the part played by the USA, IMF and World Bank in bailing out some of these 'tigers' including, within a few months of 1997, Indonesia, South Korea and Thailand).

In this process of redistribution there is much evidence of alliances and interpenetration between erstwhile 'first-world' corporations and those of other parts of the world, and stronger evidence of two-way cultural flows. This process of redistribution can be viewed as a process of democratic, pluralistic levelling between nations; alternatively it may be seen as evidence of the reformation of a global economic power elite, now more broadly based, ethnically, but otherwise intensifying processes of corporate concentration without regard for national division and geography, as corporate giants battle it out on a global field of commercial war.

This changing configuration has implications for two principal models of media imperialism which were generated by scholars in the 1970s. The first was closely associated with Herbert Schiller (e.g. Schiller, 1976) and a group of Latin American scholars (e.g. Mattelart, 1979). Schiller's model understood US media imperialism in terms of its functions of selling media-related US hardware and software, promoting an image of the USA and of the world that was favourable to American interests, and of advertising American goods and services – directly through the provision of more channels for advertising, and indirectly through the display of consumer lifestyles.

More forceful than European models of political economy of that period, this view was a radical departure from the hitherto effects-dominated literature. It did not deal well with issues of meaning, audience and reception, which were to be the province of European cultural studies, but in its confident and comprehensive grasp of political economy and its relevance to media, it was unrivalled. It can be seen within the context of domestic and international opposition to the Vietnam War, which created a receptive environment for critiques of all forms of US expansionism. The thesis was simultaneously enriched and diluted by Tunstall's book, *The Media are American* (Tunstall, 1977), which explored a broader Anglo-American ambit of influence uniting old and new imperialisms, while also identifying significant centres of independent production. Latin American scholars (e.g. Mattelart, 1979) helped to locate media imperialism within a debate about how requirements of first-world economies, led by the United States, stunted the development of third-world economies. Just as Schiller's political economy undermined the effects paradigm in media research generally, so the Latin Americans undermined the 'modernization' paradigm, whose premise was that Western-style media expansion has a benign influence for national development.

The 'Schiller' model was based on powerful cases, particularly that of the USA, and also the influence of Great Britain and France. It can be critiqued for its restrictions of time and space (history and geography). In calling Schiller's model 'totalistic' (Boyd-Barrett, 1981/2) I drew attention to its presumption of continuing US dominance across time and space, a model so circular that it left no room for change or meaningful resistance. I also noted the uncompromising negativity of the analysis. An alternative approach would have been open to relative benefits and losses. There are many examples where US media influence arguably has had a liberating effect: for example, in countries where media systems are subject to authoritarian controls or to the cultural preferences of class elites (e.g. Schou, 1992).

An alternative model – I will call it the 'generic' model – developed in Europe. It also attributed great influence to the media expansion of major powers. It was rooted in Marxist theory and the media history of colonialism. It foregrounded the diversity of different dimensions of media expansion. It was committed to empirical demonstration above political rhetoric. Generic media imperialism is associated with my 1977 publications (Boyd-Barrett, 1977a, 1977b) and is also addressed in a 1980 publication by Chin-Chuan Lee. In my view it is widely applicable, across space and time, so that it can apply to UK–Ireland media relations or to those of Germany–Austria, Australia–New Zealand, China–Hong Kong–Taiwan, Egypt–Sudan, South Africa–Lesotho, Thailand–Laos, Russia and other republics of the Russian federation, etc.

This empirical model acknowledges the multidimensionality of media forms (see below) and degrees of dependence/imperialism. Therefore it allows for both high and low dependence – in this model, it does not really matter if there is a lot of it, or not much of it (it can be used to demonstrate the sometimes *weak* charges of media imperialism) nor need it be especially important whether the focus is the so-called 'third world' or the developed world. My starting point in 1977 was the preponderance of Hollywood products in UK cinema and the popularity of US soaps in British television. We can also apply this approach to media practices within nation-states, expressed territorially, or in such terms as inter-ethnic, inter-cultural, inter-class relations.

# Both models are still useful

Both these models of media imperialism are still useful. Although I want to push the argument beyond nation-to-nation relations, there is considerable evidence still of unequal international media activity, coupling strong media exporters to heavy media importers, and the USA still figures, unquestionably, amongst the former. I will give some examples:

(i) The British film industry, which in the late 1990s is stronger than it has been for many years, is still overshadowed by the success of Hollywood products, not least because the main distribution chains are linked with Hollywood. Although 103 UK films were produced in 1997 (of which 17 were US backed), the 193 US films on release in the UK in 1997 commanded 73.5 per cent of box-office revenue (an improvement at least on the 91–3 per cent typical of the early 1990s) (*Financial Times Screen Finance*, 1998). Control of distribution and exhibition fosters the success of other US commercial activities, including film-related branding of toys, clothes and other goods (Wasko, 1994), and fast-food franchises, often located side-by-side with exhibition outlets. Hollywood film dominance inevitably carries over to video sales and television replays. In cinema, video, pay television, interactive television and multimedia markets, dominated largely by North American products, the best expectation of the European Commission is that European products could see an increase in their market share rise from only 13 per cent in 1995 to a still very modest 21 per cent in 2005; programme-makers expect to see their share of the industry's total revenue rise from 28 per cent in 1995 to 30 per cent in 2005 (private communication from Tony Robinson, 4 November 1997). Puttnam (1997) notes that in 1995 the European Community ran an audio-visual trade deficit with the USA of $6.3 billion, possibly growing to $10 billion by 2000. What this deficit means, argues Puttnam, is 'a fundamental dislocation between the world of the imagination, created by the moving image, and the everyday lives of people around the globe' (Puttnam, 1997: 8), one that is supported by an alliance between Hollywood (the Motion Picture Exporters' Association of America) and Washington.

(ii) Major 'wholesale' suppliers of international television and print news to television and radio stations and daily newspapers throughout the world are news agencies (AP and APTV, Reuters and Reuters Television, WTN), whose headquarters are in New York, London and Paris, which directly or indirectly represent a lineage of global hegemony that reaches back to the middle of the nineteenth century. In addition to these are a few international satellite broadcasters, including BBC World, CNN, MSNBC, Fox Television and BSkyB, which are clients of the wholesalers but Bloomburg have significant news-gathering staffs of their own whose services are sometimes redistributed by local television channels (Boyd-Barrett, 1997).

(iii) Global manufacture of personal-computer operating systems is almost entirely in the hands of one US corporation, Microsoft, whose annual revenues in 1997 were $11.4 billion. Microsoft was the world's fourth largest corporation in 1998, worth $99 billion (Farrelly and Ryle, 1998). Production of chips for such machines is largely controlled by another American corporation, Intel, which in 1998 was the world's seventh largest corporation valued at $93 billion. Gateway services to the Internet are mainly controlled by two US software products, Microsoft Internet Explorer and Netscape, and 96 per cent of all Internet sites are located within the rich twenty-seven-nation OECD area (with English its lingua franca), dominated by the USA (Keegan, 1997).

In a critique of Microsoft, Newman (1997) argues that it threatens to control the standards of the Internet. Web-page designers tend to support software standards that are compatible with the dominant browser, and Microsoft has been paying Internet service providers to bundle Explorer with their services. It has signed exclusive deals with companies like Time Warner and Disney where Microsoft's Explorer will be required for access to parts of the web sites which those companies are establishing. Through control of desktop operating systems and Internet browsers, Microsoft seeks to control the business computers managing web sites at the other end. It also represents a threat to the computing standards of the Internet-oriented Java language – an open standard for running software over the Internet created by Sun Microsystems and supported by hundreds of other companies. Java was designed to be platform-independent. Microsoft's goal, argues Newman, is to undermine this multi-platform function, using its combination of browsers, operating systems and developer tools to divert Java into a new Microsoft-controlled proprietary system that runs best only on Windows-based machines.

When Microsoft invested in Apple Computer in 1997 it agreed that in exchange Apple would bundle Explorer with every Apple computer and support Microsoft's Java standards. (Further battle for the Internet waged between Internet giants Microsoft and Netscape in 1998 with Netscape's development of a flexible software platform which would give users access to the programming in order to develop customized versions.) Over 65 per cent of new intranet sites are deployed on Microsoft Windows NT servers (Newman, 1997). Microsoft control extends beyond operating systems and software applications to development tools used by a majority of programmers and has strong dominance of the training programmes of IT professionals. It is increasingly involved in other media delivery systems, including Dreamworks SKG (Hollywood movies), WebTV Networks, low-orbit satellite (Teledesic), Comcast Corp – these last three will extend Internet access to non-PC consumers – and many others, even including Black Entertainment Television.

(iv) Principal global media companies identified by Herman and McChesney (1997) are News Corporation ($10 billion in 1996 sales); Time Warner ($25 billion in 1996 sales, of which two-thirds are from the USA); Disney (with $24 billion in 1997 sales, of which some three-quarters are from the US market); Viacom ($13 billion in 1997 income, four-fifths of which comes from the US market); Bertelsmann, the one European firm among the 'first tier' of media giants, with sales of approximately $15 billion in 1996, of which 66 per cent derives from Europe and 24 per cent from the USA; TCI (1996 income of $7 billion) – the leading US cable provider; Universal, bought from Seagram for $5.7 billion in 1995; General Electric, with total sales of $80 billion in 1996, of which 62 per cent were from the USA, and included by Herman and McChesney because its owns NBC, which had $5 billion in sales in 1996.

These sales figures are modest if hardware, computing and telephony are included, as they must be if we are to establish the extent of current colonization activities in the communications industries. In the case of telephony, for example, US–SBC Communications, the Texas-based telecoms company, offered $4.4 billion early in 1998 simply for the purchase of Southern New England Telecommunications, in a move into the long-distance telephony market. SBC had just previously made a $16.5-billion acquisition of PacificTelesis Group, giving it California, Nevada and undersea access to Asia and land access to Mexican and South American markets. In early 1998, US telecoms group GTE was set to raise its $28-billion cash offer for long-distance telecoms specialist MCI, in the event that rival group WorldCom's $37 billion agreed bid failed to proceed. We are talking here about sums of money that range between two to four times the entire size of News Corporation's annual revenues, bigger than the size of many individual national economies, such as those of Malawi, Angola, Bangladesh, Bolivia, Bulgaria, Ireland, Kenya, Malaysia, New Zealand or Pakistan.

Herman and McChesney identify three tiers of global media players. In the second tier, nearly half of the listed companies are from North America. The success of companies in the second and third tiers partly depends on strategic alliances among themselves and with companies in the top tier. Herman and McChesney argue that the global media market is still dominated by US interests and by the US domestic market, although its proportionate importance is bound to decline as other nations grow more prosperous and more media-active. Yet the world media system will continue to have a strong US flavour well into the next century. US companies can generally recoup costs from their domestic market and can then manipulate prices in overseas markets according to what each market is prepared to pay and the intensity of local competition. What these authors do not tell us, however, is the overall, global size of the media market and what proportion of this is commanded by each of their three tiers.

Even if such phenomena are historically specific, the concept of media imperialism is appropriate for the investigation of any periods in which access to or control of any dimension of media activity is controlled by any one nation or group at the expense at others. What I am indicating here is a reconceptualization of imperialism as a process having to do with the colonization of communications space. This may have an international character, as in the above examples, or may be represented by instances such as the dominance of television markets by single, home-grown corporations which dominate production and transmission within national markets, as in the cases of Brazil and Mexico (cf. Cole, 1996; Fox, 1997).

In this framework, communications space has no necessary relationship with territory nor with technology, but it does necessarily have to do with the resources and fora for human expression. In its analysis of those who gain control over such resources and fora, it is proposed that we can identify structural consistencies which do often relate to territory and other markers of identity, but more importantly have to do with political and economic power. It is in the relationship between communications space and power that we find justification for retaining the vocabulary of imperialism, especially upon investigation of the giant, intensifying and global concentrations of capital that have driven the development of media industries in recent decades. The model also insists on multidimensionality and on empirical measures: it can reveal the extent to which specific activities within particular sectors of the communications industries are controlled by identifiable agents or interests; final judgement as to whether the findings amount to 'colonization' of communications space is a relative judgement, one that takes account of the overall context and the values of different affected interests.

Territorial imperialism has as its object the conquest of a finite territory; the ambitions of conquerors may lead them to annex yet more territory; eventually they are stopped – by oceans, impassable or impregnable mountains, overwhelming adverse military power, etc. The object of ambition in the case of communications space does from some perspectives seem deceptively finite: a limited range of national newspapers, for example, can be said to be financially viable. One may add a further title, define a new audience or seduce one from existing publications, often at great cost and risk. Yet communications space demonstrates astonishing elasticity. Technical innovation, especially, often generates more space, and there have been many periods in which such space is radically extended – as in the case of the introduction of radio, for instance, or of the Internet – and temporarily there may seem to be enough space for every claimant.

But the value of communications space is enhanced relative to the size and quality of audiences which can be attracted to any given message for which the space is used. Those interests which have the resources and skills to attract large audiences and the revenues which attend such success typically gain great influence over regulatory structures governing producer and audience access. They achieve the power to define what the space is and how it should be used. We are beginning to see this happen with the Internet.

A feature of this model, therefore, is the symbiotic tension between the physical potential for communication, on the one hand, and technology, control and skills, on the other. That is to say, the physical potential for communication is itself extended or limited by particular choices as to the technologies that are employed for its exploitation, the regulatory structures which govern communication space and its uses, and the skills that users bring to the processes of communication. Technologies, regulatory structures and skills are resources of control, each of which has discriminatory tendencies: technologies may be more or less expensive, more or less suitable for certain forms of communication, even for certain languages of communication; regulations tend to favour certain categories of use and user over others; skills are the product of experience and training which are often in restricted supply.

Such inequalities are a common feature of trade relationships and have sometimes been attributed to the economics of competitive advantage, where success is often self-reinforcing. Such explanations do not render the phenomenon politically and culturally neutral in the way that some economists seem to imagine. In the case of media there are unique reasons for concern, having to do with relativities of power in access to mass audiences and to the infrastructures of any communications which are independent of physical proximity. Access to mass audiences is related to opportunities for the construction of dominating symbolic imagery, cognitive persuasion and affect, for political, economic and cultural purposes. Access to infrastructures has implications for the kinds of communication that are possible, and for the economic conditions under which use of such communications is permissible.

We can distinguish between media imperialism as an objective, empirical phenomenon and as a *discourse*. Worries about the import of popular US soaps may sometimes seem out of proportion when consideration is given to the decreasing proportion of audience attention – in some regions – that is spent in viewing them (see Goonasekera, 1996), the greater popularity of local productions, and strong evidence of local production and control of other areas of media activity, such as in radio or the press. Nonetheless, the discourse of concern about the presence of North American popular culture (or of any culture considered as 'other'), the dangers attributed to the values that this is said to represent, and the measures taken to reduce or off-set it, is worthy of serious study in itself, and especially for what insight it affords into the struggle for power over communications space, its resources, uses and audiences, or into the way in which such issues are incorporated within wider struggles.

The concept of 'imperialism', burdened by a weight of ideological baggage, sometimes unhelpful to this investigation (notably in its predisposition always to assume negative implications) helps us to (i) concentrate on *agency*; (ii) have regard for inequalities; (iii) be alert to communications regulation as conquest, never less so than when it is expressed as part of a natural or inevitable state of affairs (e.g. the 'scarcity of airwaves' justification for pre-1980s broadcasting monopolies; 'guarantee of universal service' for telecommunications monopolies; 'free market' for deregulation and privatization, etc.); (iv) and to be conscious of communications space as the site for struggle and resistance.

# Definitions

My provisional definition of media imperialism (Boyd-Barrett, 1977b) was a sentence somewhat out of context of the main body of my work on this subject at that time, and does not well represent the overall argument. For example, the definition makes no explicit reference to authors or readers. This omission was not an endorsement of a 'hypodermic-needle' model of media effect; indeed, the article itself called for much more sophisticated treatment than was then common of the encounter between audiences and international media texts.

In choosing to talk of 'media imperialism' as opposed to 'cultural imperialism' I was not suggesting that we should consider media without full reference to their broader social, cultural, economic and political contexts, which would indeed have been a regressive step. Instead, I was concerned about the necessity for a focus on the media industries: only by taking into account the full complexity of this economic sector, by getting inside the 'black box' of meaningful production, could we generate theory that was adequate to the task and take us beyond the fairly crude political rhetoric that was part of the NWICO debate then at its height. Cultural studies was beginning to embark on a line of enquiry that led towards notions of the autonomous reader and polysemy of texts. Important and necessary though that development was, it diverted attention away from the political economy of communications production at a crucial moment of history in which the entire infrastructure and superstructure of communications industries, whose value ultimately rests on their audiences, were subject to egregious assault by gigantic concentrations of national and international capital.

## *Benefits of the concept*

For all its limitations, there is a certain heuristic value in revisiting my original definition of media imperialism: 'The process whereby the ownership, structure, distribution or content of the media in any one country are singly or together subject to substantial external pressures from the media interests of any other country or countries without proportionate reciprocation of influence by the country so affected' (Boyd-Barrett, 1977b: 117).

One of its main strengths, I believe, is that it recognized that imperialism could vary between different media, and between different levels, dimensions or spheres of activity within any one sector of the media industries. The definition in itself refers to ownership, structure, distribution or content. It was quite possible, indeed common, for example, to find national ownership coexisting with high dependence on imports.

My 1977b article further differentiated between: the shape of the communication vehicle, a set of industrial arrangements, a body of values about ideal practice, and specific media contents. Placing the most manifest element of media activity, content, at the end of the list, this breakdown highlighted the relativity of media technologies: technologies as the products of commercial and other interests, not independent, inevitable or unalterable variables. It called attention to the structure and organization of media industries as matters of cultural, commercial and political convention (this could apply to the relationship between advertising and content, the contracting-out of production, etc.) which could and have been exported to other contexts. It also highlighted the relativity of professional and occupational ideologies and definitions of best practice: for example, Anglo-American construction of news-as-fact (selected according to values of eliteness, negativity, and so on) in opposition to French journalism of opinion, socialist journalism of agit-prop, or third-world journalism of development news.

In 1980, Chin-Chuan Lee differentiated between television-programme exportation, foreign ownership and control of media outlets, transfer of dominant broadcasting norms, media commercialism, the invasion of capitalist world views and infringement upon indigenous ways of life in adopting societies (Lee, 1980). This work demonstrates a general tendency in the literature to deal with only one medium at a time, whereas from the point of view of the whole culture, and of the audience, what matters is balance across available communications space. Internet and media convergence have extended the boundaries of traditional academic discourse about media. For example, we now need to allow for such concepts as gateway provider and telecommunications carrier. One model (KPMG, 1996) suggests a 'convergence value chain' that differentiates between: content, production, packaging, service provision, conveyance and consumer interface. There is scope for considerably more complexity, if we wish: content can be broken down into various stages of production, component supply (for example, animation, graphics, news-film, library services, still photographs) and programme formatting. We should also include factors to do with 'production' and 'readership' competency (for instance, IT skills) and consider who is involved in defining these, in relation to whose technologies, for what purposes or functions, and the distribution of such skills across relevant populations.

My 1977 model (Boyd-Barrett 1977a, 1977b) combined the elements of 'cultural invasion' and 'imbalance of power resources' between countries; imperialism could result through either deliberate export or through unintentional influence. There was nothing in the definition itself that proposed positive or negative values associated with the concept, except possibly in the choice of the term 'imperialism' to describe it.

## Problems with the concept

There were some significant problems with the definition. It talked about inter-*media* relations, and excluded non-media interests. So in itself it did not invite consideration of the extra-media powers or interests (political, or related to non-media commercial activities of media owners and their business and propaganda goals) that had invested in media companies. The definition also talked about reciprocity of cultural trade-relationships between named countries. This privileges international relations, and ignores other relevant dimensions, including the range of choice available on domestic markets between sources of local origin. It assumes that nation-states are the basic building blocks within the field of global media activities, and that it is possible simply to associate particular media with particular countries. The globalization debate certainly raises questions about the sovereignty of nation-states, challenged as they are by both centrifugal forces from within (such as secessionist movements) and centripetal forces from without (through regional trade associations such as the EC, ASEAN, NAFTA, WTO, etc.), although I believe it exaggerates the extent to which this is a new problem.

However, too often there is a blurring of the distinction between global activity of corporations which have no strong domestic base, and corporations which do have strong domestic bases – generally in first-world countries – and have extensive (but rarely spread evenly) global activity. This raises the possibility to my mind that in this period to which we refer as globalization, the sovereignty of some nation-states is undermined to support that of others, another manifestation of neo-imperialism. But substantial powers are still invested in issues of sovereignty, whether in domains of trade, culture or politics, and the mapping of the place of media with respect to such issues is a live and legitimate topic for investigation. Because media systems are often complex hybrids of different agencies and actors, it is not advisable to make simple identification of whole corporations with particular national identities – this is precisely why we need to take account of the multidimensionality of media activity. At the same time, the media-imperialism thesis needs to encompass neo-colonialisms of inter-ethnic, inter-cultural, inter-gender, inter-generational and inter-class relations.

My 1977b definition ignored the question of audience; this is a significant but not irreparable omission. The model needs to take account of audiences, audience preferences; audience consumption of specified cultural products as a proportion of total media and non-media consumption. Yet we must not assume any simple correlation between colonization of communication space and the attitudes, beliefs and behaviours of audiences. We might expect in some circumstances to find precisely the reverse – it is in the nature of imperialism to provoke violent resistance. It is not in the area of effects that we need to look for justification of an enquiry into colonization of communications space, but in relation to the question: whose voices get to be heard, and which voices are excluded? That is all. Whether the voices that do get to be heard are popular with audiences, try to manipulate them, are honest or dishonest, intelligent and entertaining or otherwise, etc., is of great interest and importance, but within an overriding concern for the democratization of communication it is the obstacles in the way of access to mass audiences that should have research priority. Regardless of the sophistication of technologies, the degree of development and democratization, only a tiny fraction of the world's population possess the resources, opportunity and skills that permit such access. In an age of democracy we have media tyranny.

Not even the Internet is a response: access to the Internet requires equipment, gateway subscriptions and skills, but no amount of access to the Internet guarantees mass audiences: that requires the kind of technical and production skills that we associate with the large media corporations.

# Applications

In recent years the global–local mix looks more complex than in the 1970s. In the 1990s as in the 1970s there are significant centres of media production which enjoy international influence in what used to be called the developing world: for example, Bombay for Hindi film, Cairo for Arabic television, radio and print production, Mexico and Brazil for *telenovelas*. Some new centres have appeared, as in the case of Hong Kong as supplier of television programming for mainland China, Taiwan and the Chinese diaspora; also, Australia, which in addition to a state-subsidized film export trade has generated several soap operas which have proved successful in various other countries, generally English-speaking (but not the USA), notably Britain (Cunningham and Jacka, 1996). Major domestic broadcasters which used to be heavily dependent on imports now produce more of their own, or their spread of dependence on imports has extended to include sources that are alternative to traditional first-world offerings.

Many parts of the world enjoy an extended choice of programme and media products that would have been inconceivable in the 1970s, at least in terms of quantity. Cities such as Buenos Aires, where most households are served by multi-channel (fifty to sixty channels) cable television, or India, where local cable network clients have a choice of several international and domestic satellite-delivered television services in a variety of local languages, as well as in English and Hindi, are actually now more 'advanced' in this respect than the UK, where most of the population still receives only a range of four or five (depending on area) terrestrial networks, despite increasing availability of direct satellite broadcasting and cable. In Europe generally the number of television stations doubled in the period 1990–6 from approximately 125 to 250. Digital services increased from 10 in 1996 to 330 in 1997 (Agence Europe, 24 October 1997). Such increases in quantity are accompanied by increasing capacity and falling costs. For example, the cost to transmit one analogue channel on Astra in 1997 was roughly £4m p.a.; this falls to £500,000 with digital 8 to 1 compression, falling to £250,000 by 1998 (Singer, 1997). In some parts of the world, such as India, television-set ownership is now ahead of radio ownership (although half of all adults in India still possessed neither in 1993–5, cf. Mytton, 1996).

For the Middle East there are now several satellite television stations, catering mainly for Arabic populations, of which the most successful are based in Beirut, Cairo, London and Rome; many others are planned. In 1996 almost every Arab state operated at least one satellite television channel, and by 1997 there were over forty Arab commercial satellite channels (Ayish, 1997). In the United Arab Emirates, the bulk of the population is made up of immigrants from India and Pakistan. Locally available Arabic programming takes little account of their presence. Instead, this worker force has a choice of ten satellite channels beamed from the Indian subcontinent. In the USA, Canada, Australia and Great Britain, on the other hand, major ethnic groups are comparatively well catered for through ethnic broadcast, video and print media, and opportunities for specialist communication needs are increasing with the development of Internet websites.

The identity of major players, while still heavily represented by corporations with close links to the USA and other first-world countries including Japan, has also become more complex. Nowhere is this more evident than in the changing panorama of telecommunications growth, where privatized ex-PTTs such as those of Spain, Italy, Malaysia and others are increasingly involved in complex alliances (often with the giants, such as AT&T, British Telecom, Sprint or MTI) for the capture of overseas markets in local and long-distance telephony and related services, which increasingly include such activities as cable, subscription TV and mobile telephony.

The phenomenon of international journalism is still associated mainly with prestige titles (e.g. *Wall Street Journal, Financial Times, Time, Newsweek, International Herald Tribune*) selling to elite business audiences (Sparks, 1997), and most national press systems are still strongly 'local' in terms of ownership and structure; but the influence of international press corporations such as Murdoch's News Corporation (especially in the USA, Britain and Australia), or O'Reilly's Independent group (with strong interests in South African press and radio, for example) and Conrad Black's domination of the Canadian press through the Southam newspaper group, testifies to the continuing importance of corporatism in press journalism.

Growth of local production in, say, television content, may coexist with dependence on the purchase of programme-formats developed in the West and managed by first-world franchise agents and consultants. Centres that were once strong in local production may now be threatened and overtaken by international satellite distribution (Fox, 1997), which, because it reaches larger markets, attracts more advertising revenue and can sell more cheaply. This may now be a threat to hitherto Latin American giants. Availability of cable television, international satellite and video in India is weakening the influence of the Bombay film industry. Overall growth in capacity increases dependence on imports to fill available time, especially formulaic imports which guarantee the interest of large, international advertisers. Television today is increasingly a high-technology, low-personnel business run from modest offices and even private villas, where many of the essential operations, including programming, advertising sales, news provision and transmission, are contracted out to other companies, greatly complicating the issue of identities of origin.

Charting this growing complexity is a major task for scholars of international communication and may be the just cause for at least some element of celebration (Sreberny-Mohammadi, 1991). Persisting through this complexity, however, are the highly visible, imposing brand-names of transnational media power with indisputable first-world associations, incorporating such household names as Microsoft, News Corporation, Twentieth Century Fox, US Fox, HarperCollins, Asian Star Television, BSkyB, Times Warner, Viacom, HBO, Atari, Sony, Bertelsmann, NBC, EMI, Disney, ABC, Dreamworks, Bell South, America Online, ESPN, MTV, TCI, Polygram, DirecTV, New York Times, Reader's Digest, Mcgraw-Hill, Dow Jones, Reuters, British Broadcasting Corporation, Axel Springer, Canal-Plus, Reed-Elsevier, Pearson, and many, many others.

It is precisely to help make sense of this complexity that application of the framework of media imperialism continues to be relevant. In applying this conceptual framework, we are likely to find evidence of (i) considerable disparity between different areas of media activity, and (ii) considerable internal variations within any single area of media activity.

In the case of news agencies, for example, I concluded (Boyd-Barrett and Thussu, 1992; Boyd-Barrett, 1997) that this sector of the communications industry mapped better than many to patterns of 'imperialism', both in the past (in the nineteenth-century cartel operated by Reuters, the French Havas and German Wolff), and, in effect, though under much more open market conditions, still today, and I noted that:

(i)   The total number of global print agencies has diminished rather than increased.

(ii)   There has been a growth of television and Internet news providers but these are either closely tied to existing major media players in the USA and UK, principally, or represent new formations of capital, principally representing the USA.

(iii)  There is little evidence to suggest that major imbalances with respect to distribution of resources or attention, or arising from the application of Western news values, have grown weaker; indeed, they may have grown stronger.

(iv)   There is little encouraging evidence that alternative media (for example, DepthNews, Gemini, Inter Press Service) have had a significant impact on mainstream media.

The maintenance or even the intensification of evidence of media imperialism with respect to news agencies may coexist with an increase in, say, overall domestication of television content (although content is only one variable in the multivariable phenomenon of television production, text and supply). We would still have to take account of the fact that television is host to many different sources of material, and that national news programmes may contain much material taken from international news agencies; or that domestically produced television may be based on specific formats that have been 'bought in' from international players who hold copyright claims to those formats.

Even within the relatively strong-case context of news agencies, on further enquiry I have found that issues of media imperialism are enormously complicated and multivariable, and if this is the case with news agencies then it is almost certainly the case with other spheres of media activity. In a previous article (Boyd-Barrett, 1981/2) I identified three core dimensions in news-agency activity, and their component variables, with a view to demonstrating how different variables may move in different directions with respect to their significance for media imperialism. The core dimensions were:

(i)    the extent to which the media in a country are dependent upon services imported from and provided by the major news services (<u>dependency</u> dimension

(ii)   the extent to which the nondomestic activities of the major agencies are affected by factors brought to bear on them by the national government or other indigenous powers within any specific client area (client countries or individual clients should not be regarded as wholly passive) (<u>production/processing</u> dimension)

(iii)  the extent to which the content of major news services is culturally, politically, morally, or in any other way 'alien' to their clienteles (content or <u>cultural</u> dimension).

Illustrating the complexity, I will briefly summarize the findings relating to one of these three dimensions, namely dependency variables, where I concluded that in relation to how far developing countries are dependent, we can say that there is likely to be a high degree of cultural dependency by news-media clients on the services of the major Western news agencies under the following conditions:

(i)     when a high consumption of agency material exists, this consumption representing a high proportion of all news provided by retail news media, both across the various categories of news and across most news media

(ii)    when agency material represents a high proportion of all news made available to domestic client media from exogenous sources and a high proportion of all such news actually consumed for retail purposes

(iii)   when alternative news sources also depend heavily in various ways on the activities of the major agencies and share important similarities with these (NB: this would affect much of the news available through available sources on Internet)

(iv)    in terms of news contents, dependence in general is reinforced by dependence in the identification of which stories are to be considered 'really important', and with respect to the general priorities ascribed to different categories of news, and if stories are not appreciably altered, shortened or augmented from other sources

(v)     retail media are unable to achieve alternative patterns of supply and consumption, and local political forces are not engaged in, or do not succeed in, establishing alternative supply patterns that also meet the legitimate requirements of news media and the general public.

We can also identify the following dependency variables:

(vi)    whether the services of all four major Western agencies are or are not equally available, and in practice whether dependence is intensified to reliance on only one or two of the major agencies

(vii)   whether dependence upon the agencies as sources of *in situ* 'wholesale' news is or is not extended to their other services, such as those provided to foreign correspondents, consultancy, training, equipment assistance, the effective sub-leasing of agency communications to retail media, translation and so forth.

# Conclusion

In arguing for the reformulation of the theory of media imperialism I am not saying that we should or need fail to take into account some of the flimsier elements of the cultural-imperialism theory generally or of the media-imperialism theory in particular. It should be said, nonetheless, that some of the arguments that have been rehearsed against both cultural and media imperialism (cf. Sreberny-Mohammadi, 1991) were only typical of cruder manifestations of such theories. For example, generally speaking, it is not true that the media-imperialism theory assumed a hypodermic-needle model of media effects, nor does the theory require such a model to justify its importance. Nor is it true that those who argued about cultural and media imperialism held a simplistic view of non-Western cultures, assuming them to be pure and unsullied from previous cultural influences. This charge is a red herring.

The significance of media-imperialism theory is in part premised on the necessity to understand the nature of the relationship between national economies and the global capitalist economy, and the role of culture and media in helping to sustain and reinvigorate that relationship. It is not true that media imperialism focused only on relations between first and third worlds and ignored relations of cultural inequality and imposition within the first world, as I have already indicated with reference to concerns about the influence of North American media in countries such as Canada and Britain and the rest of Western Europe. Nor is it true that the media-imperialism theory typically ignored sources of local production: such awareness was very much part of Tunstall's work, for example, at the very beginning of the debate.

There were two principal defects of the media-imperialism theory, in addition to those that I have already discussed. The first is that in the early days it was too much embedded in a radical political discourse against the USA. Less restrictively, it was embedded in a radical dependency discourse that grew from the work of Latin American scholars. This had value, as we have seen, in that it took account of the integration of the work of media as agents of political, cultural and commercial ideology and propaganda, and their value as hardware and software commercial products.

To this could be added the place of media within a discourse of national political and economic 'development': this is a controversial discourse, but we can certainly conclude from recent literature that media do have a role to play in constructions of nation and national identity (e.g. Scannell and Cardiff, 1991; Das and Harindranath, 1996), and that in a wide variety of ways, from fostering a demand for electricity through to facilitating business communications across modern telephony and computer networks, the media contribute to economic development and, at the very least, to the integration of business elites with the global economy. It is also important to take serious account of media contributions to education and information across a wide range of 'pro-social' contexts.

The media-imperialism theory was concerned initially with media inequalities between nations, and with how such inequalities reflected broader problems of dependency, but the metaphor of imperialism and colonialism was not sufficiently extended to include intra-national media relations (although the co-option of local elites into transnational business enterprise in opposition to the interests of non-elites was dealt with), or media fostering of inequalities between men and women, different ethnicities and between capital and labour. Arguably, the theory did not stress sufficiently the systematic patterns of ownership, industrial and technical structure, and ideology of practice that help to explain the extraordinarily limited opportunities for access to the means of production and transmission for addressing mass audiences – a scarcity of voices, a lack of diversity, that is characteristic of *all countries* of the world, and it is to this concern that the present chapter is mostly committed. The phenomenon of imperialism therefore is geographically all-pervasive.

The second major defect of the media-imperialism theory is that it has never been empirically applied to a sufficiently comprehensive degree. True, the field has benefited from a relatively modest number of individual case studies, generally focusing on single media in single countries, and sometimes focusing solely on one dimension of media activity, usually content.

In company with political economy and radical theory generally, the media-imperialism theory was set back by developments in the 1980s, including the reinvention of capitalist rhetoric by Reagan and Thatcher, the short-lived boom of the late 1980s, the growth of the 'tiger economies' in Southeast Asia and the decline of the communist East, all of which fed a growing scepticism about the validity and relevance of dependence and imperialism theories, scepticism which infected academe. In a changing climate of deregulation and enhanced communications capacity, there were significant increases in media production within some developing countries, alongside high population mobility and intensification of trade – promoting an increasing hybridity of global culture, ever more complex and more commodified, but everywhere more complex and commodified in the same sort of way. For a time these processes threw investigators off the scent, disguising the inevitability of global concentration behind a smokescreen of local proliferation. Cultural studies and postmodernism inspired facile counsel on the basis of notions of textual polysemy that there is nothing to fear from oligopolization, commodification and, too often, the moronization (or worse) of global communication space. The media-imperialism theory is a first step towards the measurement and evaluation of such trends with a view to holding responsible agencies accountable for what they do.

# References

Ayish, M. (1997) Arab television goes commercial: a case study of the Middle East Broadcasting Centre, *Gazette*, 59.6, Dec., pp. 473–94.

Baran, P. and Sweezy, P. M. (1970) *Monopoly Capital*, Penguin, Harmondsworth.

Boyd-Barrett, O. (1977a) Mass communications in cross-cultural contexts, Unit 5 of *Mass Communication and Society*, Open University Press, Milton Keynes.

Boyd-Barrett, O. (1977b) Media imperialism: towards an international framework for the analysis of media systems, pp. 116–35 in Curran, J. and Gurevitch, M. (eds) *Mass Communication and Society*, Edward Arnold, London.

Boyd-Barrett, O. (1981/2) Western news agencies and the 'media imperialism' debate: what kind of data-base, *Journal of International Affairs*, 35.2, pp. 247–60.

Boyd-Barrett, O. (1997) Global news wholesalers as agents of globalization, pp. 131–44, in Sreberny-Mohammadi, A. et al. (eds) *Media in Global Context*, Arnold, London.

Boyd-Barrett, O. and Thussu, D. K. (1992) *Contra-flow in Global News*, John Libbey, London.

Cole, R. (1996) *Communication in Latin America: Journalism, Mass Media and Society*, Jaguar Books, Wilmington.

Cunningham, S. and Jacka, E. (1996) *Australian Television and International Mediascapes*, Cambridge University Press, Cambridge.

Das, S. and Harindranath, R. (1996) Nation-state, national identity and the media, Unit 22 of the MA in Mass Communications (by distance learning), Centre for Mass Communication Research, University of Leicester, Leicester.

Farrelly, P. and Ryle, S. (1998) Drug giants merger puts 10,000 UK jobs at risk, *Observer*, 1 Feb.

*Financial Times Screen Finance*, 8 Jan. 1998.

Fox, E. (1997) *Latin American Broadcasting: From Tango to Telenovela*, University of Luton Press, London.

Goonasekera, A. (1996) Asian audiences for Western media, Unit 44b in the MA in Mass Communications (by distance learning), Centre for Mass Communications Research, University of Leicester, Leicester.

Herman, E. and McChesney, R. (1997) *The Global Media: The New Missionaries of Corporate Capitalism*, Cassell, London.

Keegan, V. (1997) What a Web we weave, *Guardian*, 13 May, pp. 2–3.

KPMG (1996) *Public Policy Issues Arising from Telecommunications and Audiovisual Convergence*, European Commission.

Lee, C. C. (1980) *Media Imperialism Reconsidered: The Homogenizing of Television Culture*, Sage, London.

Mattelart, A. (1979) *Multinational Corporations and the Control of Culture*, Harvester Press, Brighton.

Mytton, G. (1996) Audience research, Unit 25 in the MA in Mass Communications (by distance learning), Centre for Mass Communication Research, University of Leicester, Leicester.

Newman, N. (1997) *From Microsoft Word to Microsoft World: How Microsoft is Building a Global Monopoly*, A NetAction White Paper, Nathan@netaction.org.

Puttnam, D. (1997) Terminated, too, *Guardian*, 9 May, pp. 8–9.

Scannell, P. and Cardiff, D. (1991) *A Social History of British Broadcasting: Volume One 1922–1939: Serving the Nation*, Basil Blackwell, Oxford.

Schiller, H. (1976) *Communications and Cultural Domination*, M. E. Sharpe, New York.

Schou, S. (1992), Postwar Americanization and the revitalization of European Culture, pp. 142–58 in Schroder, C. and Skovmand, M. (eds) *Media Cultures*, Sage, London.

Singer, A. (1997) Speech to Royal Television Society, Cambridge Convention, 18–21 Sept.

Sparks, C. (1997) Towards a global public sphere? Paper presented to course conference, MA in Mass Communications (by distance learning), University of Leicester, 22 Nov.

Sreberny-Mohammadi, A. (1991) The global and the local in international communications, pp. 118–38 in Curran, J. and Gurevitch, M. (eds) *Mass Media and Society*, Edward Arnold, London.

Sreberny-Mohammadi, A. (1996) From globalization to imperialism and back again, Unit 19 in the MA in Mass Communications (by distance learning), Centre for Mass Communications Research, University of Leicester, Leicester.

Tomlinson, J. (1991) *Cultural Imperialism: A Critical Introduction*, John Hopkins University Press, Baltimore.

Tunstall, J. (1977) *The Media are American*, Constable, London.

Wasko, J. (1994) *Hollywood and the Information Age*, Polity Press, Cambridge.

# 10

# *Global and regional dynamics of international television flows*

STUART CUNNINGHAM, ELIZABETH JACKA AND JOHN SINCLAIR

A sea-change in television systems around the world began in the late 1970s. An integral element in the various complex phenomena usually captured under the rubric of 'globalisation', this transformation has forced the West to confront the television cultures of the more 'peripheral' regions of the world. Shifting geo-political patterns within the world system, most notably the partial dismantling of national boundaries in Europe, the demise of communism and the rise of the Asian economies, are having a profound effect on cultural ecologies and the consequent receptiveness of many regions of the world to new cultural influences, including new sources and kinds of television. Alongside this, and related to it, the last 10 years have seen major changes in the television cultures of many countries as technological innovation, industrial realignments and modifications in regulatory philosophy have begun to produce a new audio-visual landscape.

## The transformation of the audio-visual landscape

All these changes in turn have been part of a broader movement in the Western world, spearheaded by the USA and the UK, towards a 'post-Fordist' mode of organisation of the economy, composed of four major elements – globalisation, trade liberalisation, increased national and international competition, and a decrease in the centrality of the state as a provider of goods and services. These tendencies in the advanced Western

This chapter is based on material first published in chapters 1 and 7 of John Sinclair, Elizabeth Jacka and Stuart Cunningham (eds) *New Patterns in Global Television: Peripheral Vision*, Oxford University Press, Oxford and New York 1996, by permission of Oxford University Press.

economies were all reflected in the arena of communications and the cultural industries, but with the added factor of a revolution in technology which promised, at least according to its enthusiasts, to abolish spectrum scarcity and bring about a new era of diversity and choice in broadcasting services.

At the forefront of the technological changes in broadcasting technology was the satellite, which abolished distance and allowed for the first time the linking of remote territories into new viewing communities. There is no doubt that the satellite has acted as a kind of 'Trojan horse' of media liberalisation. Although evidence from Europe and elsewhere indicates that satellite services originating outside national borders do not usually attract levels of audience that would really threaten traditional national viewing patterns, the ability of satellite delivery to transgress borders has been enough to encourage generally otherwise reluctant governments to allow greater internal commercialisation and competition.

The most significant innovation has undoubtedly been the advent of STAR TV, the pan-Asian satellite service which operates from Hong Kong. Asian television cultures traditionally have been heavily controlled politically and protected from a high level of Western programming, but STAR TV has introduced them to new sources of programming, especially from the West, and exposed them to diverse sources of news reporting. Although the advent of STAR TV seems to demonstrate that attempts to control the national television space are fruitless, some Asian governments still seek to maintain bans on satellite receiver dishes, notably China, Malaysia and Singapore.

In this new era, global, regional, national and even local circuits of programme exchange overlap and interact in a multifaceted way, no doubt with a great variety of cultural effects which are impossible to conceptualise within the more concentric perspective appropriate to previous decades. Instead of the image of 'the West' at the centre dominating the peripheral 'third world' with an outward flow of cultural products, we now can see the world as divided into a number of regions which each have their own internal dynamics as well as their global ties. Although primarily based on geographic realities, these regions are also defined by common cultural, linguistic and historical connections which transcend physical space. Such a dynamic, regionalist view of the world helps us to analyse in a more nuanced way the intricate and multidirectional flows of television across the globe.

By the mid-1980s it had become evident that the cultural-imperialism discourse, within which international cultural influence had been framed, had serious inadequacies, both as theory and in terms of the reality which the theory purported to explain. Actual transformation of the world television system made it less and less sustainable on the empirical level, and shifting theoretical paradigms, including postmodernism, post-colonialism, and theories of the 'active' audience, made its conceptual foundations less secure (Sinclair, 1990; Tomlinson, 1991; McAnany and Wilkinson, 1992; Naficy, 1993).

To take the empirical aspect first: even in Latin America, virtually the cradle of the theorisation of cultural imperialism, US imports were prominent only in the early stages. As the industry matured in Latin America, and as it developed 'critical mass', US imports were to a significant extent replaced by local products, a pattern that can be found repeated many times over around the world, and currently shaping Europe's new privately owned services. Of course, not all countries in Latin America have the capacity to develop sizeable indigenous television-production industries. Rather, the pattern in Latin America, as in Asia and the Middle East, is that each 'geolinguistic region' as we shall call them is itself dominated by one or two centres of audio-visual production – Mexico and Brazil for Latin America, Hong Kong and Taiwan for the Chinese-speaking populations of Asia, Egypt for the Arab world, and India for the Indian populations of Africa and Asia. The Western optic through which the cultural-imperialism thesis was developed literally did not see these non-Western systems of regional exchange, nor understand what they represented.

As theory, the cultural-imperialism critique tended to identify the USA as the single centre of a process of mediacentric capitalist cultural influence which emanated out to the rest of the world in the form of television programmes. It also assumed that these programmes had an inevitable and self-sufficient ideological effect upon their helpless audiences in the periphery. Although this rationale established a theoretical connection between US television programmes and 'consumerism', it did not address the question of just how such a mechanism of effect might work, nor how it could be observed in action upon actual audiences. In the discourse of cultural imperialism, the mystique of television entertainment's multivalent appeal for its audiences, and how specific audiences responded to it, was never on the agenda.

Other shortcomings arose from the theory's emphasis on external forces from the USA, and the corresponding disregard for the internal sociological factors within the countries seen to be subject to them. In its eagerness to hold US companies, and behind them, the US government, responsible for regressive sociocultural changes in the 'third world', the cultural-imperialism critique neglected the internal historical and social dynamics within the countries susceptible to their influence. This left out of consideration the strategic social structural position of the individuals and interest groups who benefited from facilitating US market entry or even from taking their own initiatives. Some of these have subsequently built up their own international media empires, some notable cases of which will be discussed further on.

Cultural-imperialism theory failed to see that, more fundamental than its supposed ideological influence, the legacy of the USA in world television development was in the implantation of its systemic model for television as a medium – the exploitation of entertainment content so as to attract audiences which could then be sold to advertisers. American content may have primed this process, but as the experience of many parts of the peripheral world shows, it is not required to sustain it.

If the discourse of cultural imperialism has proved inadequate to understand the more complex international patterns of television production, distribution and consumption as they became evident in the 1980s, and the responses which audiences make to the television available to them, what new theories have become available which might serve these purposes? As Richard Collins has observed, there has been no adequate replacement for the fallen 'dominant ideology paradigm' in which cultural-imperialism theory had grounded its view of the world (Collins, 1990: 4–5). One important reason for this is that in the process by which postmodernism has succeeded neo-Marxism as the master paradigm in social and cultural theory, the new orthodoxy has taught us to be sceptical of such 'grand narratives' or totalising theories as that of cultural imperialism.

Yet, it must also be said that within postmodernism itself, there is no clear theoretical model with which to understand the international trade in television programmes. On the contrary, postmodernism has tended to valorise the fractured cultural meanings of all images and goods, and to conflate the actual processes by which they are produced, distributed and consumed. In this context, it is ironic to recall the exhortation of Jorge Schement and his colleagues more than a decade ago that we disengage from the 'grand theory' of both the 'free-flow' and the 'American-hegemony' paradigms in favour of Robert Merton's 'theory of the middle range' (Schement et al., 1984), yet this now appears to be just the level of abstraction to which we should now climb down.

## Home on the middle range: geolinguistic regions

A striking feature of the new international media landscape beyond the traditional anglophone centre is the consolidation of the trend to regional markets. As noted above, these also are geolinguistic rather than just large, geographically contiguous regions, as international satellite networks enable the television production centres of the major domestic markets in the world's largest language regions to beam programmes across the world to the 'imagined communities' of their diasporic concentrations and former colonial masters in the metropolises of Europe and the USA. It is worth noting, too, how far these new regional centres have been built upon already existing centres of film production identified with characteristic popular tradeable 'hybrid' genres of their own, such as the Hong Kong action movie or Hindi musical film. Latin America, which the 'geolinguistic-region' explanation fits particularly well, also has had its film production centres, but its tradeable hybrid became the *telenovela*, a commercial television serial genre, reflecting the longstanding commercialisation of Latin American broadcasting.

Although some of these regions appear to have been victims of cultural imperialism in the past, at least in terms of their heavy importation of US films or television programmes, the pattern which had emerged by the mid-1970s was that 'The countries which are strong regional exporters of media tend themselves to be unusually heavy importers of American media' (Tunstall, 1977: 62). This suggests a process of indigenisation in which the US generic models, in establishing themselves as 'international best practice', also invite domestic imitation. However, the substitute products become adapted to the local culture in the process, whether for market reasons, for the sake of diversity or to diminish foreign influence, and new 'hybrid' genres are created.

The resulting situation is not the passive homogenisation of world television which cultural-imperialism theorists feared, but rather, the heterogenisation. Within the anglophone world, Australia, Canada and even the UK produce programmes which have assimilated the genre conventions of US television, but with their own look and feel. Outside of it, US genres (such as the MGM musical and the soap opera) have been adapted beyond recognition in a dynamic process of cultural syncretism. For it is cultural similarities in general, not just language in particular, that binds geolinguistic regions into television markets. Pan-Sino cultural elements allow programmes produced in Cantonese to cross easily into Mandarin, just as Spanish and Portuguese readily translate into each other in 'Latin' markets.

Religion, music, humour, costume, nonverbal codes and narrative modes are all elements in what Joe Straubhaar calls 'cultural proximity'. He hypothesises that audiences will first seek the pleasure of recognition of their own culture in their programme choices, and that programmes will be produced to satisfy this demand, relative to the wealth of the market. Similar to Tunstall's prediction of the growth of a level of hybrid programme choice between the global and the local, Straubhaar argues that, in general, audiences will tend to prefer programming which is closest or most proximate to their own culture: national programming if it can be supported by the local economy, regional programming in genres that small countries cannot afford. The USA continues to have an advantage in genres that even large third-world countries cannot afford to produce, such as feature films, cartoons, and action-adventure series (Straubhaar, 1992: 14–15).

This is consistent with Hoskins and McFadyen's prognosis that US production will continue to increase, finding its strength especially in the prosperous 'North American/West European/Australasian market' but that it will also 'constitute a smaller share of an expanding market' in world terms as regional and national production also expands (Hoskins and

McFadyen, 1991: 221). This expansion will occur to the extent that competitors also develop comparative advantages such as the USA has enjoyed historically. As well as dominance of the largest market within a geolinguistic region, these include economies of scale, high levels of commercialisation and 'first mover advantage', especially where that is based on technical and stylistic innovation.

## Australia: an 'in-between' television producer

The case of Australia illustrates why a more nuanced 'middle-range' analysis is necessary in order to understand the complexities of global media flows. Australian television programmes have begun to be a quite visible presence on the stage of world television. The success of *Neighbours* and *Home and Away* in Britain are the most dramatic sign of the export successes of Australian television, but there are few territories in the world now that do not contain Australian material as part of their programme mix. Following the initial acceptance of Australian cinema as an art-house favourite in the 1970s, the next decade saw a large number of prestige Australian mini-series on screens in continental Europe, Britain and New Zealand and, to a much lesser extent, North America. Since the mid-1980s, Australian serials and series have become standard fare in many of these territories and Australia is well represented worldwide in genres like children's drama, documentary, science and technology programmes, comedy and nature programmes.

Australia shares some characteristics – the English language and high levels of commercialisation – which have produced the metropolitan (US and UK) dominance of television trade, while also sharing characteristics of other peripheral nations, such as being a substantial net importer of film and television. This 'in-between' status arises from its Anglo-Celt, white-settler-dominion history which places it between 'core' and 'peripheral' countries in the world system.

Australian production costs are relatively low compared to other English-language production markets, particularly the USA. Because Australia's population (and therefore production) base is small, the industry has to be efficient to survive. Its relative efficiency is largely a function of sophisticated technical and creative resources. However, its domestic market is small relative to the amount of television material produced and this, combined with the rising cost of all forms of television, but particularly high-end drama, necessitates the search for external financing and markets. The subsidy, investment and regulation infrastructure in Australia for film and television has contributed over the years to the diverse portfolio of formats and genres produced domestically, allowing the production industry and the viewing public to retain their own voice despite the small population base. Australia's high level of commercialisation from the inception of its television system (which has meant the development of one of the largest advertising bases per capita in the world), in tension with its small market, has also meant that the production industry had to develop relatively cheap production protocols for a variety of long-form and one-shot drama.

It is significant that this predominantly anglophone country is an English-language production centre. This is becoming increasingly important because the more internationalised television becomes, the more crucial the language of production becomes. An English-language production centre automatically lowers its product cost and potentially increases its markets. Australia is not limited to export within its geolinguistic community or region – its biggest aggregate market is Europe (including Britain, it accounts for 40 per cent of total export trade), while the anglophone North American market is resistant to Australian (as well as most other foreign) imports. Language is neither the major enhancer nor the main inhibiter of export success in these territories.

While it is probably a support for the 'geolinguistic hypothesis' that Australia clearly enjoys a certain comparative advantage by producing in English and being primarily an anglophone culture, several factors parallel to the 'geolinguistic hypothesis' are relevant to Australia – opportunities for export to rapidly expanding and commercialising territories (Europe in 1980s and early 1990s; Asia in the 1990s) and export to cultural as much as linguistic 'common markets' (the UK and New Zealand). A further point concerns the hybridity or recombinant nature of the Australian television system (Cunningham, 1992: 28–32; O'Regan, 1993). Having been largely modelled on and influenced by high levels of imports from the two premier television centres, the USA and the UK, it has internalised best practice in both commercial and public-service practices.

It is possible to argue that '[w]hen Australia became modern, it ceased to be interesting' – 'interesting, that is, to an international cultural intelligentsia and anthropological audience' (Miller, 1994: 206). Equally, it is arguable that the country has attracted international interest again at present, due in no small part to its audio-visual output. What made the country interesting in the nineteenth century was the radically premodern cultural difference of its indigenous peoples set against a transplanted white-settler colonial culture. What has produced interest again is its emerging profile as a post-colonial and multicultural society – a postmodern 'recombinant' culture – well suited to playing a role in global cultural exchange.

This view is put strongly by Andrew Milner, who argues that social and cultural modernity was only ever partially realised in Australia. Thus Australia has been catapulted towards post-industrialism at a speed possible only in a society that had never fully industrialised; towards consumerism in a fashion barely imaginable in historically less affluent societies; towards an aesthetic populism unresisted by any indigenous experience of a seriously adversarial high culture; towards an integration into multinational late capitalism easily facilitated by longstanding pre-existing patterns of economic dependence; towards a sense of 'being "after"', and of being post-European, entirely apposite to a colony of European settlement suddenly set adrift, in intellectually and imaginatively uncharted Asian waters, by the precipitous decline of a distant empire' (Milner, 1991: 116).

Although it underlines reasons why Australian popular culture has a certain dynamism within globalising and postmodern cultural exchange, this view is a partial and rhetorical account. There remain strong modernist institutions and structures, to which the public-broadcasting sector is a major contributor, as well as a strong, if constantly deprecated, reliance on a central state as well as a ramified series of local and regional structures which arose out of the prototypically modernist project of nation-building.

John Caughie's comments on the way postmodernist trends overlay rather than eclipse modernist traditions in British broadcasting are even more appropriate for Australia, because it has had an embedded commercial ethos for longer than Britain, so the 'overlay' process has been a less traumatic one: British television, and much European television, is still rooted in modernity, the concept and practice of public-service broadcasting, part of an unbroken tradition of 'good works' dating from the administration of capitalism in the latter part of the nineteenth century. 'While that tradition is clearly under threat from the readministration of capitalism and the redistribution of power in global markets, nevertheless the scenario of magical transformation – the marvellous vanishing act of deregulation: now you see "quality", now you don't – in both its optimistic and its pessimistic variants seems naive' (Caughie, 1990: 48).

Australia's central public broadcaster, the ABC, exemplifies this combination in its performance of its charter functions as a modernist, nation-building instrument, while also enthusiastically exploiting commercial and corporate opportunities in new markets and new media. Australian historical mini-series of the 1980s (some of them exported widely, as we have noted) are also prime examples of this combination. Extremely popular commercial successes, screening almost exclusively on commercial networks in Australia, they were nevertheless imbued with the modernist educational public-service ethos of reconstructing popular memory about major defining moments of the nation's history.

International exposure of Australian television products and representative figures span the modernist/postmodernist spectrum. Those stellar few who enjoy mogul status in world television include, pre-eminently, Rupert Murdoch, since 1985 an American citizen, but whose Australian patrimony and business roots are the subject of considerable review as commentators and antagonists alike seek to chart the causes and effects of his success as 'ringmaster of the information circus', as William Shawcross called him. Supposedly 'Australian' traditions of sharp practice and derring-do, anti-establishment commitments and brash populist beliefs are held to contribute to his interventions in British television and press, the establishment and hard-won success of BSkyB and the continuation of that success with the take-over of STAR TV and his lead in the major expansion and commercialisation of television in East Asia, Eastern Europe and India. His mastery of populist press traditions is credited with underscoring the invention of tabloid television: 'Tabloid television, as the term is generally understood, was born in the United States. But before anyone cries Yankee cultural imperialism, they should consider this: if the Americans nurtured the genre, Australians fathered it' (Lumby and O'Neil, 1994: 152).

The Australian system seems to have bred a talent for successful low-budget commercial television and has attracted a reputation for it, for better or worse, throughout the world. Australian producers, like some Latin American and Egyptian companies, have churned out a considerable body of soap-opera hours which occupy considerable space in terrestrial and satellite schedules. In many situations, this means being able to substitute for and possibly even compete with US programme offers. This attracts criticism from countries which perceive themselves to be threatened by the Trojan horses of US culture. In New Zealand, the view is put that 'Australian programmes are merely American programmes once-removed . . . as a consequence of the internationalization of television, Australian television networks had readily adopted formats and styles "born in the USA". Such formats and styles have now been passed on to New Zealand in the form of Australian-made programmes or as local adaptations of Grundy productions' (Lealand, 1990: 102). When a recent study showed Australia to be a significant supplier of light entertainment into Europe, this was seen as setting an unfortunate precedent for the further development of a local production industry: 'The question is whether the European programme industry has to follow the Australian recipe: imitation of American TV formulas, thus stimulating the globalization and homogenization of the international TV market' (de Bens et al., 1992: 94).

At the other end of the spectrum, producers of quality drama in the British tradition have enjoyed a royal road to the BBC and ITV, and have established long-term co-production and co-venture arrangements with such central public services based on the highest-quality values of television practice. Australian producers can 'play at being American' – the two-edged sword of the post-colonial condition, playing a game of reverse imperialism, but within the rules of subordination (Caughie, 1990: 44) – without reserve. They can equally strongly eschew that path. The first model is exemplified by the advocates of increased off-shore production in Australia, or by those productions, like *Paradise Beach*, made primarily for the US market. The second finds no better exemplar than the Kennedy Miller company, whose outstanding historical mini-series of the 1980s were found too 'parochial' by many international buyers, who expressed bewilderment that a company with a world reputation for feature-film successes (such as the *Mad Max* films) should evince no interest in 'modifying' their television output for the international market. In some cases, as with Village Roadshow/Warner Roadshow group, these two traditions can even exist under the same corporate umbrella (for example, with Village Roadshow producing *Paradise Beach* and Roadshow Coote and Carroll, *Brides of Christ*).

The Australian system has neither the depth of public-service ethos and product of the UK system, nor the universalist appeal and range of talent of the US system, but its recombination of both systems affords it certain strengths beyond that seen in similarly medium- or small-sized, peripherally placed industries.

## Cross-cultural textual and audience analysis

We have argued in general, and the Australian case illustrates the point, that the flow of peripheral production is not so much displacing US production as finding its own, intermediate level. The way is then open to inquire into how these levels might be impacting upon the cultural identification and restratification of television audiences on a global scale.

In recent years a tradition of micro-situational audience analysis, influenced in some measure by 'ethnographic' anthropological methodologies, has been used to demonstrate the great variety of ways in which programmes are interpreted by different audiences in different 'places'. The best-known of these is undoubtedly the Tamar Liebes and Elihu Katz (1990) study of the reception of *Dallas*, the series which became 'the perfect hate symbol' of cultural-imperialism critics in the 1980s (Mattelart et al., 1984: 90). While this line of investigation is welcome as far as it goes, we want to argue that, just in itself, a micro approach is also inadequate to track the fortunes of the television exports of peripheral nations.

We must ask what precisely it means, and how might it be possible, to carry out research on how audiences respond to television programmes from other cultures, and not just from the dominant ones either. Methodological protocols central to this line of investigation need modification to account for peripheral programme reception. When studies are restricted to reporting and analysis of the self-understanding of selected audience respondents, wider factors affecting the impact of programmes are often bracketed out, or treated superficially as just 'background'. Instead, the middle-range research advocated here should look at the broader context of viewer reception set by the social environment; the professional practices of trading in, marketing and scheduling television programmes; and the strategic role played by the 'gatekeepers' of the television industries, including owners, managers and programme buyers.

# 'Gatekeepers' and cultural industry factors in television flows

Far more than for the USA, the success or otherwise of peripheral nations' exports is contingent on factors other than those captured by established modes of audience study. This explains why so little audience-reception research has been able to be conducted on their products in international markets, and why we need instead middle-range analysis to do so. In the middle range between political-economy approaches and reception analysis, a number of factors are mediating. How are programmes acquired overseas? Who engages in their appraisal and acquisition and what perceptions have they formed of peripheral programming? This 'primary audience' is the major source of informed 'gatekeeping' which regulates (in the widest sense) the flow of peripheral programming in international markets. And what are the characteristics of the major territories which influence the success or failure of such programmes internationally? All these mediating factors embody legitimate, indeed central, aspects of cultural exchange, as virtually all the significant research on nondominant nations' television production and reception indicates (Lee, 1980; Silj, 1988; de la Garde et al., eds, 1993).

The actual structure of major international television trade markets is central to middle-range analysis (Cunningham and Jacka, 1996). There is an ever-wider variety of modes of contracting for international programme production and exchange: off-shore, co-production, official co-production, co-venture (including presales), and straight purchase of territorial rights for completed programmes in the major trade markets such as MIP-TV and MIPCOM. These run on annual cycles suited to the programming and scheduling patterns of the major northern hemisphere territories, but a notable shift in the patterns of global television traffic was indicated in 1994 when the first MIP-Asia was held. At such events, programming is often bought (or not bought) on the basis of company reputation or distributor clout, in job lots and sight-unseen. Very broad, rough-and-ready genre expectations are in play; judgements may seem highly 'subjective' and arbitrary.

Explanations cast in terms of 'universal' appeal, such as those of Liebes and Katz, may prove useful in accounting for the international successes of historically universal forms like US series drama, but there is solid evidence that cultural specificities, along with other middle-range industrial factors, are unavoidable and at times enabling factors for international success in peripheral countries' export activity. Studies which compare viewers' engagement with US-sourced as against otherwise sourced television programming confirm that there tends to be a more distanced realm of 'pure entertainment' within which US programmes are processed – as markers of modish modernity, as a 'spectacular' world – compared to more culturally specific responses made to domestic and other sources (Biltereyst, 1991).

To be sure, the structure of content and the form of internationally popular serial drama in particular are widely shared and may even be 'borrowed' from US practice, as the *telenovela* was decades ago. But the 'surface' differences, almost always, are nevertheless consequential, and contribute to the acceptance or rejection of non-US material, depending on whether the 'primary audience' of gatekeepers and the viewing audience respond positively or negatively to those differences. As Anne Cooper-Chen (1993) has shown, even that most transparently internationalised of television formats, the game show, contains significant differences in the widely variant cultures in which it is popular. After looking at popular game shows in fifty countries, she regards them as having at least three structural variants – the East Asian, Western and Latin models – and innumerable surface particularities.

The 'export of meaning' is not just a matter of viewer reception. Many nations, both core and peripheral, place special importance on the international profile they can establish with their audio-visual exports. These are fostered both as a form of cultural diplomacy, and for intrinsic economic reasons, although national cultural objectives and audio-visual industry development are not always compatible, as Australia and Canada have long been aware, and some Asian countries are now learning. In the case of the Middle East, one commentator has observed that the popularity of Egyptian television exports in the Arab states has a number of cultural and even political 'multiplier effects'. This popularity was preceded by the success of Egyptian films and carries with it a potential acceptance and recognition of Egyptian accents and performers that can operate as 'a soft-sell commercial for Egyptian values' which is then translated into indirect political leverage (M. Viorst, quoted in Tracey, 1988: 12). While it might be difficult to isolate and measure them, it is not unreasonable to infer cultural, trade and political multiplier effects from what can be seen of peripheral nations' products on the world's television screens.

## 'Globalisation': more than meets the eye

While it is fundamental that we recognise the new patterns of television programme exchange and service distribution to be global in their scale, this does not mean that we must therefore conceive of them in any facile framework of 'globalisation'. Globalisation has already become a cliché that it is high time to move beyond, and analysis of the new patterns discernible in global television show a useful way in which this can be done.

Discussions of globalisation often counterpose the global with the local, and the local is in turn equated with the national. However, in the analysis of television production and distribution on a world scale, it is important to distinguish not just the local from the national, but the regional from the global. Of these distinct but related levels, it is the local and the regional which have been most neglected in the literature to date. We need to give more attention to the local characteristics of the television industries of significant non-metropolitan countries that have built a presence outside their own borders. This includes the phenomenon of 'contra-flow' (Boyd-Barrett and Thussu, 1992), where countries once thought of as major 'clients' of media imperialism, such as Mexico, Canada and Australia, have successfully exported their programmes and personnel into the metropolis – the empire strikes back.

Similarly, we need to give more recognition to the regional level, and the national within the context of the regional, where 'region' must now be understood to be geolinguistic and cultural as well as geographic. A regional perspective on the development of television markets brings to light national similarities, such as the widespread adoption of commercial television across the nations of Latin America in the 1950s, or to take a familiar example from the old metropolis, the wave of privatisation and new services which has transformed television in Europe since the mid-1980s. For one thing, a regional, rather than a global, perspective elucidates the connections between trade and culture, particularly in the potential impact which the formation of regional free-trade zones might have upon programme exchange, and in the clash of free-trade rhetoric with national cultural objectives.

So long as television remained a terrestrial technology, there was less distance between the local and the national levels on one hand, and the national and the global on the other. However, satellite distribution has opened up regional and transcontinental geolinguistic markets, while terrestrial broadcasting and video cassettes have provided an additional but less immediate means for the distribution of television products to diasporic communities, notably those of Chinese, Arab and Indian origin. Attention to this regionalization of markets gives greater insight into what is happening in the world than does the hollow rhetoric of globalisation. Two instances of trends elucidated by a regional perspective are the rise of the regional entrepreneurs and the restratification of audiences into 'imagined communities' beyond national boundaries.

Although Rupert Murdoch severed his national ties with Australia by taking up US citizenship in 1986, it remains the case that his rise to become perhaps the world's most spectacular media entrepreneur was based upon his initial accumulation of media assets in Australia, where he still controls almost 70 per cent of the daily press. From this base, literally on the periphery of the English-speaking world, he launched his ventures into the largest countries of that geolinguistic region, first Britain and then the USA.

Even more peripheral in origin were the two generations of Azcárragas whose dominance of the world's largest Spanish-speaking market in an erstwhile 'third-world' country has been turned into a platform for extensive operations in the USA as well as South America, and a toehold in Spain. In this respect, 'El tigre' (the tiger) Azcárraga is not 'Mexican' any more than Murdoch is Australian. If the term globalisation is to mean anything, it must take account of such deracination of corporations and entrepreneurs from 'their' nation-states, and furthermore, the more recent moves of these entrepreneurs in particular even beyond their geolinguistic regions. With Murdoch's purchase of STAR TV and Azcárraga's return to partnership in the PanAmSat international satellite corporation, we see both of them ratcheting up the scale of their operations so as to establish a strong presence in Asia, expected to be the fastest-growing regional media market of the next century. Also of note is the strategic alliance which they have made to exchange programming from each other's regions.

Benedict Anderson's concept of 'imagined communities' has been one of the most influential tropes in theories of national consciousness for more than a decade (1983), but as satellite television distribution transcends the borders of the nation-state, there is some value in applying it to the new audience entities which that process creates. Similarly, in the decades since Nordenstreng and Varis first drew attention to the transnational media's action upon 'the nonhomogeneity of the national state' (1973), there have arisen international services which stratify audiences across national boundaries not just by class and education, but by 'taste culture' and age – the ostensible international youth-culture audience for MTV, for example. Of more interest to us are the imagined communities of speakers of the same language and participants in similar cultures which form the geolinguistic regions exploited by the media entrepreneurs, especially the diasporic communities of émigrés on distant continents.

Even amongst the globalisation theorists, it is becoming a commonplace to observe that the globalising forces towards 'homogenisation', such as satellite television, exist in tension with contradictory tendencies towards 'heterogenisation', conceived pessimistically as fragmentation, or, with postmodernist optimism, as pluralism. Thus, 'identity and cultural affiliation are no longer matters open to the neat simplifications of traditional nationalism. They are matters of ambiguity and complexity, of overlapping loyalties and symbols with multiple meanings' (Castles et al., 1990: 152).

To the extent that we can assume that television is in fact a source of identity, and that audiences for the same programme derive similar identities from it, it becomes possible to think of identities which are multiple, although also often contradictory, corresponding to the different levels from which the televisual environment is composed in a given market. An Egyptian immigrant in Britain, for example, might think of herself as a Glaswegian when she watches her local Scottish channel, a British resident when she switches over to the BBC, an Islamic Arab expatriate in Europe when she tunes in to the satellite service from the Middle East, and a world citizen when she channel-surfs on to CNN.

In both the positivist mainstream and critical traditions of communication theory in the past, disregard for actual content, disdainful stereotypes of 'lowest-common denominator' programming, and dichotomous thinking about tradition and modernity, all have prevented this more pluralistic conception of audience identity to surface. What it has required has been, first, the more recent theorisation of multiple social identities being overlaid in the individual subject, and then the perception argued for here, that these identities are related to the local, national, regional and global levels at which cultural products such as television programmes circulate.

# References

Anderson, B. (1983) *Imagined Communities: Reflections on the Origin and Spread of Nationalism*, Verso, London.

Biltereyst, D. (1991) Resisting American hegemony: a comparative analysis of the reception of domestic and US fiction, *European Journal of Communication*, 7, pp. 469–97.

Boyd-Barrett, O. and Thussu, D. K. (1992) *Contra-flow in Global News: International and Regional News Exchange Mechanisms,* John Libbey, London.

Castles, S., Kalantzis, M., Cope, B. and Morrissey, M. (1990) *Mistaken Identity: Multiculturalism and the Demise of Nationalism in Australia,* 2nd edn, Pluto Press, Sydney.

Caughie, J. (1990) Playing at being American: games and tactics, in Mellencamp, P. (ed.) *Logics of Television: Essays in Cultural Criticism,* Indiana University Press, Bloomington and Indianapolis.

Collins, R. (1990) *Television: Policy and Culture,* Unwin Hyman, London.

Cooper-Chen, A. (1993) Goodbye to the global village: entertainment TV patterns in 50 countries, paper presented to the conference of the Association for Education in Journalism and Mass Communication, Kansas City, Aug.

Cunningham, S. (1992) *Framing Culture: Criticism and Policy in Australia,* Allen & Unwin, Sydney.

Cunningham, S. and Jacka, E. (1996) *Australian Television and International Mediascapes*, Cambridge University Press, Cambridge.

de Bens, E., Kelly, M. and Bakke, M. (1992) Television content: Dallasification of culture?, in Siune, K. and Truetzschler, W. (eds) *Dynamics of Media Politics: Broadcast and Electronic Media in Western Europe*, Euromedia Research Group, Sage, London.

de la Garde, R., Gilsdorf, W. and Wechselmann, I. (eds) (1993) *Small Nations, Big Neighbour: Denmark and Quebec/Canada Compare Notes on American Popular Culture*, John Libbey, London.

Hoskins, C. and McFadyen, S. (1991) The US competitive advantage in the global television market: is it sustainable in the new broadcasting environment? *Canadian Journal of Communication*, 16.2, pp. 207–24.

Lealand, G. (1990) 'I'd just like to say how happy I am to be here in the seventh state of Australia': the Australianization of New Zealand television, *Sites*, 21, Spring, pp. 100–12.

Lee, C. C. (1980) *Media Imperialism Reconsidered: The Homogenising of Television Culture*, Sage, London.

Liebes, T. and Katz, E. (1990) *The Export of Meaning: Cross-Cultural Readings of Dallas*, Oxford University Press, New York.

Lumby, C. and O'Neil, J. (1994) Tabloid television, in Schultz, J. (ed.) *Not Just Another Business: Journalists, Citizens and the Media*, Pluto Press and Ideas for Australia, Marrickville.

Mattelart, A., Delcourt, X. and Mattelart, M. (1984) *International Image Markets*, Comedia, London.

McAnany, E. and Wilkinson, K. (1992) From cultural imperialists to takeover victims? Questions on Hollywood's buyouts from the critical tradition, *Communication Research*, 19.6, pp. 724–48.

Miller, T. (1994) When Australia became modern, *Continuum*, 8.2, pp. 206–14.

Milner, A. (1991) *Contemporary Cultural Theory*, Allen & Unwin, Sydney.

Naficy, H. (1993) *The Making of Exile Cultures: Iranian Television in Los Angeles*, University of Minnesota Press, Minneapolis.

Nordenstreng, K. and Varis, T. (1973) The nonhomogeneity of the national state and the international flow of communication, in Gerbner, G., Gross, L. and Melody, W. (eds) *Communications Technology and Social Policy*, Wiley, New York.

O'Regan, T. (1993) *Australian Television Culture*, Allen & Unwin, Sydney.

Schement, J., Gonzalez, I., Lum, P. and Valencia, R. (1984) The international flow of television programmes, *Communication Research*, 11.2, pp. 163–82.

Silj, A. (1988) *East of Dallas: The European Challenge to American Television*, British Film Institute, London.

Sinclair, J. (1990) Neither West nor Third World: the Mexican television industry within the NWICO debate, *Media Culture & Society*, 12.3, pp. 343–60.

Straubhaar, J. (1992) Asymmetrical interdependence and cultural proximity: a critical review of the international flow of TV programmes. Paper presented to the conference of the Asociacion Latinoamericana de Investigadores de la Comunicacion, São Paulo, Aug.

Tomlinson, J. (1991) *Cultural Imperialism*, Johns Hopkins University Press, Baltimore.

Tracey, M. (1988) Popular culture and the economics of global television, *Intermedia*, 16.2, pp. 9–25.

Tunstall, J. (1977) *The Media Are American*, Constable, London.

# |11|

# *Trends in global media reception*

ANANDAM P. KAVOORI

The process of media globalization is often invoked to signify sweeping social, cultural and institutional change, the end results of which are sometimes said to define our age. While the institutional and programming aspects of media globalization have been examined from a variety of theoretical perspectives, issues of media effect and use have been largely underexplored. Although exploring issues of media effect across the range of global media programming is needed, the research reported here focuses on only one genre – television news.

This chapter presents empirical data from two media-reception projects. Three aspects of global media reception are dealt with – these are termed the 'national' question, the 'cross-cultural' question and the 'power' question. The aim in each section is not a theoretical mapping of the issues within each of those areas but the presentation of data and how they relate to some of the issues addressed in the literature on media globalization.

## The national question

In a recent study of globalization, media audiences and television news, focus groups were used in the USA, UK, Israel, Germany and France to investigate both issues of the commonalities of media reception across cultures and those of local mediation.[1] Groups in each of these countries were shown three international news stories that had been broadcast on their respective national channels. In the manner of Liebes and Katz's groundbreaking study (1990) on the US television drama *Dallas*, audiences were asked to retell the story in their own terms. The central idea was to read audience accounts alongside textual accounts and contextualize those readings in terms of contemporary debates in reception theory and the literature on nationalism and globalization.

In dealing with 'the national question', the analysis focused on the cultural function of foreign news. Two general questions informed the reading of the audience transcripts. One concerned the terms in which the nation is referenced in contemporary news discourse and its reception. The second, larger question was whether the nation-state is still the most viable form of social collectivity that is addressed by audiences living in a globalized and information-saturated society. The findings across these countries showed a sweeping culture of audience criticism of the news broadcasts (this is discussed in the next section) rather than the discourse embodied by the text itself. The anomaly, however, was the case of Israel, where discussion of the news texts were constantly referenced back to core cultural concerns of nationhood and cultural identity. Here, it was found that the reception of international news does indeed serve a specific cultural function: it creates a community of the self, one that is continuous with local national identity.

While space does not allow for textual analysis here, each of the news texts across all five countries presented images of the 'other', within what was termed 'discursive practices of representation'. Drawing on much of the critical textual-analysis literature, the data showed that television news was an 'agency of socialization' (Dahlgren, 1981: 102), which showed the audience 'what the *nation* already presumes . . . (functioning) as the principal circulator of the cultural mainstream' (Gitlin, 1986: 3, emphasis added).

The key issue from a reception perspective became to identify the dynamics that created this relative homology between textual and audience interpretations. Analysis of the focus-group material offered explanations as to (a) the specific processes by which such national referencing takes place and (b) the cultural basis for such referencing. Taken in combination, these two allow for understanding the cultural function of international news from an ethnographic, audience-based perspective.

# Processes of national referencing

The Israeli audience was shown three stories dealing with political conflict. The stories dealt with 'South Korean student unrest', 'Gulf War refugees' and 'South African train violence', and were aired on the nightly news broadcast *Mabat* (which means 'view' or 'outlook') broadcast by the IBA (Israel Broadcasting Authority).[2] In each case, the respondents were asked to retell the story and then discuss it more contextually. Across the six focus groups, three interconnected contexts of national referencing were identified.

These were categorized as follows: (a) 'event-based' referencing (the Intifada, the Temple Mount in the Korea unrest story, Jewish refugees in the Gulf refugee story and the Gulf War itself, various violent acts in Israel in the case of the South Africa train-killings story); (b) 'identity-based' referencing (the Holocaust, Arab–Israeli wars, Jewish identity and religion);

and (c) 'media referencing' for the three stories (how the media portrays Israel in a negative light). Some details from each story follow, with sample responses included in the end notes.

The Korea student-unrest story dealt with student protests against the then president, Chun Doo Hwan. The story's narrative dealt with how some students had attacked police while others had taken refuge in a Catholic church. To help make sense of the Israeli audience discussion of the story, three Israeli citizens (living in the United States) were asked to read and help interpret the story. The one common theme across all the focus groups was the almost immediate localizing of the news story in terms of Israeli political and identity issues. The Israeli citizens (who were used as cultural interpreters) said this was a typical practice amongst Israelis, whose daily life and view of the world were filled with concerns over security and the Intifada. As one of them put it, 'Israelis are always worried about how something affects them.'

Thus in the Korea unrest story, the focus groups did not focus so much on the Korean students as on the Intifada ('It's not our students', said one respondent. 'It's Arabs.') and how that was affecting the Israeli body politic. Rather than referencing the Catholic church in Seoul, the audience focused on the religious status of the Temple Mount in Jerusalem – a site of conflict between Muslims and radical Jews.[3] Both identity-referencing and media-referencing were tied into how the topic was discussed. The Temple Mount issue became an index of how portrayals of Israel are skewed in the media and how this was reflective of the unfair treatment Israel had received in the past. One participant saw the Korea story and said that 'they [South Koreans] kill many soldiers and no one in the world [says anything] but here one Arab gets killed . . .'. Additionally, the audience used the Intifada as event referencing rather than the Korean student riots. Discussion of specific incidents from the Intifada were interlaced with extrapolation to incidents from other anti-Jewish incidents in the region, the Holocaust and other repressions of Jews worldwide. These composed the bulk of the identity referencing in the story's mediation. Finally, the audience offered media referencing by repeatedly linking the continuation of the Intifada to television coverage.[4]

The Gulf refugee story focused on the efforts of Asian families to return to their homelands after the invasion of Kuwait by Iraq. The audiences discussed the story in the Israeli context by focusing on the conflict itself and Israel's role in it. The event referencing focused on how the refugees were one element in a complex regional problem. One concern was the possibility that Israel may have to take in refugees.[5] Other discussion focused on the strategies that Iraq used in the conflict; the allied forces' bombing raids and different phases of the conflict.

While identity referencing was implicit in all of these discussions, it was especially evident in discussions of the status of Palestinian refugees.[6] Media referencing was implicit both in discussion of the extensive media coverage, but more crucially in how the media coverage was helping Jordan to gain more international currency and boost its image globally. Jordan was seen as using the refugees to generate support – financial, political and in the media.[7]

The South Africa train-violence story dealt with a massacre of passengers on a commuter train. Event referentiality in this case focused on parallels between the South African conflict and the Israeli–Palestinian conflict.[8] Identity referencing, while inherent in the above discussions, was also invoked in discussing the role of colonialism in South Africa and Israel and in the reiteration of historical incidents dealing with persecution of Jews.[9]

## Cultural basis for national referencing

In examining the repetitious quality of the referencing across the three stories, it became evident that an overall pattern of self-referentiality was taking place – of what it is to be Israeli. Israel is not of course unique in its self-orientation; what is different, however, are the direct equivalences between self and nationhood. In discussions with the cultural translators and a reading of the literature on Israeli society and culture, the emergence of the nation as a category of structural relevance was apparent. To quote from one of the early communication studies on Israel:

> It is a nice paradox that the establishment of modern nationhood was probably easier – psychologically speaking – for the Jews than for the embryonic nations that were living on their own soil. Jewish nationalism did not have the difficult job of overcoming loyalties to village and region that stood in the way of the unification of other nations. Jewish loyalties always reached beyond the local community to regional, national and international alliances with other Jewish communities everywhere. The nation is united not only by the fact of the State and not only by memory of collective experience of long ago, but by more recent experiences as well.
>
> (Katz and Gurevitch, 1976: 31)

The nature of those recent experiences is not hard to identify: wars with its neighbours; conflicts inside Israel between Arabs and Jews, between secularists and fundamentalists, and between political parties. These different conflicts have developed along with other processes of modernization, secularization and globalization leaving identification of the nation-state as perhaps one of the few points of convergence for all Israelis.

To better understand how such a convergence may have a cultural basis, the analysis turned to relevant anthropological categories that assist such national referencing. Some suggestions as to what these may be were offered by the work of Tamar Katriel and other scholars. Based on her own life in Israel and field work in a variety of settings, she identifies a number of key cultural processes that provide a relevant frame of reference for understanding Israeli culture – and, for our purpose, understanding patterns of national referencing. The two that were used are those of *gibush* (crystallization/cohesion) and *kiturim* (griping).

By *gibush*, Katriel implies the idea that social cohesion is the product of work and effort by everybody. As she puts it, 'the quasi-utopian ideal of Gibush, suggests that social life is not a given, but something that must be continuously made and remade' (Katriel, 1991: 15).[10] Both event referencing and identity referencing of the three stories played on the idea of comparing conflicts abroad to those in Israel and the need to both tackle them and reinforce a sense of self despite them. The extensive media referencing was a more direct criticism of both local and international media as obstacles to greater national cohesion or greater *gibush*.

All three modes of referencing related to the notion of *kiturim* or griping. Katriel finds that griping rituals and communication rituals are closely related and 'functionally comparable in that they each provide a major context for members . . . to give expression to, and form an experience of, a central problem in their lives (ibid.: 38). Audience mediation of the stories was framed around a set of gripings about the problems in Israeli society (whether it was the Intifada, perceived incompetence of national politicians, criticism of local media) or abroad (reminders of persecution, criticism of Israel abroad, criticism of coverage by foreign media). Such a process has been seen as a 'trademark of Israeli society' (ibid.: 37) and is manifest in a comment by Israel's first president, Chaim Weizmann, who said his task of governance was very difficult since he was a 'president of about six hundred thousand presidents' (Cohen et al., 1990: 9).

Griping is not an end in itself, and much like the notion of *gibush*, is oriented towards the collectivity. 'Griping parties are unofficial, unrecognized ceremonies of communal participation, in and through which the gibush-ethos plays itself out' (ibid.: 36). Their function is largely the original use of the term 'ritual' which refers to the 'patterned symbolic action whose function it is to reaffirm participants' relationship to a culturally sanctioned sacred object' (ibid.: 36), the object in question here being the nation itself.

# The cross-cultural question

One of the key questions that theorists of media globalization have left unaddressed is that of global patterns of media use. It is presumed in the literature that audience predilections must follow patterns of format convergence and genre development. While other studies have looked at the global reception of soaps, the reception of news has gone relatively unexplored.

The chief finding from the analysis of the data across the four Western countries was the sweeping similarities of the critical or 'reflexive' treatment of the news stories. Audiences across these countries showed similar trends of media referencing. These criticisms were labelled as follows: (a) criticism of the discursive content of the broadcast, (b) criticism of textual strategy, (c) criticism of institutional principles (of journalism). It needs to be emphasized that these different criticisms were not independent of each other. Discussion of one topic often flowed into another.

## Criticism of discursive content

The two dominant themes in the Korean unrest story ('a violent world' and 'the fight for democracy') and the dominant theme in the South Africa train violence ('a barbaric world') were critically reviewed by respondents. Respondents said that stories with such themes were unclear, repetitive and largely negative about the 'other world' and provided little context to events.[11]

## Criticism of textual strategy

Respondents across the four countries focused on specific textual features in the news stories. Criticism of the news stories' structures focused on issues of framing (discussion of a story's key verbal and visual elements) and perspective (discussion of how television news itself is a construction of events rather than an objective report).[12]

## Criticism of institutional principles

Respondents used the stories to raise questions about the rules governing journalism as a profession. The main criticism was the news value accorded to violence. Respondents said repeatedly that television has too much violence and too little concern for violence victims.[13]

In each case, what stood out was the detailed critical attention paid to different issues by the audience. There was limited evidence of homologies between textual and audience meanings. Instead, the texts' preferred meanings were considered reflexively, as media constructions rather than reality. Addressing the 'cross-cultural' question, then, the study revealed that watching television news institutes a persistent social practice through which audiences carry out considerable rhetorical, political and cultural work (Saenz, 1992). The data presented here clearly indicate that part of the political and cultural work that television news audiences perform is reflexive, re-articulating the terms of the news texts through a specific pattern of media referencing.

# The power question

This section deals with an ongoing project examining news reception in India, with specific attention paid to emergent patterns of reception in terms of the traditional debates around theories of media imperialism. The history of this debate, which started in the 1970s, has been based on the unequal balance in the flow of media products. Underlying the debate is the assumption that audiences in the third world are 'under siege . . . facing the relentless flow of Western media' (Schiller, 1991: 13), resulting in a process of 'cultural synchronization' (Hamelink, 1983). As some scholars have recently suggested, this is a simplified perception of a process of mediation that is vastly more complex – of which processes of localization are only the first step. While recent work on India has focused on these issues in terms of popular culture (Mankekar, 1993; Sen, 1993; Mitra, 1994; Rajagopal, 1994), the study of news remains relatively unexplored.

A pilot study in India (consisting of a mall intercept and thirty in-depth interviews in January 1997) explored some of these issues in terms of the changed news environment. The project began with the proposition that major global services such as CNN and BBC and cable services such as STAR TV have created sets of audience preferences and predilections that had little basis even as late as 3 years ago. The overall aim of this project is to understand how audiences have mediated, internalized and transformed these sets of global messages and to theorize how broadcast news can create conditions for structuring national consciousness and thereby impinge on the process of democracy and political change.

The pilot study attempted to identify patterns of television-news viewership across three stations – BBC, CNN and the Indian state-controlled network, Doordarshan. The survey was conducted as a mall intercept in an upscale shopping area in New Delhi. A total of 180 cable viewers filled out the questionnaires. The major finding was that BBC was the leading choice among respondents. CNN and Doordarshan came second on different variables. The survey had two sections – 'media viewing habits' and 'news performance'. A quantitative summary of the findings follows.[14]

## News viewing habits

1 Hours all TV programming watched: 86 per cent of respondents said that they watched four hours or less of television.
2 Hours TV news watched: 94 per cent of respondents said they watched less than two hours of news every day.
3 News source: 90 per cent of respondents said they got their news from newspapers. BBC came next with 8 per cent, followed by Doordarshan and CNN at 1 per cent each.

4 News channel watched most: 68 per cent said BBC, followed by Doordarshan with 29 per cent and CNN with 3 per cent.
5 Rank by programming: for world news, BBC was considered the best broadcast (88 per cent), followed by CNN (8 per cent) and Doordarshan (4 per cent). For business news, BBC was considered the best broadcast (65 per cent), followed by Doordarshan (31 per cent) and CNN (5 per cent).
6 Channel watched when a major news story breaks: 88 per cent said they would tune to BBC, followed by CNN (9 per cent) and Doordarshan (3 per cent).

## News performance questions

1 Comprehensiveness: BBC was ranked as the network that provided the most comprehensive coverage of international news (87 per cent), followed by CNN (10 per cent) and Doordarshan (3 per cent).
2 Objectivity: BBC was ranked as the most objective (76 per cent), followed by Doordarshan (16 per cent) and CNN (8 per cent).
3 Comprehensive coverage across regions: Asia: BBC (70 per cent), Doordarshan (19 per cent) and CNN (11 per cent); Europe: BBC (89 per cent), CNN (10 per cent) and Doordarshan (1 per cent); USA: CNN (82 per cent), Doordarshan (14 per cent) and BBC (5 per cent); Africa: BBC (81 per cent) and CNN (19 per cent).

The in-depth interviews helped to contextualize some of the findings in the survey. Four basic points with reference to the cultural/media imperialism debates emerged.

First, the idea that the choices provided by global media programming radically alters established news consumption patterns was problematic. Perhaps the key finding from the survey is how highly significant the print news media remains to Indians who have the choice of cable television. Newspapers and magazines remain overwhelmingly the choice for news consumption. One respondent cynically enquired, 'What media revolution are you going to study?' It needs to be emphasized that global news media must counter not only competition from local media but from established regimes of reading – which are heavily skewed to the print media.

Second, in all the interviews conducted, respondents did not choose either BBC or CNN or Doordarshan as their top choice of broadcast news programming, but rather private Indian news-media programming. Respondents said that of the English-language programming they preferred *STAR News* put out by a leading Indian production house, NDTV (New Delhi Television) and in the Hindi-language news programming they preferred either *ZEE News* or *Aaj Tak*. All three shows are produced by Indian production houses but mimic the editing and reporting styles of

Western news programming. These choices clearly indicate what has already emerged in many other studies – that audiences given the choice between programming developed by traditional state-run media, global media conglomerates and local private media usually choose the last one. What Robertson (1994) has called 'glocalization' – the use of global formats, genres and news values mediated and framed by local thematic and cultural contexts – emerges as the preferred choice of viewers.

Third, interviews helped contextualize the choice of the BBC rather than CNN or Doordarshan. There seem to be two reasons for this preference. The first is linguistic and the second is historical. Respondents said that the BBC is a more international channel not only in terms of coverage and its approach to stories (angle, information, persons interviewed) but also in its performative aspects. In other words, it approximated to what a news broadcast should sound like. This mirrors much work in discourse analysis, which has suggested that news discourse is as much about the ideology of presentation as it is about information. Respondents said that the BBC's formal, paced style, with a heavy emphasis on context and elaboration (and the British accent itself) helps *BBC News* to be seen as a more authoritative news broadcast. This is evident even in those survey questions – concerning breaking new stories and economic news – in which (given the US role as economic superpower) CNN might be expected to be the preferred choice.

The naturalization function of language, then, can be seen as how a certain news discourse (the BBC style) gets translated as news. By contrast, CNN with its heavy attention to graphics, sharp editing and the centring of the anchor as icon suffered as much by its implicit connection to 'entertainment' as from a near ubiquitous ambivalence towards the heavy American accent (this was especially pointed out with regard to the Indian CNN reporter). Audience preferences for the BBC were linked also to the programmers' long history of broadcasting in the country and to a backhanded allegiance to colonialism. In the post-colonial era, the BBC has the advantage of certainty (the Indians know what to expect) and authenticity (this is how 'English' should be spoken). Doordarshan news, by contrast, was criticized both as a government mouthpiece and as failing to approximate – perhaps only as mimicry – to the discourse of British news. As one respondent put it, 'BBC is after all BBC. How can you compare the commentators on CNN or Doordarshan with them?' This avowed enthusiasm for the BBC should however be seen in context. The BBC is not the first choice of news, but the third at best (after print and local private news programming). It is only when we look beyond glocalized regimes of readings that global media programming has an impact.

Fourth, a strong perception existed that CNN is an American network and speaks largely to American interests. From the in-depth interviews, it appears that younger respondents (aged 20–25) may prefer CNN's American-style coverage of news as opposed to the more formal style of the British programmes. However, that question needs to be addressed in a future study. The central critique of CNN lies in its unabashedly American focus. Details about American politics (Senate hearings, presidential meetings and visits), economy (American labour issues, automation, depression fears) and social issues (abortion, affirmative action) were seen as fundamentally American concerns and not international ones.

# Conclusion

To summarize, this chapter's aims were primarily empirical and attempted to address one aspect – media use and effects – that has been left underexplored in the burgeoning literature on media globalization. Three aspects of news reception – the national, the cross-cultural and the power question – were identified and findings relevant to each of them were presented. In terms of the national question, it was suggested that media audiences confirm the nation through specific modes of referencing but only when the nation-state is already overdetermined. In terms of cross-cultural commonalities in the reception of news, it was suggested that there is an emergent culture of critical media referencing. This referencing takes place around issues of news content, textuality and the news industry itself. Finally, the issue of whether global news media creates a hegemonic presence in the third world was examined and it was suggested that media audiences persist in traditional reading practices followed by a preference for glocalized media products. The relative importance of the BBC over CNN also was discussed.

Needless to add, these three aspects only scratch the surface of what needs to be attempted if we are to better understand the varied aspects of media reception in a global context.

# Notes

1 This research was part of a larger study called 'The Global Newsroom' conducted at the College of Journalism, University of Maryland at College Park, and the Department of Communication, Hebrew University, Jerusalem. The primary investigators for the project were Professors Michael Gurevitch and Mark Levy at the University of Maryland and Professors Akiba Cohen and Itzakh Roeh at the Hebrew University. The author is grateful to them for their help and for permission to use this research material. The study examined comparative television coverage across countries that are part of Eurovision. In addition, focus groups were conducted in five countries. Parts of the transcript material and analysis in the 'cross-cultural' section are reproduced with permission from Kavoori (1996, 1997). For other reports from this project see Gurevitch and Kavoori (1994), Gurevitch

(1991), Gurevitch et al. (1991). In the fall of 1990, six focus groups were conducted in each country in conjunction with the Centre National de Recherche Scientifique (Paris), the Technical University (Berlin), Independent Broadcasting Authority (London), the Hebrew University of Jerusalem (Jerusalem) and the University of Maryland (College Park, United States). The six focus groups consisted of nine to twelve people from different occupations (school teachers, bank clerks, sales people, factory workers) and income levels, and were recruited by each institution. This study was not designed to provide any social-scientific measures, and to echo Liebes (1988: 278), 'one cannot make claims of formal randomness or representativeness, but, on the other hand there is no reason to suspect any systematic bias'. Naturally, given the complexity and difficulty of comparative work, these focus groups can perhaps provide a good sample, but can never fully represent all the diversity that makes up a nation. The focus-group transcripts were analysed for issues of variance (across countries) and issues of power (the extent to which the audience reiterated the discursive features of the text). Each question by the moderator was followed by discussion. Each transcript was divided into discussion segments. Summary statements about issues of variance and power were written for each discussion segment. These statements then were used as the basis for identifying the modes of referencing discussed in the paper.

2 The IBA is an independent body modelled to a large extent on the British Broadcasting Corporation but its organizational structure allows for greater influence from the government than is exercised on the BBC. While it is considered largely Western in its journalistic orientation, it also has a developmentalist orientation typical of Southern countries. This stems from the charter issued to it by the Israeli Knesset, which saw its function as 'reflecting the life, struggle, creative effort and achievements of the state; to foster good citizenship; to strengthen the ties with, and deepen the knowledge of, the Jewish heritage and its values' (Cohen et al., 1990: 204). At the time of the study, *Mabat* had a near monopoly of the audience. Surveys conducted from time to time in Israel consistently report that about 85 per cent of the adult viewing population watch the news on any given evening, a remarkably high rate of viewing (ibid.: 206–7).

3 The Temple Mount issue was related to the activities of the Gush Emunim (the 'bloc of faithful'), a religious and militant group who had planned to blow up mosques on the Temple Mount in Jerusalem because they claimed it was situated on the site of the Second Jewish temple. The Muslims in turn considered the mosques highly sacred, second only to Mecca and Medina. In May 1984, twenty members of the Gush Emunim group were arrested and three of them were found guilty of murder and sentenced to life imprisonment (Melman, 1992: 121–2).

4 For example: 'Look at what's happened in Israel. I think television

influenced the Intifada generally. A child that sees a young man throwing stones on television, and nothing happens. He is famous on TV. Why shouldn't he throw stones the next day? And when he sees the cameraman he gets even more excited and will do it. That shows how much influence TV has.'

5 For example: 'It left an awful feeling, the dominant feeling is the parallel, the frightening story repeating itself. They mentioned World War II. It ended in 1945 and 3 years later the same pictures returned. I was only 3 then but we learned about it in history. These pictures happened here where we are sitting today. Also refugees before the state of Israel was created and these pictures are repeated today, every day, every week and every month all over the world.'

6 For example: 'I wonder what would happen if all of these guys running away from Iraqi rule would get permission from Hussein to cross the Jordan river and reach us through one of the bridges that can still be crossed, and they would come in here. I wonder what would happen.'

7 For example: 'It is propaganda for Jordan, so that it can ask for money for all kinds of things to show that it has refugees and does not have money to give them.'

8 Two examples: 'It reminds me of the situation between us – between the religious and the secular. Between those that want to give up land for peace and those that do not.' 'There are extremists and there are those that are willing to compromise. There are also extremists and moderates.'

9 For example: 'The white government, just like the British one in Israel, created such conflicts. Here between the Arabs and the Jews – thus they could rule. The same thing is happening in South Africa, there are two tribes in conflict.'

10 The notion of *gibush* is also related to the general valence towards 'work' in Israeli society and is tied to a long history of ideas in Jewish theology, Zionist philosophy and contemporary politics (Harpaz, 1990).

11 For purposes of brevity, sources of quotes are identified by means of abbreviations (for example, the British Focus Group number 1 is referred to as BFG1). With reference to the Korean unrest story, one respondent said, 'You never hear why they were rioting and only they want democracy' (AFG3) while another one, referring to repetitiveness, said, 'In any political demonstration, average or big, they are the same images. I think these same scenes are filmed, no matter what event, whether it's the Middle East, in Seoul or in Africa, because they are the same demonstrations' (FGF3). Similarly, in discussions of 'a barbaric world' in the South African train-violence story, one respondent pointed out how such stories are 'so confusing that you hardly know who is doing what. The reasons given are very confusing' (BFG1). Making a similar point, another respondent said, 'It didn't quite become clear to me who was actually fighting against whom. It also didn't become clear

why they're fighting each other and what their demands are' (GFG5). With reference to the South African train-violence story theme of 'A barbaric world' respondents emphasized the effects of using violence without a context to understand it. Two examples: 'It's about violence. I can't exactly say why there are such problems. I only understand that this violence is for nothing. This reporting is unbearable. They are sensationalistic and do it in order to make people watch. It's a kind of absolute violence' (FFG4). 'It totally makes no sense. There are more than twenty dead people, the reasons we don't know, it's totally crazy. The message that is probably being transmitted is that in South Africa when the blacks recover all their rights, and when the whites will no longer have the upper hand, there will still be problems as there always will be this inter-ethnic conflict, instead of fighting between blacks and whites, the blacks will fight between themselves' (FFG4).

12 On news as a construct: 'Television news is like an iceberg, they only show us a little part and I always ask myself what they haven't shown us. Behind these images, we could only imagine what they did not show us' (FFG1). 'I mean what I find is that as I keep seeing this, [it] makes me think more about what I see on television. I mean, how close to any truth is this bulletin? You don't know about what other footage there was or what other people could have been interviewed or how many people refused to be interviewed' (AFG5).

13 Some examples: 'If there is blood then it is good. This is a characteristic sample of broadcasts from abroad. A lot of disasters, a lot of wars' (GFG4). 'The news shown on TV. Its all gloom and doom. Very rarely do they show real news which is not gloom and doom. Some things are interesting which are not necessarily violent' (AFG3). 'They have no inhibitions about filming directly into their open wounds or to interview the woman mourning for her shot husband five minutes ago with the camera ten millimetres from her face asking if she is still sad' (BFG2). 'When someone is gunned down, murdered, victimized give them a little bit of dignity. Don't flash them on the screen' (AFG4).

14 The respondents were split by gender (59 per cent of respondents were male and 41 per cent were female) and age (50 per cent were under 30 and 50 per cent were above 30). No significant variance was found on the questions for either gender or age.

# References

Cohen, A., Adoni, H. and Bantz, C. (1990) *Social Conflict and Television News,* Sage, Newbury Park, Calif.

Dahlgren, P. (1981) Television news and the suppression of reflexivity, in Katz, E. and Szecsko, T. (eds) *Mass Media and Social Change,* Sage, London, pp. 101–14.

Gitlin, T. (1986) Looking through the screen, in Gitlin, T. (ed.) *Watching Television*, Pantheon, New York, pp. 3–8.

Gurevitch, M. (1991) The globalization of electronic journalism, in Curran, J. and Gurevitch, M. (eds) *Mass Media and Society*, Edward Arnold, London, pp. 178–93.

Gurevitch, M. and Kavoori, A. (1994) Global texts, narrativity and the construction of local/global meanings, *Journal of Narrative and Life History*, 4, pp. 9–24.

Gurevitch, M., Levy, M. and Roeh, I. (1991) The global newsroom: convergences and diversities in the globalization of television news, in Dahlgren, P. and Sparks, C. (eds) *Communication and Citizenship*, Routledge, London, pp. 195–215.

Hamelink, C. (1983) *Cultural Autonomy in Global Communications*, Longman, New York.

Harpaz, I. (1990) *The Meaning of Work in Israel: Its Nature and Consequences*, Praeger, New York.

Katriel, T. (1991) *Communal Webs: Communication and Culture in Contemporary Israel*, State University of New York Press, Albany, NY.

Katz, E. and Gurevitch, M. (1976) *The Secularization of Leisure: Culture and Communication in Israel*, Harvard University Press, Cambridge, Mass.

Kavoori, A. (1996) How different audiences understand foreign news, in Cohen, A., Levy, M., Roeh, I. and Gurevitch, M. (eds) *Global Newsrooms, Local Audiences: A study of the Eurovision News Exchange*, John Libbey, London, pp. 119–42.

Kavoori, A. P. (1997) Between narrative and reception: towards a cultural/ contextualist model of foreign policy reporting and public opinion formation, *Journal of International Communication*, 4.1, pp. 99–115.

Liebes, T. (1988) Cultural differences in the retelling of television fiction, *Critical Studies in Mass Communication*, 5.4, pp. 277–92.

Liebes, T. and Katz, E. (1990) *The Export of Meaning: Cross-Cultural Readings of 'Dallas'*, Oxford University Press, New York.

Mankekar, P. (1993) National texts and gendered lives: an ethnography of television viewers in a North Indian city, *American Ethnologist*, 20, pp. 543–62.

Melman, Y. (1992) *The New Israelis: An Intimate View of a Changing People*, Birch Lane Press, New York.

Mitra, A. (1994) An Indian religious soap opera and the Hindu image, *Media, Culture & Society*, 16, pp. 149–55.

Rajagopal, A. (1994) Ram Janmabhoomi, consumer identity and image-based politics, *Economic and Political Weekly*, 2 July, pp. 1659–68.

Robertson, R. (1994) Globalization or glocalization, *Journal of International Communication*, 1.1, pp. 33–52.

Saenz, M. (1992) Television viewing as a cultural practice, *Journal of Communication Inquiry*, 16, pp. 37–51.

Schiller, H. I. (1991) Not yet the post-imperial era, *Critical Studies in Mass Communication*, 8, pp. 13–28.

Sen, A. (1993) The impact of American pop culture in the Third World, *Media Asia*, 20.4, pp. 208–17.

# Acknowledgement

The author would like to thank the University of Georgia Research Foundation for funding this pilot study. He would also like to thank Dr James Rada for running the statistical tests on the data.

# |12|

# *Feminist internationalism*

## *Imagining and building global civil society*

ANNABELLE SREBERNY

There is no single dynamic of globalization but many, complex, interlocking skeins of global interactivity. Appadurai's (1990) well-known schema of five 'scapes' of interaction (ethnoscape, technoscape, financescape, ideoscape and mediascape) can be extended with the sacriscape of global religious networks (Waters, 1995) and a genderscape of social and sexual roles (Sreberny-Mohammadi, 1996). Globalization also embodies contradictory processes, powerful pressures towards homogenization and sameness as well as counter-tendencies towards 'disjuncture and difference' (Appadurai, 1990), heterogenization, localization and diversity.

It remains important to map out the dynamics of and actors in 'globalization from above'. Globalization includes global economic restructuring, a complex international division of labour and increasing economic interdependence (Krause, 1996). Analysis of the global media environment shows transnationalization and increasing conglomeratization of media corporations; the convergence of technologies, and thus actors, in broadcasting, telecommunications, information provision, and a potential consequent narrowing of the global cultural and ideological environment (Herman and McChesney, 1997).

But often globalization models are far too simply top-heavy and reductionist. It is evident, as Krause (1996), amongst many others, has argued, that the terms of political debate and action are being transformed as a new agenda of issues in international politics develops. Hence, it is important to acknowledge the dynamics of 'globalization from below', to borrow Richard Falk's phrase, emergent 'alternative globalizations' that provide new spaces for political action and global solidarity and articulate what is concealed – and provide alternative meanings for what is revealed – by dominant media. This kind of activity has been labelled a 'global solidarity culture' (Waterman, 1995: 5); Brecher et al. (1993) discuss the emerging 'global visions', and Falk (1994) is concerned with 'the making of global citizenship'. Of course, internationalism in itself is not a new phenomenon but the old forms were largely 'nationalist internationalism' (Waterman, in Brecher et al., 1993), trying to win states for peoples without them, or, as in the labour movement, battling for rights of workers *within* states. The emerging global solidarity culture is organized towards addressing problems for which no national solution alone can be adequate.

The focus on 'globalization from below' is important theoretically, as it punctures any too simplistic grand narrative of 'globalization from above' and raises questions about global power relations and the political significance of popular movements. It is important politically because, in the imagining of new possibilities, alternatives become less impossible. Indeed, if we recognize theoretical discourses as themselves domains of practice, then analyses of the processes and potential of other globalities serve to actualize and diffuse them.

Mediated communication can be used to articulate the local with the global in unprecedented ways, and aid the extension of the new social movements such as the women's movement (amongst other actors) into transnational networks. These networks prefigure a global civil society, occupying a space (like its namesake at the national level) between global markets and transnational corporate activity and the formal organizations that represent global political interests. Moreover, I want to suggest that the decentralized women's movement, using a variety of mediated forms, is a particularly interesting articulation of the new global networking.

# The notion of 'global civil society'

While debates about globalization have burgeoned within the social sciences, the notion of 'global civil society' is not yet a well-developed or widely used notion. Elise Boulding has argued that the growth in 'globe-spanning associations of private citizens' is one of the most striking phenomena of the twentieth century, growing from the 176 international non-governmental organizations in 1909 to the scores of thousands active as we approach the end of the century (Boulding, 1988: 35). The diversified landscape of Ingos, Bingos and Pingos is an increasingly important part of the interdependent political landscape of the late twentieth century (Hamelink, 1994: 38–9). Ingos are intergovernmental organizations such as the UN, NATO, OPEC, the OAS and EU; Bingos are business interest organizations, predominantly transnational corporations. Pingos are the professional and public-interest organizations which include not only Amnesty International and Greenpeace, but also the International Olympics Committee, the World Federation of Trade Unions, the World Council of Churches, the Organization of the Islamic Conference and many others. Many of these are based on forms of participation and civic consciousness which start at local level but build to globe-spanning – if not universally inclusive – networks.

The changing, transnational forms of political action mean that concerns about global governance, global citizenship and global civil society are debated in a number of academic discourses. Some are concerned with the possibilities for truly global institutions that can deliberate upon and act on global problems – that is, a reconstituted UN system. So, for example, Archibugi and Held (1995) ask whether it is possible to develop democratic relations among sovereign states and whether decisions which affect the whole world can be taken democratically; they propose rather formalist suggestions for 'cosmopolitan democracy' as a new model of global political order.

The meaning of citizenship is challenged, to be conceived of as participation in public life and society at large, not just in political life. That is, citizenship implies mainly social participation and integration, which prompts the need to explore the possibilities of citizenship in a broader context than just the national (van Steenbergen, ed., 1994). A narrow definition of party/parliamentarian politics has long been challenged as issue groups, social movements and alternative media claim new spaces for action and new formations of actors. But that challenge no longer operates within national boundaries but increasingly across them; the new social movements have gone global.

Falk remains concerned with the rights of citizens, and wonders how the rapidity of global change and unevenness of circumstance, perception and awareness will allow for popular participation in the governing process: 'Citizenship is tied to democracy, and global citizenship should in some way be tied to global democracy, as leading to a process of democratization that extends some notion of rights, representation and accountability to the operations of international institutions and gives some opportunities to the peoples whose lives are being regulated, to participate in the selection of leaders' (Falk, 1994: 128). He readily acknowledges that energy, resource and environment issues require global solutions, or effective global citizenship in order to redesign political choices on the basis of an ecological sense of natural viability. And he goes further, to acknowledge a politics of the imagination, normative visions of planetary unity and a politics of (im)possibility, of 'dedicated action that is motivated by what is desirable, and not discouraged by calculations of what seems likely' (ibid.: 132). Falk describes the transnational activism of the social movements of the 1980s as sharing 'a conviction that upholding human rights and building political democracy provide the common underpinning, although adapted to diverse circumstances, for the types of transnational developments that are desired' (ibid.: 138).

He argues that such activism is producing a 'new orientation toward political identity and community, which cumulatively can be described as global civil society' (ibid.). What people identify with, in this institutional construction of new arenas of action and allegiance, is no longer bounded by any formal relationship that individuals have to their own territorial society, so that traditional citizenship is being challenged and remoulded by this transnational political and social activism. Falk suggests that while 'traditional citizenship operates spatially, global citizenship operates temporally, reaching out to a future-to-be-created, and making of such a person "a citizen pilgrim", that is, someone on a journey to "a country" to be established in the future in accordance with more idealistic and normatively rich conceptions of political community' (ibid.: 139). This global activism, what Falk calls 'globalization from below', is a future-oriented project, a functional utopia, 'a global citizenship of the positive variety implies a utopian confidence in the human capacity to exceed realistic horizons' (ibid.: 140). He considers the new social movements as 'not political in any conventional sense'.

Beck (1997), however, prefers to acknowledge a profound 'reinvention of politics' which is producing a new reflexive, rule-altering kind of politics, operating from the local level, which is 'below' the national, up to the global level 'above'. Not necessarily progressive, indeed often counter-modern, this form of politics requires, in the face of the collapse of old institutions, 'the formation of support networks crossing the boundaries of systems and institutions . . . networks, which must be connected together and preserved' as new formations of power.

Arguments about whether there is one or many public spheres (Sreberny-Mohammadi, 1996) surface in this context also, with concern about the presumed 'singularity' of 'global civil society'. As Lipschutz (1992) suggests, there is not one but many heteronomous transnational (and potentially, in my own view, conflictual) political networks being established. Yet he too recognizes that civil society is becoming global and therefore a political force to be reckoned with, 'not only as a challenge to the nation-state system but also in its reconstruction and reimagining of world politics'.

These kinds of global identifications and involvements are integral to the processes of globalization, and while pressurizing the state from above and below, also produce and diffuse new global signifiers of political commitment and identification. Turner summarizes these dynamics neatly:

> The state is caught between the global pressures, which challenge its monopoly over the emotive commitments of its citizens, and local, regional and ethnic challenges to its authority. The question of political sovereignty is of paramount importance for understanding the nature of citizenship and human rights. The traditional language of nation-state citizenship is confronted by the alternative discourse of human rights and humanity as the normatively superior paradigm of political loyalty. The idea of human rights is itself partly a product of this globalization of political issues.
>
> (Turner, 1994: 157)

Within debates about the role and impact of transnational forms of media and communications, the main critical concern has been about imbalance in cultural and informational flows and their cultural effects. Concerns with the democratization of communication as well as the potentially democratizing role of communications in political life have been very nationally focused and only slowly is interest growing in the ways new forms of communications technologies can be used by emerging transnational social movements. Some examples include Frederick's work (1997), which focuses on the growth of the APC (Association for Progressive Communication) and specifically the way in which Mexican NGOs have used computer technologies and the Internet to develop and coordinate policies in relation to NAFTA talks, the Chiapas uprising and other matters. He too argues that community is no longer linked to place and that civil society as the political and juridical space for private citizens is expanding beyond national boundaries and playing an important role in international relations to challenge government and market hierarchies. Serra's research (1996) examined the way one prominent Pingo, Amnesty International, briefed by local organizations on the killing of street children in Brazil, got the issue onto the international media agenda, mounted a campaign of international pressure and so forced political debate and finally new strategies to cope with the problem inside Brazil. Her study shows the dynamic and complex interactions between local activists, the international organization, the international media (particularly the press) and international public opinion, and is an excellent illustration of how global solidarity can be invoked through concerted campaigning and hard work.

Thus debates about globalization have helped to focus attention on emerging forms of politics and the redefinition of what constitutes 'the political'; on the internationalization of new social movements; on the growth of new identifications beyond the nation-state and on the roles that various forms of media can play in the possible expansion of a global civil society. I want to go further and suggest that the women's movement in particular offers a different kind of structure than other 'new social movements': one that I characterize as including similarity-in-difference, latency, and a lateral network-of-networks model of organization.

## Global discourses, global networks

An alternative way of thinking that seeks a consensual approach to international institutions can arise only out of the existence of a transnational political culture that can create a transnational public opinion. To some extent this does already exist through the horizontal networks created by green/peace/human rights groups.

(Kaldor, 1995: 94)

The increasingly globalized discourse of human rights has encouraged a plethora of national groupings, regional monitoring groups, etc., but the international debate is symbolized, if not spearheaded, by Amnesty. There are countless ecological and enivronmental groups active around the world, but two key organizations again tend to push the global debate, or collar media attention: Friends of the Earth and Greenpeace. Greenpeace's 1994 report suggests that the organization now has 4 million regular supporters worldwide, more than the population of many countries, with twenty-four regional offices that generated £12 million in 1994.

The women's movement, I want to suggest, operates with a different model. There is no central organization with national branches, not even for public-relations purposes (there may, of course, be national organizations, such as NOW in the USA, but nothing that functions at the transnational level). Rather there are a variety of regional and locally based and focused women's groups, many centred around media production, often in the context of development.

As should already have become evident from the preceding discussion, the notion of a 'network' has become a key trope of contemporary social theory. Castells, in his three-volume analysis of the information age (1996–7), is concerned to map out the *global* networks of wealth, power, information and images that cross boundaries and shape ever more lives. But at the same time, he also recognizes as counter-hegemonic forces the social movements which resist global capitalist restructuring, uncontrolled informationalism and patriarchalism (Castells, 1997: 361). These offer a 'networking, decentered form of organization and intervention' which both mirrors and counteracts the 'networking logic of domination' in the information society (ibid.: 362).

Melucci, long a key theorist of new social movements, not only returns to the needs for identification and belonging that movements now fulfil, but also their global focus, although for him this implies raising issues that do not concern specific groups but the 'system as such' and multiple affiliations, whereby actors move from one association to another, from one network to another without permanent commitment (1996: 308). More specifically, he also acknowledges considerable variation within the women's movement, from affective support structures to professional groups feminizing public space, those producing female culture and those offering public services, etc., and precisely echoes my own description, that 'The "movement" is then a network of networks' (ibid.: 144; see also Moghadam, 1996).

There is a huge range of women's media and cultural activities on the ground, often ignored by mainstream and malestream commentary, that nevertheless are channels for women's empowerment and thus for social development. Examples would include the ways in which Zimbabwean women use radio for development; or how the Tamania Mars collective in Morocco used their press to carve out an area of feminist debate and pressure for improved legal rights in an Islamic context; or how Sistren use theatre to explore Jamaican women's lives, giving them a feeling of empowerment and through performance begin to articulate social critique and formulate social policy (Sreberny-Mohammadi, 1994, 1996).

Then there are also a number of more formal women's information and communication networks, many of which were developed after the first UN World Conference on Women in Nairobi in 1975 which established the Women's Decade. Many are organized on a regional level: for example, Femnet and TAMWA in Africa; ISIS International in the Philippines; DepthNews and Women's Features Service in Asia; the South Pacific Commission/Pacific Women's Resource Bureau (SPC-PWRB) in the Pacific; ISIS International in Peru; Fempress in Latin America; DAWN (Development Alternatives with Women for A New Era) and CAFRA (Caribbean Association for Feminist Research and Action) based in the Caribbean; Women in Development Europe (WIDE) in Brussels; Women Living Under Muslim Law (WLUML) in France, with a base in Pakistan (see also Moghadam, 1996).[1]

These organizations have built linkages, networked and exchanged ideas and skills over the years and in 1992 established a network of networks called WomeNet (consisting of ten key networks based in nine countries) with the express purpose of sharing research and exchanging information around the world, fast. Its members include CAFRA, Trinidad and Tobago; DAWN and WAND, Barbados; IWTC, New York; ISIS International, Manila; ISIS International, Santiago; Sistren, Jamaica; SPC/PWRB, Fiji; TAMWA, Tanzania, and WFS, India. By 1997, WomeNet comprised twenty-nine members in twenty countries. Between them they regularly produce a wealth of materials including quarterly journals, news magazines and newsletters; books, booklets and comics; posters and postcards; resource kits, manuals and training resources; occasional papers, research papers and bibliographies; news features and videos. Considerable training and support for technical development, especially in relation to computerization and the Net, has been provided by the APC Women's Networking Support Programme established in 1993. It has trained trainers, supported women's training at APC member and partner sites in twenty countries, and trained more women in the preparatory meetings for and at the Beijing conference. It has facilitated the development of networks, supported seventy electronic conferences in three languages and networked to over twenty countries and developed a number of WWW sites (APC, 1997). All of this organizational development, preparation and planning came into its own at and around the Beijing conference, a key example of a feminist global civic culture at work.

# A network of networks: a compelling case study

The Global Faxnet case is one example of how rapid and extensive a response this global network of networks can make.

(Frankson, 1996)

Important gains were made by and for women at various UN conferences (on the environment, 1992, Rio de Janeiro, Brazil; on human rights, 1993, Vienna, Austria; on population, 1994, Cairo, Egypt; and the Social Development Summit, February/March 1995, in Copenhagen, Denmark). A lot of preparation was being made for the UN Women's Conference in Beijing, and for the parallel NGO forum, when the Chinese announced at the end of March 1996 that the NGO forum was being moved out of Beijing. The change of site threatened the possibility for effective lobbying at the official conference, would prohibit meaningful plenary sessions and offered very limited telecommunications facilities. IWTC developed a very simple petition urging governments to speak out against the controversial site-change decision and to support NGOs and sent it out to thirty women's media networks in twenty-one countries across Africa, Asia, the Pacific, Latin America and the Caribbean and the European Community. This Global Fax Network project became the principal vehicle for alerting the international women's movement to the UN Fourth World Conference on Women and NGO Forum '96.

When it reached the communications desk of the Pacific NGO Coordinating Group in Fiji, it prompted two actions. First, it was re-faxed out to eight local, four national and twenty-four regional women's groups and NGOs, and to media focal points in Polynesia, Melanesia and Micronesia. Second, a news release was drafted and disseminated to national media houses. Within the week, in Fiji alone, these actions had resulted in several newspaper articles, two live radio interviews and a mention in a radio documentary about what was now fast becoming a global controversy. Within three weeks, forty-one signed petitions from Papua New Guinea, Vanuatu and Fiji had been sent to the offices of United Nations Secretary General Boutros Boutros-Ghali and to the China Organizing Committee.

In Costa Rica, the women producers at FIRE (Feminist International Radio Endeavour) translated the petition into Spanish and re-faxed it to the Ombudswoman's Office, media outlets, women's organizations and NGOs at national level, and human rights and women's human rights groups in Central America – and broadcast the news in Spanish and English via short-wave to listeners in over 100 countries. Fempress in Chile reached over 4000 organizations, researchers, politicians and journalists across Latin America, using press and radio services and its monthly magazine. The Tanzania Media Women's Association (TAMWA) mobilized signatures via phone and fax, while the London office of the World Association for Christian Communication (WACC) contacted ten international groups by fax and 'snail' mail. The speed with which the momentum grew worldwide amongst women's groups, human rights organizations and NGOs was spectacular.

Within four days signed petitions and petitions adapted into letters from 111 organizations in forty countries of eight world regions had been faxed to IWTC for re-faxing to the offices of the UN secretary general in New York and to the China Organizing Committee in Beijing. Within six weeks, the WomeNet had evolved into a Global Faxnet, servicing over 500 organizations, groups and individuals, and it had generated an estimated 3000 signed petitions and protest letters from women's organizations, global networks, NGOs – and even governments – in over 100 countries of every region of the world. Several organizations took the initiative of translating the petition, into French, Spanish, Portuguese, Greek, Russian, Chinese, Japanese and even local languages such as Kiswahili.

It also stimulated collaborative actions and pressure groups as women took action to ensure the news reached their governments: the Tanzania Media Women's Association (TAMWA) asked the Chinese Embassy and Xinhua news agency to keep them informed of developments 'as a strategy to let them know we know!'; Austrian Women's Human Rights fed the Faxnet information to the Austrian government, which expressed full support for the NGO protest against the site change, and in turn used the information at meetings of the European Committee; Fiji women informed IWTC that, 'Our government has sided with the NGOs and awaits all information coming down the line'; and in the Caribbean, women's coalitions lobbied Caribbean Community government ministers in charge of women's affairs to support the appeal. In Kenya, women's organizations approached a former minister and women's leader to get the government to write to the UN secretary general, while in Barbados, the deputy prime minister, herself a feminist, was kept abreast of developments by women's groups linked to the Faxnet.

By May, in order to keep down costs and to make the information more widely available, IWTC augmented the Global Faxnet with GlobalNet, a website of e-mail addresses. The Global Faxnet now stands at almost 500 information-multipliers worldwide but mainly in the South, while the GlobalNet is mainly used by a Northern audience. The Global Faxnet/GlobalNet proved to be the most valuable communications tool for alerting women's networks, governments, donors, journalists and other participants to late-breaking news and issues related to plans and preparations for the conference and NGO forum.

Between 3 April and 30 November 1995, IWTC disseminated forty-four Global Faxnets, although the number was approaching 100 by August 1997. The beauty of the fax alerts has been their instant accessibility and the simplicity of their format. In most cases information was edited to fit one page (except where newspaper clippings or focal-point lists were added). These one-page bytes were not only easily digested but could also be shared with others very quickly – slapped straight back onto the fax machine; photocopied and mailed; read over the telephone, on the radio or TV; easily adapted into press releases and protest letters – ideal in every way for the busy women activists who form the major part of the audience.

The Beijing Process towards the Fourth World Conference on Women was the most democratic one ever mounted by the United Nations. None of the other major decade meetings included regional conferences and forums. It was in this regional process that women consolidated national plans and forged them into regional platforms. Phenomenal growth had taken place in the international women's movement since the 1985 Third World Conference on Women in Nairobi: in the networking capability; in the numbers of networks, organizations, alliances and groups formed; in the development of women's skills as lobbyists and strategists; in the diversity of our ranks and in our confidence to demand transparency. These factors both fed into and were in turn nurtured by the Beijing process.

Some 36,000 women registered for the NGO forum in Beijing; 1700 e-mail accounts were registered; 60,000 e-mail messages were sent and received during the period of the conference; over 30,000 conference forum participants visited the conference WWW site; while over 100,000 'visits' were made to the APC international conference website. The ability to keep in rapid touch with what was happening in Beijing was summarized in the pithy epithet 'China seems close from my computer screen' (quoted in Gittler, 1996). The Global Faxnet and the GlobalNet services – run by women for women – indicate the speed at which women are moving along the 'information superhighway'.

# GK97: spiderwomen activate their Net again

A less globally visible but nonetheless significant moment of global feminist reaction was in relation to the Global Knowledge (GK)97 conference organized by the World Bank and the government of Canada in June 1997. When the line-up of plenary speakers and panelists was first made public in the spring, there was a rapid reaction by women's groups about the lack of women speakers and the North-centric nature of the topics, odd for a conference purporting to deal with 'global knowledge'. An online discussion developed, which by the end of June 1997 included 1100 members from more than 65 countries, 25 per cent of whom were from developing countries compared with 2 per cent participation in the Internet overall (APC, 1997). If the decentralized structure is taken seriously, and women really do act as information 'translators' for others in their physical locality, then such uses of the Net can articulate the global and the local.

The APC site is invaluable for the material posted and the discussion that focuses on gender and information technology; debates have centered on the need for network support, gender-sensitive training and the creation of women-friendly software and websites in IT; the tension between preserving tradition and women's rights of access to and liberation through new technologies; concerns about social and gender inequality and the need to integrate gender considerations within all spheres of national policymaking;

and examples of positive practical applications, especially where different forms of communication and activity intersect.

One evocative case (APC, 1997) described a young Ivoirian woman who had been married under the legal age to an older man by her parents, who, after being subjected to conjugal rape and violence, rejected the marriage and finally cut the husband's throat. She was jailed, but a women's group in the Ivory Coast lobbied for her freedom. IPS Harare circulated the story in English, and ENDA translated it into French. WULML, in contact with the group by telephone (since they had neither fax nor e-mail), helped mount an international solidarity campaign, and the girl was pardoned by the president of the Ivory Coast at the beginning of 1997.

The GK97 conference organizers, under pressure, accepted many new panels with a gender focus. 'Promoting Grassroots Women's Entrepreneurship' discussed a number of projects, including the 'Virtual Souk', which helps women market their products directly online, so avoiding any middlemen; an initiative among Moroccan women to develop a marketplace for the direct sale of rugs; and Empowering Information Tools for Grassroots Women, with participation from members of many of the networks already cited. More women were invited as plenary speakers, and an early-morning woman's breakfast was organized, well attended by many (men) perhaps because of the generous welcome breakfast of fruits and cakes.

It could be said that there was the usual bland agreement, once again, that development could not work without women, and that women's participation in the emerging information society was paramount. Even James Wolfensohn, the head of the World Bank, repeated the old adage that 'if you educate a man, you educate one person, but if you educate a woman, you educate the family and nation'. Soon after the conference, the World Bank launched a website on women and development; the government of Canada already supports women and development issues through CIDA (as do a number of other Northern countries) and the on-going and shifting debates from GAD to GID to WID (see Moghadam, 1996) about gender, development and information technologies find yet new spaces for articulation.

## Global feminism as part of the 'network' society

In its confrontation with difference women's collective action has spread all over the world, crossing conditions and cultures and becoming a planetary phenomenon.

(Melucci, 1996: 144)

The women's movement suggests a particular model of global activism, in itself prefiguring the construction of global civil society. It is built upon grassroots organizations, which combine into networks, build networks of networks, and then utilize communications technologies to exchange information as quickly and cheaply as possible and in ways that facilitate greatest access and therefore mass participation. It is thus a prime example of the articulation of local and global, whereby intensely local issues can be made globally public and often elicit a global response leading to a local resolution, and potentially universal issues can receive local discussion and inflection.

It is able to manifest what I would label 'a solidarity in difference', whereby broad support for general issues, such as improving the global legal instruments in relation to the abolition of discrimination against women (CEDAW), can be mobilized, alongside specific struggles, with particular or differently prioritized sets of concerns within each national or cultural context (violence, rape, trafficking in women, enforced prostitution, forced pregnancy, for example). One of the great achievements of the women's movement is getting women's rights accepted as part of the broader rubric of human rights, and activities such as those listed above recognized as war crimes in a permanent International Criminal Court.

While much is indeed based on some recognition of the identity of women, it seems to me to be too much of a reduction to call this simply an 'identity movement', especially given the enormous critique that concept has had within feminist writing. Part of the movement could be characterized as a 'strategic essentialism' (Spivak, 1987) – not asking what gender means, but asking how to improve the position of women. This provides a powerful latency to the movement, which can mobilize rapidly when called upon.

Of course, many significant issues and difficulties remain, including the fact that much of this activity is still unrecognized; while the development literature and development planning now manifests a necessary obsequiousness to the need to involve more women, it often shows a lack of awareness of how much women are already mobilizing and what already exists. In a sense, the opposite tendency is also an issue: while huge advances have been made, access is the first concern to be raised at any mention of the use of new technologies, including by women themselves. It is, of course, a valid and important concern, which has to be creatively addressed. Yet endemic problems, such as illiteracy, which hinder women's access to cultural and political participation far more than lack of access to comunications technologies, are articulated far less often.

There is also a question about the internal democracy of such alternative groups and media. Women's groups may not all be internally democratic; indeed, many print-based activities could themselves be criticized for elitism. Yet that is both to ignore the huge challenge for women to organize themselves, and to be over-schematic about the 'correct' forms that activity should take. However, issues around women's leadership styles, dominance of Western discourses and methods, and class and race hierarchies all exist within the complex sphere of 'global feminism'.

Finally, all the organizing did not persuade the Chinese to alter the venue for the NGO forum. The story was picked up by the global media, and, of course, Beijing did garner quite a lot of coverage, although the women's conference was often the peg for many other stories – on China's human rights record, the memory of Tiananmen and China's incapacity to hold a major international conference. Global networks are not always effective or successful – but history does not come with guarantees. The global interactivity of women continues to provide support to local and national groups struggling to achieve specific goals within nation-states but also as a global movement: the ratification of CEDAW; the recognition of women's rights as fundamental human rights; the development of international instruments and actions against violence against women and the sex industry – these have become part of the global ideological and political landscape. Difference-in-solidarity remains the women's movement's mode of operation.

# Conclusion: the importance of recognizing 'globalization from below'

Many analysts end with the reminder that many of the most cataclysmic changes of the end of the twentieth century (the fall of communism, even the end of apartheid) were hardly anticipated and suggest that one of the functions of discussing the emergence of global civil society is because its very articulation creates a space of possibility. Melucci (1996) and Castells (1997) both describe the decentred, subtle character of networks of social change and argue that a key contribution of such movements is to challenge accepted codes. Thus Castells says that the new movements do more than organize activity and share information, 'they are the actual producers, and distributors, of cultural codes' (1997: 362) and he credits the women's movement in its varied forms and expressions for the demise of patriarchy. (If I have focused so much on Melluci and Castells, it is because I find it relevant, and heartening, that two major male social theorists should so emphasize the women's movement within the context of new global political networks.)

Let me reiterate that the logic of globalization itself produces antagonism and resistance, which take many forms but also have global dimensions. By examining globalization from above and globalization from below, we see more clearly the current dialectics of history, and it is evident that global feminism is one strand. Women do seem particularly adept at articulating the global and local, and their imaginings have moved towards the construction of something that is global in outlook, civil in manner and location and societal in impact. It becomes harder to argue against a concept such as global civil society when so many are actively involved in making it a reality; it is salutary to remember that social theory most often lags behind social practice.

# Note

1 The information in the section that follows draws heavily on articles by Gittler (1996) and Frankson (1996) in Sreberny-Mohammadi (ed.) 'International Feminism(s)', a special issue of the *Journal of International Communication*, 1996, 3.1.

# References

APC (1997) APC GK97 Online living summary, Issue 6, 25 June–2 July 1997; to be found at http://community.web.net/gk97.

Appadurai, A. (1990) Disjuncture and difference in the global cultural economy, *Public Culture*, 2.2, pp. 1–24.

Archibugi, D. and Held, D. (eds) (1995) *Cosmopolitan Democracy*, Polity, Cambridge.

Beck, U. (1997) *The Reinvention of Politics*, Polity Press, Cambridge.

Boulding, E. (1988) *Building a Global Civic Culture*, Syracuse University Press, Syracuse, NY.

Brecher, J., Childs, J. B. and Cutler, J. (1993) *Global Visions: Beyond the New World Order*, South End Press, Boston.

Castells, M. (1997) *The Power of Identity*, Blackwell, Oxford.

Dickenson, D. (1997) Counting women in: globalization, democratization and the women's movement, in McGrew, A. (ed.) *The Transformation of Democracy?* Polity Press/Open University, Cambridge.

Falk, R. (1994) The making of global citizenship, in van Steenbergen, B. (ed.) *The Conditions of Citizenship*, Sage, London.

Frankson, J. R. (1996) Women's Global Faxnet, *Journal of International Communication*, 3.1, pp. 102–10.

Frederick, H. (1997) Mexican NGO computer networking and cross-border coalition building, in Baillie, M. and Winseck, D. (eds) *Democratizing Communication? Comparative Perspectives on Information and Power*, Hampton Press, New Jersey.

Gittler, A. M. (1996) Taking hold of electronic communication, *Journal of International Communication*, 3.1, pp. 85–101.

Hamelink, C. (1994) *The Politics of World Communication*, Sage, London.

Herman, E. and McChesney, R. (1997) *The Global Media: The New Missionaries of Corporate Capitalism*, Cassell, London.

Kaldor, M. (1995) Europe, nation-states and nationalism, in Archibugi, D. and Held, D. (eds) *Cosmopolitan Democracy*, Polity, Cambridge.

Krause, J. (1996) Gender inequalities and feminist politics in a global perspective, in Kofman, E. and Youngs, G. (eds) *Globalization: Theory and Practice*, Pinter, London, pp. 225–38.

Lipschutz, R. D. (1992) Reconstructing world politics: the emergence of global civil society, *Millenium*, 21.3, Winter, pp. 389–420.

Melucci, A. (1996) *Challenging Codes: Collective Action in the Information Age*, Cambridge University Press, Cambridge.

Moghadam, V. (1996) Feminist networks north and south, *Journal of International Communication*, 3.1, pp. 111–26.

Serra, S. (1996) Multinationals of solidarity: international civil society and the killing of street children in Brazil, in Braman, S. and Sreberny-Mohammadi, A. (eds) *Globalization, Communication and Transnational Civil Society*, Hampton Press, New Jersey, pp. 219–43.

Spivak, G. (1987) *In Other Worlds*, Routledge, New York.

Sreberny-Mohammadi, A. (1994) *Women, Media and Development in a Global Context*, UNESCO.

Sreberny-Mohammadi, A. (1996) Globalization, communication and transnational civil society: an introduction, in Braman, S. and Sreberny-Mohammadi, A. (eds) *Globalization, Communication and Transnational Civil Society*, Hampton Press, New Jersey.

Turner, B. (1994) Postmodern culture/modern citizens, in van Steenbergen, B. (ed.) *The Conditions of Citizenship*, Sage, London.

van Steenbergen, B. (ed.) (1994) *The Conditions of Citizenship*, Sage, London.

Waterman, P. (1995) Holding mirrors out of windows: a labour bulletin, a feminist agenda and the creation of a global solidarity culture in the new South Africa, Working Paper Series No. 188, Institute of Social Studies, The Hague, March.

Waters, M. (1995) *Globalization*, Routledge, London.

# Discussion questions

1 How relevant is the concept of media imperialism to an understanding of globalisation of the media in the 1990s?

2 What does Boyd-Barrett mean by 'colonisation of communications space'?

3 How far can a regional perspective provide an alternative analysis of media globalisation?

4 Can you think of any television programmes from the so-called third world which have been shown on Western television? Discuss a recent example.

5 Assess the potential for 'globalisation from below', focusing on the international women's movement. How might women in the developing world benefit from media globalisation?

6 Why is there a need for a gender perspective on globalisation?

7 Are round-the-clock international news channels such as CNN creating a global audience?

8 Watch a television documentary with a group of international students to study audience reactions. How far do race, nationality and gender influence media reception?

9 What can the case of Australian television tell us about international television flows?

10 Examine the limitations of quantitative audience-research methods. What other perspectives are needed to measure media reception in a global context?

# SECTION

# IV

# GLOBAL MEDIA AND LOCAL RESISTANCE

# Introduction to Section IV

The chapters in this final section of the book investigate the possibilities of resistance to the monopolising power of electronic empires, looking at some areas in which media globalisation is being contested or at least adapted in a variety of sociocultural contexts, and whether viable alternative sites for media can be evolved. Reflecting the perspectives of professionals – three of the four chapters in the section are by contributors who have professional experience in the media – the chapters look at how far media empires can be either challenged or culturally mediated by local and 'alternative' actors.

The issue of how new technologies can enable the media to empower and liberate is taken up by Anuradha Vittachi, a journalist and activist, and daughter of a famous journalist. In a personal account, Vittachi, who is editor and co-director of OneWorld Online, examines how electronic communications, especially the Internet, can be used to create a counterbalancing diversity to the homogenised media empires created by the global conglomerates. She challenges the prevailing pessimism among critical political economists about the power of media empires and argues that falling costs of telecommunications can potentially provide an outlet to a widening range of voices, with the Internet as a prime example.

As a case study, the chapter analyses the Internet supersite OneWorld Online, which gives a platform to those with alternative agendas, providing a voice for a range of perspectives – such as feminist and Southern – on issues of global significance. Drawing on her own experiences, Vittachi recounts how this supersite has become a tool for activists across the globe and among international non-governmental organisations, bringing a much-needed plurality of opinions to cyberspace at the same time as lowering costs. The idea of a supersite was conceived out of frustration with the impermeability of the mainstream media and the disappearance of issues affecting the majority of the world in the increasingly superficial and entertainment-led news media. The concept of a supersite must be seen, she argues, as a facilitating substructure and not as a gatekeeping superstructure. Will this diversity of the new media, she asks, help replace the sense of the nation-state with a sense of 'one world' and thus contribute to the development of an alternative global media sphere?

The theme of creating an alternative globalisation is further developed by Tony Dowmunt, himself an 'alternative media' activist, who edited the critically acclaimed television series *Channels of Resistance*, shown on Britain's Channel 4 television in the early 1990s. In looking for concrete examples of resistance to media empires, Dowmunt focuses on projects involving young people, as the category of youth not only provides a useful framework for looking at alternative media within diverse international contexts but is a key market for exploitation by global media.

He reports on how groups working with alternative video and television have found ways to challenge the monopolies of electronic empires by becoming producers instead of just consumers of media. One such project is 'Rebeldes con Cauce' in Colombia, which trains young people to produce television programmes which are then shown on national television. Another example that Dowmunt discusses is the Media Training and Development Trust in South Africa, which trains young people to make programmes for regional community TV as an alternative to mainstream television.

Apart from these national projects, Dowmunt also reports on attempts to internationalise alternative news and media systems such as the New York-based Downtown Community Television Center, which makes programmes for public-access cable channels in the USA. The chapter draws on the experiences of a DCTV producer in Russia whose experiment with a private Russian television channel demonstrates the complex processes of cultural translation necessitated by the encounter of US alternative media values with Russian culture. Dowmunt acknowledges the limitations of such global efforts which, although they promote transnational solidarities among media professionals, do not address the problem of getting the work shown more widely than within and between the communities that produced them. In this respect they pose no significant challenge to global empires.

However, he also looks at a few emerging prospects for the distribution and exhibition of alternative material, such as a Canadian government-funded scheme which distributes programmes to partner broadcasters at national and regional levels across the world. Alpha TV, an Eastern European consortium, which is in the process of setting up a satellite channel dedicated to indigenous production, and Mondial, a proposed Europe-wide channel, which is aiming at promoting this alternative agenda to young people across Europe, are other key examples covered in the chapter.

These examples of work by young people, Dowmunt argues, show that alternative media provide a space in which groups whose presence is excluded from or distorted by the mainstream media can gain some power over how they are represented. More importantly, when these groups network internationally or distribute these representatives to a wider audience, they begin to create an alternative globalisation. While acknowledging its limitations, Dowmunt argues that an investigation into alternative media activity is essential to understanding the context of inequality in which the mainstream global media operate.

In examining Islamic encounters with the expansion and influence of electronic empires, Ali Mohammadi sees patterns of political or cultural resistance in terms of the continuing response to the legacy of colonialism and to the incursion of Western modernity into the traditional societies of the Middle East. The reaction in the Islamic world to globalisation of media conglomerates, he argues, has varied from muted criticism to hostility, reflecting the pro-Western and anti-Western camps. He divides Islamic countries into three categories – modernist, mixed and traditionalist, with most Islamic nations torn between Islamic tradition and secular modernity.

Focusing on the Arab world, Mohammadi examines how, like many other Islamic countries, the Arab nations have copied media systems imported from Western powers, however inappropriate to their societal needs. He surveys these developments in the Arab world within the context of shifting power and influence. Restricting his analysis to developments in television, Mohammadi looks at the changing mediascape in the Middle East, arguing that globalisation of media products was only possible once the culture became open to mass consumption.

Tracing the evolution of pan-Arabic television networks and their changing contents, Mohammadi argues that the 1990 Iraqi invasion of Kuwait transformed the television scene in the region, leading to liberalisation of broadcasting systems and the development of direct broadcast satellites, necessitating change in the style and content of television programming in relation to the globalisation of the market. The chapter also looks at the key pan-Arabic satellite television channels such as Middle East Broadcasting Centre and Orbit.

With the globalisation of culture as commodity, the rhetoric of market forces has become a new dogma, threatening national interests. The emergence of a few megacorporations, Mohammadi argues, is instrumental in establishing the domination of Western culture, which is being resisted by many Islamic countries concerned about the impact of electronic empires on cultural identity in the Islamic world. The availability of global channels is perceived in some Islamic countries as a threat to the Islamic way of life and culture, and this has found expression in anti-Western rhetoric. Mohammadi examines Islamic responses to this media globalisation, from the extreme of banning Western satellites (as, for example, in Iran and Saudi Arabia) to coming to terms with the global culture promoted by US-dominated television programming.

Adapting the global to suit local media conditions and contexts is the key theme of the last chapter in this volume. Daya Kishan Thussu examines the impact of globalisation on electronic journalism in India through the example of Zee TV, a subscription-based news and entertainment channel which is now half-owned by Rupert Murdoch. The chapter analyses the spectacular rise of Zee TV and examines the reasons for its success. Launched in 1992 from the backrooms of Bombay to rival the Indian operations of Murdoch's pan-Asian network, STAR TV, this private television channel now reaches into millions of living rooms in India and to the Indian diaspora globally. Thussu analyses the development of Zee TV's strategy of indigenising Western media formats to Indian languages and contexts – a process that provides a key example of hybridisation as a result of interactions between global and local media systems.

The chapter content-analyses the news output of this popular channel to examine how far and in what ways availability of Western television channels has influenced broadcast news agendas in India. Thussu locates his discussion within the evolution of Indian media, which has a long tradition of independent journalism. Journalistic practices and training, already much influenced by Western journalism, he argues, are being further Americanised as a result of media globalisation.

Thussu looks at how elements in the Indian media are countering this trend. With growing literacy the regional-language press (in many respects the more authentic voice of India than the English-language 'national' press) is booming, and in broadcasting there has been a proliferation of channels making programmes in Indian languages. The process of liberalisation and privatisation has also opened up space for local production and interchange between media professionals. He proposes that the experience of the media in India could provide a useful model for developing a framework for analysing global–local interactions.

# |13|

# *The right to communicate*

## ANURADHA VITTACHI

In this chapter, I make some observations on media democracy from my personal experience as a journalist and an activist. I also draw from the work of people I have known well, particularly my father. One especially important thing I have learned from them is this: that traditional media are not conducive to democracy by their very nature. Can the Internet do better? This chapter discusses the limitations of the traditional media in democratising international communication. Based on my work at OneWorld Online, the alternative website which has more than 280 partners from across the globe – non-governmental organisations, grassroots groups, academic and journalistic communities – I will suggest how the Internet can contribute to global justice.

## 'Keeping governments honest'

In some parts of the world, the matter is straightforward. There is no media democracy because the government simply will not allow journalists and broadcasters to speak up.

A senior Bosnian media adviser, Maurice Linnwood Todd, visited OneWorld in early 1997. I asked him what he thought was the most important thing to know about media democracy. He did not hesitate. 'Without an independent, pluralistic professional media, you cannot have a democracy, or even a process of democratisation', he said. 'The key to democracy is taking away the control of information from governments and from political parties. Anything you can do to take information out to citizens and to educate them as to what to expect from the media – keeping governments honest! – is a major contribution to democracy.' It was heartening to hear a media adviser still speaking out so strongly and so idealistically about the purpose of journalism: to keep governments honest. It is a world away from most of the newspapers I see now in the UK, increasingly pushing what sells. Wherever there is war – or rather, the spectre of death that rides close to journalists during war – journalists have powerful reminders that it is their duty to be vigilant about what really matters, and not waste their time on fashionable trivia.

'What really matters' was a phrase drummed into my head throughout childhood. My father, Tarzie Vittachi, who created the first Asian programme for the International Press Institute, fought not only for press freedom but for a press that deserved that freedom. 'Information without transformation', he used to say, 'is just gossip.'

## The press we need

As far back as the 1960s Tarzie Vittachi was teaching journalists that they needed not only to focus on the topics that mattered but also to go deep enough to make sense of them. Their duty was to 'explain the process', not to indulge in cheap 'event journalism'. It was never good enough to throw our hands up in horror that people were dying of famine. We had to work out why – to chase the story back to its roots, and write about its origins, fearlessly, even if it turned out that the ultimate beneficiary of the people's suffering was a politician or a proprietor who had power over your own livelihood, or even your own life. A journalist's right to investigate was not God-given: it was earned by playing one's part responsibly in guarding the values of a humane society.

He was tickled by how unpopular he made himself, not only with Sukarno, but Marcos, Bandaranaike, Indira Gandhi – the many heads of state in Asia who, he believed, misused power for their own ends. But it was not really a joking matter. He put his life – and his family's – in constant danger. When I was 13, he bundled us hastily onto a plane at Colombo airport in the middle of one fraught night, after the twice-daily child-kidnap threats had turned even nastier.

He was well aware, however, that it was not just governments that limited democracy. He promised himself that he would, one day, write a book called The Press We Need, challenging the North's domination of the global media. That domination was evident, he taught me, not so much through the fact of Northern ownership but through the subtler tyrannies of Northern agendas, Northern values, dominated by Northern prejudices. When Rupert Murdoch offered him a job, he publicly turned it down flat. He argued instead for a 'new information order' to parallel the New Economic Order – though the one being proposed then, in the 1970s, based on Southern governments as the guardians of global fair play, was hardly his idea of progress. 'Ministers of Information', he said, 'are not in the business of providing information but of suppressing it.' It was journalists themselves, as individuals who cared ardently for the right to speak freely, who had the job of guarding media democracy.

But what did all these years of courageous service amount to? Did it really change anything? In the last year of his life, these were the questions that tormented him. His words had reached far – Harold Evans wrote, in his loving obituary to my father, that 'His global vision and unaffected love for humanity had made him at all levels [academic seminars, the UN, the villages of South Asia, the press rooms] a brilliant mobiliser for action on questions of poverty, the environment and especially for children . . . In some parts of South India, the make-up sheet for planning the next day's page is still called a "Vittachi".' But people seemed still as narrow-minded, as full of sectarian prejudices, as war-mongering, as they had ever been. He was fast losing heart in the power of journalists to change anything.

## Participatory communication

During the last months of his life, he abandoned both his trusty typewriter and his book on the press. He wrote his last pieces, in a surprising leap into the digital age, on a laptop computer – propped up on a tray on his bed. Even more startlingly, his subject was participatory communication: no longer was he writing about media professionals being the sole guardians of democracy but only as facilitators helping ordinary people, especially poor people in the South, to operate a medium through which they could speak up for themselves.

Some new, more effective mass medium was necessary. At one point he thought it might be video, when cheap camcorders arrived that allowed people to tell their own stories directly, without the need for jet-setting journalists from the media conglomerates of the North to get in the way. What was especially good about this medium was that the viewer would have pictures and sound – they could see the real people who told or re-enacted their own stories, not just face grey text.

'But how', I asked him, thinking all this completely impractical, 'would such stories get broadcast out to the world?' He replied that the stories could be broadcast by satellite, so that everyone around the whole globe could see villagers in the South speaking up for themselves. He was in touch with idealists who wanted to make this happen, though they knew it was a very expensive and technically complex solution. Looking back, it was not a perfect answer, but it was probably the best one available at the time – and was prophetic of the coming of Internet-based television-on-demand.

Interactive CDs offered another potentially interesting medium, because here people could get the deep background they needed for proper 'process journalism', not just the daily soundbites of 'event journalism'. The interactive, hypertext medium was marvellous for providing information stacked at different levels, from broad sweeps to the very detailed, as required by different researchers. But this technology too had the disadvantages of being expensive, high-tech and static.

What were the characteristics of the perfect mass medium needed to nudge democracy along? It had to be a people's medium – participatory, cheap, fast, global, interactive. It needed 3-D space, wide enough to offer a whole range of truths (not just Mr Murdoch's) and deep enough to offer information for audiences who needed more or less background. What would such a medium look like? What he was yearning for, of course, was the World Wide Web. It arrived the year after he died.

# Whose agenda?

I wish I had known earlier about the Internet. But I grew up as a writer, not a 'techie'. So I knew nothing about it till I was introduced to the Net in 1994 by another media visionary, Peter Armstrong. Peter was a producer at the BBC, pioneering television documentaries on development like the *Politics of Compassion*, and groundbreaking series on global justice like *Everyman* and *Global Report*.

When the BBC Micro computer arrived and was offered to schools across the UK, it dawned on him that it had an unprecedented potential for interactive networking. Under his direction, a million people – schoolchildren, teachers, parents and a whole floor of technicians and editors at the BBC – came together to create the Domesday discs: a digital, interactive snapshot of Britain in 1986, exactly 900 years after William the Conqueror had done something similar (though he took it a little slower).

Despite this prodigious task, neither the BBC nor the media then believed in interactivity or multimedia: many of the media pundits of the time in the UK delighted in tearing the concepts apart. Indeed, the BBC sold off the interactive unit that Peter founded. Now, of course, it is spending millions on re-inventing a multimedia centre, and it regards the Internet as 'the third broadcasting medium'. But Peter was one of the few media people who had a sense of the potential of hypertext-based multimedia many years before, as Sir David Puttnam ruefully acknowledged in his BAFTA speech to broadcasters about the Internet in 1996.

The television industry, unfortunately for democracy, labours under a powerful but publicly uncontested form of censorship. Censorship is not limited to the sort carried out by repressive governments, forbidding the transmission of politically sensitive programmes. There are also media gatekeepers working within the industry: channel controllers who commission programmes in the first place and who find transmission slots for a chosen few.

The number of such gatekeepers is depressingly small. A handful govern the broadcast output of the whole of the UK – and, unlike politicians, they are not even elected. But if they do not want your programme, you are doomed. We keep hearing how expensive the Internet is – you have to be able to afford a good computer, a modem, a few more pounds on your phone bills each month – but making a television programme costs many tens of thousands of dollars. And that is just for a single programme, transmitted just once. To keep your agenda high in the audience's consciousness by producing repeated programmes could cost you millions. Some direct action groups manage to keep their costs down to a few thousands through 'blagging' equipment and pre-shot footage. But this usually has to be a short-term game plan, for a single issue, or a single programme: it is rarely sustainable in the long run. And, as Ken Loach pointed out, this kind of production is unfair on conventional workers in the industry.

The biggest catch of all is yet to come. Even if a group manages to beg or borrow enough resources to make a film, they still cannot get it screened unless one of the channel controllers likes it – and a film that languishes on a shelf, however brilliant, does not do anything to further democracy. As for international transmission, what people often forget is that television and radio are national institutions. By definition, your audience is not an international one, unless you are one of the even luckier few whose programmes are sold abroad. It is of cold comfort to most producers that, if their programme is not chosen, it does not reflect too much on the quality of the programme or of its producer. The gatekeepers' choices are mostly determined by commercial pressures – the notorious ratings war. One senior producer, for example, gave up trying to get any more development ideas commissioned after years of battling, and asked instead to make a programme on his other love, sailing. The response: why just one programme? Have a series!

Television executives like Paddy Coulter of the International Broadcast Trust (IBT) wring their hands in despair because they find the amount of development programming being pushed further and further into the wings, as infotainment takes centre stage. Every 2 years the IBT monitors the numbers of development programmes that get past the gatekeepers, and each time the numbers plummet further. Global justice just is not fashionable any more.

There is another drawback. Television is not an amateur's medium. You have to be a professional even to be allowed on the track, never mind to run in the race. Home-made movies are only welcome to Jeremy Beadle – or if you happen to be holding a video camera when a bucketful of gore is spilled in front of you. Event journalism of the most sensationalist kind or entertainment (are they the same thing?) are all the average citizen is thought to be good for.

## Citizens' spaces

Neither newspapers nor television offer citizens serious amounts of space in which to speak intelligently about their own agenda. A few letters (on an edited page), or fifteen minutes' worth of 'Points of View', or the occasional open-access programme – however excellent in itself – do not qualify these media as democratic fora. Mostly, members of the public are wheeled on to perform, to entertain the viewers, in ways that suit the producer.

Squeezing entertainment value out of citizens, like toothpaste out of stiff tubes, is the job of the modern broadcaster. He or she is looking for someone with a bit of 'personality' who can deliver a predictable, ready-made package, consisting of three facts, two anecdotes and a nice, crisp soundbite. And then clear off quickly without making a fuss. Most members of the public are not good media performers. They are therefore 'too boring' to be given a lot of precious airtime. Oddly enough, I have never yet met a person who did not have very moving and important things to say, when they had the chance to say them in their own time and in a sympathetic setting. But people are not performing fleas.

In some cases, speakers feel they have been deliberately tricked by the producers into saying things that are then used against them unfairly – not in order to make an important point but in order to make 'provocative television'. The appearance of offering a range of views, under circumstances like this, is deceptive. It is not about helping people to hear, respectfully, other people's genuinely held points of view: it is about creating artificial conflicts in order to raise ratings. It is about one channel competing with another, not about media democracy.

Perhaps this is why 'real-life' soaps and daytime shows like Oprah Winfrey's are so popular. They are often accused of being prurient and nastily confessional. But perhaps they go some way towards meeting a real need for citizens' spaces – places where people can do a necessary kind of 'confessing': sharing, in dramatised, heartfelt language, what they feel most strongly about. Of course the producers have picked subjects and formats that heighten sensationalism, but that may be, again, the requirement of the medium (to entertain) interfering with the need of people (to speak out together).

To sum up, our traditional mass media are spaces for entertainment professionals, like circuses with lion-tamers and trapeze artists. They are not genuine citizens' spaces because it is not much fun up on the high wire if you are not a professional. Occasionally, though, members of the audience are invited into the ring – to play among the clowns.

## CD-Roms and the shelf-space crisis

It is not just in the broadcast media that ratings-minded gatekeepers are tightening their grip. Publishers, too, are feeling the commercial heat: the 'best book' may soon be synonymous with the 'best-selling book'. And sadly, this vicious circle operates just as powerfully in CD-Rom publishing – for an unexpectedly practical reason: the size of the CD-Rom box.

Ciaran Doyle, managing director of the MultiMedia Corporation (MMC), explained it to me like this:

> The trouble is that the boxes are so big – but the computer stores only have a small amount of shelf space for CD-Roms. How many boxes can you fit on it? Maybe just 100 non-games boxes – and since space is so precious, then you have to be sure that these boxes will earn their keep by turning over fast. So what concerns you is whether enough people in your catchment area will be stimulated into purchasing products in your store. A publisher who can guarantee a mass-media campaign to support a product is more likely to achieve shelf space than a publisher who shows a very good product. The big boys like Microsoft or Dorling Kindersley can afford to spend millions of dollars on advertising campaigns, so they will always get most of the shelf space – maybe 80 per cent. All the thousands of small producers, however good their products, will be fighting for space among the other twenty. What chance do they have?
>
> You could say that the controller of the retail channel is the store owner. But the store probably belongs to a big US chain – so perhaps the chain's owners are the real gatekeepers. Or you could say that Microsoft and DK, who can afford the biggest promotional budgets, control the choices made by these chainstore owners! Just like independent broadcasters, small CD-Rom producers cannot get past the channel controllers.

Does it matter? Yes, it does, if one cares about media democracy. If the emphasis on advertising means that the more famous you are, the more a publisher will love you, then the undemocratic corollary is that the less famous you are, the less the publisher will care about publishing – or (even more important) promoting your work. Because even if you get your best friend's cousin to desktop-publish your tract, unless a major publisher who has the money and the means publicises and distributes it, who will ever know just how brilliant it is? So how will you ever become famous enough to be taken seriously by a publisher? It's a vicious circle.

In sum, communication about human rights (by which I include the broad sense of social justice) is crucial if we are to maintain democracy. But even media professionals cannot usually broadcast or publish what they feel they must on these urgent issues because what they want to say is so often censored – either by commission (say, by repressive governments, or those who kowtow to them), or by omission, if their subject matter is deemed by a small elite of gatekeepers to be unfashionable and uncommercial.

As media products are, by their very nature, so expensive to produce, promote and distribute, you almost certainly have to be a media professional to get through the gatekeepers' hoops – unless you are happy with a circulation limited to your immediate circle of friends and whoever you can meet on a street corner. Which means that a citizen who is not a media professional has virtually no chance of getting his or her voice publicly heard through today's mass media. My father (idealistic to the end) may have argued for video-cameras for villagers – but how many broadcasters would ever transmit their footage?

In these ways, not only is communication about human rights shamefully restricted in our supposedly democratic societies, but media communication as a human right is barely recognised.

# Cybercitizens

On the Net, words are cheap and distribution is easy – distribution worldwide, what is more, not just within national borders. I could go out in the morning, interview someone, and upload the interview onto the OneWorld site later that day, broadcasting out to the world at large. And no gatekeeper, either in the government or at the BBC, could tell me not to. This is not theory: we have done it, often. For the first time, any one of us who is reasonably affluent and educated, by Northern standards, can – with a little bit of training – become a journalist or broadcaster in our own right, addressing a potential audience of many millions, saying what we want to say and how we want to say it. And we can do all this without leaving the comfort of our own mouse. The Internet has provided us with an extraordinary leap towards empowerment and democracy. It is the first truly citizen-based mass medium.

Of course the Net does not just broadcast text: audio and video services are improving rapidly. When B-92, a local radio station in former Yugoslavia, was banned by the government, the broadcasters got out a message telling other Net-users that they were in trouble. OneWorld broadcast their radio programme instead – as did various other Net broadcasters – and so the messages could not be silenced. The government caved in.

As Lin Todd, the Bosnian media adviser, said:

> Traditional media cannot do the job [of democratisation] any more: they are too easy to control. So you have to look at new ways to get fair, accurate and balanced information to people. When I see the situation in Bosnia, that is where I see the value of e-mails or chat-lines – or whatever we can do! I do not doubt that at a certain point the governments will try to shut these down too. But the Internet is such a fast-moving thing, perhaps we can keep ahead. The propaganda that is put out now to incite enmity and hatred is unforgivable. Anything that can stop that is worthwhile.

Naturally, governments have already tried to gag the Net. But the tradition of freedom is so strong on the Net, that freedom is guarded zealously. At present governments cannot do too much damage without being prepared to be blatant about reducing public freedom. In China, the government feels no shame in insisting you have to get a licence to get online, but there would be an outcry if Western governments tried that trick. Singapore's authorities, too, are not ashamed to admit how much they would love to censor the Net, but they have not worked out a way to do it yet that would be politically acceptable to their citizens.

A more immediate threat is that of commercial censorship. By squeezing out the small operators, the multinationals are moving in as gatekeepers again. However, this is difficult, since, unlike in the computer stores, there is almost unlimited 'shelf' space in cyberspace ... Or is that true? Cyberspace may be vast, but there is one area that is very limited: the Net-user's screen. It has become possible for a handful of large corporations – like Microsoft, of course, and the BBC and Virgin – to position themselves so that their icons come up on viewers' computer screens as the screen flickers to life. Click on the icon for, say, the Virgin channel, or for the BBC's channel, and you are dropped at once into their site. Of course you do not have to be diverted by these icons: you could still seek out the website of your choice by typing in its address, or storing it in your favourite bookmarks list. But if you are the Web equivalent of a couch-potato, the chances are that you will take the easy way out – and just a few corporations will steal an enormous number of lazy viewers.

Is there anything that the alternative media can do? Well, we probably cannot become channel controllers who can compete with these corporations. But we can still become high-profile gatekeepers on the Net – benevolent ones, motivated by democratic rather than commercial considerations. It is what we have tried to do at OneWorld.

# OneWorld Online

OneWorld was founded by Peter Armstrong and myself. In December 1994 we were appointed directors of the OneWorld Broadcasting Trust, a charity devoted to promoting understanding between South and North through broadcasting. In January 1995, we launched OneWorld Online as the Internet arm of the Trust, to supplement the work of the two traditional broadcast media, television and radio, with this exciting new medium. We had absolutely no idea how it would take off. Quite wrongly we assumed that this would be a very small project and we launched with just one full-time worker (myself) and three part-timers (Peter, our secretary, and an inexperienced young journalist). Three years later, there are now twenty of us – and we could do with twice as many.

Within six months of the launch, the OneWorld partnership had become the world's leading website on human rights. Within 2 years, the partnership's pages were being read in over 100 countries, sixty of them from the South. We have stopped being able to count precisely how many accesses the partnership receives but we know it is many millions each month.

Why did it take off so? Because we created it as a gateway, rather than as a site promoting just the work of the Trust. Most websites followed the usual media pattern: just as a newspaper promotes its own editorial line, each organisation uses its website to promote the aspirations of the parent organisation: Amnesty International tells you about Amnesty's work. Oxfam about Oxfam's. OneWorld, however, tells you about the work of both – and also of the other 280 OneWorld partners from all over the world working in the field of global justice. And it is a place where readers can react to the partners' data. OneWorld's job is to provide a citizens' space – and one with a sufficiently high profile, so that people know that this is an open space where readers from NGOs, research bodies, schools, universities, journalists, broadcasters, or people who are just casual surfers can speak, or listen, seriously to their fellow human beings on issues of global justice.

But how does one create a gateway, even with the best of intentions, without ending up as a dictatorial gatekeeper who simply includes the voices of people one likes? The solution: to create a model that was simultaneously united and diverse, like a hand with independently moving fingers.

Each of OneWorld's partners has their own, independent website, where they have complete editorial autonomy. The OneWorld editorial team never changes a word of their documents. But there is also a shared, communal area, called the 'supersite', through which a reader can approach partners' material in all kinds of ways – and this area is managed by the editorial team. Via the Gallery, for example, you can find all the partners' photo-exhibitions gathered together. Via the Guides, you can find the partners' material gathered by theme – like child labour, for example, or racism. Via the News Service, you can find the partners' hot news. The Blast Chamber is a citizens' space where young people can blast off their opinions, the Think Tank Colloquia is where development experts can do the same.

It is important to note that the material that is available on OneWorld reflects a broad church: the editorial team by no means always agrees with the views of all its partners. Our editorial policy is to include considered material that constitutes serious debate. So, for example, on the issue of 'dying rooms' in China's orphanages, we included the television transcript denouncing the practice as well as the Chinese government's official rebuttal – and we even included the 'middle-path' opinions offered by international organisations like UNICEF who had been working with orphanages in China. The editors do, however, exclude mere hate-speech.

In this way, a wide-ranging community of people from all over the world are able to attend a kind of standing conference on global justice, available twenty-four hours per day, 365 days per year. It is available to millions of delegates from all the continents – and this is achievable without fund-raising for airfares and hotel bills, or creating impossible queues at coffee breaks.

In 1998, one of our most active partners, the European Centre for Development Policy Management, will be launching OneWorld Europe, and OneWorld will then become seriously multilingual. Other OneWorld offices (for example, in India, Central America, the Middle East and Southern Africa) are expected to follow soon. A sophisticated system of remote searching and remote authoring will mean that partners will be able to self-enter material from all over the world, and editors will be able to organise this material on the supersite to make it easy for readers to navigate it.

Devolution is the objective: the OneWorld team does not want to expand indefinitely in the UK, with obedient outposts 'overseas', like some multinational corporation. We do not want to become a superstructure, imposing a central will from above: we want to be part of an expanding partnership, facilitating that process as a supportive substructure. And we think the supersite structure will help this devolutionary wish, because it has been conceived and built from the start as a structure that promotes maximum autonomy for each partner while also providing a simple mechanism for sharing when that is appropriate.

# A baby with powerful lungs

It will not be long – perhaps just another year or so – before the courtship that has begun between television and the Net results in a noisy and spectacular birth. The baby that is born of this union will be a baby with very powerful lungs indeed.

No longer will you have to peer at a computer screen to call up the Net. You will be able to recline on your sofa, your channel-surfing handset in one hand and a glass of something cool in the other. You might watch your favourite soap till 8.30. Then you might surf the Web till 9 – perhaps taking in something more serious, like reading OneWorld's Guide on child labour. You could instantly buy a book on child labour online from OneWorld's Earthscan site with your credit card, since that gives you a 10 per cent discount. And then you could sign an online petition to help stop children being exploited as underpaid workers, run by, say, Oxfam, or by a grassroots group like Katha in India. All this would take you just a matter of moments, since you would not need to find a pen or a stamp. You would have plenty of time to refresh your drink before flicking back from the Web to the *Nine O'Clock News*, where you would watch the news item on child labour with a more educated eye. During this process you will not even notice that you will have switched seamlessly from one broadcast medium to another and back again. But you will have been able to choose – to a far greater degree than ever before – what you wanted to see on your screen (rather than what was chosen for you by a channel controller) and also to have performed with ease a couple of learning and networking actions that could benefit the cause of global justice.

No individual, and no NGO, could ever hope to challenge the media conglomerates powerfully enough single-handedly to make much of a dent in their awareness. But it is just possible that millions of disparate individuals and organisations all over the world, by Net-working together, could create a small but crucial shift in that mysterious climate known as 'public opinion'. Politicians and corporations care about that climate. Isolated, we have not a chance. But when people have a forum where we can speak up, and hear others speak up, we can build a sense of solidarity.

One last point. Good liberals in the North worry that they should not indulge in the Net when people in the South have so much less access to it than they have. It is a kind thought, but probably pointless. The North will get online as fast as it can – and so will the South. When OneWorld was launched three years ago, Latin America was already well connected and the industrialised areas of Asia were fast getting online. Only Africa had a void in the middle. But already that has substantially changed. Three-quarters of the capital cities in Africa now have some form of connectivity, and others will be connected soon.

Of course we are only talking about an urban elite gaining access, not rural people or urban people who are poor. But that is true of the North too. Never fear: the Net has not been around very long yet, and it will be a different story in a few years' time. In the meantime, we have to push hard to share out its benefits across the globe and along the economic range. We have to, because it is the only mass medium left where human rights are allowed to stay high on the agenda – because it is the only medium where we, the people, still have the right and the means to say it should.

I'd like to end with my father's favourite quote about journalism, as it is also mine:

> The free press is the omnipresent open edge of the spirit of the people, the embodied conscience of a people in itself, the articulate bond that ties the individual with the state and the world . . . It is the ruthless confession of a people to itself, and it is well known that the power of confession is redeeming. The free press is the intellectual mirror in which a people sees itself, and self-viewing is the first condition of wisdom.

# |14|

# *An alternative globalization*

## *Youthful resistance to electronic empires*

TONY DOWMUNT

This chapter looks at how groups working with 'alternative' video and television in different parts of the world have found ways to subvert or overcome the pressures towards commercial, cultural and political conformity that the 'electronic empires' exert. I want both to celebrate this work as an achievement in the face of the considerable cultural power ranged against it, and at the same time to write about it realistically, acknowledging the problems and contradictions that it raises.

It is tempting – as an 'alternative media' activist myself – to become rhetorical and utopian when writing about alternatives to the 'mainstream'. In a lot of our writing in the past there has been what Ron Burnett calls a 'sense that video will somehow break through the smoke screens manufactured by mainstream media and communicate directly to people in the community' (Burnett, 1996: 12). This way of looking at the work undervalues both the obdurate power and pleasures of the 'mainstream', and the complex processes of negotiation between producers, texts and audiences that happen, of necessity, in both mainstream and 'alternative' media production and consumption. Audiences who watch – and often enjoy – mass media are not simply and unproblematically duped by its 'smoke screens', nor is there any simple guarantee that because a production process is 'alternative' it will transparently communicate a radical message to its desired audience.

All the same, alternative media do give us specific, dynamic and lived examples of practices that challenge mainstream models – of how cultural consumers can become producers as well. The aim of this chapter is to give a concrete glimpse of the considerable current strengths of the 'alternative' movement globally, but to try to discuss it in a way that refers to relevant discourses in media studies. My hope is that discussion of both the production and reception of 'alternative' media can take its place alongside analyses of the mainstream industry from 'political-economy' or 'audience-research' perspectives. For me there is little point in understanding the behaviour of transnational media conglomerates, or of the audiences of mainstream television (however active or empowered), if this work is not also accompanied by an investigation into how to change the context of inequality in which the mainstream global media operate. A close and considered look at 'alternative' media activity is an essential part of this investigation.

An initial difficulty with this project is defining more precisely what the 'alternative' label actually means – though there is clearly an increasing amount of activity across the world that can be grouped under it. Diverse forms of media resistance have grown up, keeping pace with the process of globalization in the mainstream. Camcorder-based video activism of different sorts is now a feature in most countries in the world (Harding, 1997; Dowmunt, ed., 1993). There is a worldwide movement of indigenous peoples' media organizations, from the Amazon to the Arctic and the Australian outback. There are growing international networks of alternative media groups – for example, Tactical Media working out of Amsterdam, or Vidèazimut out of Montreal – and a marked increase in regional networking across Latin America, Southern Africa and South-East Asia.

Vidèazimut are one of a number of international groups leading an initiative to establish a 'People's Communication Charter' (Vidèazimut, 1996) which 'aims to bring to cultural policy-making a set of standards that represents rights and responsibilities to be observed in all democratic countries and in international law'. The charter asserts that: 'All people are entitled to access to the resources they need to communicate freely within and between their societies; All people need to develop their own communication skills, channels, and institutions through which they can speak for themselves with dignity and respect, and tell their own stories.'

The charter makes these demands in the context of global inequality in which:

> unless resources are re-allocated, new communication technologies tend to further widen the gap between the rich and the poor. In a growing number of countries, the concentration of commercial operators displaces public media, erodes the public sphere, and fails to provide for cultural and information needs, including the plurality of opinions and the diversity of cultural expressions and languages. (Ibid.)

It is clear that any definition of the 'alternative' has to be informed by a sense of this 'context of global inequality'. Rafael Roncagliolo defines the 'alternative' as 'what defends our cultural identities against the transnational homogenization of culture' and locates it in the (political, rather than geographical) South: 'It is the South that is coming to the defence of humanity's cultural plurality and of the rights of all peoples and sectors of society to express themselves through the mass media by word, image and voice' (Roncagliolo, 1991: 207).

Of course, one of the effects of globalization is that the old polarities –
North/South, transnational/national, global/local, indigenous/'foreign' – are
no longer so reliable as precise indicators of where inequalities in the
distribution of cultural power lie, of where the boundaries between the
powerful and the powerless are located at the end of the twentieth century.
Roncagliolo himself refers to this uncertainty when he talks of 'that part of
the South located in the North' (ibid.: 208). Geographical polarities also
leave out other structured inequalities, for instance those determined by age
or gender. Chido Matewa notes, from her research in Africa, that a primary
distinction between the mainstream and the alternative is that of 'the
mainstream media being generally dominated by men and the alternative by
women' (Matewa, 1997, personal communication).

So any useful definition of alternative media, or of what constitutes
resistance to the empires, is bound to be complex, and will need to be
informed by detailed investigation of what exactly is being resisted, by
whom, in what contexts. Maybe we have to move away from generalized
assertions, towards analysing alternative media more 'ethnographically', in
particular contexts, mirroring the way that audience research now
concentrates on 'the investigation of television consumption in its "natural"
setting, as a contextualized activity' (Morley, 1992: 173).

The importance of looking at concrete conditions in particular contexts
is one reason why in this chapter I am looking at projects involving youth.
Although 'youth' remains a broad and general category, it provides a
potentially unifying focus for looking at alternative media within diverse
global contexts, and a way of looking in more detail at specific instances of
the distribution of cultural power – in this case between older and younger
people.

The dominant, adult world has contradictory responses to young
people's relationship with the media; they are seen by some as a primary
market to be exploited, and by others as in need of protection from
manipulation or exploitation. So young people are very much at the cutting
edge of 'media imperialism': they are indeed often the first to be 'colonized'
or 'exploited' (for instance by MTV or the marketing of computer games),
and, at the same time, much of the 'moral panic' that surrounds public
debate about media 'effects' is focused on their supposed vulnerability.
Neither response is concerned very much with young people's agency or
control over their own images.

MTV's worldwide success is based on the enduring appeal of popular
music for its young audience (combined with the economic advantage
provided by the fact that the channel does not have to pay the production
costs of their basic programme ingredient – music videos). Their own
'worldwide reach estimates' for June 1997 show 296.7 million households in
the 84 territories they cover. Of course these figures do not tell us how many
of the young people in these 300 million or so homes actually watch MTV, or
with what regularity, but they do suggest a potentially enormous audience.

The figures are impressive in the USA (66.8 million households) and Europe (57.4 million), but equally so in other parts of the world: Brazil – 16.2 million; Russia – 80 million; China -16.7 million; Thailand – 12.1 million. Allowing for the relatively low figures in India (6 million) and the complete absence of Africa, this indicates a powerful, if selective, global reach.

Broadcasters are desperate to emulate the success of MTV and attract the attention of young people, as a new audience to be won for their ratings and their advertisers. To take one particular example, Stephen Marshall, director of the Canadian news organization Channel Zero is developing a new form of news programme designed to appeal to a youthful audience used to surfing the Internet and watching MTV. He challenged his more conservative – but undoubtedly anxious – colleagues at a recent conference: 'Why do so many young people watch MTV and not the news? Well, because they would rather watch that style of picture and design. Take a look at that. Don't get mad at it' (Marshall, 1996).

Plenty of adults generally do seem very willing to 'get mad at it'. The panic about young people's apparent vulnerability to new media forms seems to grip both 'conservative' and 'progressive' social groups with equal vigour. Both fear the media's apparent power to seduce young people away from values that these groups hold dear. David Buckingham points out that 'it is possible to trace this concern about the impact of new popular media on young people throughout history' (Buckingham, 1993: 3). Currently these media seem to threaten traditional, adult authority in minority or indigenous cultures threatened by 'outside' media, at least as much as they challenge the moral guardians and authoritarian structures within dominant cultures.

This provides a tricky contradiction for 'alternative' institutions such as the Inuit Broadcasting Company (IBC) in the Canadian Arctic, who 'see children as an important target group. If the culture is to survive, Inuit youth and children must understand and identify with their history, language and people. Therefore two of IBC's six programmes are directed towards the Inuit youth and children' (Christinsen and Sorensen, 1997: 20). IBC avoid setting up their own local media authoritarianism by working with elements of the media culture from the South that their young people watch and enjoy: they created a local 'superhero' – Super Shamoo – who wears a cape and a T-shirt with a big 'S' on the front, but whose magic powers (flying and seeing into the future) owe more to the traditions of Inuit shamanism than to Kryptonite origins; his side-kick is not Robin but a black raven, a traditional Inuit spirit helper.

To see young people merely as passive dupes of global media products and to undervalue the uses that they make of them undermines the democratic and empowering aims of alternative media. As Buckingham points out, 'To define young people as merely vulnerable and credulous . . . represents a forceful legitimation of adult power and control' (Buckingham, 1993: 4).

Young people in many different parts of the world, and with varying degrees of self-awareness, already use their consumption of mainstream TV as a way of subverting 'adult power and control' over how they define their lives. Marie Gillespie describes the uses Asian teenagers in the UK make of *Beverly Hills 90210* to build 'an ideal of teenage freedom' (Gillespie, 1995: 45). Corinna Sturmer speculates that the popularity of MTV in Sweden comes from the way that it provides 'voluntary exile for bored Swedish youth' (Sturmer, 1993: 58). Thomas Tufte's research in the Gaucho communities in Southern Brazil reveals how 'some young Gauchos identify with the transnational urban cultures of young Americans or young Paulistas (inhabitants of Sao Paulo) than with the national Brazilian discourse with which their parents perhaps identify' (Tufte, 1997: 26). What is clear is that young people actively use the media products at their disposal to help them build their own culture, often in opposition to the cultures of family and community that immediately surround them.

Nevertheless, however active young people are as viewers of global television, their agency and power remains limited in most cases to their role as the consumers – rather than, say, the producers or schedulers – of programmes. As David Morley points out, 'the power of viewers to reinterpret meanings is hardly equivalent to the discursive power of centralized media institutions to construct the texts which the viewer then interprets' (Morley, 1995: 313). The importance of alternative production is that it represents an appropriation – however limited and tentative – of some of this discursive power.

# Rebels with a cause

'Rebeldes con Cauce' is the name of a project currently underway in Bogota, Colombia. It is a response to the particular situation of the media in that country, and to wider social factors. The project has been training a representative group of 140 young people in the city (mostly between 15 and 25 years old), with no previous experience, to make their own films. Project organizer and film-maker Felipe Aljure indicts the global television available to young people in Colombia for promoting 'unrealizable dreams' which are 'only a focus for frustration which clog their souls and choke their capacity for self-expression' (Aljure, 1997, personal communication). His aim is to turn a group of people who have been 'traditional audiovisual message receivers' into 'audiovisual message producers', to alter the imbalance between the small number who produce, and the large number who consume television programming. He sees this imbalance operating both within Colombia, and internationally through 'local, foreign and imperial forms of information which manipulate culture and public opinion, usually towards tendencies and behaviors that favour their particular interests and views of the world' (ibid.).

Aljure characterizes Colombia as 'an atomised society in which social and group action have decreased, while individuality and selfishness have grown excessively' (ibid.). So an important secondary aim for the project was to use the necessarily collective nature of film-making to provide a spur to group action, 'to construct spaces in which people have to work together to achieve a common goal'. This enabled them to attract a high level of funding (US$500,000) from the Departamento Administrativo de Acción Communal de Bogotá. 'Communal action' has become a vote-winning platform for local politicians, and Aljure and his team (Sylvia Amaya, a 40-year-old professional film-maker like Aljure, and a young producer, Pablo Duque) were able to exploit this to further their project.

The majority of the young people who participated were from economically disadvantaged backgrounds, seven from each of the twenty localities that make up the city. They began by watching films, discussing their reactions, then deconstructing what they had seen so they could understand more clearly how their responses had been structured by the various techniques that went into making the films they had viewed. Then Aljure and his colleagues 'reversed the process and asked them to identify a concept, idea or sensation that they wanted to convert into an audiovisual message' (ibid.). All 140 young people came up with outline proposals from which each of the groups from the twenty localities chose their favourite, and all but one of the groups then went on to produce their own ten to fifteen-minute films using new digital production and editing equipment provided by the city government.

The films were dramas and comedies in a range of styles, from those that challenged traditional images of Colombia and Bogota, to those that reinforced them. Aljure comments that there were 'of course a great percentage of visions implanted from foreign images and programmes' and he was concerned by the fact that the majority of the 140 initial outline proposals had a narrative line resolved by violent death. His conclusion after analysing the proposals was that 'as material for social diagnosis we can foresee a society that has no space to solve its conflicts by dialogue or conciliation, no way but death' (ibid.).

The films were screened at 7 p.m. on Bogota's TV channel Canal Capital and attracted 'outstanding' ratings, according to the station manager. Aljure's ultimate aim was that the young people he works with would, under their own leadership, become legally organized, inherit the equipment donated by the city to the project and start to produce professionally for a recently licensed network of local TV stations. (At the time of writing they have just received the equipment from the city, on loan for a 5-year, extendable period.) From that kind of institutional base young people in Bogota may be able to imagine and represent ways – other than death – out of the conflicts that face them. Aljure himself has been appointed National Director of Cinematography at the newly formed Ministry of Culture and is using the experience of Rebeldes con Cauce as a pilot for a similar programme all over the country.

The recent political transformation in South Africa has opened up similar opportunities. For instance, the Media Training and Development Trust (MTDT) in Cape Town are in the process of training young people, mainly activists from political and Labour organizations, to service a regional community TV station which will have an initial audience reach of 2 million. In the presentation paper for the project, Peter Heller refers to 'the historical imbalances of the distribution of power, by which South Africa is deeply affected. These imbalances are especially clear in the media sector, which is highly monopolised by Western and Afrikaaner business interests' (Heller, 1997: 3). He comments that 'community media in South Africa play an essential role in providing an alternative to SABC (the South African Broadcasting Corporation) and the mainstream press, which are seen as one-sided and "sterile" when it comes to monitoring the real conflicts and challenges of this country' (ibid.: 1). MTDT plan to address this by screening programmes 'produced by members of the communities themselves, thereby revealing their special life-situations and experiences' (ibid.: 3).

Rebeldes con Cauce and MTDT offer models of working within one city or region that oppose national and global media regimes at a local level. But in the same way that trade unions have had to learn to organize internationally to deal with transnational capital, it is clear that effective challenges to mainstream media globalization will need to be mounted globally. The work of organizations like Vidèazimut cited above represents an aspect of global resistance to the global media empires, but there are also projects using media which span more than one country or region which have gone some way towards setting up international links.

Development Education for Youth (DEFY), an organization based in Dublin, recently completed a video project called *Living on the Edge*. DEFY is interested in enabling young people to reflect on 'the structural causes of inequality in our interdependent world, by linking local and global issues, by imagining a better future and by taking action towards change' (Kelly, 1997: 25). The project, in the words of DEFY worker Kevin Kelly, is 'a collection of documentary films made by young film makers from Ireland and Brazil and so contains the unmediated voices of young people as they try to make sense of their lives' (ibid.). The films were made in Limerick and Recife and feature young people from both cities talking to camera and showing their daily lives in a fresh and direct manner. They were produced by professional film- and video-makers working in close collaboration with the young people concerned. Kelly adds: 'Without compromising the reality of poverty, the films show images of vibrant communities, images that show that young people in the South can have the same hopes, live under the same hardships, and share the same visions as young people living in Ireland, thereby drawing common threads between both societies' (ibid.)

One of these threads is enthusiasm for 'world' music of different kinds – not necessarily the predictable kinds. Jason from Limerick is a Reggae fan, and relates the messages of hardship in the Jamaican music and lyrics to conditions in Ireland: 'It's hard over here too', he says, after singing Bob Marley's track: 'Half the story has never been told / So now you see the light / Stand up for your rights'. In the Alto *favela* (slum) in Recife we see two young women performing in punk-rock bands, and discussing how they have to overcome sexist prejudices to do so. The films have been widely shown in Limerick and Recife, and DEFY distribute them to schools and youth organizations all over Ireland. They have yet to persuade RTE (Radio Telefis Eireann – the Irish national broadcaster) to show them.

Downtown Community Television Center (DCTV) in New York has been a focus for alternative media for over a quarter of a century, enabling the diverse communities in the city to 'study television production on inexpensive equipment and make videos about issues large and small that matter to them. In addition, they can air their work on one of four public access cable channels New York media activists fought to create' (Lucas, 1996: 1). DCTV was set up in 1972 by Jon Alpert and Keiko Tsuno 'to empower disempowered communities in New York through providing access to video equipment and training' (ibid.). Jon and Keiko were among the first American film-makers to produce documentaries in countries like Cuba and Vietnam, but it is only in recent years that DCTV has begun to work on international community projects, notably in Brazil and Siberia.

They set up a 'video-letters' exchange scheme between young people in a *favela* in Sao Paolo and a poor neighbourhood in New York. The resulting 'letters' are an amazing testament to cultural difference, laced with generational similarities and solidarity: two 14-year-old Paulista girls deliver a rooftop rap on survival in the *favela*, followed by a young man working in a Manhattan MacDonalds, secretly filming himself taking out the garbage late at night – messages from the South, and from 'the South in the North', delivered with an exuberance and directness rarely seen on mainstream television.

Martin Lucas of DCTV travelled to Russia in 1996 with an assignment to set up a community video training centre with TV-2, a small independent television station in the Siberian city of Tomsk. The US federal government paid for the equipment costs out of a programme designed to encourage 'independent' broadcasting in the former Soviet bloc. 'Needless to say this was the only case that I could find where independent was also "alternative"', comments Lucas, in his account of setting up what would be the first community media centre in Russia and DCTV's first sister centre (Lucas, 1997, personal communication).

The TV station he was working with, Tomsk TV-2, is independent but commercial part of a loose network of independent stations. There are also four commercial networks based on large Moscow stations, as are the two state-owned systems. The commercial programming varies, but most of it tends towards game shows and music shows. The soap operas are foreign, mainly from Brazil, Mexico and the USA, the Brazilian ones being the most popular: 'There are also lots of American shows on the screens, and there is a big US involvement, from both business and government, in developing an American style television system in Russia.' As Lucas explains, TV-2 was very unusual in its interest in developing an 'alternative' media approach: 'On one level alternative media just has more to do with the mind set of the people who work at the station. Almost everyone at the station is young. Tomsk is a university town. The editor-in-chief is a lecturer in medieval Chinese philosophy. The chief engineer got his training in control and guidance systems.'

The other important factor is that the station wants to remain politically independent and in order to do so needs a 'media-literate' audience. According to Lucas, the station is regularly attacked by local politicians who do not like the coverage they are getting:

> While I was in Tomsk this fall a politician made a speech, aired on TV-2, attacking the station for 'Americanism'. This is based on the fact that the station shows the *X-Files*, which are quite popular, and the *Simpsons*, which is not. (Arkady, the station president, told me the most popular thing on TV is still old Soviet films.) They also show WTN Evening News for their international news. Except for a series of special reports from Chechnya financed directly by a local progressive businessman, and occasional reports from Moscow, the station has no correspondents outside the city.

Some of the problems that Lucas encountered related to the fact that the idea of the press as a 'fourth estate' was only 5 or 6 years old and almost all training by foreign or national organizations is devoted to developing a commercially based 'professional' media. In addition, they were working with young people for whom the only 'oppositional' culture with a popular base was music: 'for young people in particular, oppositional culture is heavily co-opted by corporations'.

One of the stories covered by the Tomsk Media Center participants was evangelism – a live issue, with many evangelistic groups proselytizing across Russia. Another 'intriguing' piece was about a young homeless man: homelessness is not a widespread phenomenon in Siberia. Lucas comments: 'Historically it was illegal, and climate-wise it is tough. The man in question actually is living in the forest, the *taiga*. The story deals with complex notions of the nature of alienation and social expectations in a society both opening and in some ways collapsing.'

The stories made by the young people involved in the Media School were aired in a fifteen-minute slot on TV-2 once a week – the local equivalent of 'public access', the home of so much of American alternative media: 'The impact was limited but real. Tomsk, with a half million people, is small enough that the media center is known throughout the city, but big enough to generate an urban anonymity. The stories didn't create a city wide sensation, but they were watched, noted and discussed around town' (Lucas, 1997, personal communication). As an alternative practitioner, Lucas acknowledges that

> . . . producing for television has dangers. I spent a lot of time arguing with the Siberians about the dangers of focussing our efforts on producing 'television' without redefining the kind of television involved. There was a strong tendency to re-inforce stylistic notions from mainstream, usually foreign, models. Since Russian news is still given to 5-minute stories on trade conferences and the like, there's some virtue to a zippier approach, but I was worried that they were just slotting kids into a commercial network approach.
>
> (Lucas, 1997)

Among the most interesting aspects of DCTV's experiment in Tomsk are the complex processes of cultural translation necessitated by the encounter of US alternative media values with Russian culture. Lucas comments that 'Bakunin may have lived here, but the anarchist spirit is hardly flourishing, except in the under 20 crowd' (Lucas, 1996). In his training work with the young people, he had to fight a prevailing attitude amongst some of the older people directing the scheme that 'sees learning as a hierarchical activity with fear as an important motivation' (ibid.). Hearing himself arguing vigorously with these people for an open-access policy, Lucas comments that 'the irony of an American telling a group of Russians to trust "the masses" to have intelligent ideas they will express in the medium of video doesn't escape me'.

The work of DEFY and DCTV suggests a use of transnational networking that fosters equality of exchange and generational solidarity. But these networks are still relatively limited: they do not address the problem of getting the work shown more widely than within and between the communities that produced them. In that respect they pose no challenge at all, at the moment, to the global empires whose enterprises are driven by their exploitation and dominance of enormous global audiences. There are, however, a few emerging prospects for the distribution and exhibition of 'alternative' material on a wider scale. WE-TV was initiated by a Canadian development organization – International Development Research Center (IDRC) – after the Rio Summit in 1992. It is already distributing programming to partner broadcasters at national and regional levels across the world, and is planning to make use of DBS – direct broadcast satellite – to offer a full service to individual subscribers. Alpha TV is an Eastern European consortium (with twenty-five member countries) in the process of setting up a satellite channel dedicated to indigenous production with cultural and social objectives, in a competitive market already heavily penetrated by MTV and CNN. Alpha will potentially be a home for the kind of production work initiated by the partnership of TV-2 and DCTV in Tomsk.

A lot of the youth-oriented programming featured in this chapter will certainly find a willing distributor in Mondial, the proposed new European-wide satellite channel. Mondial was originally conceived as 'the first truly global channel' (Fountain and Stevens, 1994), with the aim of creating 'the possibility of equality of communication – within Europe, between North and South, between East and West' and of harnessing 'the vast potential of advanced new technologies to the cause of democratic communication'. As such it built on the international work of one of its founders, Alan Fountain, when he was Senior Commissioning Editor for Independent Film and Video at Channel 4 in the UK. The plan was to base Mondial on 'a network of global partnerships' in which 'producers and managers from the South are intimately involved from the beginning'. This initial vision has undergone some modification, as Fountain (1998, personal communication) explains:

At the outset Mondial's aim was to attempt to create a pan-European channel which would draw on independent programming from all parts of the world, and an initial feasibility study was made with support from the European Union. The cost of creating such a channel, even though it was based primarily on acquired programmes, was very considerable and immediately confronted the project with its most fundamental problem: is it possible to create a channel with cultural values and objectives historically associated with public-service television in an environment defined by commercial imperatives?

At the beginning it was thought that it might be possible to launch the channel with a mix of public and private backing. The European Union had shown some interest in the development of pan-European cultural channels through its support for Euronews. However, although there was very strong support from the cultural sector of the European Parliament, it rapidly became clear that there was no corresponding will in the European Commission to go beyond low-level development support.

During the 1990s most European governments have presided over the rapid development of commercial television systems and, in most cases, have created a climate in which public broadcasters have felt obliged to develop commercially driven policies in order to survive. The expanding private sector, although it often cloaks itself beneath the language of choice for viewers, has demonstrably failed to widen the range of programmes available to viewers and is extremely wary of anything not easily classified as mass entertainment. Unsurprisingly, it is very difficult to raise sufficient levels of money to launch a project like Mondial in a period when the very idea of the 'public sector' across the whole range of public services is under severe ideological and financial pressure and when the profit-driven values of 'the market' reign supreme.

Mondial has also been investigating the possibility of finding space within the new world of digital television and this has offered some grounds for optimism. One often reads that the vast televisual space opened up by digitalization has created a desert wilderness desperate for the water of new content. However this is not as straightforward as it might seem. The audience take-up of new digital channels has so far been rather slow and most digital operators are extremely conservative in their judgement of what type of content might attract viewers to these – mainly subscription – services. Whilst Mondial remains convinced that there is a consistent minority audience for such a channel it is far from easy to convince digital gatekeepers of such a view.

Even so there might well be the possibility of creating blocks of Mondial programming for use in various parts of the digital world even if not, in the short term, the launch of an entire channel and service. A recent feasibility study conducted by Mondial into digital television indicates that if carriage in the major European territories was obtained as the network develops, a financially viable channel could be created. There remains the ideological rather than financial problem of convincing a commercial system to risk supporting a Mondial-style initiative.

In the face of the difficulties of achieving carriage and financial backing for either analogue or digital television at present, Mondial has in recent months been considering the potential of the Internet to achieve some if not all of its cultural objectives. Over the next year Mondial will establish a website which will provide a focal point for independent producers around the world, create a database of independent work, initiate a distribution system using the Internet and focus on the use of the Internet as a production medium in its own right.

This activity will also prepare Mondial to take advantage of technological developments which will lead to new forms of distribution, whether this be Web TV, or accessing television via the PC.

Mondial's recent feasibility study confirmed their own instinct to go for a schedule that would appeal to a 'youthful' audience (in attitude as much as age); the study concluded that the channel could be commercially viable in the long term (after initial public investment), assuming the core audience would be in the 16–35 age-range. Mondial are currently conducting specific audience research in that range and devising production strategies that are particularly responsive to input by young people.

It is not my intention to make large claims for the work outlined in this chapter: the 'electronic empires' are not immediately about to transform themselves in response to these or all the other diverse initiatives of media activists throughout the world. We remain, in Martin Lucas's phrase about Deep Dish (the alternative satellite network in the USA), 'hitchhikers on the edge of the eight-lane information superhighway' (Lucas, 1993; part

3). But what these examples of work by young people do show is that alternative media provide a space in which groups whose presence is excluded from or distorted by the mainstream media can gain some power over how they are represented; and that when these groups have a chance to network internationally, or distribute these representations to wider audiences, they begin to create what have been called, elsewhere in this book (p. 208), 'alternative globalizations'.

Rather than being imprisoned by an exclusively 'top-down' concept of globalization, we need to imagine and create global networks where cultures can meet and interact in conditions of relative equality – relative, that is, to the conditions of global dominance and one-way flow imposed by the electronic empires. With Martin Lucas, I believe that

> what we are doing is 'rehearsing' for a media universe that barely exists, one not controlled by large corporations and the governments that serve them. The media culture of the corporations defines desire as something that can be quenched through consumerism. It is mainly circular: TV's reality is itself. Our hope is that the kids we work with will articulate their own realities, their needs and their desires in a way that is about their own lives and the world they live in, the world they want to create.

# References

Buckingham, D. (1993) *Reading Audiences: Young People and the Media*, Manchester University Press, Manchester.

Burnett, R. (1996) 'Voice of the voiceless' and other well worn clichés, *Zebra News*, 27, pp. 10–13.

Christinsen, L. and Sørensen, L. (1997) Of the Inuit, for the Inuit, by the Inuit – aboriginal network making headway in Canada, *Zebra News*, 32, pp. 18–21.

Dowmunt, T. (ed.) (1993) *Channels of Resistance: Global Television and Local Empowerment*, British Film Institute and Channel 4, London.

Fountain, A. and Stevens, S. (1994) *Mondial Television – Launch Document*, London.

Gillespie, M. (1995) *Television, Ethnicity and Cultural Change*, Routledge, London.

Harding, T. (1997) *The Video Activist's Handbook*, Pluto Press, London.

Heller, P. (1997) *MTDT Community Television Project*, Presentation Paper, MTDT, Cape Town.

Kelly, K. (1997) DEFY TV: living on the edge, *Zebra News*, 31, pp. 25–6.

Lucas, M. (1993) Interview in the television documentary *Tactical TV*, APT Film & Television for Channel 4, London.

Lucas, M. (1996) Letter From Siberia, *Scanlines*, winter 1996, pp. 1–2.

Marshall, S. (1996) All mouth and no future, *Guardian* (G2), 9 Dec., p. 15.

Michaels, E. (1994) *Bad Aboriginal Art – Tradition, Media and Technological Horizons*, University of Minnesota Press, Minneapolis.

Morley, D. (1992) *Television, Audiences and Cultural Studies*, Routledge, London.

Morley, D. (1995) Theories of consumption in media studies, in Miller, D. (ed.) *Acknowledging Consumption*, Routledge, London.

Roncagliolo, R. (1991) Notes on 'the alternative', in Thede, N. and Ambrosi, A. (eds) *Video: The Changing World*, Black Rose Books, Montreal.

Sturmer, C. (1993) MTV's Europe, in Dowmunt, T. (ed.) *Channels of Resistance: Global Television and Local Empowerment*, British Film Institute and Channel 4, London.

Tufte, T. (1997) Gaucho life in the global communication era, *Zebra News*, 32, pp. 22–7.

Vidèazimut (1996) The People's Communication Charter, Vidèazimut, 3680 Rue Jeanne-Mance/ bureau 430, Montreal, Quebec, Canada H2X 2K5 (Tel: 1 514 982 6660 / Fax: 1 514 982 6122 / email: videaz@web.net).

# Acknowledgement

Thanks to Felipe Aljure, Ursula Biemann, Shareef Cullis, Alan Fountain and Signe Byrge Sørensen for help with this chapter; and particularly to Martin Lucas for the wealth of material he provided.

# |15|

# Electronic empires

## An Islamic perspective

ALI MOHAMMADI

This chapter attempts to analyse how Islamic countries encounter electronic media and discusses the various approaches of these countries to modern media systems. It will also focus on the rapid growth of international television in the Islamic countries in general and the Arab world in particular, and finally will examine the impact of international television on different Islamic countries. It is argued that the priorities of national interests become secondary to global market forces, and that the emergence of a few powerful mega-corporations is instrumental in establishing the domination of Western culture and consumer society in the Islamic world.

The purpose of this chapter is to analyse the Islamic responses to the expansion and influence of electronic empires. Electronic empires are presented here in terms of the legacy of colonialism and the continuing response to the incursion of Western modernity. After the independence movements of the 1950s and 1960s, many newly independent countries copied media systems from their colonial masters as part of the process of building nationhood. While total domination by colonial powers was gradually diminishing, a new colonisation emerged in the form of 'zones of influence'. In the past, most of the colonial powers did not limit themselves only to their own colonies but were always eager to extend their influence beyond the limitations of their colonial territories. Some of the countries of the developing world that were not among the colonies, such as Iran, were clustered within these zones. They, too, were eventually affected by rivalry among the international powers.

Over the past 50 years the form this power and influence has taken has shifted from military force to economic power, and into the dimension of cultural power. With the globalisation of culture as commodities for trade, the rhetoric of market forces has become a new dogma for the end of the twentieth century. John Berger described this process:

The editor and publishers would like to thank Icom Publications for permission to use the data for Tables 15.2 and 15.6.

As the global plan advances, it increasingly demands a global de-politicisation. Otherwise, the protests of the suffering majority may become too insistent. Our decoy politicians are the agents of such de-politicisation. Not necessarily by choice, but by compliance. They accept the global market's projection concerning the future as if it were a natural law, instead of examining it for what it is.

(Berger, 1995)

In order to find out 'what it is', we need to look at the policy shifts of the major international institutions, such as the World Bank and the International Monetary Fund. Lending mechanisms are used as an instrument to push forwards the policy of privatising national assets for the benefit of the few emerging mega-corporations such as Time Warner, Disney, Bertelsmann, Viacom and News Corporation (Herman and McChesney, 1997).

During the 1980s, the ideology of corporate capitalism forced through deregulation of markets, and the expansion of the mainly Western-based transnational corporations beyond existing geographical boundaries was seen as the answer to unemployment and economic stagnation (Mohammadi, ed., 1997). As in the beginning of colonisation, economic structures in every corner of the world were profoundly affected, disturbing traditional patterns of production and consumption in order to integrate economies into the competitive world markets demanded by the West. The development of a communication infrastructure became a necessity to bring the labour force of the colonial regions of Asia, Africa and Latin America into the single market of Europe (Latouche, 1996).

In order to do this, the West used whatever means it had to destroy the very fabric of social systems which were functional in traditional economies (Latouche, 1996: 20). Thus, the old way of being was destroyed and a dependent way of life was born. What was not considered very important was the question of 'culture', or any sort of cultural resistance to the adoption of a Western way of life. Yet globalisation was not possible unless the culture became open to mass consumption – the foremost instrumental means for the globalisation of culture. With the end of the Cold War and the demise of the Soviet Union, there was no longer any powerful ideological opposition to preaching the free market and preparing public opinion to support these policies of privatisation and deregulation.

In the early 1980s, communication technology accounted for about 18 per cent of world trade, which is roughly equal to $350 billion. By the mid-1980s, because of deregulation and the rapid expansion of corporate capitalism, the value of communication technology and information industries had jumped to $1600 billion (Herman and McChesney, 1997: 38).

## Islamic states' attitudes to globalisation

Islamic states must consider to what extent they will accept the rule of the market economy and the penetration of Western cultural industries. In order to establish the precise operation of market forces, it is helpful to divide Islamic countries into three categories or trends: modernist, mixed and traditionalist.

According to Alwani (1981), in relation to cultural strategy, there are three modes of response to Western secular modernity prevailing in the Muslim world. None of the Islamic countries is at ease in accepting the mores of Western consumer society, but these categories indicate how flexible they are towards the expansion of electronic empires. The first can be described as the traditionalist approach. Some Muslims would like to follow the 'straight path' of Islam as in the period of Mohammed 1400 years ago, ignoring all technological and cultural developments since then. This approach could also be described as a search for an authentic religious culture, which is antithetical to modern secular culture. The second approach is one of modernisation, adopting a Western view of 'modern' culture and civilisation, but, at the same time, trying to adapt the Islamic view of life in relation to the modern world. The impact of developments in communications technology and media content is to encourage the adoption of this modernist worldview in Islamic countries. The third approach to modernity can be described as a 'mix' of the more compatible aspects of Islamic thought with modern Western thought. Most of the Islamic world is struggling between tradition and modernity, torn over the method of reform and adaptation.

Table 15.1 briefly indicates the variety of responses in the Islamic world to modernisation. The majority of Muslim countries are slowly adopting modernity, though many are still at the 'mixed' stage. At the end of twentieth century, with the rapid expansion of information technologies and international television, the number of traditionalists among the Islamic states is shrinking.

The countries of the Arab world from the Nile valley (Egypt, Sudan, Somalia, Djibouti) to the West (Morocco, Tunisia, Libya, Algeria and Mauritania), to the fertile crescent (Syria, Lebanon, Jordan, Palestine and Iraq), to the Persian Gulf region (Saudi Arabia, Kuwait, United Arab Emirates (UAE), Bahrain, Qatar, Oman and Yemen) all share one language, one religion and a single civilisation. Their traditions and cultures generally are the outcome of the interaction between the Islamic religion and the Arabic language. They are intimately connected with Islam, as are the non-Arab Muslim countries around the world, through the Quran, which still sets the standard of good Arabic-language usage. However, while they may be very nationalist, they do not necessarily share the same politics, especially in relation to the Western world. In economic terms, the Arab world has its share of inequalities – from thinly populated and oil-rich Gulf states to densely populated and relatively poor Egypt and Jordan.

Among the twenty-one Arab countries, those adopting the modernising approach are Egypt, Tunisia, Morocco, UAE, Bahrain, Qatar, Kuwait, Oman, Jordan, Palestine and Yemen. They are all modernist in terms of the

**Table 15.1** Attitudes of Islamic states towards modernity

| Country | Modern | Mix | Traditional |
|---|---|---|---|
| **Arab states** | | | |
| Algeria | ✓ | ✓ | |
| Bahrain | | ✓ | ✓ |
| Djibouti | | ✓ | ✓ |
| Egypt | ✓ | ✓ | |
| Iraq | ✓ | | |
| Jordan | ✓ | ✓ | ✓ |
| Kuwait | | ✓ | ✓ |
| Lebanon | ✓ | | |
| Libya | ✓ | | ✓ |
| Palestine | ✓ | ✓ | |
| Qatar | ✓ | | ✓ |
| Saudi Arabia | | ✓ | ✓ |
| Sudan | | ✓ | ✓ |
| Syria | ✓ | ✓ | |
| UAE | ✓ | | ✓ |
| Yemen | | ✓ | ✓ |
| | | | |
| **Non-Arab states** | | | |
| Afghanistan | | | ✓ |
| Azerbaijan | ✓ | | |
| Bangladesh | ✓ | ✓ | |
| Indonesia | ✓ | | |
| Iran | | ✓ | ✓ |
| Kazakhstan | ✓ | | |
| Kyrgyzstan | ✓ | | |
| Malaysia | ✓ | ✓ | |
| Pakistan | ✓ | ✓ | |
| Somalia | | | |
| Tajikistan | ✓ | | |
| Turkey | ✓ | ✓ | |
| Turkmenistan | ✓ | | |
| Uzbekistan | ✓ | | |

development process and are markets for Western consumer goods, yet at the same time are keen to keep their Arab traditions.

After the fall of the Shah in Iran in 1979, who was the guardian of Western interests and a modernist figure in the Persian Gulf region, UAE has become strategically very important for the global market and Sheikh Rashid, the ruler of Dubai, has become the advocate of modernisation in the region (Brewer, 1994). From the mid-1980s Dubai became a new global hub and a commercial centre for the promotion of Western communication hardware and software. As a result, the media industry, especially television, which was introduced to the Emirate only in 1969, became very significant. In the Emirates, as elsewhere in the Arab world, television was state-owned and state-run and the programming was largely local. However, by the mid-

1980s when a second channel was launched several foreign programmes were routinely broadcast, in English, partly to cater to the large number of expatriates from the Indian subcontinent who worked in Dubai. The availability of satellite technology made this new programming accessible to the wider Arab community. The Space Network of Dubai, part of the Arabsat system, began operations in 1992. This pan-Arabic network spans from the Indian subcontinent to the Islamic republics of Central Asia to Southern Europe, and broadcasts round the clock. Its main programmes consist of news services – both in Arabic and in English – entertainment programmes, films and drama, both in English and in Arabic (Amin, 1996: 121).

However, it is Egypt, the most populous Arab country and once a champion of pan-Arab ideology, which has gained more support from the Western governments, particularly the USA, not only for recognition of Israel but also for supporting the Western model of development – it is one of the highest receivers of US aid. With its rich cultural resources, Egypt has been a key centre for Arabic film and television production and thus a catalyst for advocating the modernist trend in the Islamic world in general and the Arab region in particular. The country's emphasis on secular entertainment, coupled with a pan-Arab perspective, has made Egypt the most important producer of Arabic media artefacts in the region. In addition, the Egyptian media is also promoting Western images for expansion of tourism, a significant sector of the country's economy (*Middle East Broadcast and Satellite*, 1993a).

# Growth of national television

As elsewhere in the developing world, the colonial legacy skewed the development of the communication network among the Arab nations. Every national broadcasting establishment was the outcome of the colonial power and its zone of influence. As a consequence of this process, some Muslim countries not only adopted similar media systems in terms of institutions but, despite the policy implications, had no other choice than also to accept the electronic systems of their colonial/zone masters. Systems such as PAL, SECAM and NTSC were born as a consequence of colonial divisions, which continue to be reflected in the sharp divisions in consumption in the global market in the use of electronic manufacturing goods. Even today many Islamic countries lack the expertise for selecting technology in general and communication technology in particular.

In the Arab world, television broadcasting started in the 1950s with Morocco being the first Arab nation to acquire TV, in 1954, followed by Algeria, Iraq and Lebanon in 1956. Television was introduced to Egypt in 1960 and to Saudi Arabia 5 years later. In all countries, governments played a key role in the development of television and consequently controlled the programming content and delivery systems. Such support from governments made television organisations less dependent on advertising. Educational programming, news and information and cultural and religious awareness became professed aims of broadcasters while entertainment was considered only marginal. The state control of news and information channels ensured compliance by Arab journalists to the policy prescriptions of the often undemocratic rulers, obstructing the evolution of any public space for democratic debate.

## Arabsat

Arabsat – the pan-Arab satellite network – emerged as a result of deliberations within the Arab League and the establishment in 1969 of the Arab States Broadcasting Union, a regional mechanism to exchange cultural and educational television programmes in the Arab world. Some national television services, such as those in Saudi Arabia and Egypt, became part of Arabsat for direct broadcast to homes across the Arab world because of powerful transmission and their respective claims on the Arab leadership.

In 1976, when the Arab Satellite Communications organisation was established in the Middle East region they were ahead of other Islamic countries. They aimed to have the first international satellite for providing information, education, religious and entertainment services from the perspective of the Arab culture and society (Warwick, 1993).

As the demand for satellite technology grew, from 1981, after a fierce international competition, France became the first contractor to deploy the three first-generation Arabsats. These three satellites were specially made to meet the needs of the member-state countries particularly for domestic TV reception, using antennae less than 2 m in diameter, as well as for regional and international telecommunication (ibid.: 8).

Arabsat consists of twenty-one member states holding various shares, the lowest (0.1 per cent) belonging to Djibouti and the highest (36.66 per cent) to Saudi Arabia. Table 15.2 shows the shareholdings of individual countries. The Arabsat organisation consists of a general assembly, whose delegates are ministers of telecommunication and chairs of the national post, telegraph and telephone services (PTT) of all members. Every year the general assembly meets to discuss policy and review strategy. The headquarters of the consortium is in Riyadh, the capital of Saudi Arabia. After 1979, with the signing of the peace treaty with Israel, Egypt was no longer a member of Arabsat until it rejoined the Arab League in 1988.

In 1985, Arabsat 1A and 1B were launched into orbit and became operational – such was the keenness to have access to new information technology. Two Arabsat ground stations, one in Dirhab in Saudi Arabia and one in Eddikhilaat, Tunisia, became operational solely in the domain of the Arab people. Now for the first time the Arab world had access to what was to become known as the 'information highway'. The Arabsat

Table 15.2 Member-state shareholdings in Arabsat

| Country (by rank) | Share (%) | Country (by rank) | Share (%) |
|---|---|---|---|
| 1 Saudi Arabia | 36.7 | 12 Yemen | 1.6 |
| 2 Kuwait | 14.6 | 13 Egypt | 1.5 |
| 3 Libya | 11.3 | 14 Oman | 1.2 |
| 4 Qatar | 9.8 | 15 Tunisia | 0.7 |
| 5 UAE | 4.7 | 16 Morocco | 0.6 |
| 6 Jordan | 4.0 | 17 Sudan | 0.3 |
| 7 Lebanon | 3.8 | 18 Mauritania | 0.3 |
| 8 Bahrain | 2.4 | 19 Palestine | 0.2 |
| 9 Syria | 2.1 | 20 Somalia | 0.2 |
| 10 Iraq | 1.9 | 21 Djibouti | 0.1 |
| 11 Algeria | 1.7 | | |

Source: *Middle East Broadcast and Satellite*, 1.1, Jan. 1993
(Note: During the Gulf War Iraq was suspended temporarily)

consortium is the only organisation in the Islamic world that has acquired satellite launch vehicles and control systems and has full control of pan-Arab orbital broadcasting and telecommunication systems (*Middle East Broadcast and Satellite*, 1993a).

# The arrival of commercial television

Arabsat had acted as a kind of filter for the flow of satellite television into the Arab world, but from the mid-1980s the liberalisation of broadcasting systems and the development of direct broadcast satellite (DBS) had a profound effect on media in Middle Eastern countries. First, there was a major change in the style and content of television programming in relation to the globalisation of the market. Popular access to some television programmes was perceived, in some Arab countries, as a threat to Islamic and Arab national culture. With the expansion of international television and the rapid increase of the various satellite footprints, with a satellite dish people could have access to various uncontrolled channels. This easy access caused serious criticism of the performance of the Arabsat and of some Arab national television services (Warwick, 1993: 9).

The Iraqi invasion of Kuwait, in August 1990, had a dramatic impact on national broadcasting services in the Persian Gulf region. As a consequence of the Kuwait crisis, the Middle East became a key focus of the international news agencies and the people in the region were exposed to an extensive international TV; the spread of satellite became inevitable. Bahrain, in competition with the rest of the Arab world, and regardless of the impact on Islamic culture, began to rebroadcast CNN's twenty-four-hours-a-day service on conventional terrestrial systems with the signal boosted to allow reception across Saudi Arabia and the other Arab states. The government of

Saudi Arabia was not happy about allowing CNN to broadcast the destruction of the Iraqi forces and Bahrain's initiative was a significant spur to Arab countries to acquire their own satellite television systems.

Egypt was the first to launch an international broadcasting service for the Arab world when the Egyptian Space Channel (Space Net) started transmission on Arabsat at the end of 1990. ESC offered a wide variety of programming including news, sports, religious, educational and cultural programmes, as well as entertainment, the most popular being serials and Egyptian films (Amin, 1996: 112). Nile TV is another Egyptian international satellite service, launched in 1993 with the prime aim of promoting Egypt's image for tourism.

Less than a year after the establishment of ESC, Saudi Arabia established the Middle East Broadcasting Centre (MBC), whose main shareholder is King Fahd's brother-in-law, Sheikh Walid Al-Ibrahim. Broadcast from London by satellite to Europe, North Africa and the Middle East, it is a news-led service but also offers family entertainment and 'aspires to become an Arab version of the American networks' (ibid.: 114). Given its professional standards, the channel is very popular with the Arab diaspora and also within the region, where it can reach more than 100 million people. More importantly, this international Arabic channel gives the advertisers access to upmarket Arab homes to promote their products, since MBC is partly dependent on advertising. Some MBC programmes are also rebroadcast by terrestrial channels in the Arab world. In 1997, MBC claimed to be broadcasting to 50 million homes and among its key advertisers were Pepsi, Nissan and Coca Cola (*Advertising Age International*, 1998).

The other Arab states in the region started to compete with each other over the establishment of international television via satellite. KSC, the Kuwaiti Space Channel, began transmission in 1992, as did Dubai's Space Network and Tunisia's TV7; JASC, the Jordanian Arab Space Channel, started transmission in 1993. Morocco, Oman and the United Arab Emirates have joined them, with the Moroccan Satellite Channel, Oman TV and UAETV, respectively.

The Orbit Communications Company's Orbit Satellite, owned by the Mawarid Group of Saudi Arabia, was launched in 1994. Orbit covers all the countries in the Middle East and North Africa, a population of around 291 million, and also caters to a population of 5 million Arabs across Europe and about 1.25 million Arabic households in North America (Zilo, 1994). Orbit carries sixteen television and four radio networks, including such transnational English-language channels as CNN (International), Disney's Entertainment and Sports Channel (ESPN) and Discovery Channel, catering largely to the foreign expatriates in the region. In addition, Orbit also offers a wide variety of programming – from news to current affairs, from music to cartoons – in Arabic language. In 1997, Orbit Satellite was being watched by 3.1 million homes across the Arab world and among the Arab diaspora (*Advertising Age International*, 1998).

There are new deals in progress with commercial television in Syria and Lebanon. Lebanon is rapidly becoming one of the key producers of programming for pan-Arab delivery, regaining some of the ground lost during the 16-year civil war. Jordan's United Satellites Company (USC) plans to build a factory for the assembly of satellite dishes for sale on the regional markets. In Jordan by 1992 there were only 700 large parabolic antennas, mostly in the capital Amman where one-third of the population is concentrated. There are also about twenty companies selling receiver equipment for satellite. Jordan is also in a prime location to receive programmes from Eutelsat2, Intelsat, Arabsat and Asiasat with ninety channels available (*Middle East Broadcast and Satellite*, 1993b).

Table 15.3 indicates the number of TV channels for each country in relation to population. (The number of TV sets has not been included here as it is increasing constantly.) The extent of national and international television reflects the attitudes of governments to having TV networks as an important national priority and a matter of prestige; there is also fierce competition to have satellite television.

As is clear from Table 15.3, most Muslim countries now have access to global television channels. However, the reception and interpretation of television messages, especially on such controversial subjects as gender

**Table 15.3** Television systems in the Arab world

| Country | Est. population (millions) | TV networks/ satellite | Terrestrial TV channels |
|---|---|---|---|
| Algeria | 25 | RTA-1 | 2 national |
| Bahrain | 0.5 | Bahrain TV | 2 national |
| Egypt | 59 | ESC, Nile TV | 2 national 5 local |
| Iraq | 17.2 | none | 2 national |
| Jordan | 4.1 | JASC | 2 national |
| Kuwait | 2 | none | 2 national |
| Lebanon | 2.7 | none | 40 private |
| Libya | 3.8 | LIBTV | 1 national |
| Morocco | 25 | MorTV | 1 national |
| Oman | 1.6 | OmanTV | 1 national 1 local |
| Qatar | 0.7 | QatarTV | 1 national |
| Saudi Arabia | 10.5 | Saudi TV1 MBC x 2 ART Orbit | 2 national |
| Sudan | 20.5 | none | 1 national |
| Syria | 10.6 | none | 2 national |
| Tunisia | 8 | TV7 | 2 national |
| UAE | 1.6 | UAETV | UAETV |
| Yemen | 11.3 | none | 1 national |

Source: UNESCO Statistical Yearbook, 1993

equality, human rights and political pluralism, has created social and political tensions in some Islamic countries. Though a pro-Western nation, Saudi Arabia, for example, stopped backing for BBC Arabic, part of the BBC World Service Television's Arabic network, for its coverage of human rights issues in the kingdom.

However, the most striking example of an anti-modern Islamic nation is Iran, which after the fall of the Pahlavi regime in 1979 took an anti-democratic stand on media with the rhetoric of anti-Westernisation and anti-consumerism (Sreberny-Mohammadi and Mohammadi, 1994). During the Shah years, Iranian National Radio and Television was one of the largest broadcasting institutions in the region. Television became a 'multiplier of Western and consumption values. These were overtly displayed in advertisements for new consumer products and were also embedded in the depiction of Western lifestyles carried by American films and television series' (Mohammadi, 1995: 371). But the post-revolution Islamisation of media content and purging of all progressive elements on the electronic media have affected the quality of programming, making Iranians clamour for foreign satellite channels, for news and information and, most importantly, for entertainment (Mohammadi, ed., 1997).

The Islamic government has even used coercion to 'protect' Islamic values from Western cultural 'pollution'. The country's Islamic Council Assembly decreed in 1994 that watching international television was a 'sinful act', and banned the manufacture, import or use of satellite dishes. Yet technological advances, which have made globalisation of consumer culture an international reality, ensures that many homes still use their satellite dishes, despite heavy fines. On the other hand, Iranian radio and television has to broadcast via Intelsat in order to cover all the remote areas in the countryside. They have increased the number of TV networks from two (national) to five (provincial) networks in order to compete with international TV broadcast. As a consequence of the attraction of international television, Islamic Republic of Iran Broadcast (IRIB) has lost about 67 per cent of television audiences (*Middle East Broadcast and Satellite*, 1997).

Apart from Iran, only two other Islamic countries – Malaysia and Saudi Arabia – have banned access to Western television by dish. This may be more for political than cultural reasons. The Malaysian government, however, allows only selected DBS offerings, such as *Asian Business News* (ABN) and CNN *World Report* among news programmes. It has employed its efforts to protect their culture from the onslaught; at the same time as wishing to protect Malaysian culture, it is sensitive to global market changes and wants Malaysia to have a share, particularly in information technology. In addition, more programming is needed to fill the rapidly proliferating television channels to keep the audience happy (Hashim, 1994).

The growth of satellite broadcast television has been much faster than the production and distribution of satellite dishes. During the 1990s, the satellite dish and the decoder box have become the most important commodities in the electronic market in the Middle East, especially in those countries banning access to international television. Due to the significant expansion of satellite broadcasting, demand for broadcast equipment is rising (Steel, 1994). The Middle Eastern region has now become the centre of rivalry for satellite manufacturing companies and broadcasting equipment producers – particularly for US manufacturers. There are about 129 corporations active in the various businesses of broadcasting and audio and video manufacturing in the Middle East. Among all these manufacturers of communication technologies in the region the British and Canadians each have three companies; Israel and Australia have one each. But the rest of 121 firms in the communications market are American (*Via Satellite*, 1994).

The trend in exports of broadcasting equipment during 1993 showed a steady increase. Saudi Arabia paid over $5.4 million for broadcasting equipment in 1993, almost double what it paid in 1992. The World Bank has made loans available to those Islamic countries that could not afford to buy the technology. The growing demand and the rapid increase of international satellite services provided a healthy growth in satellite transponders, from seventeen in 1994 to forty-five in 1997 (*Middle East Broadcast and Satellite*, 1997). There has also been a boost in launch-vehicle production. Of the European Ariane space agency's 1995 output, accounting for $650 million in 1995, 45 per cent was for export. In 1995, Arianespace launched ten communications satellites, seven of which were for Middle East countries and Intelsat. In 1996, thirteen out of fifteen communications satellites launched by Ariane were for export. It seems this trend will increase steadily over the next few years, with twenty-one out of forty-one being exported (*Executive Summary in Space Business*, European edn, 1996/7).

Given that more and more hardware is being developed to make television accessible to larger numbers of Muslim homes, it is important to recognise how these new channels will sustain themselves. The increasingly privatised nature of broadcasting and the entry of major media corporations into the Arab world could mean a spurt in advertising expenses in what remains one of the post prosperous regions of the developing world, thanks to petrodollars, especially in the Persian Gulf region.

# Advertising

Media entertainment and advertising have become part of the global market development because media are the window to the outside world. The trends in more or less all Arab countries indicate a rapid move towards a consumer society. Expenditure is increasing in all the main categories of advertising. The expansion of private satellite television is highly dependent on gaining a bigger share of the advertising market. And it is not surprising that the Middle East is a key target for advertisers – there are more millionaires in Jeddah than in Hollywood. It is quite clear that the market for consumer goods has grown dramatically with the expansion of commercial television channels. Advertising agencies are generally tuned to the promotion of Western consumer goods, for which there is huge demand unmet by domestic products. As a result of advertising revenue, the variety of media and the level of consumption has increased.

Table 15.4 shows comparative spending on the three main advertising media for the first half of 1994 in four key countries where commercial media are dependent on advertising for survival.

Though newspapers dominated, with advertising transactions accounting for 75 per cent of the total, advertising expenditure in television alone was just over $60 million. In UAE, advertising expenditure overall was $68 million, which is proportionately large for a very small country, 80 per cent of whose population consists of foreign workers and expatriates (*Arab Ad*, 1994). In Saudi Arabia alone the total advertising expenditure reached $142.8 million by mid-1994, a 16 per cent increase on the previous year (ibid.).

Table 15.5 shows advertising expenditure in UAE for the top twenty product categories, and the increase from the previous year. Since the demise of the Soviet bloc, Dubai has become a vacation and shopping mall for the Russian *nouveaux riches*. The expansion of seaside resorts and the relaxation of Islamic codes of conduct in UAE have not only encouraged tourism, but have made it a popular shopping destination for neighbouring Persian Gulf countries. This has encouraged transnational advertisers to use the local media to promote their products. Consequently, advertising revenues across the Gulf region rose up to 20 per cent in 1996, with UAE showing the fastest growth. In 1996, ad spending in the emirate was $117 million (Bidlake, 1997).

# Media entertainment

Entertainment is at the heart of the success of most of the private channels now operating in the Arab world. The expansion of satellite television

Table 15.4 Advertising spending by media in four key countries, Jan.–June 1994

| Country | Total spending (US$000) | Television | Newspapers | Magazines |
|---|---|---|---|---|
| Bahrain | 13,332 | 7,466 | 5,600 | 266 |
| Kuwait | 56,335 | 6,197 | 38,308 | 11,830 |
| Saudi Arabia | 142,781 | 31,412 | 84,241 | 27,128 |
| UAE | 68,901 | 15,847 | 43,408 | 9,646 |

Source: *Arab Ad*, 4.10, Nov. 1994

Table 15.5  Advertising expenditure by category, UAE, 1994

| Categories in order of expenditure | 1994* ($000) | 1993* ($000) | % increase |
|---|---|---|---|
| Road vehicles | 13,612 | 12,539 | 9 |
| Cosmetics and beauty products | 12,704 | 10,981 | 16 |
| Retail stores | 10,654 | 8,626 | 24 |
| Publishing/media | 9,318 | 7,313 | 27 |
| Jewellery/accessories | 7,567 | 5,636 | 36 |
| Dairy products | 6,164 | 5,283 | 17 |
| Professional services | 6,009 | 4,443 | 35 |
| Insurance/real estate | 5,267 | 3,720 | 42 |
| Travel/hotels and resorts | 3,761 | 2,265 | 66 |
| Office equipment/accessories | 2,939 | 2,116 | 39 |
| Adult/hair products | 2,824 | 2,127 | 33 |
| Cooking/seasoning | 2,784 | 1,839 | 51 |
| Food/beverages | 2,768 | 2,347 | 18 |
| Major electrical | 2,557 | 2,057 | 24 |
| Soft drinks | 2,522 | 1,706 | 48 |
| Restaurants/hotels | 2,499 | 1,499 | 67 |
| Health services | 2,368 | 1,739 | 36 |
| Organisations | 2,288 | 2,108 | 9 |
| Prepared/convenience food | 1,733 | 1,226 | 41 |
| Confectionery/snacks | 1,667 | 1,259 | 32 |

Source: *Arab Ad*, 4.10, Nov. 1994
*First 6 months

broadcasting and the spillover from satellite footprints has distracted national television audiences by exposing them to more attractive programmes and interesting entertainment shows. As a result of a rapid expansion of delivery channels to the Middle East countries, viewers with the necessary receiving equipment are no longer restricted to domestic programmes.

Entertainment is a predominant feature of Arab international television. Almost 42 per cent of the entire weekly broadcast of the Egyptian international satellite programming is entertainment and only about 3 per cent is about religion (Amin, 1996: 112). Every week, at least one or two Western soaps are on the menu. Arab identity is often the underlining theme of popular serials, most originating from Egypt and steeped in a secular culture of visual entertainment. However, on international channels most of the programming is imported from the West and contains material such as sex, nudity and violence, which is not acceptable to most Islamic societies, especially to their conservative religious establishments. This has often created tension in countries where Islamists are gaining ground – notably in Algeria.

In addition to the various entertainment programmes offered by domestic channels in the Arab world, there is also an extensive variety of programmes for children on the commercial television channels. Now a new range of satellite stations are all pushing to extend television audiences among children. Many of these children's programmes are versions of European or American programmes, dubbed into Arabic. TNT/Cartoon Network provides various youth and children's programmes for Middle East countries. Orbit broadcasts twelve hours of children's programmes per week. MBC also broadcasts children's programmes, with 20 per cent being dubbed from English to the local language.

Table 15.6 shows the percentage of children's in relation to other programmes on terrestrial television in four different countries in the Middle East.

It is important to note that there is no tradition of children's television in these countries. The programmes were made originally for European children with reference to their familial, social and cultural contexts but exported to an audience with totally different cultural and social experiences. Children of these Arab countries will be exposed to toys and numerous other products which are non-existent in their countries. When the children are the target audiences, pressure is put on parents to provide their children with the products advertised. There is no clear government policy on supporting national culture, particularly in the context of children's television and dubbed cartoons. The critical issue for national governments in the Islamic countries is how to protect their children from the pressures of the global market and the cultural values of a consumer society and uphold the values of a culture under attack.

# Conclusion

In the context of the electronic empires, the Islamic countries are facing a difficult task. In the process of globalisation, for the protection of Islamic cultural identity, it is necessary to formulate an Islamic cultural strategy. In

Table 15.6 Middle East terrestrial TV programming mix (%)

| Country | Children | Sport | Drama | Films | News | Doc. | CA | Variety | Games | Other |
|---|---|---|---|---|---|---|---|---|---|---|
| Kuwait (KTV) | 21 | 5 | 42.5 | 10.5 | 10.5 | 3 | 3 | 4.5 | n/a | n/a |
| Lebanon (MurrTV) | 5 | 10 | 10 | 15 | 3 | 3 | 2 | 10 | 10 | 15 |
| Saudi (STV) | 15 | 10 | 15 | 10 | 10 | 10 | 10 | 12 | 8 | n/a |
| UAE (UAETV) | 12 | 5 | 12 | 15 | 20 | 5 | 5 | 5 | 15 | 6 |

Source: *Middle East Broadcast and Satellite*, 4.5, 1996

order to achieve this objective, there is a need for a redefinition of knowledge in terms of Islamic cultural epistemology in a way that will be acceptable to the Muslims all over the world. The dominant theory of knowledge, rooted as it is in Western intellectual traditions, affirms that there is only one possible source of scientific knowledge – the tangible universe. Islamic epistemology stresses that knowledge has two sources: the tangible universe and revelation. Revelation is the source of absolute facts and truth which are not subject to relativity.

The failure of the Islamic revolution in Iran to bring equality, justice and political freedom provided a fertile ground to establish a dialogue between Western culture and Islam on the question of 'doubt' instead of absolute truth. The only way culture can grow is to open itself up to other cultures, to interact critically and freely. It is important to draw our attention to Mahatma Gandhi, who suggested: 'I want the cultures of all lands to be blown about my house as freely as possible but I refuse to be blown off my feet by any one of them.' Today, many Muslim countries in the world support Gandhi's line, particularly with regard to dialogue and gradual rational modernisation – and possibly alternative development, because their cultures, civilisations and historical experiences are different. Unfortunately the impact of the powerful images broadcast by the electronic empires have promoted the predominance of capitalist culture around the world.

In response to the global market and the power of promotional culture, Islamic countries have attempted to resist or provide an alternative, as in the case of international broadcast television for Muslims living in Europe. However, the evidence is that the chance of success in the highly competitive world of international television is slim. Muslim countries are finding that it is impossible to survive the process of globalisation without accepting to a certain degree some kind of modification of their culture in order to maintain their own cultural identity. Summing up, the response of various Islamic states around the world to the expansion of electronic empires shows that the traditionalist approach is losing ground to a mixture of adaptation and modernisation.

# References

*Advertising Age International* (1998) Europe and Middle East TV lineup, 9 Feb., p. 20.

Alwani, T. J. (1981) *The Outline of Cultural Strategy*, International Institute of Islamic Thought, Occasional Paper 1, Washington.

Amin, H. (1996) Egypt and the Arab world in the satellite age, in Sinclair, J., Jacka, E. and Cunningham, S. (eds) *New Patterns in Global Television*, Oxford University Press, Oxford.

*Arab Ad* (1994) 4.10, Nov., p. 18.

Berger, J. (1995) The *Observer* essay, *Observer*, 17 Dec, p. 4.

Bidlake, S. (1997) Middle East's resurgence earns it debut in rankings, *Advertising Age International*, June, p. i18.

Brewer, T. (1994) The state of the satellite market in the Asian & Pacific Ocean region, *Via Satellite*, 9.10, Oct.

Hashim, R. (1994) *Direct Broadcast Satellite and its Implications for Malaysia*, IAMCR, 19th General Assembly, Seoul, July 3–8.

Herman, E. S. and McChesney, R. W. (1997) *The Global Media: The New Missionaries of Corporate Capitalism*, Cassell, London.

Latouche, S. (1996) *The Westernization of the World*, Polity, Cambridge.

*Middle East Broadcast and Satellite* (1993a) 1.1, Jan.

*Middle East Broadcast and Satellite* (1993b) 1.2, April.

*Middle East Broadcast and Satellite* (1996) 4.5, Sept.

*Middle East Broadcast and Satellite* (1997) 5.4, July.

Mohammadi, A. (1995) Cultural imperialism and cultural identity, in Downing, J., Mohammadi, A. and Sreberny-Mohammadi, A. (eds) *Questioning the Media*, Sage, London.

Mohammadi, A. (ed.) (1997) *International Communication and Globalisation*, Sage, London.

Sreberny-Mohammadi, A. and Mohammadi, A. (1994) *Small Media and Big Revolution*, University of Minnesota Press, Minneapolis.

Steel, J. (1994) Export of broadcasting and satellite equipment to the Middle East, *Middle East Broadcast and Satellite*, Oct.

*Via Satellite* (1994), 9.10, Oct.

Warwick, M. (1993) Arab Sat: ATV broadcasting dream only partially realized, *Middle East Broadcast and Satellite*, 1.1, Jan.

Zilo, A. B. (1994) Understanding the Arab world, *Multicultural News International*, 3 Oct.

# |16|

## Localising the global

### Zee TV in India

DAYA KISHAN THUSSU

This chapter examines the challenges and opportunities that globalisation has opened up for media industries in India. It analyses how the entry of media empires into India has transformed broadcasting, as is evident in the exponential growth in the number of television channels from one state-controlled channel in 1991 to more than seventy in 1998, necessitating an overhaul of broadcasting strategy as India adapts its media industries to the competitive, deregulated and privatised environment of the late 1990s.

The first part of the chapter sets the debate about the impact of globalisation on the Indian media in the context of its evolution and its role as a fourth estate in the world's largest democracy, where the past 50 years of multi-party polity have ensured a diverse and relatively free media. In the second part, news reports from Zee TV, the most successful of the private television channels, and partly owned by Rupert Murdoch's News Corporation, are content-analysed to examine whether and in what ways the availability of transnational media channels has influenced television news – until recently the exclusive domain of the state broadcaster.

By focusing on Zee TV, a channel which has evolved, in the words of Don Atyeo, channel manager of STAR TV, from 'a less than shoestring operation . . . to without a doubt probably the most successful story in broadcasting history' (Channel 4 Television, 1995), this chapter aims to provide an example of how local media can indigenise global products by developing derivatives of programmes broadcast on international television.

This localisation of the global works at different levels – in employing metropolitan visual codes and conventions, in broadcast language and in programme formats, such as game- and chat-shows, unknown on television in India before globalisation. Zee TV was one of the first Indian channels to understand the value of locally produced entertainment-based television, as is also reflected in its news bulletins, which tend towards 'infotainment', as I discuss below. To contextualise the growth of Zee TV, it is important to locate it within the development of the media in India.

## The historical context

From the advent of mass media in India, with the publication of the *Bengal Gazette* in 1780, newspapers acted as a harbinger of modernity, contributing significantly to the construction of a national identity. Despite very low literacy rates and strict press laws introduced by successive British colonial administrations, the press played a key role in the nationalist movement, even if its pioneers came from a small, Westernised elite. Within a century of the publication of the *Bengal Gazette*, more than 140 newspapers in Indian languages were articulating a nascent nationalism which grew as nationalist leaders became involved in campaigning journalism. Most notable of these was Mahatma Gandhi, who used Gujarati, his mother tongue, as well as English, to spread the message of freedom. By 1941, about 4000 newspapers and magazines were in print in seventeen languages, and the underlying theme was the end of colonial rule.[1]

Even after independence, the legacy of anti-colonialism continued to influence Indian media, which inherited from the British the combination of a private press and a government-controlled broadcasting system. The press demonstrated relatively greater critical awareness and, by and large, acted as a fourth estate in a fledgling democracy, while the electronic media was used by the state for what came to be known as 'nation-building'. The task of the media was to help in overcoming the immediate crisis of political instability that followed independence and to foster the long-term process of development, reflecting the dominant ideology of the newly emergent and activist state. In a vast, geographically and culturally diverse, multilingual and multireligious country, it was argued by the leadership that the All India Radio (AIR), Aakaashvani, the only medium of mass persuasion at the time, be employed to develop 'national consciousness'.[2]

As elsewhere in the developing world, Indian leaders did not relinquish control over broadcasting after independence, arguing that an uncontrolled broadcasting system could destabilise the country, given its traumatic birth during which 1 million people were killed and more than 15 million displaced as a result of the partition as the British divided and left India in 1947. The violent legacy of partition demanded that AIR had to be extremely sensitive to ethnic, cultural and religious considerations in a hugely illiterate country (Chatterjee, 1991). However, in the name of achieving this worthy goal, the leadership more often than not used the radio to promote its own ideology. Consequently, AIR became little more than a propaganda service for the government, over-bureaucratised, with dull and drab programming. How far it succeeded in serving any developmental purposes is also open to debate.

The introduction of television in 1959, as a UNESCO-sponsored, pilot educational project, reflected the initial attitude to the medium as an educational tool and a means for disseminating state policies and public information. The state television channel, Doordarshan, formed part of AIR until 1976 when it became a separate department under the information and broadcasting ministry. The aim of the national broadcasters was to educate, inform and create a feeling of national identity and help maintain national unity. Doordarshan followed the AIR broadcasting code, which prohibited, among other things, criticism of friendly countries, attack on religions or communities, incitement to violence or the broadcast of material affecting the integrity of the nation.[3]

While the broadcasters toed the official line, the privately owned and politically plural press provided the critical framework within which Indian journalism evolved. The relative autonomy of the print media was a significant factor in strengthening democracy in India, and more importantly, the investigative, often adversarial, role of some journalists contributed to the creation of an early-warning system for serious food shortage and thus a preventive mechanism against famine (Ram, 1990).

Given the linguistic and cultural diversity of India, state support was invaluable, especially for the regional and small-scale newspapers and magazines. The government-subsidised national news agencies – Press Trust of India and United News of India in English, and Samachar Bharati and Hindustan Samachar to cater to regional languages – which were a lifeline for newspapers across the country. As one commentator put it: 'without their solid and unfailing service over the decades, the Indian press could not have possibly retained its diversity and pluralism, and small and medium newspapers could not have survived or come up in various Indian languages' (Ram, 1994: 2790).

During Jawaharlal Nehru's prime-ministership (1947–64), Indian media seemed to follow the democratic agenda set by the government. Unlike in most other developing countries, the government accepted criticism and encouraged open debate in the press. This tolerance gave Indian journalists a space in which to engage in critical debates on national and international issues. Nehru, himself a distinguished writer, had a genuine interest in promoting consensus through the mass media. His intellectual stature and charisma as the undisputed leader of the country further strengthened his position. However, the political manipulations which became the hallmark of Nehru's daughter, Indira Gandhi, prime minister from 1967 to 1977 and again from 1980 to 1984, strained this national consensus. During her tenure the national broadcasting organisations were reduced to becoming the mouthpiece of the ruling Congress party and its leader – prompting critics to call the AIR the 'All Indira Radio'.

Expanding the reach of television was a high priority for Indira Gandhi, who invested heavily in developing satellite technology. Following the launch of the Indian National Satellite (INSAT) in 1982, the number of transmitters increased from 19 to 199 in 1987 and as a result Doordarshan was able to cover 70 per cent of the population, as against the 26 per cent it could reach in 1982 (Doordarshan, 1997: 2). This spree was intended in part 'simply to spread the magic and myth of the ruling family' (Pendakur,

1991: 248). Doordarshan became increasingly commercialised during the 1980s, a process that had already begun in 1976 with selling of airtime for advertising and which continued with commercial sponsorship for programmes from 1980. This commercialisation was intensified by the increasingly neo-liberal governments of the 1980s, making television entertainment-oriented to meet the needs of advertisers (Rajagopal, 1993). As a result, Doordarshan began to draw large audiences and its commercial earnings rose nearly twenty-fold from 159 million rupees in 1982 to 3006 million rupees in 1992 (Doordarshan, 1997: 2).

Like other Indian industries, the media and telecommunications sectors were transformed by the liberalisation of the economy introduced in 1991 by the government of P. V. Narasimha Rao, as India was forced to open up its economy in the wake of the disintegration of the Soviet Union, with which New Delhi had close economic and security ties during the Cold War. Rao announced a new economic policy that began the process of privatisation, dismantling state controls and liberalising these sectors, under the influence of the World Bank and the International Monetary Fund, paving the way for the entry of global media empires into India (Mody, 1995: 119).

## Impact of globalisation on the press

The entry and steady expansion of such empires created unease in some quarters of the traditionally left-of-centre mainstream press, as they weighed up the implications of foreign ownership in a country where traditionally the media had been owned by indigenous capital (Ram, 1994). Among the main bidders were London *Financial Times*, which planned to team up with the *Business Standard* of Calcutta to start a new business daily, and *Time* magazine, keen to produce an Indian edition in collaboration with Living Media group, publishers of *India Today*, which has already launched an Indian edition of *Cosmopolitan* magazine.[4]

One key area of concern has been that competition from transnational media empires will drive regional and small-scale publications out of the market, or at least reduce the rich diversity of a press that represents a multiplicity of interests and political opinions – Delhi alone has more than a dozen daily newspapers. Already, the serious and staid Indian press is copying US-style sensational journalism, with an emphasis on entertainment-oriented news agendas. The increasingly vicious circulation wars and the managerial approach to running editorial operations, most acutely seen in the venerated *Times of India*, are symptoms of how globalisation is affecting even the most traditional of Indian newspapers.[5] The *Times*, wrote one observer, 'is no longer the newspaper for the most authoritative reports on government and politics, the most timely op-ed pieces and the best book and arts reviews. The most successful circulation-booster has been a weekly colour magazine insert called *E-Times*, full of gossip about film stars and the coming week's cable TV programming. Markets follow the market' (McDonald, 1995: 25).

However, while the English-language elite publications are experiencing a declining circulation and a dilution of content, the newspapers and magazines in Indian languages have witnessed something approaching a renaissance (Jeffrey, 1997: 78). Media globalisation hit India at a time of extraordinary growth in the vernacular press. The changing contours of national politics, with regional parties taking centre-stage, has given a new impetus to newspapers in Indian languages. According to the Indian Newspaper Society, in 1996 publications in Indian languages sold four times more than English-language publications.[6]

# The satellite 'invasion'

A more profound consequence of media globalisation has been the entry of foreign, mainly Western, commercial satellite television in what used to be one of the most closed broadcasting systems in any democracy. The first major event to be shown via these satellites was the 1990–1 Gulf crisis, covered live by the Atlanta-based Cable News Network (CNN), which found a ready audience among the Indian metropolitan elite.[7] This was followed in 1991 by provision of a five-channel satellite service (Plus, Prime Sports, Channel V (an Indianised imitation of MTV), BBC World, and Movie, India's first pay channel) by Hong-Kong-based STAR TV (Satellite Television Asian Region), now part of News Corporation.

The satellite channels, not bound by public-service conventions, became an instant hit with Indian middle classes because of their entertainment-led and mainly Western programming and, more importantly, with advertisers, who saw India as an 'emerging market' for transnational corporations. According to industry estimates, television's share of advertising expenditure in 1997 was 32 per cent. Total television advertising expenditure was estimated to be $485 million, of which $157 million was spent on satellite channels (*Cable & Satellite Asia Yearbook 97/98*, 1997: 76). Industry estimates predict that Indian advertising will increase from 15 billion rupees in 1990 (of which TV accounted for 2.5 billion rupees) to 86.6 billion rupees in 2000, with television advertising accounting for 30 billion rupees (*Business India*, 1997: 59).

Buoyed by advertising revenues, cable and satellite television has increased substantially since 1992, when only 1.2 million homes had it. By 1996 the figure had reached 14.2 million (Doordarshan, 1997: 48). Moreover, satellite TV, once considered the exclusive preserve of urban consumers, is now targeting the well-heeled in India's villages – particularly those in the southern states. In Tamil Nadu, for example, nearly 32 per cent of rural TV viewers are tuning into satellite channels (Chatterjee, 1997: 30).[8]

By 1998, more than seventy cable and satellite channels were operating in India, including major transnational media players, notably STAR, BBC, Discovery, MTV, Sony, CNN, Disney and CNBC, and scores of Indian companies. Just as India has adapted to global media forms and firms, the media empires, too, have had to adjust their strategies to suit the Indian context. STAR, for example, felt that its mainly US-originated programming was only reaching a tiny, though influential and wealthy, urban audience (Mullick, 1995). It therefore started adding Hindi subtitles to Hollywood films broadcast on its twenty-four-hour channel STAR Movies and dubbing popular US soaps into Hindi. In October 1996, STAR Plus began telecasting locally made programmes in English and Hindi, in addition to Western programmes. Such efforts seem to have worked as STAR today claims to be available to approximately 16 million cable homes, though this has created tensions with Zee, since both channels are aiming to reach the Hindi-language audience, even if STAR's is more middle-class (Mullick, 1996).

Other global players have followed the market leader in Asia by 'localising' their products to reach a wider market and increase advertising revenues. The Discovery channel, which started beaming to India in 1995, now dubs its documentaries into Hindi. BBC World regularly broadcasts 'India-specific' programmes, including news in Hindi. The NBC and its business affiliate CNBC – launched in India in 1996 – also produce such daily programmes as *Taking Stock India*, a half-hour business programme with an intention to reach, in the words of NBC vice-president Richard Reingold, 'well-educated above-average income viewers' (Bhandare, 1997a).

## Zee network: Indianising the global

Unlike these elite-centred channels, the Zee network has aimed to reach the mass market by pioneering entertainment television based on popular culture. That movie-based entertainment was the key to the success of any television channel, in a country whose popular culture has been defined for the past six decades by the hugely successful Hindi film industry, was perhaps best understood by a small-scale Indian entrepreneur, Subhash Chandra Goel, the chairman of Zee TV, India's first private Hindi-language and most successful satellite channel.

Launched in October 1992 and owned by Goel's Essel Group, Zee TV initially depended on recycled programming – Hindi films and old Doordarshan serials – and its own, mainly down market, programmes made by young and inexperienced staff. But the channel broke television taboos by broadcasting programmes about such topics as sex, relationships and horoscopes. From such modest beginnings the channel has come a long way. By 1995, Goel was being called a 'TV tycoon' whose 'entertainment empire' has 'changed the face of television in India' (Agarwal, 1995). Projecting itself as a family entertainment channel, Zee set the standards for private television, thriving on a mixture of Hindi film and film-based programming, serials, music countdowns and quiz contests. Catering for a young audience has been a key factor in Zee's success. It developed an Indianised version of the global youth channel, Music Television (MTV), using Hindi pop and film music, creating an urban youth culture hitherto unknown in the country. As Subodh Lal, executive president of Zee between 1993 and 1995 remarked, 'Zee TV is a young, youthful, dynamic, at times irreverent channel, which needed to be there as there was nothing like this' (Channel 4 Television, 1995). Zee's innovative programming, including the news in 'Hinglish' (a mixture of Hindi and English), became very popular with its growing audience. Entertainment remains central to its broadcasting philosophy, as its 'mission statement' proclaims:

> To be the leading round-the-clock airtime properties provider, delighting the viewers on the one hand, and providing value to the advertisers for their time and money, on the other. To establish the company as the creator of entertainment and infotainment products and services to feast the viewers and the advertisers. Through these services, we intend to become an integral part of the global market. As a corporation, we will be profitable, productive, creative, trendsetting and financially rugged with care and concern for all stake holders.
>
> (http://zeetelevision.com)

Zee's flexible and frequent advertising breaks and its practice of putting sponsors' names on programmes made it popular among advertisers. The channel broke even within the first year of its launch, making it a prize target for media conglomerates, and in 1993 Rupert Murdoch's News Corporation became a 49.9 per cent partner. This facilitated the network's expansion and the launch in 1995 of EL Television, showing movies and music videos, followed in 1996 by Zee Cinema, a pay-to-view channel. In 1996, Zee TV had revenues of about $74 million (Wanvari, 1997: 74).

An audience survey conducted in nine major cities of India in March 1997 showed that among the private television channels Zee was the most popular (see Table 16.1). According to market analysts, in 1997 Zee network had 29 per cent of audience share in cable and satellite homes. It also owns Siti-cable, India's largest cable company, a music production company called Zee Music and the Asian Teleshopping Network, with tie-up outlets throughout India (Ninan, 1997).

By 1998, Zee TV was claiming to be 'the world's largest Asian television network', covering Asia, Europe, the USA and Africa, catering to the 24-million-strong Indian diaspora who live outside the region but retain linguistic and cultural links with the subcontinent. In Asia, the network spans more than forty countries and offers round-the-clock programming on four channels – Zee TV, Zee Cinema, Zee TV India and Music Asia. It was reaching approximately 18 million homes in India and another 5

**Table 16.1** Top ten channels by number of viewers,* March 1997

| Channel | Number of viewers (000s) |
| --- | --- |
| Doordarshan 1 | 33,911 |
| Doordarshan 2 | 29,980 |
| Zee | 5985 |
| Local cable | 4468 |
| Sony | 2798 |
| Zee Cinema | 1596 |
| Sun | 1596 |
| Star Plus | 1319 |
| EL TV | 937 |
| Eenadu | 937 |

*Viewers who watched the channel for some time during the week in nine cities. Total viewers: 39,896,000.
Source: Doordarshan, 1997

million in Pakistan, Bangladesh and United Arab Emirates. Zee TV Africa, which started in 1996, transmits via PAS-4 satellite to thirty-five African countries in Hindi, Urdu and Tamil, for eight hours every day, catering to more than 2 million African-Asians – the Indian diaspora alone comprises 400,000 households.

Zee TV's strategy now is to expand its operations in the lucrative Northern markets. After it took over the London-based TV Asia in 1995, it became the only pan-European channel available on both cable and satellite, providing programmes in Hindi, Urdu, Punjabi and Gujarati to over 1 million viewers across Europe (Zee TV, 1997). In the USA, where Zee TV is available through the cable operation International Channel, it is planning to raise its daily output from the current one-and-a-half hours to twelve hours (Ravindran, 1998).

# News on Zee TV

When Zee started, news and documentaries were not considered popular genres and were therefore not priority areas. However, over the past 6 years the channel has invested in factual programming, aware that control over television news can bring enormous political influence (Shivdasani, 1998). One of its early programmes *Aap Ki Adalat* (People's Court) gave the channel considerable clout and raised its profile beyond a merely entertainment network.

This made business sense too, given the need to fill the existing vacuum in electronic journalism, and the potential for supplying news and current affairs programming to the proliferating channels. Before the entry of global news channels into India, television news was a monopoly of the state broadcaster and rarely aspired to a role beyond that of the government's public-relations department, disseminating official policies and covering state visits and functions. The news bulletins were remarkably unimaginative, with very limited visuals and little on-the-spot reporting. More often than not, the news was about putting the government's view across and generally marginalising any dissent. The journalists who worked on Doordarshan news were government employees, who would rarely question state policies, preferring to steer clear of controversial subjects, in contrast to the print media which excelled in investigative reporting.

The availability of transnational television news channels, such as CNN and the BBC, with high professional standards, a range of visual material and freedom from the codes and conventions of a public-service broadcaster, challenged this self-imposed, uncritical approach to electronic journalism. Moreover, it gave a necessary fillip to private television, still in its infancy in the country in the early 1990s. The expansion of video had ensured the development in the late 1980s of privately owned video news magazines such as *Newstrack* and *Eyewitness*, first attempts by print journalists to explore the visual medium, which were emerging as the only alternative to the state broadcaster, but their reach was limited as the market for independent news was very small.

With the availability of satellite television, CNN and the BBC brought the outside world into urban living rooms across the country, creating demand for international material. Small private companies, such as New Delhi Television (NDTV) started to fill the gap in this influential genre with such programmes as *The World This Week* for Doordarshan, adding a dose of professionalism to news and current affairs on the state broadcaster (Kumar, 1996).

## Analysing Zee news

In an age when television is the main source of information for most people, it can be argued that TV news is essential to the existence of a public sphere, and that the quality of public debate is likely to be influenced by the quality of the information available on the electronic media. In a country where only half the population is literate, the visual medium acquires added significance. We have already noted how politicians have used the electronic media to further their own political interests.

Even for an ostensibly entertainment-oriented network like Zee, news remains a key component of its daily schedule. However, the question arises of whether its entertainment-led approach influences the way the channel perceives its news programming and constructs its news agendas. How do private channels like Zee, unrestricted by the state broadcaster's remit, deal with issues of public information? Are their news priorities significantly different from those of the state broadcaster? Has the availability of global television news channels made much difference to news presentation? Has globalisation spurred a greater coverage of foreign issues?

In order to examine these issues, Zee TV's main evening Hindi news bulletin was content-analysed for the week from Monday 18 August 1997 to Friday 22 August 1997. This twenty-minute news programme, broadcast at 10 p.m., was chosen since the Hindi news bulletins are the news programmes most regularly watched, by the largest number of people. Weekday bulletins were chosen as the focus, since they usually contain more news and features than weekend news programmes. The week was chosen at random, and the week's news was used as the major data for the analysis.[9]

Zee TV broadcasts from 6 a.m. to midnight. Most of the programming is entertainment-based, including two hours of Disney programmes. There is a news bulletin at 6 a.m., a news update at 8 a.m. and the main evening news is at 10 p.m., followed by ten minutes of Zee business news.

## News presentation

The presentation is in a format derivative of Western news programmes, with a signature tune of upbeat, repeated chords similar to those for Western news broadcasts. The opening title sequence takes up to ten seconds, panning around a virtual studio with a series of screens showing news footage, including the Indian prime minister, Inder Kumar Gujaral, followed by the US president, Bill Clinton, Pakistani prime minister, Nawaz Sharif, a shot of Indian army soldiers walking through fields and a scene from a cricket match.

The screen has the Zee logo at the right-hand corner and on the left the words 'The News', under which is the Indian flag and written in small letters '50 years' in English, a reference to the fiftieth anniversary of India's independence. In the background is a map of the world, with India in the centre, suggesting that the news is from around the world but that India is the main focus. The whole of the news bulletin is fronted by one presenter. During the week's coverage, the newscasters alternated between Kapil Batra, dressed in suit and tie, and Nidhi Kulpati, dressed in a sari. Both are smart, young, fair-complexioned and with a polished delivery.

The headlines (thirty seconds) are immediately followed by a commercial break, which lasts for two to three minutes. This seems to pick up on a trend visible in Western news networks of offering viewers the easy soundbites of headlines as a product in themselves (cf. CNN's Headline News channel). After another eight to ten minutes of news there is a second commercial break for two minutes, mid-way through the bulletin. The commercials, which included a public-service advertisement about voluntary disclosure of income for taxation, are mostly Indian-made (during the week in question, there was one visuals-only advert for DHL that was obviously made for international use) and the majority are in Hindi. The most-often-occurring products are saris, suiting and motorcycles. The images presented are of young, urban professionals living a free-and-easy Westernised lifestyle, reflecting Zee's target audience.

The last item on the news is the national weather, the captions for which are in English. News reports constituted approximately 70 per cent of the broadcast while advertisements accounted for another 20 per cent and the remaining 10 per cent was taken by headlines, weather and other presenter-talk.

The news bulletins generally used Western formats of delivery. The majority of stories were introduced by the presenter and then reported by a news reporter, including actuality footage to create an impression of authenticity and authority, usually with a commentary spoken by the reporter. The reporter's name, in English, was credited in a caption on the screen, although they did not speak to the camera. Occasionally there was footage with a reporter's commentary, credited as a 'Zee Bureau report', which could mean that footage was not Zee's own but from a national news provider such as Asian Television News, a Delhi-based supplier of news footage to Indian and foreign broadcasters. However, there were no live one-to-one interviews with those in the news, a normal feature of news reports in the West, but only one interview with a political leader that had been pre-recorded.

## News agenda

In order to analyse the news content, the news reports were divided into six categories – domestic/political, foreign, cultural, development/environment, sport and human-interest news – and the proportion of the news broadcast for each category of story was calculated (see Figure 16.1). Despite claims of globalisation, much of the news had a very domestic agenda, preoccupied with party politics and a very Delhi-centric view of India. Of the total fifty-seven stories during the week, thirty-three were on domestic and political subjects and a majority of these originated in India's capital city, accounting for 66 per cent of total newstime. However, given the dynamics of Indian politics and the high levels of politicisation in the country, it is perhaps not surprising that political stories emanating from the centre of power seemed to dominate the news from as avowedly an entertainment-oriented channel as Zee.

Political news was mostly based on public personalities and staged events in Delhi. Developmental and cultural stories too appeared to have a Delhi bias. Most news was sourced to what Hartley calls 'institutional voices' (Hartley, 1982: 110), i.e. the political and cultural elite. Two factors may be operating in this: availability of material and perceptions of what is newsworthy. Given India's limited telecommunications infrastructure, even

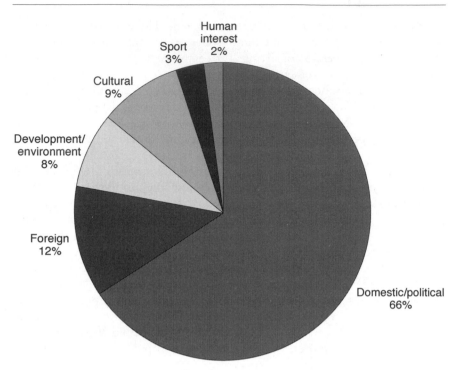

**Figure 16.1** Zee news by category of story (during the period 18–22 August 1997)

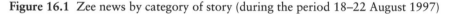

a national broadcaster such as Zee is constrained by the availability of footage. And in Delhi, as the hub of political activity, such newsworthy material – from the perspective of broadcasters – is readily and cheaply on offer. That such elite-centred footage might also be politically useful could be a consideration for a new commercial channel eager to establish its credentials.

## Foreign news

Despite the existence of more than seventy channels in India and the fact that Zee itself has ambitions to be an international broadcaster, the national agenda seems to far outstrip the global in the case of Zee news. During the week only two foreign stories – both about neighbouring countries – were given adequate coverage. Instead, foreign news was 'covered' in a daily slot called 'World Briefs', with less than two minutes of 'human-interest' stories (usually two) from around the world, such as monkeys being used to catch fish in Japan, or a multiple-births festival in France, with no apparent news value except infotainment.

Analysing the Indian newspapers of the week showed that several foreign stories which had received prominent coverage in the national press were absent from the Zee news schedule. These included: 160 people killed in Sri Lanka by a stinger missile used by the Tamil guerrilla group LTTE (Liberation Tigers of Tamil Eelam); rebels surrendering in Tajikistan; civil conflict in Cambodia; religiously motivated violence in Algeria; and the appointment of a new Iranian cabinet led by moderate president, Mohammed Khatami. Some of these stories are of direct relevance to India. The LTTE story, for example, is significant because the Tamil guerrilla group was implicated in the assassination of former Indian prime minister, Rajiv Gandhi. Similarly, developments in the Islamic world are important for a country which has millions of expatriate workers in the Persian Gulf region.

## The use of 'Hinglish'

One area where the influence of globalisation is most evident is the language of the news. Linguistic purists in India may disapprove, but a hybrid media language, a mixture of Hindi and English, is increasingly being used by news broadcasters, especially on Zee channels. Hinglish, whose roots are in the spoken languages of north India, has been steadily gaining acceptance among the urban youth across the country. Arguably it was a major factor in making Zee popular with this audience. In the past 5 years Hinglish has become the standard language in serials and game- and chat-shows on television, but Zee TV was the first channel to elevate this new language by using it in a more serious genre such as news.

Every story that Zee news covered during the week included English words and phrases interspersed among standard Hindi. Such terms as 'press release', 'press conference', 'temperature', 'break', 'headlines', 'news room', 'bureau report' and 'committee', appeared in every bulletin monitored during the week. Most stories had an average of three to five key words in English, which might occur several times through the story. The more specialist features and sport could have up to ten key words and many of the 'World Briefs' were almost entirely dependent on English for the key words (for example, an item about bullet-proof clothing in Columbia, 22 August 1997). This is a significant departure from the traditional approach of Doordarshan, where only Hindi is used in Hindi news bulletins.

However, Zee is reflecting popular speech and making its news accessible and easy to understand, avoiding the use of Sanskritised Hindi, the hallmark of the national broadcaster. By using English words, Zee is also expanding its reach beyond the Hindi-speaking regions of the country, to the south – something which may be more influenced by motives of profit than any altruistic efforts towards national integration. The language issue remains an emotive one in India, where the constitution recognises sixteen languages and hundreds of dialects are spoken across the country. National television has been often perceived as 'Hindi- and Delhi-centric' (Mitra, 1990: 174), and therefore an instrument of northern hegemony, especially in the southern state of Tamil Nadu where anti-Hindi sentiments are still prevalent. However, given that Zee is targeting a younger urban audience less concerned with issues of local/regional identity and more likely to use Hinglish, the channel may be contributing to a new hybridised pan-Indian lingua franca.

## Private vs. public broadcaster

In order to examine whether competition from private channels has had any impact on the presentation of news from the national broadcaster, the Zee bulletin of Tuesday 19 August was compared with the main Hindi news bulletin, *Samachar* (news) on Doordarshan shown at 8.30 p.m. on the same evening. Both Zee's and Doordarshan's bulletins ran for around twenty minutes (to be precise, twenty-one and twenty-two minutes, respectively).

Before the Doordarshan news bulletin, there were two promotional advertisements for public campaigns, the National Literacy Mission and primary education, celebrating 50 years of independence. Both were slick and professional with high production values. These values were carried through into the fifteen-second Doordarshan opening titles, showing the TV transmission mast and a dynamic sequence establishing the logo (based on a globe), giving an image of authority and credibility.

However, this level of presentation and production values was not carried through into the Doordarshan news bulletin itself. The studio had a plain background with a 'window' used for graphics and visuals but which often only showed the Doordarshan logo. The news was read by two alternating announcers – on this day, one male and one female, both middle-aged and sombre-looking. The dress code was less Western in that the man did not wear a jacket. There were no advertisements and the only break in the news presentation was for a dull and didactic government-information film warning about vehicle pollution. Much of the news was read by announcers from the studio, with only one location report in the bulletin. Even where there was footage, the commentary was read by the presenter. Often the visuals would show a speech being made at a press conference, but instead of broadcasting the speech itself, the commentary would paraphrase what was being said. The quality of visuals and the production values were inferior to those of Zee. Despite facing competition from transnational and private Indian news organisations, the state broadcaster continued to display an amateurish approach to news delivery: at times there was a gap of several seconds between the visuals and the start of the commentary; the graphics used were very basic and at times there were no visuals at all.

In contrast with the language employed on Zee news, which, when not

Hinglish, tended to be more informal (one report called the defence minister by his first name), Doordarshan used only formal language and that in 'pure' Hindi. Hindi was also used for all captions or legends on maps, charts and graphs shown during the bulletin.

In terms of news stories, the emphasis for both networks was on domestic and, within that category, mostly on political stories, as the running orders indicate (see Figure 16.2). The most significant difference lies in the time allotted to foreign news (see Figure 16.3), where the state broadcaster has more than four times the number of stories in comparison to Zee.

The reason for this disparity could be the availability of foreign footage for the two channels. Doordarshan receives regular feeds from international government-to-government news-exchange programmes, such as Eurovision and Asiavision, and it also buys footage from international commercial suppliers such as Reuters Television and Worldwide Television News. Zee, on the other hand, is dependent solely on commercial television news agencies, and appears to cut costs on foreign coverage, since

| Zee news | Doordarshan *Samachar* |
|---|---|
| Titles | Titles |
| Headlines | Headlines |
| **Break:** Adverts | 1. **Veerapan – smuggler to surrender** |
| 1. Congress to support United Front | 2. **Environment minister on pollution** |
| 2. Reactions to Congress decision | 3. Clinton may visit India, Pakistan |
| 3. **Murder of builder in Bombay** | 4. War in Cambodia |
| 4. Queen's planned visit | 5. Attack on Israel by Hizbollah |
| 5. **Veerapan – terms for surrender** | 6. Sri Lanka – former minister released |
| 6. Rebel Congress leader in Calcutta | 7. Problems on Mir spacecraft |
| **Break:** Adverts | 8. Commemoration of freedom fighter |
| 7. Award for folk singer | **Break:** Advert on pollution control |
| 8. Chief of Hezbol Mujahaddin in Kashmir | Business news |
| 9. **Environment minister on pollution** | 9. Attack on minister in Uttar Pradesh |
| 10. World Briefs: | 10. **Murder of builder in Bombay** |
| a: Rolling Stones tour starts in USA | 11. Environment minister at rural development seminar |
| b: Vietnam imports crocodiles from Cuba | 12. Festival of Thailand in New Delhi |
| **Break:** Trailer for drama serial; advert for Konica, sponsor of weather | 13. New organisation to promote culture for youth |
| Weather | 14. Cricket – one-day series in Canada |
| | 15. Cricket – profile of bowler Srinath |
| | Weather |
| | Headlines repeated |

**Figure 16.2** Running order of stories on Zee news and Doordarshan *Samachar*, 19 August 1997

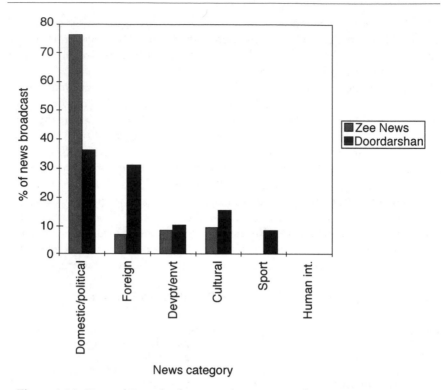

**Figure 16.3** Zee and Doordarshan news by category of story (19 August 1997)

international news is not a priority area for its audience and a private channel driven by considerations of ratings is more likely to report stories which interest its viewers.

Unlike Zee, which generally seems to cover a wider range of political perspectives – several stories included quotes from representatives of the main political parties on both left and right – Doordarshan news appeared still to be wedded to putting forth the view of the government of the day. The Indian state broadcaster sees its primary function within the discourse of nationalism (McDowell, 1997) and tends to cover stories – both domestic and foreign – which it considers relevant to the national audience.

It can be argued that Zee news's greater degree of professional presentation reflects the adoption of Western broadcasting codes and values and helps it to establish a credibility as a news provider, which for Doordarshan is automatically conferred by its relationship to the state. The key factor in this, and the primary difference between the two programmes, is the use of on-the-spot reporting and inclusion of alternative voices, which has the potential to open up a wider news agenda. However, at present in both channels government officials and political elites are still the 'primary definers' of the news.

The most significant difference in relation to the impact of privatisation of broadcasting appears to be that, while the state broadcaster views news as public information, Zee news tries to make its programme more 'entertaining', i.e. more visually appealing and varied, to attract a wider audience. This emphasis on infotainment and the absence of serious foreign coverage may lead to omission of issues of major public concern such as policy prescriptions of the World Bank, critical in a developing country like India. In addition, the news is also a vehicle for delivering a target audience for its advertisers, and Zee news could be seen as part of the project to open up the huge Indian market to a global consumer culture which is being promoted by the media empires (see Chapter 4).

## Doordarshan's dilemma

With increasing competition from private channels Doordarshan's public-service role is under pressure, as, in order to remain competitive, it now has to provide mass entertainment as well as education. That infotainment is becoming a dominant factor in news and current affairs is shown by the fact that Doordarshan has named one of its new channels 'Infotainment'.

Because of the reach of the terrestrial broadcasting network – it now covers nearly 450 million people in 87 per cent of the country (Doordarshan, 1997: 2) – the government has been supportive of Doordarshan, for example, by banning Direct to Home (DTH) reception, although it insists that the ban is temporary and once the rules have been laid under the Broadcast Bill, DTH will be allowed through bidding.[10] The Broadcast Bill, introduced in 1997, seeks to bring order to the broadcasting industry, currently regulated by the archaic Telegraph Act of 1885, and to create an independent broadcasting authority to regulate broadcasting services.[11]

It has been suggested that the bill be replaced by the 1990 Prasar Bharati (Broadcasting Corporation of India) Act, which came into force in September 1997 and led to the creation of Prasar Bharati Corporation, promising to give autonomy to Doordarshan and AIR. Surrindar Singh Gill, a former information and broadcasting ministry secretary and the chief executive of this new body, is keen to fulfil the 'social obligations' of Doordarshan and reduce entertainment programming (Bhandare, 1997b: 23).

This has become imperative as, although Doordarshan's reach has been extended and new channels added (in 1997 it had nineteen channels), the percentage of public-service programmes has declined and entertainment of a hybrid variety has flourished, a trend disapproved of by the old guard. The comment of P. V. Krishnamoorthy, first director general of Doordarshan, is typical: 'imported content has increased considerably and even the local content is highly influenced by the imported content . . . our sitcoms have very little relevance to the Indian situation, the Indian milieu and the Indian culture. This is what bothers me' (Broadcast 50, 1997).

A public-service broadcaster has a crucial educational role in a country where, even after 50 years of independence, nearly half of the population is illiterate. This role involves not just expanding literacy but exploiting the educational potential of such a powerful medium as television to promote awareness about, for example, health, rural development, gender equality and ethnic and religious tolerance. The egalitarian potential of the mass media remains hugely unexplored in India, home to the world's largest number of poor people: in the period 1981–95, more than half the population – about 500 million people – lived on less than $1 a day (World Bank, 1997: 214).

Apparently, the government is still committed to such an agenda for its electronic media. There has been a five-fold increase in the number of transmitters in the past decade – from 200 in 1987 to 1000 in 1997 (Doordarshan, 1997: 4) – and state television, the government says, must concentrate on 'priority areas of national concern' like 'eradication of illiteracy, environmental protection, healthcare, agriculture and rural development' (Government of India, 1997: 1–2).

The need for developmental television is so vast that private channels such as Zee may chart out areas of co-operation with transnational media companies to provide much-needed factual programming. Already, Zee has considerably expanded its news operations and in January 1998 it converted its EL channel into a twenty-four-hour news and current affairs channel called Zee India TV (Hebbar, 1998).

Its main rival, NDTV, the most professional producer of indigenous news programmes, and since 1996 part of STAR network, has also started a round-the-clock news and current affairs channel. A survey of 300 cable and satellite homes in Delhi conducted in December 1997 by *Cable Waves*, the industry newsletter, showed that TV audiences are slowly but surely moving from 'entertainment to infotainment'. Exploiting the demand for more news during a period when the political situation in the country is in flux, the networks have timed the launch of their news operations shrewdly (Singh, 1998). Other entertainment-oriented channels such as twenty-four-hour Sony Entertainment Television (SET), 60 per cent owned by Sony and the second most popular private national channel after Zee, is also planning to enter the news and current affairs arena (Chakraborty, 1998).

But is more news necessarily good news? Converting news into a 'show' and adopting news formats, values and agendas that reflect subservience to centres of power, nationally and globally, could undermine the liberating and empowering potential of the electronic media. Nevertheless, despite fears of a loss of identity under the avalanche of Western television, it is instructive that Zee TV, as the most successful private television channel, is nevertheless making programmes on Indian themes in Hindi, although the formats may be derivative and the language hybrid. The expansion of private channels in regional languages and the extraordinary growth of the regional-language press in India – the largest selling daily in the country continues to be *Malayala Manorama*, a regional newspaper – is a testimony to the cultural complexity of the nation.

Globalisation has provided Indian journalistic talent opportunities for professional advancement and expansion beyond the borders of India. As output from a reinvigorated Indian television becomes available outside the country, India, given its competence in English, the language of international media, its traditions of critical debate and its marketable film-based popular culture, is well placed to become the first Southern nation to achieve a significant presence in the US-dominated global media market. Zee, the network named after the last letter of the alphabet, may emerge as the first Indian media corporation with global ambitions, further complicating the discourse of globalisation.

# Notes

1 For a discussion on the role the press played in developing nationalist consciousness see Desai (1976: 221–39). During the closing days of the British administration, the press could be broadly divided into three categories: establishment newspapers such as the *Statesman* and the *Times of India*; the nationalist press, *Hindustan Times*, the *Indian Express* and *The Hindu*; and Indian-language publications, notably *Anand Bazaar Patrika* in Bengali, *Kesari* in Marathi, *Sandesh* and *Bombay Samachar* in Gujarati, *Matribhumi* in Malayalam and *Aaj* in Hindi.

2 At independence, All India Radio had only six stations; by 1996, there were 185 broadcasting centres, covering more than 97 per cent of the population (All India Radio, 1997: 17).

3 Other sections of the electronic media were also employed by the state for propaganda purposes. Newsreels produced by the Indian Film Division, a wing of the ministry of information and broadcasting, were used to promote government policies. As a study by the Press Institute of India observed, newsreels 'are not only controlled by the government but their theme and content are also dictated by it' (Bhattacharjee, 1972: 21).

4 *India Today*, a weekly magazine, has the largest circulation of any English-language news magazine in the country. It also has editions in five Indian languages – Hindi, Telugu, Gujarati, Malayalam and Tamil – making it the most widely read publication in India, with a circulation of 1.2 million copies and a readership of 11.4 million (Purie, 1997).

5 According to one account, Samir Jain, the chief executive of the *Times of India*, is credited with 'Americanising' the *Times of India* and imposing Harvard Business School techniques that he picked up during a short

internship at the *New York Times*. For an interesting description of how he runs his newspaper empire see Coleridge, 1993: 220–41.

6 According to the figures from the Indian Newspaper Society, in 1996 there were 70 dailies, 26 weeklies, 23 fortnightlies, 56 monthlies in English alone, accounting for a circulation of 9.3 million. There were 324 dailies, 79 weeklies, 33 fortnightlies, 96 monthlies in Indian languages, with a circulation of 37 million (*Business India*, 1997).

7 It was not CNN, though, that brought satellite television into India for the first time but SITE (Satellite Instructional Television Experiment), launched in 1975 to expand the reach of Doordarshan's social educational programmes to remote villages. See Agrawal, 1981.

8 One reason for such success is the widespread perception in Tamil Nadu that television emanating from Delhi reinforces the cultural and linguistic hegemony of the north. It is no coincidence that the most successful regional channel has been Sun TV, the first Tamil-language satellite channel, launched in 1993.

9 This limited survey was based on a small sampling. There is enormous scope for further research on the impact of globalisation on television news in a complex and rapidly changing media situation in India.

10 STAR TV is leading the private channels which are lobbying to launch DTH. It has reportedly invested $8 million to provide forty channels through ISkyB (India Sky Broadcasting), set up by Rupert Murdoch.

11 The bill divides broadcast services into six categories: terrestrial radio, satellite radio, terrestrial TV channels, satellite TV channels, DTH broadcasters and local delivery services. An operator can get a licence for only one category. Foreigners are allowed up to 49 per cent on foreign equity in satellite channels but cannot invest in terrestrial networks. This is opposed by media corporations, as one of their key representatives, Rathikant Basu, a former director general of Doordarshan, who became chief executive officer of STAR TV's India operations in 1996, argued: 'It is impractical for transnational broadcasters to get into join ventures with varying equity structures in each country where their signals are downlinked' (Basu, 1997).

# References

Agarwal, A. (1995) Catering to the masses, *India Today*, 15 Jan., p. 114.

Agrawal, B. C. (1981) Anthropological applications in communication research and evaluation of SITE in India, *Media Asia*, 8.3, pp. 136–46.

All India Radio (1997) *All India Radio 1996*, Audience Research Unit, Directorate General, All India Radio, New Delhi.

Basu, R. (1997) Have rules, not curbs, *India Today*, 30 Jan., p. 39.

Bhandare, N. (1997a) Indian season, *India Today*, 6 Oct.

Bhandare, N. (1997b) New waves, *India Today*, 8 Dec.

Bhattacharjee, A. (1972) *The Indian Press: Profession to Industry*, Vikas, New Delhi.

Broadcast 50 (1997) Documentary on 50 years of Indian broadcasting, *STAR Plus*, 16 Aug.

*Business India* (1997) Message for the media, March 24–April 6, pp. 54–60.

*Cable & Satellite Asia Yearbook 97/98* (1997) Pearson Professional Ltd, London.

Chakraborty, A. (1998) SET for a tie-break, *Business India*, 12–25 Jan., p. 166.

Channel 4 Television (1995) *Bazaar Television*, part 2 of *Satellite Wars* series, Channel 4, UK, 2 April.

Chatterjee, A. (1997) A new tele(view) of the villages, *Business Today*, 7–21 Sept.

Chatterjee, P. C. (1991) *Broadcasting in India*, Sage, New Delhi.

Coleridge, N. (1993) *Paper Tigers*, Heinemann, London.

Desai, A. R. (1976) *Social Background of Indian Nationalism*, 5th edn, Popular, Bombay.

Doordarshan (1997) *Doordarshan 1997*, Audience Research Unit, Directorate General Doordarshan, New Delhi.

Government of India (1997) *Ministry of Information and Broadcasting, Annual Report, 1996–97*, Director Publications Division, New Delhi.

Hartley, J. (1982) *Understanding News*, Methuen, London.

Hebbar, M. (1998) Zee to make EL channel 24-hr news, *Asian Age*, 6 Jan.

Jeffrey, R. (1997) Hindi: taking to the *Punjab Kesari* line, *Economic and Political Weekly*, 18 Jan., pp. 77–83.

Kumar, K. (1996) International news on Indian television: a critical analysis of *The World This Week*, in French, D. and Richards, M. (eds) *Contemporary Television, Eastern Perspectives*, Sage, New Delhi.

McDonald, H. (1995) Paper tigers, *Far Eastern Economic Review*, 5 Oct., pp. 24–30.

McDowell, S. (1997) Globalization and policy choices: television and audio-visual services policies in India, *Media, Culture & Society*, 19, pp. 151–72.

Mitra, A. (1990) The position of television in the cultural map of India, *Media Asia*, 17.3, pp. 166–76.

Mody, B. (1995): State consolidation through liberalisation of telecommunications services in India, *Journal of Communication*, 45.4, Autumn, pp. 107–24.

Mullick, A. (1995) STAR TV goes all out to double viewership base in Asia, *Times of India*, 20 Jan.

Mullick, A. (1996) STAR–Zee relations touch rock bottom after board meeting, *Times of India*, 8 Nov.

Ninan, S. (1997) Tough going, *The Hindu*, 12 Oct.

Pendakur, M. (1991) Political economy of television in India, in Sussman, G. and Lent, J. (eds) *Transnational Communications: Wiring the Third World*, Sage, London.

Purie, A. (1997) Letter from the editor, *India Today*, 9 June, p. 1.

Rajagopal, A. (1993) The rise of national programming: the case of Indian television, *Media, Culture & Society*, 15, pp. 91–111.

Ram, N. (1990) An independent press and anti-hunger strategies: The Indian experience, in Dreze, J. and Sen, A. (eds) *The Political Economy of Hunger*, Vol. 1, Clarendon Press, Oxford.

Ram, N. (1994) Foreign media entry into the press – issues and implications, *Economic and Political Weekly*, 22 Oct., pp. 2787–90.

Ravindran, S. (1998) Zee plans Hindi channel in US, *Business Standard*, 1 Jan.

Shivdasani, M. (1998) News is the 'in thing', *Business Line*, 19 Jan.

Singh, G. (1998) A newsy spin, *Economic Times*, 7 Jan.

Wanvari, A. (1997) India, in *Cable & Satellite Asia Yearbook 97/98*, Pearson, London.

World Bank (1997) *World Development Report 1997*, Oxford University Press, Oxford.

Zee TV (1997) *Zee TV and You*, press pack from Zee TV, UK.

Zee TV website (1998): http://zeetelevision.com

# Discussion questions

1 Can you think of any examples of alternative media in your country? Analyse the output of one of them and compare it with the output of the mainstream media.

2 Surf the Internet to visit other alternative media websites such as OneWorld Online. Note their country of origin. Does it matter that so much of the new media technology is based in the North?

3 Are international entertainment television channels such as MTV creating a global youth culture? How representative are these channels of youth in the developing world?

4 Why have some Islamic nations such as Iran banned Western satellite television?

5 What impact has the privatisation and commercialisation of broadcasting had on the public-service role of television?

6 What do you understand by the concept of media hybridity? Is there anything pure or authentic in cultural terms?

7 What strategies has the STAR network adopted in India to expand its reach?

8 Do you think it is significant that two of the most widely used Arabic television networks — MBC and Orbit – are based in London? What does this tell us about the state of the media in the Middle East?

9 What role do Southern broadcasters such as India's Zee TV play in the global flow of television?

10 What do you understand by glocalisation? Is glocalisation the way ahead for global media forms and firms?

# Author index

# Subject index